The New Middle Ages

The New Middle Ages is a series dedicated to pluridisciplinary studies of medieval cultures, with particular emphasis on recuperating women's history and on feminist and gender analyses. This peer-reviewed series includes both scholarly monographs and essay collections.

Henry Ansgar Kelly

The Trial and Retrial of Joan of Arc

A Judicial Review

palgrave
macmillan

Henry Ansgar Kelly
Department of English
UCLA
Los Angeles, CA, USA

ISSN 2945-5936 ISSN 2945-5944 (electronic)
The New Middle Ages
ISBN 978-3-032-07886-5 ISBN 978-3-032-07887-2 (eBook)
https://doi.org/10.1007/978-3-032-07887-2

This Palgrave Macmillan imprint is published by the registered company Springer Nature Switzerland AG.
The registered company address is: Gewerbestrasse 11, 6330 Cham, Switzerland

For Barret and Caroline

Preface

This book is the result of various natural forces, such as evolution, accretion, and tectonic shifting. It began in effect when Esther Cuenca, whom I had met at a medieval conference, asked me to contribute to a project of hers of putting out a textbook illustrating the Middle Ages through motion pictures. She assigned me the subject the trial of Joan of Arc, on which I had written some articles in the past. I had just sent off the manuscript of my latest book, *Criminal-Inquisitorial Trials in English Church Courts* (eventually published in 2023), and I had nothing else in particular to do, so I said yes.

My main interest in the trial had been violations of due process in the rules of inquisitorial procedure established at the Fourth Lateran Council in 1215. In order to get a focus on the entire trial, I started reading it from beginning to end, and, eventually, the notes "began to grow under my hand," as they used to say, into a large pile.

In due course I produced a chapter for Esther's book, comparing Joan's trial with the silent film *The Passion of Joan of Arc*—though not without some difficulty of reining in my enthusiasm for detail. In this matter, the local co-editor Anthony (or Tony) Perron of Loyola Marymount University proved indispensable. The resulting book *Law, Justice, and Society in the Medieval World* came out in early 2025.

I decided to enlarge the scope of my effort to all aspects of the trial, including illustrative judicial precedents, and extend it to the trial of nullity that followed. The latter had been mainly studied for the light that it could throw on Joan's life and trial, but the actual mechanics of the proceedings had been largely neglected. I hope that my account will remedy that neglect.

After taking emeritus status in the English Department at UCLA, I was officially declared a distinguished research professor and still able to enjoy the resources of the department in keeping my office and using the services of the department technicians, currently Chris Cabrera Thompson and Victor Samperio, for which I am very appreciative. But during the early years of putting this book together, the COVID-19 pandemic kept me mainly at home. A year or two after the plague had passed, however, another disaster struck, the Palisades fire, in January of 2025, and my home was destroyed, including the notes and books I had used to compose this book—which, fortunately, was all but completed. I am especially grateful to my family for their support, not only during that difficult time but always: my wife Marea and my daughter Sarah and son Dominic. I dedicate this book with gratitude to Sarah's daughter Caroline and Dominic's son Barret, praying that St Joan will serve as an inspiration to them, and to us all.

I would like to express my gratitude especially to my medieval colleagues in the UCLA English Department: above all Donka Minkova and Arvind Thomas, and also Matthew Fisher, Chris Chism, Erica Weaver, Debora Shuger, and Eric Jager, for their support, and also my former student Jennifer Smith, now at nearby Pepperdine University. Of these, Donka particularly excelled in linguistics, Arvind in canonistics, and Jennifer in logistics. Other supporters that should be named are Leslie Arnovick, Michael Hanly, Matthew Brosamer, and Jane Richardson. Among outside consultants, I want to express a special tribute to my dear late-lamented friend Ed Peters, whose expertise in all things canonical was unexcelled. Finally, I do not know what I would have done without the help of my former student and very-long-time assistant Claire Banchich.

Taking the long view, given my current age, I think it unlikely that I will produce many more books, so I would like to acknowledge at this point earlier influences. My parents, to begin with, Harry and Inez Kelly, who well understood the value of education. Sister Clarice, who first instructed me in Latin in my little high school in Fonda, Iowa; Ray O'Donnell, S.J., who taught me Latin at Creighton University; my Jesuit mentors, instructors, and companions in my thirteen years in the Society of Jesus; other mentors and friends at St Louis and Harvard and Rome and UCLA and elsewhere, who have stimulated and entertained and consoled me through the years. Thank you all so much. I look forward to more good times with all who are still here and all who are to come. I hope you profit from reading my take on Joan of Arc.

Los Angeles, CA, USA Henry Ansgar Kelly

Contents

Abbreviations

CF	Council of Faith, Paris 1413–1414
CIC	*Corpus iuris canonici*, ed. Emil Friedberg (q.v.)
CJC	*Corpus Juris Canonici* (q.v.)
CUP	*Chartularium Universitatis Parisiensis*, ed. Henri Denifle (q.v.).
DTC	*Dictionnaire de théologie catholique*
FM	French Minute, ed. Tisset, *Procès* (q.v.).
LR	Latin Record, ed. Tisset, *Procès* (q.v.).
NT	Nullity Trial, ed. Duparc, *Procès* (q.v.).
X	*Liber Extra*

CHAPTER 1

Introduction

The spectacular rise and subsequent fall of Joan of Arc is well known. She is arguably the most famous historical figure of the fifteenth century. The chief reason we know so much about her, a girl who was only nineteen years old when she died, is that the judicial proceedings held against her are among the most detailed of all historical trials. The entire posthumous Latin Record (LR), produced at the order of her chief judge, Bishop Pierre Cauchon, survives, as do substantial portions of the original notarial French Minute (FM). In addition, there is the testimony of over a hundred witnesses twenty years later in the Nullity Trial (NT), proceedings aimed at overturning the earlier sentences against her.[1] Yet it is often far from clear exactly what the motivations and mechanisms were behind the earlier prosecution, what laws of procedure were observed or broken, and the basis upon which conclusions were made. And the events and circumstances of the later proceedings that exonerated Joan are mostly unfamiliar. They have been mainly mined to explicate the earlier trial. But what did it mean for Joan's mother to sue the perpetrators of her daughter's death for damages to the honor of them both? Who were the actors, and how did it work? All this is the subject of the present book. Its main focus is on due process, as seen from the perspective of present-day law and experience. What were the rights of defendants, and what exactly were the wrongs that were done to them?

[1] Details of these court records are given at the beginning of Chapter 3.

H. A. Kelly, *The Trial and Retrial of Joan of Arc*, The New Middle Ages, https://doi.org/10.1007/978-3-032-07887-2_1

1.1 Inquisitorial Trial Procedure

One reason why the mechanics of the prosecution against Joan have been distorted, misunderstood, or ignored is the long-standing assumption that a special code of conduct called "inquisition" was permitted to prosecutors of heresy, in which the rules of due process were suspended. I thought so myself until I came to study the divorce trials of Henry VIII,[2] during which I learned that virtually all criminal trials in Church courts followed inquisitorial procedure, a form of trial promulgated by Pope Innocent III at the Fourth Lateran Council in 1215 in the canon *Qualiter*, and incorporated into the *Liber Extra* of Gregory IX in 1234.[3]

The rules of the procedure were simple. There had to be a public crime—secret crimes were off-limits. There had to be a suspected perpetrator, that is, general belief (*publica fama*) that a certain person was guilty of the crime. When this person was summoned for trial, the judge, usually a bishop, was first required to establish that the *fama* was reasonable, and then explain the charges that were being laid against him, before making him plead guilty or not guilty. This suspect, now defendant, had the right to reject the judge and any witnesses against him if they were his enemies. He had the right to counsel, the right to bring his own witnesses, and the right to appeal his case to a higher judge when any of the rules were violated.

[2] Henry Ansgar Kelly, *The Matrimonial Trials of Henry VIII* (Stanford 1976).

[3] Innocent III, *Qualiter*, canon 8 of the Fourth Lateran Council, contained in the *Liber Extra* (X), or *Decretals of Gregory IX* (AD 1234), 5.1.24: see *Corpus iuris canonici* (CIC), ed. Emil Friedberg, 2 vols. (Leipzig 1879–1881), 2:745–47. The English translation of *Qualiter* in *Decrees of the Ecumenical Church*, vol. 1: *Nicaea I to Lateran V*, ed. Norman P. Tanner, 2 vols. (London 1990), pp. 237–39, mistakenly renders *inquisitio* not as "inquisition" but as "inquest."

NB: Official canon law was contained not only in the *Liber Extra*, but also in the *Sext* (*Liber Sextus*) of Boniface VIII, issued in 1298; and in the *Clementines* (*Constitutiones Clementinae*) of Clement V, made official in 1317, frequently followed by the *Extravagantes Johannis XXII*; all are edited in vol. 2 of Friedberg's CIC. Vol. 1 of CIC contains the *Decretum* of Gratian of Bologna (ca. 1150–1160), a textbook collection of "canons," that is, early laws and decrees (mainly local), and extracts from Church Fathers like St Augustine. Canons were often cited from the *Decretum* as if they were authoritative and binding on present-day Christians. Glosses (commentaries) on all these texts, as well as the texts themselves, can be found in Pope Gregory XIII's edition of the *Corpus Juris Canonici* (CJC), 3 vols. (Rome 1582); see the UCLA online production of this edition: *https://digital.library.ucla.edu/canonlaw/*.

I must emphasize that the *publica fama* which served as "probable cause" for triggering an inquisitorial trial is nowadays frequently misunderstood as *mala fama*, simple "bad reputation" in general.[4] What was meant by "public fame" in this context was that the person was widely believed to be guilty of the crime with which he was to be charged. And, to repeat, there had to be a crime, not the mere *fama* of a crime. And those members of the community who believed the suspect to be guilty of it should be respectable members of the community—and not hostile to the suspect, such as, in Joan's case, the English and their sympathizers.

A flaw in the system was that the judge, or inquisitor, was supreme in his own courtroom, and there was no good way of enforcing the rules. Thus, when inquisitorial procedure was adopted for the prosecution of heresy, its due-process protections for defendants were often disregarded by negligent or unscrupulous judges. This was especially the case with the right of appeal, which heresy inquisitors (and historians after them) regularly claimed was not allowed in heresy trials, with the result that they matter-of-factly rejected any appeals that were lodged. But, of course, legally no such exemption was approved in canon law. Confirmation of this can be seen in records of appeals that were actually heard when defendants managed to circumvent the judges and get their complaints directly to the pope or other higher authorities.[5]

Other spurious claims made for heresy judges included that attorneys were not allowed to defend the accused suspect/defendant, and that the defendant could not call witnesses in his defense. Speaking of witnesses, however, heresy judges did have an advantage over and against defendants, for they were allowed to use disqualified persons (say, those with criminal records) as prosecution witnesses. But this was only because heresy was classified among serious or "exempt" crimes, which included simony and treason, or lese majesty. It by no means allowed judges, as has recently been claimed,[6] to throw off all restrictions and proceed *extra*

[4] For examples of this mistake in connection with Joan, see Colette Beaune, *Jeanne d'Arc* (Paris 2004), pp. 300–02; Daniel Hobbins, Introduction to his abridged translation of the Latin Record: *The Trial of Joan of Arc* (Cambridge MA 2005), p. 21; Jacques Chiffoleau, "L'hérésie de Jeanne: Note sur les qualifications dans le procès de Rouen," in *Jeanne d'Arc: Histoire et mythes*, Jean-Patrice Boudet and Xavier Hélary, eds. (Rennes 2014), pp. 13–55, at p. 26.

[5] See, for instance, J. M. Vidal, *Bullaire de l'inquisition française au xive siècle et jusqu'à la fin du grand schisme* (Paris 1913).

[6] See Chiffoleau, "L'hérésie de Jeanne," pp. 28, 39.

ordinem or *sine ordine*. They were still bound by the *ordo judiciarius* or *ordo juris* in all other respects, that is, they had to include all the actions and procedures demanded by law in the conduct of a trial.

However, canon law did eventually allow a relaxation of due process specifically for heresy cases: according to a decretal in Boniface VIII's *Sext* (*Liber Sextus*) of 1298, the identity of any witnesses determined to be in danger because of their testimony could be suppressed.[7] (None of this mattered in Joan's case, of course, since Bishop Cauchon brought no witnesses to prove any allegations.)

There was yet another concession in the *Sext*, which permitted heresy judges to truncate their actions by using "summary procedure."[8] But this advantage was eviscerated within twenty years by another law issued by Clement V, which extended summary procedure to all kinds of trials, while stipulating that no defenses could be omitted.[9]

Quite obviously, many heresy judges, as well as other kinds of judges, violated all of these safeguards from time to time. However, there was one deviation in particular that was particularly disastrous for defendants, which was developed by the papally appointed heresy inquisitors in France in the thirteenth and fourteenth centuries. Instead of immediately charging a suspect with the crime he was suspected of and providing him with full details, as *Qualiter* insisted should be done, they treated him as a witness, and put him under oath to answer questions not only about others but about himself (*de se et aliis*). The inquisitors were then more easily able to make people incriminate themselves, thereby avoiding the trouble of finding proofs in case of denial. It also made it possible for them to turn up previously unknown offenses, or provoke incorrect statements about the sacraments or the articles of faith—which, once spoken aloud in court, could be charged against them.[10]

This was the tactic that Cauchon used against Joan. For a whole month, he insisted that she swear an oath every day to tell the truth about whatever he would ask her "in this cause of faith," against her protests that she

[7] Alexander IV, *In fidei favorem*, *Sext* 5.2.4 (CIC 2:1071).

[8] Boniface VIII, *Statuta*, *Sext* 5.2.20 (CIC 2:1076).

[9] Clement V, *Saepe*, *Clem.* 5.11.2 (CIC 2:1200). All of the above points are explained by Henry Ansgar Kelly, "Inquisition and the Prosecution of Heresy: Misconceptions and Abuses," *Church History* 58 (1989) 439–451.

[10] See Henry Ansgar Kelly "The Fourth Lateran *Ordo* of Inquisition Adapted to the Prosecution of Heresy," *Brill's Companion to Heresy Inquisitions* (Leiden 2019), pp. 75–107, at pp. 87–96.

might not wish to respond to some questions. The final charges against her were entirely gathered from her own statements thus made under illegal duress.

Some years ago I reviewed the prosecution against Joan of Arc with this feature principally in mind, as part of a dialogue about modern ideas of the right against self-incrimination. In 1990, Richard Helmholz corrected Leonard Levy's study of the protections of the Fifth Amendment (reprinted in 1986[11]) on matters dealing with medieval canon law and the principles of Roman civil law, especially as understood in the Early Modern period.[12] I then contributed a supplementary essay on earlier medieval law in 1993, drawing on Joan's trial.[13]

In the present study I look at all aspects of Joan's condemnation, extending to what used to be called her "rehabilitation," and is now the Nullity Trial. One question I left unanswered in my earlier study was whether the "interrogation-before-trial" abuse used by Cauchon was usual procedure in his time, as it became for the Roman Inquisition in the sixteenth century. Or was the due process of charging defendants immediately still normally followed in Cauchon's time? After all, even Tomás de Torquemada insisted upon it when the Spanish Inquisition was instituted in the latter part of the fifteenth century. It would now seem that it was so, to judge from other trials of the time, especially that of Jean Ségueut, which was concluded just a month or so before the proceedings against Joan began. That, of course, complicates the question of why there was almost no mention of this violation of lawful procedure on Cauchon's part by the later defenders of Joan, since it was so important for the case. It was, however, one of the censures against his proceedings pointed out at the time by Jean Lohier.

Another question that merits more attention here is "What kinds of actions and ideas could be classified as heretical?" We will look at some previous cases within the time-span of Cauchon's career. Cauchon himself proved to be on the minimalist side when he was at the Council of Constance, whereas others, like Jean Gerson and Cardinal Pierre d'Ailly, were more than ready to view ordinary offenses as heretical. Cauchon at

[11] Leonard W. Levy, *Origins of the Fifth Amendment: The Right against Self-Incrimination* (New York 1968; repr. with new preface, 1986).

[12] R. H. Helmholz, "Origins of the Privilege against Self-Incrimination: The Role of the European *Ius commune*," *New York University Law Review* 65 (1990) 962–90.

[13] Henry Ansgar Kelly, "The Right to Remain Silent: Before and after Joan of Arc," *Speculum* 68 (1993) 992–1026.

that time also insisted on due process, contrary to his behavior during Joan's trial. A key to his inconsistency on this score can be found in his unwavering loyalty to the House of Burgundy.

In her original prosecution, Joan was sentenced twice. The first time was to life imprisonment on May 24, 1431, after being prosecuted for several months for largely undefined offenses—with a two-day aborted trial in the middle (March 27–28) when she was formally charged—being convicted of implied heresy, and allegedly abjuring all heresy. The second time was only four days later, on May 30, 1431, when, without any trial at all, she was convicted of relapse into unnamed heresy, which entailed her delivery to secular execution by fire.

When I say that Joan was condemned the second time without a trial, I rely on the common understanding that a judicial trial, whether civil or criminal, begins only when a person is formally charged with an offense, and when that person, the defendant, replies, or pleads, to the charge before a judge in court. In a civil case, this is called "the contesting of the suit," or *litis contestatio*, in which the person bringing the charge is called the plaintiff. The same term was used by analogy in the Middle Ages for criminal trials that followed inquisitorial procedure, in which the judge himself or his appointed promotor leveled the charge.[14] This distinction does not apply to the closest word for "trial" that exists in the original languages of our case, namely, *processus* in Latin and *procès* in French, meaning "any judicial proceeding" and also "the record of the proceeding." In other words, "a trial" (in our usage) does not include the arrest, detention, and grilling of a suspect, or anything else that precedes charging the defendant.

A proper inquisitorial trial therefore would be one that gave the defendant all the rights set down in the lawbooks for defending him- or herself against accusations, especially those brought without proof in the name of suspicion.

[14] The use of *litis contestatio* in inquisitorial procedure is explained by William Lyndwood in his *Provinciale, seu Constitutiones Angliae*, 1434 (Oxford 1679, repr. Farnborough 1968) 3.27.3, note k, on the word *evocato* (p. 254 col. 2 top).

1.2 The Plan of the Book

In the second chapter, I set the stage after Joan's capture, discussing the competing or complementary jurisdiction of the heresy inquisitor of northern France, on the one hand, and that of bishops and archbishops on the other, looking especially at Bishop Cauchon and his background at the University of Paris. In Chapter 3, I review various condemnations of doctrine and trials that took place before Joan's trial, to reveal some precedents of doctrinal assessment and judicial procedure that can throw some light on what will happen in her prosecution. We will see, for instance, that "beginning a trial without a trial" (i.e., questioning the defendant rather than charging him) was not a usual procedure. We will also become aware that there was much disagreement about what was heretical and not heretical in various cases, especially in the tyrannicide controversy at the Council of Constance, in which Cauchon served in effect as a defense attorney, insisting on due process and resisting attempts to find heresy in ordinary crimes.

Chapter 4 shows how Cauchon extracted testimony from Joan about herself, with the support of a team of six theologians from the University of Paris, instead of accusing her of crimes that she was suspected of, until the legality of this proceeding was challenged by the papal judge Jean Lohier. Chapter 5 details the charges that were finally leveled against Joan by Cauchon's promotor (prosecutor) Jean d'Estivet. Estivet said that he would prove those charges that Joan denied (which were all of them), but in fact nothing was made of this whole exchange; instead, the promotor receded again to the sidelines. In the meantime, as we see in Chapter 6, Cauchon's Paris colleagues put together a hostile summary of her case, the Twelve Articles, from her original responses, to be evaluated by consultants. They alleged in particular a refusal to submit to the Church Militant as a violation of the credal belief in one Holy Catholic Church.

While waiting for the consultations to be assembled, Cauchon continued his campaign for Joan to admit to wrongdoing, alleging concern for her spiritual wellbeing, but then threatening her with torture (Chapter 7). After the negative University of Paris conclusions arrived, they were read in Joan's presence, and the case against her was concluded (Chapter 8). Court was reconvened the next morning on the scaffold, where Joan's appeal to the pope was rejected, and Cauchon started reading the sentence condemning her to death for refusal to submit to the Church, whereupon she capitulated to what was being demanded of her, which was construed as an abjuration of heresy, and she was sentenced to life imprisonment (Chapter 9). Four days later, Cauchon and his co-judge visited Joan in prison and witnessed a claimed relapse into heresy (consisting entirely of resumption of male clothes and reliance on her visions), and, without trial, she was condemned of relapse the next day and handed over to the executioner (Chapter 10).

Chapter 11 narrates various reports of Joan's fate over the next twenty years, from initial propaganda put out by the reigning authorities in Rouen and Paris, to accounts at the Council of Basel, and finally to initial investigations after the French recovery of Normandy (1450, 1452). Chapter 12 examines consultations that were gathered over the next two years with a view to challenging the condemnation proceedings on legal grounds.

Chapter 13 takes up the form of trial chosen for invalidating these proceedings, namely, a papal commission authorizing Joan's mother and brothers to sue for damages to their family honor. The commission contained no reference to the hostilities between the French and the English, or Joan's intervention on the side of the French and her prosecution by allies of the English. The prosecution was characterized as sparked by local jealousy, with false charges made by Promotor Estivet and maliciously supported by the judges, Bishop Cauchon and Sub-Inquisitor Lemaistre. The plaintiffs' demand was simply to declare the trial null and void. The trial of nullity, taken up in Chapter 14, began in Rouen in December of 1455 before the papal commissioners, Archbishop Jouvenal of Rheims and Bishop Chartier of Paris, along with the present-day heresy inquisitor of northern France, Jean Bréhal, OP, with a presentation by the plaintiffs' attorneys of their libellus, or "book of charges." It consisted of 101 articles outlining the procedural defects of the trial and Joan's innocence of the charges laid against her. Because the defendants were dead or assumed to be dead, the current bishop of Beauvais was summoned each court day, as was the promotor of criminal causes for the diocese of Beauvais, and the sub-inquisitor of heretical depravity for the diocese (who by all accounts did not exist), and much time was spent in declaring them in contempt of court for failing to obey the summonses.

The Arc family case against the defendants was elaborated in January of 1456 (Chapter 15), and in February their charges were accepted by the judges. Sworn inquests were ordered to obtain depositions of witnesses, to prove or disprove the charges. The completed depositions were turned in by May, and final productions of documents received in June and July by a substitute judge (Chapter 16). The judges began their deliberations in

June. The prelates had requested Inquisitor Bréhal, who had long been working for Joan's exoneration, to prepare an assessment of the case, and the resulting treatise was one of the exhibits. The verdict, delivered on July 7, 1456, was very spare. It simply nullified the verdict of 1431, restoring Joan to her original fame, and it left to God the question of the nature of her visions. There seems to have been little publicity given to this papally commissioned trial (Chapter 17). It was only when the records of both of her trials were published in the 1840s that she began to be venerated as a saint, which led to her relatively rapid canonization (Chapter 18). The last chapter, in addition to summarizing all that has gone before, warns of new encroachments upon Joan's honor (Chapter 19).

CHAPTER 2

Questions of Judges and Jurisdictions for the Captured Joan

2.1 Claim of the "Holy Inquisition"

After the triumphant deliverance of the city of Orleans in May of 1429 through Joan of Arc's leadership, Joan continued fighting for another year, until she was finally captured at Compiègne on May 23, 1430, by John of Luxembourg. He was an ally of the Burgundians, who in turn were allied to the English occupiers of much of France and enemies of the French king, Charles VII, Joan's Dauphin. Luxembourg treated her as simply a prisoner of war, but there was an immediate eagerness on the part of at least one heresy inquisitor in Paris (fifty miles south of Compiègne) to put her on trial for heresy.

Three days after her capture, a Dominican priest, "Friar Martin," who identified himself as "a master of theology and vicar-general of the inquisitor of the faith for the kingdom of France," addressed a letter to the current duke of Burgundy, Philip the Good (r. 1419–1467), demanding that Joan be sent to Paris for trial before him, because she was vehemently suspect of heresy for propagating various errors against the faith.[1]

[1] Pierre Tisset, ed., *Procès de condamnation de Jeanne d'Arc*, 3 vols. (Paris 1960–1971), 1:8–9. Friar Martin's letter is the third of a series of letters supposedly exhibited by Joan's judge, Bishop Pierre Cauchon, on the first day of his formal proceedings against her, January 9, 1431.

H. A. Kelly, *The Trial and Retrial of Joan of Arc*, The New Middle Ages, https://doi.org/10.1007/978-3-032-07887-2_2

Friar Martin, identified as Martin Billorin, OP,[2] was subordinate to Jean Graverent, who since 1422 was one of two papally appointed heresy inquisitors (*inquisitores heretice pravitatis*), otherwise known as inquisitors of the faith (*inquisitores fidei*), in France. Graverent's district was the northern part of the kingdom of France, and he had the power to appoint deputies in various places as he chose, usually referred to as vice-inquisitors or vicars (*vicarii inquisitoris*) or sub-inquisitors (*subinquisitores*). Graverent was a doctor and professor of theology at the University of Paris, as was usual for the northern inquisitor. He was also the prior of the Parisian Dominicans (called "Jacobins," because residing on rue de St-Jacques),[3] making him Billorin's religious as well as juridical superior. He was strongly in favor of the English occupiers of France, as was evident from a sermon he delivered to the Parlement of Paris (as prior, not inquisitor) on August 29, 1429.[3]

Each heresy inquisitor in Europe operated independently of the others, and also independently of the pope. Graverent's remit at least was called "the Holy Inquisition,"[4] a name that undoubtedly helped to give rise to the myth of *The Inquisition* as a centralized and highly organized institution in the Middle Ages.[5] But the inquisitors seemed to run shoestring operations. Charles Beaurepaire has concluded that those at this time did not have their own tribunals, but made use of episcopal facilities. Graverent's usual *modus operandi* seems to have been to go to the diocese where an accused offender was being tried and serve as co-judge with the local bishop or the bishop's "official" (judge of the diocesan court). The inquisitor was nominally equal to the bishop, but always seemed to take a subordinate role. The same held true, of course, for deputy inquisitors appointed by the inquisitor for individual dioceses.[6] It may have been the case that heresy inquisitors in general by this time had fallen considerably

[2] Tisset, *Procès*, 3:312.

[3] See Alexandre Tuetey, ed., *Journal d'un Bourgeois de Paris, 1405-1449* (Paris 1881), p. 270 n. 2.

[4] Billorin's letter was "given at Paris under our seal of the Office of the Holy Inquisition" (*Donné a Paris soubz nostre seel de l'office de la sainte inquisition*). In the second Ségueut trial in Rouen in 1430 it will be called "the Holy Inquisition of the Faith."

[5] See Edward Peters, *Inquisition* (New York 1988), pp. 1–7, 122–315.

[6] Charles de Robillard de Beaurepaire, *Recherches sur le procès de condamnation de Jeanne d'Arc* (Rouen 1869; Google Books), pp. 83–84.

in importance, since there did not seem to be much in the way of heresy to combat, and the office may have been seen to be something of an honorific.[7]

But according to a record unearthed by Beaurepaire himself—the case of Jean Ségueut, analyzed below—a heresy inquisitor was perfectly able to stage a heresy trial on his own. So was a bishop. This point needs explaining, since the contrary has been held—specifically, that the constitution *Multorum querela* of Pope Clement V, from the Council of Vienne (1311–1312), in the aftermath of the prosecution of the Templars, demanded a joint process.[8] The truth is, according to the text of the constitution itself, inquisitors and bishops could try a suspect either alone or together. Or, if they wished, they could hold two trials simultaneously. But in the latter case, they would have to consult and agree on three points: first, if unusually harsh imprisonment was to be imposed, that is, the sort of constraint more in keeping with punishment than mere safeguarding; second, on the use of torture, in case the alleged crime was only partially proved; and third, in pronouncing the final sentence.[9]

Boniface VIII had already spoken of the possibility of separate trials in his *Liber Sextus* of 1198, and had specified that in case the inquisitor and bishop came to different verdicts (e.g., one for acquittal and the other for conviction), the matter should be taken to the pope.[10]

Billorin's reference to himself as a "vicar-general" rather than as a simple vicar is unusual; perhaps he had a tribunal of sorts at the University of Paris—seeing that his letter was countersigned by University notaries. Since he does not mention any role to be played by the local bishop (i.e., the bishop of Paris),[11] he may have been prepared to try cases on his own, with juridical assistance as well as moral support from the Paris masters. He notes that Joan would be prosecuted by the procurator/promotor of the Holy Inquisition, and that he himself, officiating as judge/inquisitor,

[7] Martine Ostorero, "Itinéraire d'un inquisiteur gâté: Ponce Feugeyron, les Juifs, et le sabbat des sorciers," *Médiévales* 43 (Fall 2002) 103–17, p. 110.

[8] See, for instance, Tisset, *Procès*, 3:5.

[9] Clement V, *Multorum querela*, *Clem.* 5.3.1 (CIC 2:1181–82; CJC 3:2:263–70).

[10] Boniface VIII, *Per hoc*, *Sext* 5.2.17 (CIC 2:1076; CJC 3:1:638). See also John Andrew (Johannes Andreae), Ordinary Gloss on *Multorum*, ad v. *ad sententiam* (CJC 3:2:264–65): "dicit decretalis *Per hoc* ut, si discordent in sentencia, consultatur Papa" (the decretal *Per hoc* says that if they disagree on the sentence, let the Pope be consulted).

[11] The bishop of Paris could have claimed the same sort of jurisdiction over Joan that Cauchon would, since she had besieged his city.

would be assisted by the good counsel, favor, and aid of the doctors and masters of the University of Paris. Heinrich Denifle interprets this to mean that the masters of the University hastened to compel the inquisitor to institute a trial against Joan.[12] It might also have meant that he would draw on the faculty of the University for assistance in the trial, including appointing an *ad hoc* procurator.

Whatever Billorin's intention, we do not hear from him again. I will speculate below that the visionary woman Pieronne of Brittany may have been tried and burned to death by the bishop of Paris's official, acting without the participation of the Inquisition, in September of 1430.[13]

Billorin's assertion that Joan was vehemently suspect of heresy was an obvious falsehood, clearly designed to get her into a position to find or invent charges against her. But what sorts of things were being thought of? Could this teenaged illiterate girl be framed as starting her own heresy? If so, what would it be? Or what doctrine already condemned by the Church might she be said to be proclaiming? What erroneous ideas about the orthodox Christian faith was she supposed to be advocating? Assuring her soldiers that God was on their side and against the English would hardly qualify. Everyone assumed God to be on the home side. No worries, they would come up with something, by manipulating her into saying something wrong or in some other way.

What about rumors of Joan's practice of sorcery? Would not these have been enough to involve a heresy inquisitor? That is a complicated question, and it will be discussed below. Here it is enough to point out that the word "sorcery," like "witchcraft," usually translates to the Latin *sortilegium*, "sortilege," which meant "finding or reading portents," similar to *divinatio*, "divination" (i.e., "fortune-telling" or "prognostication"). Canon law forbade heresy inquisitors to deal with such activities "unless they savored of obvious heresy."[14] In other words, there had to be heresy

[12] Henri Denifle (with Émile Chatelain), *Chartularium Universitatis Parisiensis* (*CUP*), 4 vols. (Paris 1889–1897), 4:510–14: "Universitas Parisiensis et Johanna d'Arc," at p. 512.

[13] See Chapter 11, in my account of the sermon that Graverent gave against Joan after her execution.

[14] Alexander IV (1254–1261), *Accusatus de heresi*, *Sext* 5.2.8 §4 (CIC 2:1071–72). The text reads: "Cum negocium fidei, quod summe privilegiatum existit, per occupationes alias non debeat impediri, pestis inquisitores hereticae a Sede Apostolica deputati de divinationibus aut sortilegiis, nisi heresim saperent manifeste, intromittere se non debent, nec punire talia exercentes, sed eos relinquere suis judicibus puniendios" (Since the trial of faith, which is privileged above all, should not be impeded by other occupations, inquisitors of the plague

there already. Some authorities were finding ways of linking divination automatically with heresy at this time, but there is no indication of such thinking in the records of the prosecution against Joan, even when she was charged with "invoking demons" to get her knowledge of the future. We will see that the same was basically true when the University of Paris dealt with a demon-connected case in 1398. But now the University clearly conceived something of the sort against Joan from the very start. In September of 1429, the month of her failed attack, the University composed or authorized a treatise against her, *Tractatus de bono et maligno spiritu*,[15] in which, undoubtedly, a scriptural "discernment of spirits"[16] was performed, and she was judged, because of her evil deeds (fighting the English), to be on the side of the Devil, and empowered by him.

I should note that "vehement suspicion of heresy" was also a term of art, signifying the crime of "favoring heretics or their heresies," when there is no evidence of actually holding the heresies. It was a sort of second-degree heresy, related to actual heresy as misprision-of-treason is to treason.

2.2 A Bishop Is Preferred; a Bishop Appears

Vice-Inquisitor Billorin was obviously acting in the interests of the English occupiers of Paris; but the English authorities elsewhere, especially those traveling toward Rouen with King Henry VI (still a child of only eight years), under the charge of Cardinal Henry Beaufort, Bishop of Winchester,[17] may have preferred a bishop for the job. One reason might have been that, since no heresy inquisitor had even been assigned to England, they were not familiar with the operations and implication of this nominally papal tribunal. Furthermore, they may have been aware that the heresy inquisitor's jurisdiction was technically limited to matters of faith and heresy, whereas a bishop could prosecute other crimes as well. In any

of heresy deputed by the Apostolic See should not involve themselves with divinations or sortileges, unless they clearly savor of heresy, nor punish those who engage in them, but leave them to be punished by their own judges).

[15] See Denifle, *CUP* 4:512 and 4:515 no. 2370.

[16] St Paul speaks of a gift of discernment of spirits (1 Cor. 12:10), and St John warns: "Do not believe every spirit, but test the spirits to see whether they are of God" (1 John 4:1).

[17] See Bertram Wolfe, *Henry VI* (New Haven 1981), pp. 58–60; Ralph Griffiths, *The Reign of King Henry VI: The Exercise of Royal Authority, 1422–1461* (Berkeley 1981), p. 191. The expedition landed at Calais at the end of April, 1430, and arrived in Rouen at the end of July.

case, however, it would have been important to keep the prosecution as "a cause of the faith," since heresy was the only crime that could lead to a death penalty in ecclesiastical tribunals.

A perfect episcopal candidate soon appeared: Pierre Cauchon, bishop of the diocese of Beauvais. He was an avid English supporter, who was both a canon lawyer and a theologian. One problem was that he had no jurisdiction over Joan, who had never lived in Beauvais. However, since she was taken prisoner in Compiègne, which lay on the west bank of the River Oise, the eastern boundary of the diocese of Beauvais, a very temporary presence was claimed to be as good as residence for extending his authority to her. He was assigned the commission, and it was agreed that he would be paid the high salary of ten French pounds a day by the English for his services.[18]

The University of Paris was in due course won over to this suggestion, to the extent of pretending that Cauchon was the only bishop who had a claim to try her. It produced two letters, one to Luxembourg and the other to Burgundy, pointing out that there were two judges with jurisdiction over Joan: not only the inquisitor of France but also the bishop of Beauvais, in whose diocese she was captured. The University urged Joan to be sent to one of these judges to be tried because of the errors that she was spreading against the faith.[19] In the final trial record that Cauchon ordered to be produced, the dates were stripped from these two University letters, and they were inserted before the letter of Vicar-General Billorin, giving the impression that they were written earlier. As we will see below, they were written later, to assist in Cauchon's campaign.

Pierre Cauchon was born in or near Rheims around 1371, and at the age of fourteen he entered the University of Paris, where his career was both outstanding and incomplete. After six years, in 1391 or so, he became a Master of Arts, around the age of twenty, and entered the Faculty of Canon Law, becoming a Bachelor of Canon Law in 1395 and a Licentiate in 1398 (being licensed by Jean Gerson, Chancellor of Paris). But instead of taking the short step to the doctorate, he entered the Faculty of Theology, where he stayed for many years, but did not proceed to the bachelor's degree.

[18] Richard A. Newhall, "Payment to Pierre Cauchon for Presiding at the Trial of Jeanne d'Arc," *Speculum* 9 (1934) 88–91.

[19] Tisset, *Procès*, 1:4–8.

In 1397, he was elected to a term as rector of the University, in his capacity of Master of Arts, at the usual age of twenty-six or so. This was an important though mainly honorary position,[20] and the term lasted only three months (in his case, June 23 to October 10). More unusually, he served another stint as rector in 1403, when he was in his sixth year of theology.[21]

As was normal, Cauchon started piling up benefices, becoming the nominal rector of a parish in 1403 when still only a deacon, and canon of a cathedral. In 1409, he became a canon both of Beauvais and of his native Rheims, and the next year acquired the obsolete honorific of *vidame* (vice-lord, *vicedominus*) of Rheims. By 1419 he held a large number of incompatible benefices by way of dispensations solicited for him by the University of Paris.[22] His continued close relationship with the University was demonstrated in 1420, when the rector and doctors and masters and the University as a whole notified the people and clergy of Beauvais that the splendidly worthy Master Pierre Cauchon had been appointed as their new bishop by the pope.[23]

Cauchon's first action as self-designated judge of Joan was to write a letter in July of 1430 addressed to Burgundy, Luxembourg, and a subordinate of Burgundy's, the Bastard of Vendonne, ordering them in his name and in that of the King of England and France, Henry VI, to turn Joan over to him to be tried by him; she was suspected and accused of sortileges, idolatries, invocations of enemies (i.e., demons), and other things against the faith. He expressed his willingness to accept the assistance of Inquisitor Graverent, if the need should arise, and also the assistance of theologians and canonists. Cauchon delivered the letter personally

[20] See Astrik L. Gabriel and Gray C. Boyce, eds., *Auctarium Chartularii Universitatis Parisiensis*, vol. 6: *Liber receptorum nationis Anglicanae (Alemanniae) in Universitate Parisiensi* (Paris 1964), pp. xvii–xviii, for the statutory requirements, emoluments, and duties of rectors; they held first place in functions of the University.

[21] François Neveux, *L'évêque Pierre Cauchon* (Paris 1987), pp. 28, 36–37; Jean Favier, *Pierre Cauchon: Comment on le juge de Jeanne d'Arc* (Paris 2010), pp. 113–16. His status as rector in 1397 is demonstrated by a letter he wrote in October of that year: see Denifle, *CUP* 4:26–27 (no. 1744). In 1403, the University, in supplicating for a dispensation for Cauchon to acquire an additional benefice, identified him as a Master of Arts and Licensed in Canon Law, and as a scholar at Paris in the Faculty of Theology in the sixth year of study (ibid., 4:84).

[22] Denifle, *CUP* 4:90 n. 21.

[23] Ibid., 4:387–89 (no. 2167).

to Burgundy and Luxembourg in Compiègne on July 14, 1430.[24] The wording of this letter shows that he was offering to accept the heresy inquisitor not as his fellow-judge but only as an assessor or consultant, on the same level as theological and juristic assessors.

In the preliminaries to questioning Joan, however, he would say that he was motivated by respect for the Holy See, and also assert that it was a requirement in France to invite the heresy inquisitor to join himself to the proceedings, if he considered it advisable.[25]

Cauchon probably delivered the letters from the University to Burgundy and Luxembourg on the same day. As noted above, the dates of the University letters are missing in the Latin Record, where they are exhibited before Billorin's letter of May 26, but the French Minute preserves the date of the second letter, namely, July 14, the very day that Cauchon brought his own letter to Burgundy in his camp at Compiègne.[26] Cauchon also presented on behalf of King Henry VI an offer of up to 6000 francs and a pension of 200 or 300 francs to Vendonne, and the guarantee of 10,000 francs to Luxembourg.[27]

While Joan's purchase price was being gathered, the University of Paris became impatient at the delay, and in November the rector and the University wrote a letter of complaint to Cauchon, suggesting that he was failing in his diligence to bring her to trial. The Rector *du jour* was a Bachelor of Theology working on his doctorate by the name of Thomas de Courcelles,[28] who would play a key role in the proceedings once they

[24] Tisset, *Procès*, 1:9–11.

[25] Ibid., 1:26.

[26] Ibid., 1:8 n. 1.

[27] Ibid., 1:6. Tisset, *Procès*, 3:10 calls the latter sum a ransom (*rançon*), hardly appropriate here, for it was the purchase price not of Joan's freedom but rather of her deliverance into a worse captivity.

[28] For Courcelles, see Thomas Sullivan, *Parisian Licentiates in Theology, AD 1373–1500: A Biographical Register*, vol. 2: *The Secular Clergy* (Leiden 2011), pp. 174–79, and the fiche compiled by Dr Thierry Kouamé of the University of Paris: http://studium-parisiense.univ-paris1.fr/individus/13716-thomasdecourcellis.

He was born around 1401 (Denifle, *CUP* 4:549 (no. 2423). He was probably an MA by 1421, at the age of 20 or so. He became BTh by 1425, being identified as a *cursor* in theology in that year: ibid., 4:444 (no. 2256). In 1432 he was promised a dispensation to be licensed in theology (and thereby acquire the DTh) before the canonical age of 35, but it did not take effect until 1435, so he was improperly called "doctor" when he was at the Council of Basel in 1434: ibid., 564 (no. 2457).

got under way. Contrary to many modern accounts, he was no longer rector after December (1430), and would never hold the post again.[29]

The trial was now conceived of by the University as being conducted before both judges, Cauchon and Graverent. The best place for the trial would be Paris, they said, because of its abundance of experts. Another letter of complaint of the same date was addressed to Henry VI, with even stronger representations that Paris would be the ideal site for the trial.[30]

2.3 Further Jurisdictional Questions

Inquisitor Graverent, as already noted, had jurisdiction over the whole of northern France; his headquarters were in Paris. But what jurisdiction did the Bishop of Beauvais have in Paris? As it turned out, the English command decided that the trial venue would be in Rouen. Cauchon's jurisdictional problem was solved there by requesting the diocese of Rouen to cede territory temporarily to the diocese of Beauvais for the purpose of holding the trial there. There was currently no active archbishop of Rouen, for the current holder of the title, Jean de Rochetaillée, had eventually stepped aside from the spiritual duties of the see after being named a cardinal in 1426, and thus it was considered vacant.[31] So the cathedral

[29] Gabriel and Boyce, *Auctarium Chartularii*, 6:xviii–xxx, give a list of rectors between 1424 and 1494; Courcelles is listed on p. xviii (elected 16 March 1426; cf. col. 9 n. 2), and p. xix (elected October 10, 1430). The four rectors of 1431 are listed on pp. xix–xx: Johannes Haneron, Petrus de Gouda, Johannes de Ponte, and Guillielmus Echocard. Courcelles served his first rectorship when he was twenty-five or so, a year after he received his bachelor's degree in theology. He would receive his licentiate in theology in 1435 and a month later his doctorate, becoming a master of theology. He later became a canon of Paris, in 1445 (again drawing on Dr Kouamé). Thus, Tisset, 2:394, and Favre, p. 400, are mistaken in saying that he was rector again in 1431 and 1435, and Tisset, 3:320, is mistaken in saying that he was rector from 1430 to 1432. His request for the status of master in 1433 despite his young age proves that his birthdate was 1401, not 1397 (let alone 1393).

[30] Tisset, *Procès*, 1:11–14. The second letter was from the University alone (not mentioning the rector).

[31] Rochetaillée became archbishop in 1423, and when he was made a cardinal in 1426, the chapter objected to the appointment as inconsistent with the role of archbishop; eventually therefore he kept only the administration of the diocese. It lapsed when the next archbishop was appointed, namely, Hugues d'Orges, in January of 1431, just as the proceedings against Joan were getting under way. See Conrad Eubel et al., *Hierarchia catholica medii aevi*, 8 vols. (Münster 1898–1978), 1:448, cf. Beaurepaire, *Recherches*, pp. 50–54.

chapter, consisting of the canons,[32] was in charge: it granted the petition on December 28, 1430. It is noteworthy that Cauchon's reasons for the request, which the canons rehearsed, did not include any difficulty about trying Joan in Beauvais itself.[33] Finally, a circular letter from Henry VI, dated January 3, 1431, at Rouen, told of Joan's crimes, notably the abominable offense of dressing like a man, murders, false claims of divine guidance, the spreading of false doctrines, and treason against himself; therefore, as urged by the doctors and masters of the University of Paris, he ordered her turned over to the bishop of Beauvais for trial.[34]

There was no indication in these last two letters that the "Holy Inquisition" was intended to play a role in the trial, and, in fact, Cauchon started the preliminary proceedings as sole judge. But then, on February 19, just before Joan's first appearance in court, Cauchon requested the deputy-inquisitor for Rouen, Jean Lemaistre, the prior of the Dominican house there in the city, to proceed jointly with him. Lemaistre appeared and objected that his jurisdiction did not extend to the diocese of Beauvais. The next day, Cauchon announced that the experts to whom he had shown the vice-inquisitor's commission from Graverent concluded that he did indeed have the power to participate, but Cauchon decided, for greater certainty, to request Graverent himself to participate, or to send another vicar with sufficient powers. Lemaistre continued to believe that he could not in good conscience undertake the role without further authorization; however, insofar as it was allowed to him, he agreed that Cauchon should proceed on his own until such permission was forthcoming. Cauchon then wrote to Graverent to request his participation, since the matter of heresy was pertinent to his office, or to grant the requisite extension of powers to Lemaistre or to someone else.[35]

Graverent, as it happened, was already co-judge in a much less consequential case in the diocese of Coutances, which we will look at more closely below.[36] He therefore agreed to Cauchon's alternative request by

[32] The chapter was headed by a dean, but we do not hear of him, though other officers appear in connection with the proceedings, for instance, the treasurer, Raoul Roussel. Roussel will be archbishop of Rouen when the first investigations into Joan's trial are undertaken, in 1450 and 1452 (he served from 1444 until his death on the last day of 1452; see Eubel, *Hierarchia*, 2:225).

[33] Tisset, *Procès*, 1:16–18.

[34] Ibid., 1:14–15.

[35] Ibid., 1:27–32.

[36] Graverent's case was against Jean Lecouvreur, treated in the next chapter.

specifically authorizing Lemaistre to function as inquisitor in the diocese of Beauvais. He wrote to Lemaistre to this effect on March 4: since he himself was legitimately impeded from participating in the case against the woman Joan, he delegated Lemaistre to do so.[37]

Cauchon formally accepted Lemaistre as his co-judge on March 12, after the public interrogations of Joan had ended.[38] His role, however, would be only re-active, not pro-active; he is hardly ever mentioned as doing something separately from Cauchon. This has led to the conclusion that he disapproved of the proceedings against Joan, which may be true. Nicolas de Houppeville, a priest of the Rouen diocese with a bachelor's degree in theology, would later testify that he used to speak with Lemaistre, who said that he was forced to take part in the trial, and was much afraid. Houppeville often saw him greatly perplexed during the proceedings.[39]

Other Dominicans under Lemaistre's command in Rouen may also have been favorable to Joan, especially Martin Ladvenu, her final confessor, who hardly participated at all (he appeared with Lemaistre on February 20, and not again for two months), and Isambart de Lapierre, who started to attend when Lemaistre joined the bench. We can perhaps assume that Graverent himself, if he had been able to take the case, would have been more enthusiastic because of his English leanings. A month after her execution, he gave a sermon in Paris purportedly summing up the facts of the case and expressing approval of Joan's burning, which has been interpreted as evidence that he approved of the way in which the trial was conducted. But, as we will see when we come to it, if Graverent's sermon was reported accurately by the chronicler who relates it, his alleged "facts" reveal the most appalling misinformation.[40]

We saw above that there was no canonical need for Cauchon to call on the Holy Inquisition at all. But even if he thought that there was such a need, or some advantage to it, say, in spreading the blame for the punitive nature of Joan's captivity, there was no rush. The prison conditions, after all, were in the hands of the English keepers and arguably out of his control.

[37] Graverent to Lemaistre, March 4, 1431, writing from Coutances, Tisset, *Procès*, 1:120.

[38] Ibid., 1:118–20.

[39] Pierre Duparc, *Procès en nullité de la condamnation de Jeanne d'Arc*, 5 vols. (Paris 1977–1988), 1:446, cf. 203–04.

[40] See Chapter 11 in this volume.

2.4 The Situation in 1430–1431: Archbishop, Pope, and General Council

Another point to keep in mind is metropolitan jurisdiction. Each archbishop was not only the "ordinary" judge of his own diocese but also the "metropolitan" judge of the whole province in which his diocese was situated, and a trial held before a bishop in his own diocese could be appealed not only directly to the pope but to the metropolitan instead. It happened that the diocese of Beauvais was not in the province of Rouen but in the province of Rheims (while the diocese of Paris was in the province of Sens). I have not seen that the possibility of Joan's appealing from Cauchon to the archbishop of Rheims was recorded, but it is likely that it was thought of.

Pierre Cauchon would clearly have avoided by every means any acknowledgment of the archbishop of Rheims's jurisdiction over him, because the current archbishop, Regnault de Chartres, was Charles VII's chancellor, who had crowned him at Rheims in July of 1429. Early on, he had presided over the lengthy examination of Joan by a board of theologians at Poitiers, which allowed her to continue with her mission. Houppeville, in fact, had pointed out that Chartres was Cauchon's metropolitan superior, as a reason why he should not be Joan's judge—and that was one of the reasons Cauchon imprisoned Houppeville.[41] Although Chartres often disagreed with Joan's strategies, and characterized her capture at Compiègne as allowed by God because of her willfulness, including the pride and pleasure she took in her rich clothing,[42] he presumably would have ridiculed the charges prepared against her by her enemies, for example, that her male clothing or her claimed visions and actions were heretical or against Christian faith in some way, let alone criminal in some lesser way.

Since the city of Rheims was in English hands, and the archbishop in exile, any appeal to metropolitan authority would have to be, not to the provincial court of appeals, but to the archbishop's audience, which was not limited to Rheims, but followed the archbishop's presence.

Another possible reason for Cauchon to want the heresy inquisitor as co-judge was to by-pass Rheims jurisdiction and leave the papacy as the

[41] Duparc, *Procès*, 1:445 (Houppeville's own testimony).

[42] Larissa Juliet Taylor, *The Virgin Warrior: The Life and Death of Joan of Arc* (New Haven 2009), pp. 43–44, 94, 118–19.

only destination of appeal, although no sign of such motivation is hinted at in the French Minute or Latin Record.

However, Cauchon was just as eager to keep the case out of the hands of the pope. We will see in a case reviewed below that appeal to the Roman curia in the time of the papal schism was problematic. But in Cauchon's time, the papal question had been resolved for the most part (though that would not prevent Cauchon from trying to find some heterodox view on Joan's part). There was general agreement that Martin V, the pope who emerged from the Council of Constance in 1418, was the one true pope. The fact that he died just as proceedings got going against Joan in 1431 would likely not have meant any interruption in the process of appeals to the Holy See, for the curial personnel would have remained in place to tide them over to the next pope.

The summons for a general council at Basel in Switzerland, which Pope Martin issued just before his death, was taken up and continued under his successor Eugene IV, and this looming council will have some effect on the prosecution of Joan of Arc, as we will see.

CHAPTER 3

Judgmental and Judicial Precedents

3.1 Gerson and Paris Theologians Condemn Invokers of Demons, 1398

We will now postpone our examination of the prosecution of Joan to look at a series of precedents that can throw light upon both the procedural and doctrinal aspects of her case, especially those connected with theologians of the University of Paris, who played a vital role in her condemnation.

Let us begin with the decree of the University's Faculty of Theology under the rubric *De superstitionibus* on September 19, 1398, led by Jean Gerson (1363–1429), which occurred during Cauchon's first stint as rector.[1] Gerson was not only a doctor of theology and professor (master) in the theology faculty, but also chancellor of the Cathedral of Notre Dame in Paris. Being "chancellor of Paris" made him also chancellor of the University, which, apart from ceremonial duties, entailed his granting licenses to its graduates. In fact, he licensed Cauchon that year in canon law, after which Cauchon switched fields and began his studies in the Faculty of Theology.

[1] Denifle, *CUP* 4:32–35 no. 1749, dated September 19, 1398. For an English translation, see Lynn Thorndike, *University Records and Life in the Middle Ages* (New York 1944), pp. 261–66, reprinted by Alan Charles Kors and Edward Peters, *Witchcraft in Europe, 400–1700: A Documentary History*, ed. 2 (Philadelphia 2001), pp. 129–32.

H. A. Kelly, *The Trial and Retrial of Joan of Arc*, The New Middle Ages, https://doi.org/10.1007/978-3-032-07887-2_3

A prologue to the condemnation describes at length but in vague terms an elaborate magic ceremony that had actually occurred, referring to "those who were present at the said work and took part in it," and "the principal actor of that artifice, as appears from their confessions." The participants expected to come from it "the spirit who would reveal and make known hidden treasures." The prologue ends with this declaration: "Our deliberate conclusion is as follows, that not only those who use such figments and sorceries (*maleficia*) to find hidden treasure or learn and know things secret and occult, but also all professed Christians in possession of reason who voluntarily operate and employ such things in such manner are to be held superstitious in the Christian religion, are to be deemed idolaters, are to be deemed invokers of demons and strongly suspect in the faith."[2] There is no indication that the perpetrators were in fact prosecuted and condemned under any of these heads.

There follows an open letter "to all devotees of the orthodox faith" from the Chancellor of Paris and the Faculty of Theology, who say that, because this "nefarious, pestiferous, and monstrous abomination of false insanities with its heresies (*cum suis heresibus*)" has multiplied in their day, they, "burning with zeal for the faith," will condemn some articles that bear upon it. They quote St Augustine, who says that those who practice such things "have belied their Christian faith and baptism and become pagans and apostates." They wish to extirpate and uproot "the insane and sacrilegious errors of the foolish and fatal rites that harm, contaminate, and infect the orthodox faith and Christian religion."[3]

They then list twenty-eight anonymous propositions, all of which are judged to be errors. The first few can serve as examples: (1) "That by magic arts and sorceries and nefarious invocations to seek the intimacy and friendship and aid of demons is not idolatry." (2) "That to enter on a pact with demons, tacit or express, is not idolatry or a species of idolatry and apostasy." (3) "That to give or offer or promise to demons such-and-such a thing in order that they may fulfill a man's desire, or in their honor to kiss or carry something, is not idolatry."[4]

[2] Trans. Thorndike, in Kors and Peters, p. 129. In their Introduction, Kors and Peters overread this declaration, saying that the conclusion of the theological faculty was that "witchcraft and diabolical sorcery, in all of its manifestations, could only be heretical" (p. 14).

[3] Thorndike, in Kors and Peters, pp. 130–31.

[4] Ibid., p. 130. In the original they give their reasoning by which each proposition is declared erroneous, but Denifle omits it.

Four of the propositions (nos. 10, 13, 14, and 19) are found to be not only errors but also blasphemies, for instance, the 14th: "That God himself directly or through good angels revealed such sorceries to holy men." One proposition, no. 21, is condemned as "an error in faith, in natural philosophy, and in true astrology." It reads thus: "That images of copper or lead or gold or white or red wax or other material baptized, exorcized, and consecrated, or rather execrated, according to the said arts and on certain days, have marvelous virtues which are recited in the books of such arts."[5]

In spite of all the damage that these practitioners do to the Christian faith, there seems to be no inclination on the part of these righteous defenders of that faith to consider them heretics and urge their deliverance to the secular arm to suffer deserved death in the flames. Their one mention of heresies seems more of a rhetorical flourish than an exact designation.

3.2 Bishop d'Ailly's Case Against Marie Ducanech, ca. 1399–1403

Next, let us examine an inquisition undertaken in the following year by a bishop and a vice-inquisitor against a woman, the same combination that we will see in the trial of Joan of Arc.

The bishop was a mentor of Gerson's and his predecessor as chancellor of Paris, former master of theology Pierre d'Ailly. Born in 1350, d'Ailly achieved his doctorate in 1381 at the young age of thirty-one. In 1384 he became rector of the College of Navarre (not rector of the University itself). He was chancellor of the University from 1389 to 1395, when the recently elected Avignon pope Benedict XIII appointed him bishop of Le Puy, and then, in 1397, moved him to Cambrai.

The vice-inquisitor was, as usual, a Dominican friar, named Nicolas de Péronne, an alleged vicar of the alleged Inquisitor of Northern France, with jurisdiction in the diocese of Cambrai. The woman was Marie Ducanech, who ran a money-changing business in Cambrai. After she was put on trial by d'Ailly and Péronne, found guilty of heresy, and fined a large sum of money, she appealed against them to d'Ailly's metropolitan, the archbishop of Rheims, whose court found against them.

[5] Ibid., pp. 131–32.

D'Ailly and Péronne then appealed against the archbishop, not to the pope, as might be expected in other times, but to the highest secular court in France, the Parlement of Paris. An obvious reason for not approaching the pope was that in 1398 France had withdrawn its obedience from Benedict, and, for the following five years, it recognized neither him nor the Roman pope, Boniface IX.[6] The Parlement also decided against d'Ailly and Péronne, and it is from its verdict, or *arrestum*, that we can reconstruct the case.[7]

The verdict, issued on June 30, 1403, concerned a complaint brought by the bishop of Cambrai and Vice-Inquisitor Péronne, which amounted to a civil action against Guy de Roye, Archbishop of Rheims (r. 1391–1409). Both d'Ailly and de Roye were members (clerical councilors) of the Parlement, and recognized as such in the verdict. We know that d'Ailly was in Paris as early as March 17 of 1403, when he is on record as having participated in a session of the Parlement.[8] He was central to negotiations to restore French obedience to Benedict XIII; matters came to a head in May, when Louis Duke of Orleans, King Charles VI's brother, instructed the metropolitans to poll their suffragan bishops on the matter on May 28 in Paris.[9] The participants surely included the duke's allies, the archbishops of Auch and Tours; and d'Ailly would have been a prominent discussant.[10] However, one source singles out only d'Ailly and Archbishop de Roye,[11] who belonged to the rival faction of Philip the Good, Duke of Burgundy, the king's uncle.[12] Burgundy conceded on the next day, May 29, and the king appointed d'Ailly to announce the reunion publicly in Notre Dame on May 31, which he did.[13] In due course, d'Ailly would be appointed as Charles's ambassador to Benedict along with the archbishop of Aix.[14]

[6] Louis Salembier, "Ailly (d'), Pierre," *Dictionnaire de théologie catholique* [*DTC*], ed. Alfred Vacant et al., 18 vols. (Paris 1899–1972), 1:642–54, cols. 642–43.

[7] *Arrestum* of Parlement, 30 June 1403, ed. Pierre Varin, *Archives administratives de la ville de Reims: Collection de pièces inédites*, etc., vol. 3 (Paris 1848), pp. 639–43 (lower set of footnotes).

[8] Noël Valois, *La France et la grand schisme d'Occident*, 4 vols. (Paris 1896–1902), 3:342 n. 1.

[9] *Chronique du religieux de Saint-Denys*, ed. M. L. Bellaguet, 6 vols. (Paris 1839–1852), 3:90.

[10] Valois, *La France*, 3:337.

[11] *Chronographia regum Francorum*, ed. Henri Moranvillé, 3 vols. (Paris 1891–1897), 3:224.

[12] Valois, *La France*, 3:315, 337 n. l.

[13] *Chronique de Saint-Denys*, 3:94–98.

[14] Ibid., 3:102. They arrived on 1 September 1403.

With these dramatic events in the background, Bishop d'Ailly's challenge against Archbishop de Roye was heard in Parlement in the month of June, 1403. D'Ailly and the vice-inquisitor were contesting de Roye's right to hear appeals in cases of heresy that the two of them tried together in the diocese of Cambrai. Their complaint took the form of a suit of *novel disseisin*,[15] "recent dispossession"—dispossession in this case not of landed property, but of jurisdiction. The archbishop, they claimed, had no right to recognize or respond to such appeals, which could be made only to the Holy Roman See (i.e., the papal curia).[16] The archbishop and his officials, however, in spite of being aware of the complainants' rights, had issued a cease-and-desist order against them in the preceding year (i.e., 1402), on the pretext that one Marie Ducanech claimed to have appealed against them for putting her on trial for having spoken heretical-sounding words; the bishop and vice-inquisitor were cited to appear in the archbishop's court, and commanded not to institute any further action against Marie. For this reason, the bishop and vice-inquisitor brought their complaint against the archbishop, who was consequently summoned to Parlement to respond to the complaint.[17]

When both parties, or their proctors, met in the court of Parlement, the complaint was first aired, and satisfaction ("return of possession") and court-costs demanded from the archbishop. De Roye's proctor responded that the archbishop possessed the jurisdiction to hear appeals from Cambrai, including appeals against cases heard by the bishop and vice-inquisitor, insofar as they concerned the bishop and not the inquisitor. In the specific case of Marie Ducanech (here the proctor was undoubtedly drawing on the text of Marie's appeal), she was a prominent citizen of good standing in the city of Cambrai who had been cited to appear before the bishop and vice-inquisitor, in contempt of the appeal against them to the archbishop that had been made by her and her husband, Giles de Haussy, and one of her brothers.[18]

This response on the archbishop's part is a clear indication that Marie had initiated the appeal during the course of her prosecution. She had

[15] It was called *novel disseisin* by English jurists in their "Law French." In France the Latin term for it was *casus novitatis*, as in our case. See Jean Brissaud, *A History of French Private Law*, tr. Rapelje Howell (Boston 1912), p. 340.

[16] *Arrestum*, pp. 639–40. The popes in Avignon, both before and after the schism, always referred to themselves as possessing the See of Rome.

[17] Ibid., p. 640.

[18] Ibid., pp. 640–41.

submitted the appeal directly to her two judges, and it had been ignored or rejected by them; or she had submitted it directly to the archbishop and then informed the judges; or she had submitted it directly to the archbishop after being stymied by the judges.

The archbishop's proctor characterized the action against Marie as follows: the bishop and vice-inquisitor claimed that three years previously—that is, around 1399 (the year after d'Ailly became bishop of Cambrai)—during a legal proceeding involving her business of money-changing, she was put under oath by the bishop's official, swearing to respond truthfully to a series of allegations to be put to her. In the course of her testimony, they asserted, she stated that she did not have to respond in matters that concerned her honor and interests.[19]

If there were any truth to this charge, Marie may have simply meant that she did not have to incriminate herself on unfounded implications of suspicions. What she replied, however, was that, being a fragile woman, she had no memory of saying any such thing so long ago, and that if she had spoken rashly in any way, she had referred herself to the disposition of Holy Mother Church in revoking such words.[20] By this she doubtless intended to say that she went to confession and received absolution for any sinful failing on her part.

The archbishop's proctor continued: Péronne, acting as vicar of the inquisitor-general for France, and also as a commissary appointed by the bishop, after various delays, condemned Marie to publicly recant the words attributed to her, and ordered her imprisoned in her own house for eight days, requiring her also to go on various pilgrimages and to perform other penances and mortifications; furthermore, he prohibited her from carrying on her business for nine years (subject to the bishop's "grace"), and ordered her to pay eighty gold crowns for his expenses.[21] The clause about the bishop meant that d'Ailly would be able to charge her a fine to resume her trade.

Because of this, Marie had appealed to the archbishop, and succeeded in getting the bishop cited to court in Rheims, whether to the provincial court of appeals, headed by the official (judge) of the province of Rheims, or the archbishop's court of audience, presided over by the archbishop himself or his official. The bishop's proctor had appeared and admitted the

[19] Ibid., p. 641a.
[20] Ibid.
[21] Ibid., p. 641ab.

archbishop's jurisdiction and confirmed that Marie had made an appeal. However, the proctor asked for a delay in implementing the absolution that Marie demanded, and during that delay the bishop and vice-inquisitor instituted the present action of complaint against the archbishop in the Parlement.[22]

Furthermore, the archbishop's proctor said, the alleged vice-inquisitor did not have any such authority as he claimed from the inquisitor-general in France, because there was at present no such inquisitor. If, however, he did indeed have such power, the words attributed to Marie were not of sufficient weight to justify his intervention in treating them as a matter of heresy. Péronne had been appointed as the bishop's commissary in order to defraud the archbishop of his jurisdiction—which would appear to be unnecessary in view of his claim to be the vicar of the inquisitor-general. But, supposing that he acted properly in both capacities, the said Marie could appeal to the archbishop against him as the bishop's deputy (as she had done), and to the Holy See against him as the inquisitor's deputy.[23] The latter appeal, of course, would have been difficult if no papal curia was recognized.

Finally, the archbishop's proctor asserted that the bishop and Péronne could not legitimately complain against him until he had decreed whether or not he could admit the appeal, and therefore Parlement should not hear their complaint. If, however, it was to be heard, the judgment should go against them, and all costs assessed to them.[24]

In response, the proctor of d'Ailly and Péronne asserted that their proceedings against Marie had been legitimate and justified, and Péronne had acted with both episcopal and papal authority. It was not possible for the archbishop to divide the case of appeal, since it devolved entirely to the Holy See by reason that the inquisitor's jurisdiction subsumed the bishop's ordinary jurisdiction. Because the matter properly savored of heresy (and even if it did not), the archbishop had no right to intervene, and since he attempted to hear the appeal, their complaint was justified. Moreover, he issued his citation prematurely, before determining whether he should have done so, and therefore their complaint should be heard. The archbishop's proctor responded that the argument for devolving jurisdiction was not in their original complaint and so was not valid.[25]

[22] Ibid., p. 641.
[23] Ibid., pp. 641–42.
[24] Ibid., p. 642a.
[25] Ibid., p. 642ab.

After closing arguments, June 30 was set for the verdict, and on that day the court decided, after thorough deliberation, that d'Ailly and Péronne's complaint would not be admitted; Archbishop de Roye was confirmed in his rights, and the bishop and vice-inquisitor were assessed all costs.[26]

Henry Charles Lea is doubtless correct in seeing the original prosecution against Marie as an opportunity for the Holy Inquisition to generate income at a time when heresy was in decline.[27] But it also provided an opportunity for the bishop's treasury to be enriched. In addition, it demonstrated what a forceful woman not manacled or held in prison could do against judicial persecutors.

3.3 Proceedings Against Tyrannicide in Paris, 1413–1414

An even more relevant set of proceedings occurred in 1413–1414, called the "Council of Faith," presided over by the Bishop of Paris, Gérard de Montagu, and the Inquisitor of Northern France, Jean Polet, OP.[28] It shows how an ordinary sin, like murder, could be spoken of in terms of heresy. The affair is too long to be thoroughly discussed here, but it is important because Cauchon would play an important role in it later. It all stemmed from the assassination of Louis, Duke of Orleans, in 1407 by agents of the new Duke of Burgundy, John (later called *Sans Peur*, "the

[26] Ibid., pp. 642–43.

[27] Henry Charles Lea, *A History of the Inquisition of the Middle Ages*, 3 vols. (Philadelphia 1887), 2:133–34, and see 1:479.

[28] The acts of the proceedings of the Council of Faith (CF) are printed in Vol. 5 of the badly transcribed *Opera omnia* of Gerson, ed. Louis Ellies Dupin, 5 vols. (Antwerp 1706; ed. 2, The Hague 1728), 5:49–323, beginning as an open letter from Judges Montagu and Polet, telling of the meeting on November 30, 1413 (CF 49–52), but lacking epistolary continuity and sign-off after their sentence condemning the treatise was issued on February 23, 1414 (CF 322–23). Many of the errors are corrected by Denifle, *CUP* 4:261–85 nos. 1988–2017; and see Alfred Coville, *Jean Petit: La question du tyrannicide au commencement du xve siècle* (Paris 1932), Chapter 14, "La concile de la foi de Paris," pp. 439–501. Gerson's own texts are given in corrected form in Gerson, *Oeuvres complètes*, ed. Palémon Glorieux, 10 vols. (Paris 1960–1973). Glorieux provides a valuable summary or "dossier" of the tyrannicide affair from 1407 to 1418, 10:164–70.

Fearless"), who held the dukedom from 1404 to 1419.[29] It was this deed[30] that precipitated the feud between the Burgundians and the Orleanists, the latter supported by partisans of the Count of Armagnac. Some months after the killing, in March of 1408, a doctor of theology named Jean Petit gave an oral presentation of his treatise, *Justification of the Duke of Burgundy*,[31] in Paris before an audience of nobles and University professors, in Duke John's presence.

Petit's work had been quickly and clumsily put together, and it should have proved very vulnerable to attack. It consisted, in the first part, of arguments for the necessity on some occasions of taking the law into one's own hands to kill dangerous vassals who are plotting against their king; but he misleadingly identified such traitors as "tyrants." The first and third of his Eight Truths would draw particular fire. In the first, he says that any subject-vassal who uses subterfuge or sortilege against his sovereign to take away his sovereignty commits lese majesty. In the third he says that it is licit for any other subject to kill such a disloyal traitor and tyrant (*traitre disloyal et tyrant*), especially when the traitor is of such great power that the sovereign himself is unable to take action as justice demands.[32]

The second part of Petit's treatise consists of wild charges against Orleans to prove that he was just such a traitor-tyrant. It begins with a long account of how he tried to machinate the death of Charles VI years earlier by hiring a quartet of miscreants, including a monk who called up two devils named Heremas and Estremain, who helped give noxious qualities to a saber, a sword, and a ring through various magical processes.[33]

There was no notable response to Petit's work until around the time of his death in 1411, when calls for evaluation came from some members of the Faculty of Theology of the University of Paris, while others said it would not be expedient.[34] But when the Armagnac forces took over Paris

[29] His father was the previously mentioned Philip the Bold (r. 1363–1404); he was succeeded by his son, Philip the Good (r. 1419–1467), adversary of Charles VII and Joan of Arc.

[30] For a detailed account of the killing and its aftermath, see Eric Jager, *Blood Royal: A True Tale of Crime and Detection in Medieval Paris* (New York 2014).

[31] Jean Petit, *Justification du duc de Burgoigne*, as copied in Enguerran de Monstrelet's *Chronique*, ed. Louis Douët-d'Arcq, 2 vols. (Paris 1857–1862), 1:178–242. A Latin version of it is printed in Gerson, *Opera*, 5:15–42, which greatly improves the work's arguments and citations; translator/reviser unknown.

[32] Petit, *Justification*, pp. 203–06.

[33] Ibid., pp. 224–27.

[34] Statement of Master Jean d'Achery in the consultation of November 30, 1413, CF 64–65.

in September of 1413, Jean Gerson, still chancellor, immediately called for action in an oration-treatise of his own, *Rex in sempiternum vive.* It was delivered before King Charles, and addressed to him, on September 4.[35] In it he said that he did not wish to lay blame on any particular person, and did not name Petit (or Burgundy); rather he laid out Seven Assertions, all anonymous, like the twenty-eight demon-magic theses that he and the Theology Faculty condemned in 1398. He said that they were false propositions currently rampant, which should be eradicated.

The Seven Assertions, however, were only similar to Petit's positions, not identical. Specifically, the first and most important Assertion says that "Any tyrant should and can rightly be killed by any of his subjects," etc.,[36] a much more indefensible position than Petit's corresponding statements cited above.

Some of the Assertions are simply false, according to Gerson. Saying that Phinehas, Moses, and Joab killed without authorization (Assertions 3, 4, and 6 respectively) is contradicted by Scripture. Assertion 5, that Judith and Jehu did not sin in using deception, favors the error of those who believe that lying is permissible. But the other three Assertions, he insists, contain errors of faith. Assertion 1, the injunction to kill tyrants, is against both faith and morals because it violates the Commandment "Thou shalt not kill," and falls under Christ's statement "All who take up the sword will perish by the sword," when interpreted by the Ordinary Gloss's qualification, "by their own authority." Assertion 2 (St Michael out of natural love inflicted eternal death on Lucifer, and was rewarded by God) contains several errors of faith, which he sets forth without explaining how they are against faith. Assertion 7 (it is licit to do something good even though one has sworn not to do it) is also an error against faith (unexplained).

He then elevates his polemic to the level of heresy. He appeals to Charles's royal authority and declares that every wicked doctrine and heresy should be driven out of his realm (*que toute mauvaise doctrine et heresie soit chassée hors de vostre royaume*). He then asks: "Where are our prelates

[35] Gerson, *Rex in sempiternum vive*, *Opera*, 4:657–77 (*Oeuvres*, 7:1005–30), starting with a verse from Daniel (2.4). See Coville, *Jean Petit*, pp. 433–37, for a summary.

[36] Gerson, *Rex*, cols. 669–70. Coville, pp. 440–41, displays Gerson's Seven Assertions alongside passages from Petit on corresponding subjects.

of Holy Church? Where are the inquisitors, who are bound to extirpate all the errors of the people?"[37]

An obvious reason for Gerson's anonymous approach this time was that the prelate who was meant to step forward to counter these errors, Bishop Montagu, could be impugned as a capital enemy of Burgundy, since it was under the duke's auspices that the bishop's brother, Jean de Montagu, Grand Maître d'Hôtel du Roi, was executed for treason in 1409.[38]

Two days later, on September 6, 1413, there was a congregation of the entire University of Paris, namely, proctors of the four Nations making up the Faculty of Arts (France, Picardy, Normandy, and England [= Germany]), Masters of the Faculties of Arts and Medicine, and Doctors of the Faculties of Theology and Canon Law.

There was general approval of Gerson for his oration. Then the French and German Nations along with the Faculty of Medicine asked the Faculty of Theology to approve the oration itself and to attend to the extirpation of heresies, especially those noted therein (of course, nothing was actually called a heresy); and the Faculty of Theology complied, by approving the oration.[39] Then Gerson read the Seven Assertions and his assessment of them. The Faculty of Theology approved all, and engaged to support him in any action that might arise against him because of it; and the University thanked him and committed the Assertions to the Faculty of Theology for examination.[40] Finally, the French Nation approved the oration.[41]

A month later, on October 7, 1413, King Charles wrote a letter to the bishop of Paris or his spiritual vicars or his official. It has come to his attention, he said, that many heresies and errors have been written and spoken in Paris and elsewhere. He therefore requires the bishop and his subordinates, along with the Inquisitor of France or his deputies, as well as notable masters of the Faculty of Theology and other members of the University of Paris, to inform themselves of them.[42]

[37] Coville, *Jean Petit*, p. 437; Gerson, *Rex*, col. 670C.

[38] Coville, *Jean Petit*, p. 453.

[39] Notarized instrument of September 6, 1413, CF 54–55 (garbled text with wrong date of Sept. 4); see Denifle's edition, *CUP* 4:262–63 no. 1989. Denifle notes that, although in the original vote the Faculty of Canon Law and the Picard Nation were opposed, a majority approval was sufficient for the measure to pass.

[40] Second instrument of 6 September 1413, CF 55–58 (*Oeuvres*, 10:171–74).

[41] Third instrument of 6 September 1413, CF 58–59.

[42] Letter of Charles VI, 7 October 1413, CF 52–53.

Almost two months later, on November 30, a group of twenty-nine University men, mainly Masters of Theology, including Jean Graverent, the future inquisitor,[43] appeared before the bishop's official, Jean Tudert, and Vice-Inquisitor Pierre Floure, OP,[44] who was standing in for Inquisitor Polet. Then, significantly, copies of Petit's *Justification* were exhibited, which must have displeased Gerson, who continued to insist that he did not wish to hurt anyone, or to incite any lord or prince. All present were asked to give their advice concerning the exhibits.[45]

A few days later, on December 4, Bishop Montagu and Inquisitor Polet, "…as competent judges in this matter," put the matter to a larger group of consultants,[46] and on December 19 another session was opened, now using the term *Concilium Fidei*.[47]

At the conclusion of these consultations on January 5, 1414, Official Tudert announced, on behalf of the judges who were there present and presiding, that they had found that the Seven Assertions were rightly reprobated. However, since the question of whether they were contained in Petit's treatise was raised, a committee of seventeen masters was appointed to study the matter.[48] Also at this meeting of January 5, a protest was read by the Picard Nation objecting against Gerson's tactic of first condemning the Assertions in addressing the king, and then seeking University confirmation of his judgment.[49] Specifically, they interpreted Gerson as having declared the Assertions "heretical and even contrary to Faith" (*esse hereticas et etiam contrarias Fidei*).

The Petit committee eventually produced Nine Excerpts from his treatise, which turned out to be not entirely accurate, especially the all-important First, which is a mash-up of Petit's Third and First Truths, in

[43] Graverent in his replies already shows a familiarity with the "style" of the Holy Inquisition (CF 177–80).

[44] Floure would be licensed in theology at the end of the current year, 1413: *CUP* 4:268 no. 1998. Denifle calls him Polet's vicar-general, having interpreted Ellies Dupin's "provinciarius generalis" (CF 52) as "provicarius generalis" (but this would seem to mean "deputy of the vicar-general").

[45] Meeting of November 30, 1413, CF 54–64, with responses on CF 64–69; see Coville, pp. 453–60; cf. *CUP* 4:27172 no. 2000.

[46] CF 70; *CUP* 4:272–73 no. 2001.

[47] CF 78–79. *Concilium Fidei* was also the term used when witnesses were interviewed about Petit's treatise on December 14 (CF 212).

[48] CF 215–17.

[49] Gerson, *Opera*, 5:377–78; *CUP* 4:274–75 no. 2005.

which the expression *traitre disloyal et tyrant* is deleted and replaced with *tout tyrant*, "every tyrant," thus:

> It is licit according to natural, moral, and divine law for any subject, without order or command, to kill (or arrange the killing of) every tyrant who through covetousness, trickery, sortilege, or conspiracy machinates against the bodily well-being of his king and sovereign lord to take away his high and noble lordship, and not only licit but also honorable and meritorious, especially when the tyrant is of such great power that justice cannot easily be effected by the sovereign.[50]

Copies were given to a large number of masters for comment, and over the next several days, February 12 to 19, the great majority voted for condemnation.[51] Graverent said that the matter should be taken up by the Holy See. He warned of the dangers involved in local condemnations, recalling that in 1277 Bishop Tempier of Paris condemned propositions of Thomas Aquinas. He exhibited the letter of annulment of Tempier's action issued by a later bishop of Paris in 1326.[52]

Finally, on February 23, before a great audience, Tudert explained the nature of the proceedings that had occurred "in a Council or Matter of the Faith,"[53] and Bishop Montagu and Inquisitor Polet introduced themselves once again as "competent judges in this matter." They gave a long prologue[54] to their pronouncement, calling the latter "a certain ordination for the exaltation of orthodox faith" (*certa ordinatio ad orthodoxe fidei exaltationem*). They had heard by *publica fama* that various errors ill-sounding in faith and morals had been disseminated in the city and diocese of Paris, said to have originated in the damnable treatise of the deceased Master Jean Petit, *Justification of the Duke of Burgundy*. They therefore, proceeding *ex officio*, convened masters in a Council of Faith to deliberate over the treatise and some specific errors found in it. Having examined the masters' conclusions, they hereby pronounced their own "sentence or ordination,"

[50] See Coville, *Jean Petit*, pp. 488–89.

[51] CF 219–77. All Nine Excerpts, approved for condemnation by a majority of the committee, are given and explained by Coville, *Jean Petit*, pp. 488–91.

[52] CF 314–15. See *CUP* 2:280–82. Earlier that same morning, February 17, 1414, Thomas Hobe, Master of Arts, made a similar argument, and urged that a legate be sent from Rome to deal with this matter rather than leaving it to the local diocese (CF 313).

[53] CF 322.

[54] This prologue is not given in CF; see *CUP* 4:280–81 no. 2014.

sitting in tribunal, as follows: the treatise is to be condemned, specifically Nine Excerpts from it, as erroneous in faith and morals and multiply scandalous, as is explained more fully in the record of the proceedings (*in processu*); and the treatise itself is to be burned. They give the text of the Nine Excerpts, with a short qualification or condemnation for each, which I summarize as follows:

1) It is licit for a subject to kill any tyrant who machinates against the king.
Erroneous in faith and morals, multiply scandalous.
2) All laws authorize such killing.
Erroneous in faith and morals, injurious to laws.
3) It is licit to kill such a one through deceit.
False, erroneous, scandalous.
4) It is right that such tyrants be killed in a vile manner.
Erroneous, cruel, and impious.
5) A tyrant-slayer should be applauded by the king.
Erroneous in faith and morals, detrimental to royal rule.
6) The king should honor the tyrant-slayer, as God honored Michael and Phinehas.
Erroneous in faith and morals, detrimental to royal rule.
7) The king should give the tyrant-slayer wide praise.
Erroneous in faith and morals, scandalous, detrimental to royal rule.
8) St Paul's "The letter killeth" means that following the literal meaning of Scripture always kills the soul.
Distorted and erroneous interpretation.
9) Oaths can be broken when detrimental to self or family.
False and erroneous, opening the way to perjury.

That is, five of the statements (nos. 1, 2, 5, 6, and 7) are found to infringe somehow upon Christian Faith, thus falling under the proper jurisdiction of the Inquisitor of the Faith.

All persons are ordered under pain of excommunication to turn in any copies they may have of Petit's treatise, and not to teach or defend any of the statements. All are commanded to delate those who fail to obey, either to the judges or to the chancellor of Paris.[55]

[55] CF 322–23.

The burning of all currently gathered copies of the condemned treatise was carried out two days later, on February 25, in front of "the Church of Paris."[56]

It is clear that the proceedings were not conceived of as an actual trial, with a named defendant, but only an examination of opinions in a treatise with a named but deceased author, followed by a condemnation of propositions or opinions. The comparison to the well-known action of Bishop Tempier in 1277 raised by Graverent was doubtless taken to heart by many. On that occasion, only two books were denounced by name, *De amore* (without mentioning the author, Andreas [Capellanus]), and a book on magic containing experiments of sortilege and invocations of demons, along with other books treating of similar things clearly opposed to orthodox faith and good morals (*fidei orthodoxe et bonis moribus evidenter adversantibus*).[57]

The whole process can stand as an object lesson in how easily offenses which would seem to belong exclusively to the moral sphere, like violations of the Ten Commandments, could be qualified as deviating from essential Christian belief. The next step would be, presumably, to see them not only as errors *in* faith but also as *against* faith (as in Tempier's decree), and finally as suspect of heresy or actual heresies (as the Picard Nation seemed to believe was Gerson's conclusion about his Assertions), which, if stubbornly held—or not!—might be punished by burning at the stake.

3.4 Tyrannicide, Heresy, and Cauchon at Constance, 1415–1418

3.4.1 Burgundy Appeal to Pope: Tried by Three Cardinals

Duke John the Fearless did not let the matter of the Petit condemnation rest in France, but appealed it to the pope elected by the Council of Pisa, John XXIII (in opposition to the Pope of Rome, Gregory XII, and the Pope of Avignon, Benedict XIII). Pope John appointed a commission of three cardinals to deal with it, which they did at Constance,[58] at the General Council that Pope John had summoned. As we shall see, Gerson

[56] CF 223.

[57] Denifle, *CUP* 1:543–58 no. 473, at p. 543. Those who continued to hold the condemned propositions were subject to excommunication; they were to be denounced to the bishop or the chancellor of Paris, to be punished as the gravity of the matter required.

[58] Present-day Konstanz, in southern Germany on the present Swiss border.

took the Petit matter up as well, at the Council itself. Cauchon, as Burgundy's representative, was involved in everything.[59]

Burgundy first made his appeal to the pope shortly after the Paris sentence was delivered, in March of 1414, and then renewed it in September.[60] The events of the resulting trial are summed up in the sentence given by the cardinals at its conclusion on January 15, 1416.[61] By this time John XXIII was no longer pope, having been deposed on May 29, 1415.

Cardinal Giordano Orsini of Albano, speaking for the other two commissioners (Cardinals Antonio Panciera of Aquileia and Francesco Zabarella of Florence, the latter a noted canonist), begins the sentence by giving the text of Burgundy's letter of supplication to the pope. He alleged that the bishop of Paris and the inquisitor of France, at the prosecution of some envious persons, sentenced a treatise by Jean Petit, professor of theology, to be burned as malicious and deviating from the faith. Since the condemnation touched Burgundy's honor, he appealed to the Pope to appoint a commission to summon the said judges and hear the case *ex officio*.[62] But in fact, instead of being conducted as an *ex officio* inquisition, the case would be run as a civil trial, with Burgundy as plaintiff and Bishop Montagu and Inquisitor Polet as defendants.

When Cardinal Orsini opened the trial, presumably at Constance, Pierre Cauchon was present, acting as Burgundy's proctor, and he requested that Montagu and Polet be summoned.[63] At its earliest, this request could have happened only well into January 1415, since Cauchon set off for Constance only on January 8.[64] But it could also have happened much later. We do know that it occurred before September 6, and that the date for the bishop and inquisitor to comply had not yet been reached.[65]

[59] See Coville, *Jean Petit*, Chapter 15, "Le Concile de Constance," pp. 503–61, and Sebastián Provvidente, "*Stylus theologicus et iuridicus*: La *causa* Jean Petit à Constance (1414–1418) et les débats sur le tyrannicide," *Médiévales* 77 (2019) 129–51.

[60] Coville, *Jean Petit*, pp. 504–05.

[61] The sentence is printed in Gerson, *Opera*, 5:500–07.

[62] Ibid., 5:500.

[63] Ibid., 5:501. Cauchon is identified as principal substitute of Jean de Montlyon, principal proctor of the duke of Burgundy.

[64] Coville, *Jean Petit*, p. 512.

[65] A Burgundian correspondent (intimate of Martin Porée, Bishop of Arras), writing on September 6, 1415: Gerson, *Opera* 5:382–85, at col. 385. Coville, *Jean Petit*, p. 532, says without citing a source that the Council's Commission (described below) summoned the bishop and inquisitor to appear before their tribunal on October 24.

When the day did arrive, the bishop and inquisitor were found in contempt for non-appearance, though their proctor, Jean Martinet, did appear but did not consent to the cardinals' jurisdiction, objecting orally to their commission and citation. Another proctor for Burgundy, this one from the Roman Curia, Giovanni da Montegiustino, then presented a libellus detailing Burgundy's complaint. He accused Montagu and Polet of "putting their sickle to another's crop," because the condemnation of opinions against the faith belongs solely to the Holy See. Furthermore, when they sentenced the treatise of Jean Petit to be burned, after condemning nine alleged Excerpts from it, they did not summon Burgundy, who was named in it, and did not otherwise follow due process (*ordo juris*). Burgundy therefore appealed to the pope to have the proceedings declared null. Martinet was ordered to respond to the libellus, but, not doing so, was declared in contempt.[66]

Then Montegiustino asked to have the letters or instruments that Chancellor Gerson had produced before the judges deputed by the Council of Constance in a trial of faith concerning the aforesaid Excerpts; accordingly, a notary delivered a letter of Charles VI as well as a letter by the two judges, both containing the sentence against the Petit Excerpts and treatise.[67]

It seems clear that an important aspect of the trial would be the question of the authenticity of the Nine Excerpts.[68] Extant drafts of the judges' sentences, produced in December of 1415, show that the cardinals either did not believe or were not convinced that the Excerpts had been proved to be Petit's.[69]

In their final sentence on January 15, 1416, the cardinals declared that the sentence passed by the bishop of Paris and the inquisitor of France against Jean Petit's book and contents on February 23, 1414, was null and void.[70] As usual with such sentences, no reasons were given, but the above-noted or suspected lack of correspondence of content must clearly have been one of them.

It was not, however, among the justifications given by the cardinals in their letter to Burgundy on May 15. Instead, they observed that if single

[66] Gerson, *Opera*, 5:502–04.
[67] Ibid., 5:504.
[68] Ibid., 5:385.
[69] Coville, *Jean Petit*, p. 533.
[70] Gerson, *Opera*, 5:504–07.

bishops could make declarations of doctrine it would result in great discrepancies throughout Christendom. It might have been alleged that there was a custom for such declarations in the case of the bishop of Paris, but no such argument was made in this instance, and, in fact, no one had appeared as a legitimate defender of the bishop and inquisitor. There were other reasons, too, they said, which they would not mention here. They ended by saying that if there was any dissatisfaction with the sentence, it could be appealed to the General Council.[71]

The cardinals returned to the subject of their decision in an open letter of June 26, responding to allegations that had come to their attention. One such was that they had allegedly given their approval to the Nine Excerpts, whereas they had said nothing about them; that was a question currently pending before judges commissioned by the Council (they themselves, in fact, were among those very judges). Their decision was based on their judgment that it did not pertain to the bishop of Paris to pronounce on the point, especially since the duke of Burgundy, who was implicated in the matter, had not been cited to the proceedings. They repeated what they had said in their letter to Burgundy, that no custom had been mentioned concerning the bishop of Paris, and no one had spoken in defense of the bishop and inquisitor. But instead of adding that the case could be appealed, they said that it actually had been appealed, in the name of the bishop and the inquisitor, and was now pending.[72]

On October 5, Gerson entered a complaint to the College of Cardinals, telling about the appeal made by the king of France, the University of Paris, the bishop of Paris, and the inquisitor of France (while the latter was still alive); and even though it had now been over seven months, no commission had yet been assigned to hear the appeal.[73]

3.4.2 *Council Commission Trial of Petit's Nine Excerpts*

That was late 1416. Let us go back to early 1415 and catch up with the activity in the Council of Constance that Montegiustino referred to. In mid-March of 1415, there had been an agreement between Charles VI

[71] Gerson, *Opera*, 5:585–86. At the time of the sentence, in January, and again in February, Gerson produced writings arguing that all bishops had the right to decide on doctrine: Glorieux, *Oeuvres*, 10:168.

[72] Ibid., 5:606–07.

[73] Ibid., 5:673.

and Burgundy that neither side would bring up the question of tyrannicide at the Council, which was signed off on Burgundy's side specifically by Cauchon.[74] He was Burgundy's ambassador to the Council, along with Martin Porée, bishop of Arras.

This accord was broken by Gerson on April 11, who declared to the French Nation representatives that opposers of the Paris condemnation were supporters of heresy.[75] Burgundy responded in a letter of May 15, which Porée and Cauchon presented on May 26, saying that the treatise written by Jean Petit was condemned at Paris by his enemies, in an unsafe place, and he was not summoned to participate, as he should have been; furthermore, he knew of no errors in the treatise.[76] At this, Gerson, who was present, protested and demanded to have justice here at the General Council, and Porée and Cauchon also agreed to submit to what the Council would determine (*se submittebant determinationi predicti sacri Concilii*).[77]

Gerson began to lobby for action to be taken on the Nine Excerpts, which were added to the Commission of Faith set up on June 15 to deal with Wyclif and Hus.[78] In addition to two theologians and two canonists, this Commission consisted of the same three cardinals who were appointed by John XXIII to hear Burgundy's appeal. A fourth cardinal was also appointed, namely, Pierre d'Ailly, whom we met above as bishop of Cambrai in the prosecution of Marie Ducanech; since then John XXIII had made him cardinal. However, he was challenged by the Burgundians, and stepped down as judge, but remained as a spokesman for Gerson's side.

According to the same letter-writer of September 6 quoted above, Gerson exhibited Petit's alleged Nine Excerpts to the Commission on June 25, without identifying them as such, desiring them to be condemned as anonymous errors of faith. But under challenge from Porée, he was finally forced to admit that they were the Excerpts condemned in Paris, and he exhibited the letters containing the sentence of the bishop and inquisitor (referred to above in the appeal trial before the three cardinals), and asked that the sentence be confirmed.[79]

[74] Ibid., 5:ante343.

[75] Ibid., 5:362; Coville, *Jean Petit*, pp. 515–16.

[76] Gerson, *Opera*, 5:343–46 at 345.

[77] Ibid., 5:346–47; Coville, *Jean Petit*, p. 518.

[78] Commission Judges' memo, Gerson, *Opera*, 5:636. The memo extends from June 15, 1415, to July 11, 1416 (on col. 340); Coville, *Jean Petit*, pp. 518–19.

[79] Burgundian correspondent of Sept. 6, 5:383.

On July 1, Cauchon entered a lengthy protest against the Paris sentence as invalid in matter, form, and mode, as follows (I summarize):

> In matter, because the propositions were never proposed or preached by Jean Petit; if some words in them seem to be extracted from his treatise, the extraction was and is false and done in a false and truncated manner by enemies of the duke (*extracio fuit et est falsa ac falso modo et truncato per emulos ducis facta*).
>
> In form, because no bishop or inquisitor had jurisdiction in a cause of faith by law or practice (*tam de jure quam de stilo nullam habuerint potestatem*), because a cause of faith in such matter was not condemned by the Church (*cum causa fidei in tali materia ab ecclesia dampnata non erat* [*sic*], meaning that the matter being judged had never been declared heretical or contrary to faith). Moreover, the bishop of Paris was a capital enemy of the duke, since he and his brother, the archbishop of Sens, were in a war with him at this time, and the bishop had sent assassins to kill the duke, which had been confessed to by one of them who had been caught and executed. Furthermore, the place where the trial was held was not safe.
>
> In mode (*modus procedendi*), because the masters who were used as consultants or assessors were formal adversaries of the duke or harbored ill will against him, while others, moved by a zeal for justice, were repulsed. Moreover, the Faculty of Canon Law of the University of Paris, which expressed opposition, should have been summoned, as it usually was in such cases. The Picard members of the Faculty of Theology were also opposed when the sentence was passed, and the Faculty of Medicine's approval, which was sought, was not obtained.[80]

3.4.3 Council Condemnation of Quilibet tyrannus, *July 6, 1415*

Meanwhile, there was another plan afoot, from which the Burgundians were excluded. On June 24, King Sigismund left Constance on other business, and he threatened not to return until the Petit matter was finished. This inspired the idea to bring up a single tyrannicide assertion before the whole Council for condemnation, with the hope that it would satisfy the king.[81] The chosen assertion, beginning with the words *Quilibet tyrannus*, reads in English as follows:

[80] Heinrich Finke, *Acta Concilii Constanciensis*, 4 vols. (Münster 1896–1928), 4:264–66 no. 395.

[81] Coville, *Jean Petit*, pp. 520–21; Provvidente, "*Stylus theologicus*," pp. 134–35.

> Any tyrant can and ought to be killed, licitly and meritoriously, by any of his vassals or subjects, even by means of plots and blandishments or flattery, notwithstanding any oath taken, or treaty made with the tyrant, and without waiting for a sentence or a command from any judge.

When the Burgundians found out about it, they realized that it was simply a Latin translation of the first of Gerson's Seven Assertions, which he had produced in his sermon *Rex in sempiternum vive* on September 4, 1413, and later on in the Council of Faith.

To prove this to the Council, the Burgundians on July 2 tried to exhibit one of the instruments produced on September 6, 1413, which listed the Seven Assertions, but the motion was rejected. They tried twice again, on the 3rd and the 5th, only to have it rejected again both times.[82] Then, probably on July 5 itself, they presented a long petition to the Council: since the Church is not accustomed to condemning assertions without naming their assertors, the author of *Quilibet tyrannus* should be named and punished, or it should be acknowledged that Gerson deceitfully made it up, and it should be condemned as such. Otherwise, it could be falsely attributed to another person. The Council should make clear that it does not intend to attribute this opinion to any person, dead or alive, and it should prohibit any blaming or punishing of specific persons for having held such a doctrine.[83]

Whether or not there was any debate on these points, a decree, *Precipua sollicitudine*, was passed by the Council on July 6 condemning *Quilibet tyrannus* as one of several currently dogmatized assertions erroneous in faith and good morals, causing much scandal, and threatening to subvert the state and public order. The Council defines the assertion as heretical, and declares that all who hold it pertinaciously are heretics.[84] Thus was achieved at an ecumenical level what Gerson had originally hoped for in the diocese of Paris, at least for the first and most important of his Seven Assertions.

All this happened at the end of Session 15. Before this, on the same day, Jan Hus's articles were condemned, receiving only a general characterization: "Many of them are erroneous, others scandalous, others offensive to

[82] Finke, *Acta*, 4:266, referring to the second instrument of September 6, 1413, Gerson, *Opera*, 5:55–58 (see above); it was notarized by Jacques Ysambard.

[83] Finke, *Acta*, 4:266–68 no. 396.

[84] Council of Constance, Session 15 (July 6, 1415), p. 432 (Tanner, *Decrees*, 1:432). A rubric was added to this decree mistakenly identifying *Quilibet tyrannus* as by Jean Petit.

the ears of the devout, many of them are rash and seditious, and some of them are notoriously heretical and have long ago been rejected and condemned by holy Fathers and by general councils." After this, Hus was condemned to be delivered to the secular authority (whereupon he was burned at the stake).[85] Still earlier in the session, 260 articles of John Wyclif were condemned, added to the forty-five condemned earlier, in Session 8 on May 4, 1415.[86] They were given a similar characterization: some were notoriously heretical and already condemned by holy Fathers, while others were erroneous, others scandalous, and so on.[87] A similar formula was used for the articles of Jerome of Prague in Session 21 on May 30 of the following year.[88]

We see in all of these cases that the only heresies referred to are long acknowledged ones, which gives the impression that all the other objectionable opinions of all three heretics did not rise to the level of heresy. Whether or not this impression was intended, the condemnation of *Quilibet tyrannus* stands out as giving the opposite impression, of recognizing a new heresy. What it fails to do, of course, is to explain why it is considered heretical, and not merely seditious, or offensive to the devout, or something else. This outcome should have given great satisfaction to Gerson. But he was far from satisfied.

3.4.4 Council Commission Trial, Continued

On July 7 or 8, Cauchon was back in the tribunal of the conciliar Commission, arguing that scandal would be caused by any decision about the Nine Excerpts attributed to Petit, or the Eight Truths found in his treatise, whether of approval or rejection. The Council should forbid discussion of them, nullify the Paris verdict, and decree that no one who had approved or disapproved them in the past should be held suspect of heresy.[89]

[85] Tanner, *Decrees*, 1:427, 429.

[86] See Henry Ansgar Kelly, "Trial Procedures Against Wyclif and Wycliffites in England and at the Council of Constance," *Huntington Library Quarterly* 61 (1999) 1–28 (repr. in *Inquisitions*, article V), pp. 20–21.

[87] Tanner, *Decrees*, 1:414.

[88] Ibid., 1:433.

[89] Finke, *Acta*, 4:268–69 no. 367.

But on July 9 Cauchon submitted a libellus against Gerson, which was enlarged on July 20.[90] It stated that the Eight Truths of Petit's treatise were not in opposition to kings but actually in their favor, and they contained nothing against the faith. They were different from the Nine Excerpts condemned at Paris, which were invented by the bishop of Paris and Gerson, and they were also different from *Quidem tyrannus*, condemned just now at the Council; this too had been invented by Gerson, when he preached it before the king of France. He asks that the sentence against Petit's treatise be annulled, and that Gerson be punished for calumny and making false accusations of heresies and errors.

Gerson refused to respond to the libellus, claiming to be only an evangelical denouncer, and not a party to the case.[91] On August 22 he entered a formal statement to that effect, saying that he was not a juridical denouncer.[92]

On September 2, Cardinal d'Ailly, now acting as an advocate for Gerson, submitted a statement to the commissioned judges claiming that Cauchon's libellus contained many errors in faith and morals, and enormous injuries, as many theologians would be prepared to say, but were not willing to become involved. He urges the judges to reject the libellus as frivolous. An examination of Petit's Eight Truths will show that nos. 3, 4, 6, and 7 are heretical, and no. 8 extremely scandalous. And they certainly deal with faith, the first principles of which are based not on goat's wool but natural law. What could be more pernicious than doubts about killings, perjury, and ambushes? Let the old heresies of Arius and the new heresies of Wyclif show how dangerous it is not to crush the heads of the Babylonian children against the rocks [cf. Psalm 137]. The duke of Burgundy said that he did not approve of any of Petit's errors, but now these so-called truths are being submitted in his name. They must be condemned as false and heretical.[93]

Cauchon did not respond to the cardinal, but rather a Franciscan friar named Jacques le Tessier stepped up in his place. Even though he was still only a bachelor of theology (more qualified than Cauchon, of course), and would not become a master until years later, in 1422, he was referred to as

[90] The content of the libellus is partially given in the record in Finke, *Acta* 4:269–71 (see notes on pp. 269 and 272) and in the letter of the Burgundian correspondent, 5:384.

[91] Burgundian correspondent, 5:384.

[92] Finke, *Acta*, 4:272.

[93] Ibid., 4:272–73.

"Magister Jacobus."[94] He said, first of all, that if there were any theologians who found errors in the libellus, they should offer proofs. He supported the request that the judges examine the Eight Truths. They will see that they are not heretical, he adds, but rather disputable, until such time as the Church determines one way or another. No one of sane mind will find heresies there, unless they are lying. As to what the confectors of this petition say about faith, they are wolves in sheep's wool, ready to ravage the innocent. The first principles of faith are based not on natural law but rather the articles of the Apostles' Creed. What articles are violated in those eight statements? What errors of faith can be found therein?[95] These questions could have been used to refute one of the charges against Joan of Arc, but, as we will see, Master Jacobus, under the name of Jacques de Touraine, will be a member of Cauchon's team of University of Paris theologians determined to convict her.

More fruitless discussions in the Commission tribunal would follow. On April 11 of 1416, the judges published the opinions against and for condemnation on the Nine Excerpts in a trial of faith, without identifying names. Only twenty-six of the consultants were in favor, thirteen of whom were from the University of Paris. A stunning fifty-one were opposed, a serious blow to Gerson and his allies.[96]

At last, on July 11, the Commission judges decided not to give a sentence on the question of the Nine Excerpts, but to remit the affair to the Council,[97] which both Gerson and Cauchon favored. But the Council did nothing further.

3.5 Inquisitor Graverent in Rouen and the Trials of Jean Ségueut

An "Instrument of Sentence" (Proclamation of Conviction), consisting of an open letter written on the front side of a very large folio of parchment—much bigger than an open spread of newspaper—tells of a trial of faith undergone by Jean Ségueut or Ségueult, a secular advocate of Henry VI in Rouen, completed on November 29, 1430, and signed by four

[94] Denifle, *CUP* 4:261–62 no. 1988.

[95] Finke, *Acta*, 4:273–76.

[96] Commission Judges' memo, 5:639–40. According to Glorieux, *Oeuvres*, 10:167, a proclamation of the results had been made back on January 11.

[97] Commission Judges' memo, 5:640.

notaries, including the three who worked on Joan of Arc's trial, which began a month later.[98] Such instruments as these were doubtless posted on the doors of the town's cathedral or main church, which in this case would be the Rouen Cathedral.

The letter is addressed "to all who will inspect it," by the two judges, namely, "the official of Rouen, at this time when the archiepiscopal see is vacant, and the inquisitor of the faith and heretical depravity Jean Graverent, OP, professor of theology." We know the unnamed official to be Jean Basset, a licentiate in canon law, in this post since 1429.[99] He was presumably the chief judge not only for the diocese of Rouen, but the appellate judge for the whole ecclesiastical province of Rouen, which consisted of the dioceses of Evreux, Avranches, Séez, Bayeux, Lisieux, and Coutances, as well as Rouen.[100]

3.5.1 The First Trial, ca. 1428, Judged by Graverent Alone

Embedded in the letter is a description of a trial in which Ségueut appeared before the inquisitor acting on his own, without an episcopal co-judge. In this trial, which occurred in 1428 or earlier,[101] Ségueut was convicted of holding the following positions:

1) that Christ's lordship on earth was only over the souls of men;
2) that a cleric must have received the sacrament of confirmation as well as tonsure to have valid clerical privilege;

[98] Ségueut Case: Rouen, Archives de Seine-Maritime: Seine-Inférieure, archives ecclésiastique, G 1154; Paul Doncoeur and Yvonne Lanhers, eds., *Instrument publique des sentences portées les 24 et 30 mai 1431 par Pierre Cauchon et Jean Le Maître, OP, contre Jeanne la Pucelle* (Paris 1954), Appendix 2, pp. 71–80. The proclamation consists of a single grammatical sentence, some 3400 words long (almost three times the length of the Declaration of Independence, and just under the length of the first Magna Carta), with seventy-two lines of main text, approximately fifty words per line; it is followed by certifications of the four notaries. The whole document measures some 60cm high and 69cm wide. An account of the contents is given by the archivist Charles de Beaurepaire, who discovered it: *Recherches*, pp. 70–77. "Segueut" is mistakenly spelled "Seguent" by Tisset, *Procès*, 2:411–12.

[99] Tisset, *Procès*, 2:384.

[100] Since an archbishop could hear both appeals and first-instance cases from the dioceses of his province (see Alexander III, *Cum non ignoretis*, X 1.30.1, CIC 2:183), the official would presumably have the same jurisdiction, especially when there was currently no archbishop.

[101] Beaurepaire, *Recherches*, p. 72 n. 1.

3) that Christ and his disciples possessed nothing in this world, and Christ was not king in this world, as he himself said ("My kingdom is not of this world").

He revoked the first as false and erroneous and against Christ's lordship. He revoked the second as "not well said" (as clerics say) and false, since tonsure and the sacrament of confirmation are two different things, and one can take place without the other. He revoked the third as false and against the Holy Gospel and Sacred Scriptures. He also revoked other positions condemning ecclesiastical jurisdiction, which were judged as belonging to a lower category of condemnation (i.e., "offensive to pious ears").[102]

The inquisitor sentenced him to make these revocations in the presence of two other members of the clergy. Ségueut agreed to the sentence, and did not make an appeal against it (*cui sententie acquievit, nec ab ea appellavit*)—which meant, of course, that he had the opportunity of appealing, presumably to the pope, since the inquisitor was directly appointed by the pope. He swore on the holy Gospels to bear himself in the future as a good Catholic and to show honor to the Church and its ministers and to the inquisitor, and to do nothing against the persons of the inquisitor or his officers or the witnesses produced against him (*sive testium contra eum productorum*).[103] Which tells us that witnesses *were* produced against him.

When Graverent testified in the Council of Faith in Paris in 1414, already seemingly connected with the Holy Inquisition, he did not speak of heresy, and he was very reluctant to condemn the Nine Excerpts allegedly taken from Petit's treatise, recommending instead that the Holy See adjudicate the question. But what reason for restraint was there in the present case? The first and third charges against Ségueut dealt with the poverty-of-Christ controversy; furthermore, part of the third, that Christ and the apostles had no property, had been condemned as a heresy by Pope John XXII in one of his collected decretals appended to canon law.[104]

[102] Ségueut Case, Doncoeur-Lanhers, pp. 73–74.

[103] Ségueut Case, p. 74; cf. Beaurepaire, *Recherches*, pp. 71–72.

[104] John XXII, *Cum inter nonnullos* (12 Nov. 1323), *Extravagantes Johannis XXII* 14.4 (CIC 2:1229–30). There is a new edition by Jacqueline Tarrant, *Extravagantes Iohannis XXII* (Vatican City 1983). For a translation, see Heinrich Denzinger, *Compendium of Creeds, Definitions, and Declarations*, ed. 43, ed. Peter Hünermann (San Francisco 2012), pp. 294–95.

Yet here it was only declared to be false and against Scripture, needing not to be abjured but only rejected.

The trial as described in the letter appears to be a model of due process, with which Ségueut must have been very satisfied, since he did not take the opportunity to appeal. But the new charges against him which the judges go on to relate show that the opposite was true.

3.5.2 The Second Trial, 1430, Before Official Basset and Graverent

Ségueut's new trial, just now concluded at the end of November, 1430, was initiated during a congregation of clergy of the Rouen province assembled in the archbishop's mansion, meeting for the reformation of ecclesiastical rights and liberties. It was attended by bishops, abbots, deans, archdeacons and other ranking clergy, and also doctors and masters of theology and canon and civil law. Basset and Graverent came before them accompanied by their respective promotors,[105] to consult these gathered "Fathers" concerning certain offenses that, *prima facie*, seemed to deal with faith. According to *publica fama*, they said, Ségueut was suspected of having committed them in the time since his earlier trial. The promotors then rehearsed the articled offenses, "the text of which, particularly those savoring of heresy, is given below."

Before stating these articles, however, the promotors recount his earlier trial (which we have seen above), where the articles, including one actual heresy, are only called false.

Here are the present articles:

1) He (Ségueut) made these statements:
   (a) That denial of the power of excommunication should not be cause for arrest and detention.
   (b) That the clergy used the inquisitor as a club.
   (c) That the wrong done to himself in his own trial was as bad as that done to Christ on the cross.

[105] Basset used Jean Leroy, a canon of the Rouen cathedral chapter, who was the permanent archiepiscopal promotor for Rouen, while "the promotor of the Holy Inquisition of the Faith" (*promotor Sancte Inquisicionis Fidei*) was identified as Aubert Morel. Because Morel was an advocate in Basset's court (see Tisset, *Procès*, 2:419), his appointment as Graverent's promotor may have been only *ad hoc*, just for this case.

(d) That the official who accused him at that time apologized to him and asked his pardon.

2) He said many times in and out of court that he was unjustly tried, for no reasonable cause; and asserted that things would not remain the same.
3) He repeatedly said that he did not dare to defend the king's causes in court for fear of being brought to a trial of faith and ensnared in his words (*caperetur in verbis suis*), as had recently happened to him, unjustly and deceitfully (*prout nuper injuste et dolose captus fuerat*), and that it was more for hatred of him because he supported the king that he was put on trial than for defending the faith, and that he would make a complaint about this and get satisfaction.
4) He repeatedly vowed to take action against the inquisitor and "such people" if the king came.[106]

Even though there is little that is doctrinal in these articles, the judges must have assumed that the readers of their letter would accept that these articles somehow flirted with heresy. Or at least that the Fathers of the congregation, now co-opted as court assessors, found them to do so.

After the clergy discussed the articles, it was concluded that the judges should conduct an investigation, and, if they wished, they could use two legal experts. Ready and willing to obey, as they said was their duty to do so, Basset and Graverent employed two masters and four notaries and went about swearing in trustworthy persons to testify as witnesses. When the investigation was completed, the judges themselves summoned another congregation. Articles and the depositions of witnesses were produced, but with the names of the witnesses suppressed because of the grave danger to them that the judges believed to exist (*propter grave periculum quod protunc nobis videbatur innuere*).[107] As I noted in Chapter 1, this provision was in keeping with the decretal *Statuta* of Boniface VIII in his *Liber Sextus*.[108]

The majority of the assessors wished Ségueut to be arrested and incarcerated, but Basset and Graverent decided on a milder course, simply citing him and listening gently to his responses (*citandum et dulciter audiendum in suis responsionibus*). He refused to comply with the first

[106] Ségueut Case, p. 74; cf. Beaurepaire, *Recherches*, pp. 72–73.
[107] Ségueut Case, pp. 74–75.
[108] Boniface VIII, *Statuta*, *Sext* 5.2.20 (CIC 2:1078).

citation, and was sentenced for contempt and excommunicated. He finally appeared after eight days in another congregation, but after dinner, saying that he was now willing to follow the law and respond before the judges to the interrogatories put to him (*paratus, ut dicebat, stare juri et respondere coram nobis super interrogatoriis eidem*). But the judges decided that "the matter was great and deserved to be treated maturely on an empty stomach," and he was to come back on another day at eight o'clock in the morning; and they required the prelates, masters, and doctors there present to attend, *in favorem fidei* (indicating a legal and moral obligation on their part).[109]

On the day assigned, with the clergy assembled, the parties appeared before the judges. One party consisted of the two promotors, claiming the backing of *publica fama*, and the other was the defendant (*reus*), Jean Ségueut. The promotors immediately exhibited "the aforesaid articles" against the defendant, along with the interrogatories drawn from them, so that he might be questioned upon them. The judges accordingly put him under oath to tell the truth about their contents (*de et super contencia in eisdem articulis et interrogatoriis*).[110] This questioning on the charges lasted longer than that morning and afternoon:

> It was not only on that day but also on other days and terms assigned to him by us that he was interrogated and heard. The said defendant was heard on everything he wished to say, of his pure and spontaneous will, not coerced, by his own volition; he referred himself completely to the information already gathered against him upon the aforesaid articles, and also to further information to be gained, if it pleased us. But he desired to say or allege nothing against the information or informations already in hand or to be gathered, or against the persons of witnesses produced against him or to be produced.[111]

[109] Ségueut Case, p. 75.

[110] Ibid.

[111] Ibid., 75–76: "Super quibus articulis et interrogatoriis fuisset dictus reus, nedum solum ipsa die, sed eciam aliis diebus et terminis per nos eidem assignatis interrogatus et auditus, ipsoque audito in omnibus que dicere volebat dictus reus, ejus mera et spontanea voluntate, non coactus, motu proprio, ad informacionem jam contra eum factam super articulis predictis et fiendam, si nobis placeret, omnimode se retulisset; nec aliquid contra informacionem seu informaciones contra eum factas aut fiendas, aut personas testium contra eum productorum sive producendorum, dicere, proponere, seu allegare voluisset."

The judges were clearly concerned in their proclamation to show that everything was done according to due process of law. Not only the charges but the follow-up questions based on them were made known to the defendant from the very beginning. The oath that was imposed on him bound him to respond truthfully only to the matters contained in the articles and questions, and there was no effort to force further facts or thoughts from him against his will. They obviously did not wish to give any credit to his expressed fear that he would be tricked by captious questions, as he claimed had happened to him before. Evidence was gathered by use of witnesses, and presumably their depositions were shared with him (though this is not explicitly stated). As for how he could impugn the character witnesses (and thereby disqualify them) without knowing their identity, defendants in such cases were supposed to be asked to name persons who might be inimical or prejudiced against them.

Extracts were taken from the proceedings of what was confessed and proved (*de confessatis et probatis*)—proofs, of course, would consist of the depositions of witnesses. (Beaurepaire in his summary states that the extracts were approved by the defendant, but the letter does not say so.) They were distributed to prelates, doctors, and masters of the diocese and province of Rouen, and to the Faculty of Theology of the University of Paris, and also to jurists in Paris, as well as to some doctors and masters from England residing in Rouen,[112] to advise the assessors, and these deliberations as well as the whole process—articles, interrogatories, responses, extracts (*cedule*), and deliberations—were given to certain experts in the law summoned by the judges and studied.[113]

Finally, November 17, 1430, was set for concluding the case, and Ségueut was asked if he had anything further to say; he said no. When the judges were about to set a day for sentencing, he asked for the verdict to be given immediately, and they complied.[114]

In their sentence the judges address Ségueut as not only under their jurisdiction but also as their prisoner. They recall that he admitted that he had previously been convicted in a trial of faith for having made statements which were erroneous and suspect in faith, which he had recanted, but

[112] One of these was doubtless Richard Praty, dean of the royal chapel, who witnessed the sentencing of Ségueut on November 29 (p. 80). He also served as assessor in Joan's prosecution: see Tisset, *Procès*, 2:421; 3:338. For his later career, see Janet H. Stevenson, ed., *The Register of Richard Praty, Bishop of Chichester, 1438–1445* (Woodbridge 2022).

[113] Ségueut Case, p, 76; cf. Beaurepaire, *Recherches*, p. 74.

[114] Ségueut Case, DL 76.

now, in the time since this first "purgation," he was found, not only by public fame but also through the investigation by the promotor(s) of their offices, to be not amended but rather perjurous, blasphemous, and suspect of heresy; and they sentence him to reparation for those offenses as they will decide. Furthermore, those pestiferous propositions that he had only revoked in his first trial he will have to formally abjure, using the word *abjuro*, along with the blasphemy he uttered afterwards (i.e., saying his suffering was greater than Christ's), under pain of conviction of heresy. He is also condemned to pay the expenses of the prosecution.[115]

This sentence may be read as an implied criticism of Graverent by Basset, who, as a canonist and high-ranking judge, knew more about the law than the inquisitor did. It is stated that the opinions that Ségueut had been convicted of in the first trial were condemned as "erroneous and suspect in faith" (they were not, but should have been). They were "pestiferous," and only recanted, not abjured (as they ought to have been). He is suspect of heresy (which should have been stated in the past). The heresies must be treated as such, even though no recurrence of his belief in them has been mentioned.

The threatened conviction of heresy would take place only if he failed to carry through on making the abjuration. But he did make it immediately, by reading the provided form in French. (Both it and a Latin version are included in the open letter.) He abjured only two of his earlier condemned statements: one, that Christ's power was limited to men's souls, and the other, that he was not king in this world (surprisingly, the part about his lacking possessions was left out). He also abjured his blasphemy of comparing himself to Christ suffering on the cross, and he acknowledged that his original trial was just.[116]

He was then ordered to show up for the penalty phase, likewise under pain of conviction of heresy, on November 22, which was in turn postponed until November 29. On that day he appeared and stated—sincerely, the judges thought—that he wished to return to the unity of the Church, and he asked for absolution from sentences of excommunication that he had incurred, which was granted, after he swore to fulfill the unstated penance and pay expenses.[117]

[115] Ibid., pp, 76–77.
[116] Ibid., pp. 77–78.
[117] Ibid., pp. 78–79.

We do not know what penance he was given, but whatever it was, we can be sure that it was nothing close to the life imprisonment that Joan of Arc was given after her abjuration, which named no heresies. He lived another two decades, and we hear of him in 1451 after his death, by way of his eldest son and heir, the priest Martin Ségueult.[118]

In summary, Ségueut was originally convicted, in a simple trial judged by Graverent alone, of holding ideas connected with the poverty-of-Christ controversy, specifically that Christ had power and jurisdiction only over men's souls and not over their bodies or other corporal things, and was not king on earth and possessed nothing. But Ségueut was sentenced only to retract his statements, not to abjure them as heresies. He swore an oath to that effect, but was later heard to complain that his trial was unjust, even saying that he was more wronged than Christ was when he was crucified. So, one day in 1430, Official Basset and Graverent showed up in a routine meeting of the Rouen clergy with a proposal to prosecute him. An investigation and trial followed, with charges made before any interrogation was carried out, as properly required under canon law. Ségueut was found guilty of perjury (for criticizing his trial), blasphemy (saying what he said about Christ on the cross), and suspicion of heresy. But no new instance or evidence of heresy was presented, and he was simply forced now to abjure two of the propositions he had only been required to retract before. He would be assigned penance and costs later.

3.6 Inquisitor Graverent in Coutances, 1431: The Lecouvreur Case

The trial of Jean Ségueut was hardly over when Graverent was called to a case against a citizen of Coutances named Jean Lecouvreur by the bishop of Coutances, which was why Graverent was not available to join Cauchon in prosecuting Joan. The bishop was a Burgundian nobleman named Philibert de Montjeu, much in favor of the English cause, who owed his bishopric to the duke of Burgundy and the duke of Bedford.[119] As we will see, Montjeu will be asked to weigh in on Joan's case.

The acts of the trial do not survive, but an account of Lecouvreur's appeals does exist. To begin with, Lecouvreur was represented by a proctor, a layman of Saint-Lô named Jean Beaussieu. He listed judicial

[118] Beaurepaire, *Recherches*, p. 71 n. 1.

[119] Tisset, *Procès*, 2:419.

grievances committed, and on the verge of being committed, by the judges (bishop and inquisitor) and their adherents, vicars, officials, and promotors, and he submitted a formal appeal to Pope Martin V; on February 15, 1430/1431, he demanded a formal reply (called *apostoli*) from the judges. However, instead of the *apostoli* that they were required to give by law (whether accepting or rejecting the appeal), Montjeu and Graverent issued a declaration proposing to choose an arbiter to settle the dispute between them and Lecouvreur.

In this declaration they addressed Lecouvreur directly and recounted that they had cited him to appear before them to respond to certain articles touching upon the Catholic faith; in so doing, they said, they acted not out of hatred, but rather for the benefit of his soul. In the frivolous appeal that he had lodged against one of them, namely, the bishop, recusing him, they will choose, in juridical form, arbiters to judge the matter. Lecouvreur, they say, has wrongly alleged a threat of imprisonment; they did not propose to deprive him of liberty during the proceedings, as long as he provided guarantees that he would follow the law and obey their commands; they did not wish to molest him in any way. They would give him eight days to agree to their proposal, and if he did not, they would take no notice of his appeal, except for the respect that they owed to the Holy See, to which he has appealed. This interlocutory sentence was pronounced before the portal of the episcopal manor of Coutances in the presence of Nicolas Thiébout, professor of theology and penitentiary of the diocese.[120]

The judges' attempt to quash his appeal, however, was foiled. On the following March 15 (when, as we will see, Joan was undergoing more illegal interrogation in her prison cell), another proctor standing in for Lecouvreur, a cleric named Richard Le Teneur, read a statement to the deputy of Bishop Montjeu's official[121] in Saint-Lô, to the effect that his master had lodged an appeal against the bishop and inquisitor, and had sent a message to the Holy See in pursuit of this appeal. And now he, speaking for Lecouvreur, calls on the bishop and inquisitor to desist from the proceedings that they were unduly conducting against him, to the scandal of the people. Le Teneur protests that Lecouvreur in pursuing his appeal does not wish to validate their process in any way, but only to

[120] Beaurepaire, *Recherches*, pp. 80–82.

[121] The official himself, Enguerrand de Champrond, visited Joan's trial in Rouen a week later; see Tisset, *Procès*, 2:392.

remove the scandal they have caused. His master avows himself to be a true son of the Church, and swears to obey its commands. He stands ready to put up a bond of a thousand pounds and more, if necessary.[122]

Thus we see the ease with which an appeal might be made to the pope, and how easily it could be quashed in the case of defendants with fewer resources or detained in prison.

[122] Beaurepaire, *Recherches*, pp. 82–83.

CHAPTER 4

Interrogation Instead of Trial

4.1 Judicial Investigation, January–February 1431

4.1.1 The Court Records

With the above examples of current juridical process in the background, let us begin our examination of the prosecution that Cauchon launched against Joan of Arc. We will follow the Latin Record (LR) that was created on Cauchon's orders shortly after Joan's execution,[1] and also what remains of the French Minute (FM) kept by the court's notaries,[2] supplemented

[1] The Latin Record (LR) is edited by Pierre Tisset (with Yvonne Lanhers), *Procès de condamnation de Jeanne d'Arc*, 3 vols. (Paris 1960–1971), in vol. 1; vol. 2 contains a modern French translation of LR, and vol. 3 has supplementary materials. For a complete translation of LR, see W. P. Barrett, *The Trial of Jeanne d'Arc* (London: Routledge, 1931), available online at https://heinonline.org/HOL/Page?handle=hein.trials%2Ftrijedarc0001&collection=trials. Another edition of Barrett's translation with different pagination was published in New York in 1932 (Gotham House), followed by an essay by Pierre Champion; for a transcription of this edition see: https://sourcebooks.fordham.edu/basis/joanofarc-trial.asp. A reprinting of the text of the latter (with no reference to the original), with yet different pagination, was published in 2008 (New Orleans: Cornerstone). For a recent abridgment of LR in English, see *The Trial of Joan of Arc* by Daniel Hobbins (Cambridge MA 2005).

[2] What survives of the French Minute (FM) is also edited in vol. 1 of Tisset, given in italics under the LR text. The original version of FM is lost. Much of the narrative portion was not in French, but in Latin; some of this Latin-French combination is preserved in MS U (Urfé); but in MS O (Orleans) what was originally in Latin has been translated into French. MS O

H. A. Kelly, *The Trial and Retrial of Joan of Arc*, The New Middle Ages, https://doi.org/10.1007/978-3-032-07887-2_4

with information supplied from the testimony of the 116 witnesses interviewed two decades later in the Nullity Trial (NT), proceedings aimed at overturning the earlier sentences against her, commissioned by Pope Calixtus III.[3]

One purpose of the Latin Record was to present it to the English authorities in order to collect the wages that were due to Cauchon. It was put together by Thomas de Courcelles, who, as rector of the University of Paris in November, had demanded that Cauchon get on with prosecution of Joan, and who played an active role as an assessor. The account was clearly "doctored" by him, but mainly by omission, because two of the official notaries of the process, Guillaume Manchon and Guillaume Boisguillaume, had to sign each page, attesting to its accuracy. Manchon testified that Courcelles did not interpose himself into the translation to any great extent.[4] Details must be checked, where possible, from the French Minute and the Nullity Testimony and other historical documentation.

It used to be thought that the Latin Record was compiled around four years after the proceedings. Manchon recalled that it was done "long after the death and execution of Joan."[5] But now it is clear that it was done much earlier, likely within months of her execution. It was certainly done before Cauchon became bishop of Lisieux in August of 1432, but probably finished and sealed by him in November of 1431.[6]

Following the usual format for sentences, Courcelles cast the Latin Record into the form of an open letter from Bishop Cauchon, and later, after he was joined on the bench by the vice-inquisitor Jean Lemaistre, by him and Lemaistre together.

begins on February 19 (p. 25) and MS U on March 3 (p. 94), at which point Tisset no longer follows MS O.

[3] The Nullity Trial (NT) is edited by Pierre Duparc, *Procès en nullité de la condamnation de Jeanne d'Arc*, 5 vols. (Paris 1977–1988). The original Latin proceedings are in vols. 1–2, and a French translation of them is in vols. 3–4, with commentary and indexes in vol. 5.

[4] NT 1:416.

[5] NT 1:416.

[6] Jean Fraikin, "La date de la rédaction latine du procès de Jeanne d'Arc," *Quaerendo* 3 (1973) 39–65, with an English summary on p. 66. See Hobbins, *Trial*, p. 9. This matter will be taken up in Chapter 11.

4.1.2 Joan's "Fame" Calls for Investigation

Since an inquisitorial trial should not be initiated until *publica fama* that a certain person has committed a certain crime comes to the attention of a judge, Cauchon begins his narration by saying that fame of Joan's immodest behavior in wearing male clothes, which he deems a "strange and monstrous deformity," and of her making many statements against the faith (unspecified), had reached his ears. He adds that the vicar-general of the inquisitor said that she was suspect of heresy; and therefore he has decided to complete a proper inquisition (*inquisicionem debitam explere*), that is, a full investigation.[7] He opened proceedings on January 9, 1431, in the presence of eight clergymen, who served as his "assessors," or consultants. Three were monastic superiors, and the other five were canons of Rouen, that is, members of the cathedral chapter that had voted to grant Cauchon Beauvais territory within Rouen. One of the monks was Giles de Duremort, Abbot of Fécamp, a doctor of theology, who would prove to be an especially active participant in the subsequent proceedings. The second was Nicolas Leroux, abbot of Jumièges, a jurist, and the third was Pierre Miget, prior of Longueville, a theologian. The canons of the Rouen cathedral chapter were the treasurer, Raoul Roussel, a doctor of both laws; Nicolas de Venderès, archdeacon of Eu, licensed in canon law; another jurist, Robert Lebarbier; a theologian, Nicolas Coppesquesne; and, finally, a master of arts named Nicolas Loiseleur (or l'Oiseleur, "the Birdcatcher," *Auceps* in Latin), who would achieve his bachelor's degree in theology later that year.[8] According to the Nullity Testimony of the notaries, Loiseleur, a close associate of Cauchon's, immediately set about gaining Joan's confidence by pretending to be a fellow-countryman, even hearing her confessions, but their conversations were spied upon and recorded.[9]

[7] LR 1–3.

[8] LR 3. Tisset always gives the archdeacon's name as *Venderés* in the Latin text but *Venderès* in his translation (here, 2:3). Of course, no accents were used in the original texts; such diacritical marks were developed in later times. Tisset identifies the assessors in his translation by the numbers under which they are described at the end of his volume, 2:383–425. For instance, Loiseleur is no. 90, found on 2:413–14.

[9] See the testimony of Manchon in 1450: Paul Doncoeur and Yvonne Lanhers, eds., *La réhabilitation de Jeanne la Pucelle: L'enquête ordonnée par Charles VII en 1450 et le Codicille de Guillaume Bouillé* (Paris 1956), p. 48. See Frances Gies, *Joan of Arc: The Legend and the Reality* (New York 1981), p. 159. Note, however, that Loiseleur was not "made" Joan's

The assembled consultants advised that "informations" should be gathered on the suspect, at which Cauchon informed them that some had already been collected, but he ordered more to be obtained. Furthermore, on the assessors' advice, he would appoint as promotor or prosecutor of the case his own promotor of causes from Beauvais, Jean d'Estivet, along with the two notaries mentioned above, Manchon and Boisguillaume. He then exhibited the series of letters detailed above, which, he claimed, threw light upon the foregoing matters.[10] In the letter appointing Estivet, who was not yet present, he said that Joan was publicly suspected of sortileges, incantations of demons—or invocations of, or conversations with, evil spirits—and many other things concerning the faith.[11] The letter appointing the notaries authorized them to be present in examinations of Joan and in the production and examinations of witnesses. Another appointment advised by the assessors was Jean de Lafontaine, a licentiate of canon law from the University of Paris, to serve as counselor, commissary, and examiner of witnesses. Not mentioned but also appointed that day was Jean Massieu, the urban dean of Rouen, or "dean of Christianity," as executor of his mandates and summoner.[12]

On January 13, Cauchon ordered articles (charges) to be formulated, to see if there was sufficient reason to summon her as a suspect in a cause of faith. The six assessors present—Fécamp, Venderès, Coppequesne, Loiseleur, an English theologian named William Hatton, and Commissary Lafontaine—agreed.[13]

On January 23 the resulting articles were supposedly read in open court, but they were not included in the Latin Record, even though the notaries signed off on Courcelles's version of that day's events. They should have been in a libellus formulated by Estivet, but he was not there. The same handful of assessors as before, minus Lafontaine, were present, and some of them said that interrogations should be formulated from the articles. Cauchon ordered the investigation "on the deeds of the woman"

confessor; rather he "became" her confessor. Courcelles testified that Loiseleur had told him several times about his spying efforts (NT 1:358).

[10] LR 3–4.

[11] LR 18–19.

[12] LR 4, 20–22.

[13] LR 22–23. Hatton's name occurs as Haiton, Heton, Hetton, and Hettor (the two latter forms appear in Tisset's text as "Hecton" and "Hector" because of his practice of rendering *tt* as *ct*).

to go forward, but, because he himself was otherwise occupied, he deputed Lafontaine to conduct it.[14]

4.1.3 *Six Theologians Arrive from the University of Paris*

On February 13, Cauchon swore in the officers of the court he had appointed.[15] A half-dozen masters from the Theology Faculty of the University of Paris appeared for the first time as assessors, and they were to play vital roles in the proceedings that followed. These "Paris Six," with Cauchon, will fully share in the blame for Joan's fate, as Heinrich Denifle points out.[16] One of them was Courcelles, and the others were Jean Beaupère, Nicolas Midi, Pierre Maurice, Gérard Feuillet, and, finally, Jacques Le Tessier de Touraine, who was the same Master Jacobus, OFM, who had responded sharply for Cauchon to Cardinal d'Ailly in Constance, telling him that ordinary sins should not be classified as matters of faith. Now, of course, he will be on the other side of the argument. Touraine will put the finishing touches on Midi's clever synopsis of the case against Joan (the Twelve Articles)[17] and take it across country to Paris with Midi and Beaupère (and probably Feuillet) and present it to the University of Paris. He will stay there, while Beaupère and Midi will return to Rouen with the University's verdict, and rejoin Maurice and Courcelles.

On the four days after the professors arrived, February 14–17, the unidentified witnesses were deposed. On February 19, on which day the Orleans fragment of the French Minute begins, both it and Courcelles's Latin Record say the depositions were read out before the ten or twelve assessors listed as present that day.[18] But in the Nullity Trial both Manchon and Courcelles himself would testify that no informations were ever presented to the assessors.[19] These witnesses would often be referred to in the

[14] LR 23–24.

[15] LR 24.

[16] See Denifle, *CUP* 4:512. To them should be joined Loiseleur, who was about to complete his bachelor's degree in theology at the University, but who was a resident canon of Rouen.

[17] One of the final exhibits produced in Joan's retrial was a set of five sheets of paper much marked up in Master Jacques's handwriting making many additions and corrections to the Twelve Articles, which the plaintiffs submitted to show the falsification of the said articles. Submitted June 5, 1456. NT 1:497.

[18] FM 25–26, LR 25–26.

[19] NT 1:246, cf. 356.

subsequent interrogations of Joan, but their depositions were never exhibited to her or put in the records, and no witnesses were ever called subsequently—probably because their testimony was worthless.

4.1.4 Joan to Be Summoned, Articled Charges Promised

After hearing the depositions, and allegedly consulting with the assessors, Cauchon decreed, according to the French Minute, that Joan should be summoned "to be questioned on matter of faith" (*pour estre interroguee en matiere de la foy*).[20] This could well mean that he had already decided upon his strategy: because the preliminary investigation turned up nothing to charge her with, he would have to question her at length in order to produce something damning, by hook or crook. Courcelles puts it in this way in his version: "We decreed that she was to be cited and summoned on a matter of faith to respond to certain interrogatories to be put to her."[21]

This is in contrast to the words of the citation, which were in accord with due process. Because she was delivered to the bishop as vehemently suspected of heresy, she was summoned to be heard on articles made against her and to be given to her concerning the faith (*citandam et audiendam super articulis et interrogatoriis contra eam dandis et sibi faciendis fidei materiam concernentibus*).[22] That is, she was to be charged with specific offenses, to which she would be required to plead. In other words, an inquisitorial trial.

Later that day and on the following day, February 20, the business about getting Vice-Inquisitor Lemaistre as co-judge was conducted.[23]

The February 21 meeting took place in the royal chapel within Rouen Castle, which would constitute the *ad hoc* courtroom. (The first official day of the proceedings, on January 9, had been held in the Council House next to the castle, where Joan was kept prisoner, and following meetings in Cauchon's residence.) According to the Latin Record, forty-one assessors were in attendance, including Vice-Inquisitor Lemaistre, but not Courcelles. No reference was made to the general public or to members of

[20] FM 26.
[21] LR 26.
[22] LR 34.
[23] FM 27–29, LR 26–32.

the governing English forces.[24] The French Minute in contrast omits most of the names, listing only nine assessors, including Courcelles and Jacques de Touraine, and not including Lemaistre.[25] One other attendee listed by Courcelles but not by the French Minute was Jean Basset, the high ecclesiastical judge of Rouen, who had recently finished conducting the heresy trial of Jean Ségueut. He was listed in both records on the following day, February 22. Basset's promotor, Jean Leroy, likewise appeared on February 22, and also in the following session, on February 24, and no more.[26] But Aubert Morel, who served as Graverent's promotor in the trial of Ségueut, was more industrious, and attended all six of the public sessions and another half-dozen meetings later on, and was one of only three (along with Loiseleur and Courcelles) who voted for Joan to be tortured.[27]

Proceedings began with the reading of the letter of Henry VI of January 3, making Joan available to Cauchon for trial, which indicated to the assessors the nature of the charges that would be leveled against the defendant:

> It is well known how for some time a woman calling herself Joan the Maid, putting off the habit and dress of the female sex (which is contrary to divine law, abominable to God, condemned and prohibited by every law), has dressed and armed herself in the state and habit of man, has wrought and occasioned cruel murders, and it is said, to seduce and deceive the simple people, has given them to understand that she was sent from God and that she had knowledge of His divine secrets, with many other dangerous dogmatizations most prejudicial and scandalous to our holy faith.[28]

Then followed the letter from the Rouen chapter authorizing him to hold the trial there in Rouen, which characterized her similarly:

> A woman commonly called Joan the Maid, who abandoning all modesty, has lived a disorderly and shameful life to the scorn of the estate proper to womankind: and moreover, as is commonly known, she has sown and disseminated many opinions contrary to the Catholic faith and tending to the denigration of certain articles of the orthodox belief, wherein she appears evil-thinking, suspect, and defamed.[29]

[24] LR 32–33.
[25] FM 32–33.
[26] LR 43, 55.
[27] Tisset, *Procès*, 2:419.
[28] LR 14; Barrett 1932, 30.
[29] LR 16; Barrett 1932, 33.

The citation was then read, including of course Cauchon's assertion that Joan was vehemently suspected of heresy, and that there were to be articles charged against her, based on crimes concerning the faith that she was suspected of committing. This was indeed what was supposed to happen, by law, and it is what happened in the Ségueut case, but it did not happen here. And Judge Basset was there to witness that it did not happen.

Urban Dean Massieu, who was tasked with delivering the citation to Joan, submitted a report of how he had performed his duty, and it was read. It was addressed to Cauchon, concerning the woman called Joan the Maid, whom the bishop held to be vehemently suspect of heresy. She was to be personally delivered by him to answer truthfully to articles and interrogations against her concerning matters of faith and other things upon which she was held suspect. Massieu told Joan that she was to appear before the bishop at 8:00 on Tuesday morning, February 21.

Massieu may have placed particular emphasis upon the questions she would be asked, rather than upon charges to be laid against her. At any rate, she answered that she was ready to respond to Cauchon's interrogations. But she wished Cauchon to convene alongside him the same number of churchmen from the French side as from the English side. She also asked if she could attend mass first.[30]

After the reading of Massieu's report, Promotor Estivet demanded that Joan be brought into court and "questioned according to the way of law" (*interroguee selon la voie de droit*).[31]

(Courcelles will later expand all this in his version by having Estivet intervene before Massieu's report was read, saying that Joan had been cited to appear there that day "to respond to certain questions to be propounded to her" (*super certis interrogatoribus sibi proponendis responsura*), questions to be put to her by Cauchon, "which was according to law" (*quod juris esset*).[32] Then, after the citation business, Courcelles will have Estivet say that Joan was to be questioned by Cauchon upon certain articles concerning matters of the faith.[33])

There would be questions but no articles. No charges. No warning or rationale to the questions. Estivet was supposed to present charges in a

[30] LR 33–35.
[31] FM 35.
[32] LR 33.
[33] LR 36.

libellus, but he retired from the action and left it entirely to Cauchon and his appointed questioners.

Grilling suspects before charges were leveled or even revealed was a method of self-incrimination that was first developed by heresy inquisitors in France when dealing with large numbers of suspects. But by Cauchon's time the rule of law seems to have recovered, perhaps because bishops were generally back in control, with inquisitors taking a second place, as in Ségueut's trial.[34]

4.2 Joan in Court: Mass Denied, Counsel Rejected, Chains Kept on, Blanket Oaths

Before admitting Joan to his presence, Cauchon first addressed her second request reported by Massieu, of being permitted to hear mass. After taking advice (details not recorded), he declared that, in view of the grave crimes of which she was accused and defamed—of which Joan was not informed—and also because she wore male clothes (Courcelles: because of the deformity of the clothes she continued to wear), he forbade any such attendance at mass.[35] As for Joan's demand that he include French loyalists among the assessors, a demand that was not only legitimate but legally necessary for a fair and valid trial, he simply passed over it in silence. This would be another invalidating strike against his process that the papal judge will point out, as well as the brutal circumstances of her imprisonment.

Massieu then conducted Joan into the courtroom. Neither the French Minute nor Courcelles's Latin Record mentions the fact that she was being kept manacled in her prison cell, and that her chains were still upon her when she came to court. The urban dean stationed her before the bishop and the above-named assessors (whether nine or forty-one). Cauchon immediately addressed her, telling her that because she was taken within the boundaries of his diocese, and because it was reputed not only in France but in all realms that many of her deeds were against the

[34] Whereas in Nicolau Eymeric's *Directorium inquisitorum* of 1376, forced self-incrimination was standard procedure, when the Spanish Inquisition got going a century later (a few decades after Joan's trial), Inquisitor-General Torquemada strictly rebuked the practice, saying that it was injurious to persons and to property. Tomás de Torquemada, *Instructions of Avila*, 25 May 1498, ed. Ernst Schafer, "Die älteste Instruktionen-Sammlung der spanischen inquisitionen," *Archiv für Reformationsgeschichte* 2 (1904–1905) 1–55, 109–77, pp. 109–14, no. 3 (p. 110).

[35] FM 36, LR 36.

faith, and that she was accused of heresy, she had been delivered to undergo her trial (*son procez*) concerning the faith.[36]

Courcelles will change this account, having Cauchon instead address the assessors, leaving out the accusation of heresy, and adding that it was their sovereign king (i.e., Henry VI) who delivered her for trial. Because of the fame against her and other information that he had gathered, he had her summoned *ex officio* to respond with the truth concerning certain questions concerning matters of the faith.[37]

The original record of the French Minute continues with a final statement and demand by Promotor Estivet before he seemingly withdrew, not being mentioned again as present for many weeks. He asserted that at his request Joan had been cited and convened to respond in matters of faith, as evidenced by the documents (letters and acts) that he now exhibited. Then he supplicated that she be adjured (put under oath) to tell the truth and be interrogated respecting the parties whom he would deliver (*qu'elle fust adjure de dir verité et interroguee sur les parties qu'il bailleroit*).[38] What is meant by this is not clear. Since this process was to be an *ex officio* inquisition, he himself was the denominated plaintiff or *actor* (using the language of civil litigation), and she was the defendant, or *rea*. This will be explicitly stated in the libellus he will finally produce a month later.[39] At this present point, perhaps he was promising to produce the witnesses who had allegedly been deposed against her.

Cauchon now took over. He did indeed accede to the promotor's demand and "adjure her to tell the truth," not to articles of accusation, however, but to a wide variety of questions. He first pronounced what he called a "charitable admonition": in the interests of shortening these proceedings and unburdening her conscience, to avoid all subterfuges, she must swear on the Gospels to tell the truth to everything that she would be asked about.[40]

Joan was used to dealing with dignitaries of Cauchon's stature, and, as can be gathered from the Minute, she manifested no signs of being intimidated by him and his assembly of assessors. She vigorously protested against his demand, saying, "I don't know what you want to ask me about.

[36] FM 36.
[37] LR 37.
[38] FM 36.
[39] LR 192.
[40] FM 37–38, LR 37–38.

Maybe you could ask me things that I will not tell you." She finally swore to reply only to questions concerning the faith, and not about any of her revelations.[41]

We might be tempted to conclude from Joan's initial response that she was able to divine in her unschooled way that neither Cauchon nor any judge had a right to force her to respond to unspecified questions, and that she had the right to refuse to answer them. She clearly conceded, as we can tell from this and some of her further answers, that there were certain questions pertaining to a trial of this sort that a judge did have the right to ask and that she had the duty to answer under oath. But she seems instinctively to have believed that she had a right to know what the questions were to deal with. However, her further response shows that she was concerned about a different matter: she was afraid that the all-inclusive oath being demanded of her would force her to violate previous oaths or promises she had made not to reveal certain aspects of her revelations.

It has been mistakenly thought that when Joan said that she would not tell the truth to certain questions that she meant that she would tell untruths.[42] Rather, what she meant was that she would not respond at all. Later, when she said that she was in danger of perjuring herself, she did not mean telling lies under oath, but rather violating previous oaths that she had made.

4.3 Self-Testimony Concerning Undisclosed Suspected Crimes

4.3.1 First Day of Public Interrogation, February 21

After Cauchon asked her various details about her birth and upbringing, he pressed her to recite the Lord's Prayer, but she stymied him by insisting that she would do so only to him in confession.[43] She thereby avoided being interrogated about her understanding of the content of the prayer, which could have led her to make questionable statements about the faith that would be used against her to construe into some kind of heresy.

[41] FM 38–39, LR 38–39.

[42] For example, Taylor, *Virgin Warrior*, pp. 135–36. Taylor is right, of course, in saying that Joan used equivocations throughout (p. 140).

[43] FM 40–41, LR 40–41.

Finally, according to Courcelles, Cauchon commanded her not to escape from her prison, under pain of being convicted of heresy. She stoutly responded that she did not accept that prohibition; if she escaped, she could not be accused of violating an oath. She asserted that it was the right of every prisoner to attempt to escape from custody.

Cauchon, of course, did not have the legitimate power to convict Joan of heresy without proving a case of heresy against her. His claim that he could do so simply because she escaped, however, would remain uncontested. The only penalty that a judge could inflict upon a suspect who fled from a process of faith was excommunication for contempt of court. While it is true that such an excommunication could convert into a conviction of heresy by a legal fiction, it was only after a year of remaining excommunicated.[44]

Responding to Joan's protest at being kept in fetters and chains, Cauchon justified it by her previous escape attempts, and he swore in three Englishmen to keep a close guard on her.[45]

4.3.2 Second Day of Interrogation, February 22

On the following day, February 22, thirty-one assessors were listed in the French text and forty-seven in the Latin, with Courcelles still missing from both lists but Lemaistre present. Cauchon introduced Lemaistre and brought him up to date, but the vice-inquisitor stayed off the bench until he had fuller powers from Inquisitor Graverent, as described above, for fear that if he participated, the trial would be rendered null (*ne processus redderetur invalidus*). Cauchon insisted on Joan's swearing a new oath, which she finally did, under protest, and under the same condition as the day before.[46] Cauchon then appointed one of the Paris Six, Jean Beaupère, to take over the questioning. Beaupère was a canon of Cauchon's own cathedral church of Beauvais, and had a long history with him.[47] Only two months earlier, on November 30, 1430, he had been appointed a canon of Rouen by the English government; he took possession of it a week after his arrival from Paris, on February 20, 1431.[48]

[44] Alexander IV, *Cum contumacia*, *Sext* 5.2.7 (CIC 2:1071).

[45] LR 42.

[46] FM 42–45, LR 42–45.

[47] Tisset, *Procès*, 2:385–86.

[48] Beaurepaire, *Recherches*, p. 60.

Joan answered questions about going to confession and Easter Communion, but refused to talk about Communion on other feast days, telling Beaupère to "pass on" to other matters.[49]

Beaupère's questions for the most part are missing from the records, giving the impression that Joan was speaking spontaneously. She was asked how she saw the light that accompanied her voices if it came from the side, but she did not answer and passed on, giving more details about the voices. For instance, she answered his question about what instructions the voices gave her for the good of her soul.[50]

Regarding her clothes, after the question was recorded in the French Minute ("Asked to say by whose advice she took up male clothes"), the redactor or translator intervened, and instead of stating what she answered on that occasion, he wrote that there were different answers "in the two books" (presumably the individual reports of the two notaries): "To this interrogation I found in one book that her voices had commanded her to take on male clothes, and in the other I found that when she was asked several times she always gave no other answer than, 'I don't lay this on anyone.' And I found in the same book (*audit livre*) that several times she varied (gave inconsistent answers) on that question.[51] Courcelles says that in response to this question she refused to answer several times; finally, she said that she did not lay it on anyone; and several times she varied."[52]

When she told of first meeting King Charles, she refused to respond to several questions about her revelations.[53]

4.3.3 *Third Day of Interrogation, February 24*

Two days later, Cauchon appeared in court with sixty assessors, including Courcelles for the first time, and also Joan's false friend Nicolas Loiseleur.[54] When Cauchon solemnly insisted, admonishing her three times, on her swearing another oath, she protested at greater length than before. She had sworn twice already, she said, and he was putting her in danger of perjuring herself by violating previous oaths that she had taken. She

[49] FM 45–47, LR 45–47.

[50] FM 47–48, LR 47–48.

[51] FM 50.

[52] LR 50.

[53] FM 52–53, LR 52–53.

[54] LR 54–55. FM 54 says that those who were present at the previous session were convoked by the urban dean of Rouen (i.e., Jean Massieu), but does not name them.

concluded with her own admonishment to him: "I say this to you: know well that in claiming that you are my judge, you take a great charge upon yourself and place too great a burden upon me."[55] When he continued to insist, she said that she believed that not even the whole clergy of Rouen or Paris would know how to force her (i.e., to make her break her previous oaths), unless they were in the wrong (*se ilz ne avoyent tort*)[56]—indicating her belief that Cauchon was not following the law. Courcelles has her say instead that the clergy would not be able to condemn her, except against the law (*nisi in jus*).[57]

She repeated that she would be willing to tell the truth only about her "arrival" (to fight for Charles), but not everything, which would take more than a week. Cauchon told her to ask the advice of the assessors there with him in court whether she was obliged to take the oath. She ignored this and repeated that she would willingly tell about her arrival, and that Cauchon was obliged not to say anything more about it. He warned her that not swearing to tell the truth would render her suspect.[58] He continued to warn of grave consequences from her refusal, saying that she would be found guilty and convicted of what was charged against her.[59]

The absurdity of Cauchon's position is revealed here. Joan has been charged with nothing. If, then, she refuses to swear, she can be convicted of nothing.

Cauchon finally conceded that she should swear to tell the truth about what concerned the proceedings there in court. She replied, "I am prepared to swear to tell the truth about what I know is relevant to your proceedings," and that was the form under which she swore.[60]

Beaupère then took over the questioning, concentrating on the voice she said she was hearing in her prison. She twice said that the voice counseled her to answer boldly to their questions, and then she turned to Cauchon, saying: "You say that you are my judge. Beware what you do, because, in truth, I am sent from God, and you put yourself in great danger."[61]

[55] FM 55, LR 55.

[56] FM 56.

[57] LR 56.

[58] FM 56, LR 56. He probably meant convicted of the crime of "vehement suspicion of heresy" (i.e., favoring heresy or heretics).

[59] FM 57; cf. LR 57: she would be burdened with what was charged against her.

[60] FM 56, LR 56.

[61] FM 59, LR 59.

When asked, "Do you think it displeasing to God to tell the truth," she replied that her voices told her that she could say some things to the king and not to Monseigneur de Beauvais (i.e., Cauchon).[62] At one point she said that she did not have permission to answer some of their questions, and she was not obligated to answer them by her oath. Because of this, she asked that she see in writing further questions that they wished to ask her.[63] (Of course, someone she trusted would have to read them to her.) This request, of course, was never granted. It is highly significant that Courcelles in the Latin Record transformed her demand into a request for the questions that she did not answer at that time to be put into writing and given to her.[64]

The questioning then turned to her youth, including belief in fairies; Joan said that she never saw them, to her knowledge.[65] The session concluded with her being asked whether she wanted women's clothing. She said yes, if she could be released; otherwise, she would remain with what she had on, since God approved of her wearing it.[66]

4.3.4 *Fourth Day of Interrogation, February 27*

In the next session, there were fifty-four assessors, including Official Basset, who missed the previous session.[67] Cauchon once again required Joan to swear to tell the truth, according to her compromise formula of the previous day. Joan said that she would willingly swear to say the truth about what concerned the proceedings, but would not say everything that she knew. Cauchon insisted that she should swear to tell the truth about whatever was asked of her. She responded as before, and added that he should be satisfied, for she had sworn enough.[68]

[62] FM 56; cf. LR 56: "to the king and not to you."

[63] FM 62: "Pour ce qu'elle demanda a veoir par escript les poins sur lesquelz on la vouloit interroguer." In the FM MS this statement is put out of order. The statement before it about the voices having eyes ("Interroguee se la voix a veue," etc.) goes with the response below ("Vous ne l'avez pas encoire").

[64] LR 62: "Item petivit ut sibi darentur in scriptis illa puncta in quibus tunc non respondebat."

[65] FM 66, LR 66.

[66] FM 67, LR 67.

[67] LR 68–69. FM 68 does not name the assessors, and calls it the fifth session.

[68] FM 69, LR 69.

Beaupère took over the questioning again, and asked her how she had fared since the last session on Saturday. She responded that he could see for himself; she fared as well as she could. He then asked her if she fasted every day of Lent (Lent began that year two weeks previously, on February 14). She asked if that was part of their proceedings, and, when he said that it was, she answered that yes indeed, she had always fasted that Lent.[69] This might seem like an odd question to ask a manacled prisoner, who presumably would not be able to be choosy about what she ate. Presumably Beaupère was fishing for any heterodox view that she might have on fasting obligations during Lent, which would normally consist of abstaining from animal products (meat, milk, cheese, eggs) during weekdays. Or it may be that she was being deliberately tempted to break the fast by providing her with prohibited food in the meals she was given, and he wanted to know if she had succumbed.

Beaupère proceeded to question her on her voices, and several times she referred him to the record of the interrogation that she underwent at Poitiers for confirmation of her statements here.[70]

4.3.5 *Fifth Day of Interrogation, March 1*

At the next interrogation on March 1, there were fifty-six assessors, Basset among them (for the last time). Once more, Cauchon insisted that Joan swear again. As previously, she said she would answer only regarding what concerned the proceedings, and she would respond as if to the pope himself.[71] She was then asked, presumably by Cauchon himself, what she thought about the pope, and who she believed the true pope was. She asked (perhaps sarcastically) whether there were two popes. Cauchon took the opportunity to ask about a letter to her from the duke of Armagnac, inquiring which of three popes he should obey, and about her written response to him that she would answer later. Cauchon produced the two letters there in court and had them read aloud. (This was the first use of documentary evidence in these sessions.) She said that she did not know what to answer the duke, but, for herself, she held that we should obey the pope in Rome.[72]

[69] FM 69–70, LR 69–70.
[70] FM 71–74, LR 71–74. There is a lacuna in FM (MS O) at this point.
[71] LR 80–81.
[72] LR 81–82.

(Note that Pope Martin V died in Rome on February 20, just before Joan's interrogations began, and word of it may not yet have reached Rouen. The new pope, Eugene IV, would be elected on March 3, the date of her next session.)

At one point, when questioned on predictions made by her voices, she asked that the assessors be questioned under oath whether this subject was pertinent to the proceedings. After deliberation, they concluded that it was.[73] When asked about whether St Michael had clothing or hair, she responded with mocking questions of her own: "Do you think that God could not give him clothes?" "Why would his hair be cut off?"[74] Several times she said that she could not answer without perjuring herself.[75]

4.3.6 *Sixth and Last Public Interrogation, March 3*

At the end of the previous session, those present were required to attend on the coming Saturday, but only forty-one assessors appeared. Basset, as noted, was among the missing.

Once again Cauchon pressed her to swear to answer everything, and she responded that she would swear as before.[76] When she referred to the record of her three-week-long ecclesiastical examination at Poitiers, she was asked whether she was questioned there about wearing men's clothing, and she replied to this, and to some further questions about her clothing, that she did not remember.[77] Asked whether she received the sacraments of Communion and penance in male clothing, she said yes, but did not remember whether she did so in arms.[78]

Immediately afterwards she was asked why she took the bishop of Senlis's horse, an indication that Cauchon's investigators had collected testimony that she had stolen the mount. She answered that she purchased it for a high price, but later wrote to the bishop saying that he could have it back if he wanted it, for it was no good to her.[79] She might well have asked, "What does this have to do with a trial of faith?"

[73] LR 86.
[74] FM 87, LR 87.
[75] FM 88–89, LR 88–89.
[76] LR 90–91; FM 90–91 omits the assessors.
[77] FM (now including the Urfé MS) 93–95, LR 93–95.
[78] FM 102, LR 102.
[79] FM 102, LR 102.

Another topic raised was a seemingly stillborn child in Lagny that revived for a moment and was baptized before it died. Joan was asked about the age of the infant "whom she went to visit" (Courcelles: "whom she resuscitated"). Did she believe that it was her prayer that caused "what happened" (Courcelles: "the resuscitation")? She replied that she did not inquire into the matter.[80]

4.4 Cauchon and the Clergy in Rouen

At the end of the session, Cauchon announced that he would appoint experts in divine and human law to compile Joan's testimony to see if she should be further interrogated by persons assigned by him without bothering the whole body of assessors; but he commanded all of them not to depart from Rouen without his permission.[81]

It seems to have been common procedure for a judge in a trial of faith to be able to order experts to attend trials as assessors. An example of how it might be done can be seen in the letter sent by Archbishop Carillo of Toledo in 1479 to various masters of theology commanding them to assist at the trial of Pedro de Osma, under pain of excommunication.[82] Presumably the judge's power extended not simply to clergy under his ordinary authority, but also to those who happened to be in the vicinity. In Cauchon's case, of course, he could rely on the English forces in Rouen to back him up.

The case of Nicolas de Houppeville is instructive in this matter. According to the testimony he gave twenty years later, on May 8, 1452, he had been summoned to be an assessor early on in the proceedings against Joan. Being impeded from attending the first day, he was refused admittance by Cauchon on the second day, because it had been reported that he had said that it was dangerous to participate. Cauchon then went further and had him put in the royal prison, intending to exile him to England or elsewhere. Houppeville only avoided it through the intervention of the Abbot of Fécamp and others.[83]

In further testimony five days later, Houppeville recounted that there was more to the incident. He had participated in discussions about the

[80] FM 103, LR 103. See Tisset, 3:40.

[81] FM 108, LR 108–09.

[82] José Labajos Alonso, *Proceso contra Pedro de Osma* (Salamanca 2010), pp. 98–101.

[83] NT 1:203–04.

proceedings against Joan, and he had maintained that Cauchon and the others who were promoting them could not be her judges, because they were her opponents; furthermore, she had already been examined by the clergy of Poitiers and the archbishop of Rheims, and the latter was Cauchon's own archbishop, his metropolitan or provincial superior. When Cauchon heard this, he summoned Houppeville before him to discipline him, but Houppeville asserted that he had no jurisdiction over him and was not his judge. His proper judge, he said, was the official of Rouen—namely, Jean Basset. He thereupon departed from Cauchon's court, but when he wished to appear before Basset in this connection, he was arrested and put into the royal prison. He was told later that this was Cauchon's doing, because he was indignant at the words that he had spoken to him.[84] Houppeville's informant was none other than his friend Jean Lafontaine, the very person whom Cauchon had appointed at the beginning of these proceedings to serve as his deputy (Lafontaine would also turn out to be sympathetic to Joan).[85]

What would the large body of assessors have made so far of the seemingly aimless nature of the interrogations of Joan during the past public sessions? The half-dozen assessors who heard Estivet's original articles on January 13 (if they did), and the dozen assessors who listened to the testimony gathered on her deeds on February 23—except they didn't!—might have been in the know about the crimes that Cauchon would like her to be suspected of. They would be able to conjecture how she was being led to make damaging admissions. But to the majority of assessors not in the know, the extended desultory questioning, much of the questioning, on topics far removed from what might be expected in a heresy case, could well have seemed rather pointless. Doubtless one of Cauchon's goals was to reenforce in the minds of the assessors the obviously "pastoral" approach that he professed to be taking toward Joan, assuring her that he was concerned for her spiritual welfare. But perhaps he perceived that they were getting restless and dubious about the process, even apart from those like Basset and Leroy, who were perturbed about the judicial irregularities. This may have been one reason why Cauchon decided to go underground for the next sessions.

[84] NT 1:445. He then described again his escape from being sent into exile, through Fécamp's help.

[85] NT 1:182; Tisset, *Procès*, 2:406.

4.5 Nine Prison Sessions; Lemaistre Joins as Co-Judge

On Saturday, March 10, Cauchon, making use of Lafontaine for the first time, entered Joan's prison cell along with only two assessors, Nicolas Midi and Gérard Feuillet, from the Paris Six. Present as witnesses were the urban dean, Massieu, and a lawyer, Jean Secard. Once again, Cauchon tried to get Joan to swear to answer all questions, and she insisted that she would only respond to relevant questions. She said that the more he insisted, the slower she would be to answer.[86] Lafontaine then conducted the questioning, concerning her capture at Compiègne, the sign she gave to Charles, and other matters, including her horses.[87]

It is noteworthy that the deputy inquisitor, Jean Lemaistre, who had been attending in court among the assessors, did not accompany Cauchon in the above session. But on the following Monday, March 12, he appeared at the residence where Cauchon was dwelling while in Rouen, along with one of the other friars from the Dominican house of the city, where Lemaistre himself was prior, namely, Isambart de Lapierre, and the bishop formally took him on as co-judge, as described above.[88] But when the second prison session started later that day, Lemaistre still did not accompany Cauchon and his duo of University masters.[89]

Cauchon put Joan through the same oath routine as before, and Lafontaine resumed the questioning, beginning with her visions but then moving back to her youth, when she was thirteen. He asked her why she had had a certain man cited to court in Toul (meaning the consistory court of her home diocese) in a marriage case. She replied that it was the man who cited her. She appeared before the judge, and having sworn to tell the truth, she insisted that she had never made any promise to the man.[90]

When another session was held in the afternoon, Cauchon seems not to have attended. On being asked about obedience to her parents, Joan said she never disobeyed them except in the matter of her leaving home, and

[86] FM 110, LR 110.
[87] FM 110–18, LR 110–18.
[88] LR 118–20.
[89] FM 120–21, LR 120–21.
[90] FM 121–23, LR 121–23.

in the marriage business.[91] We can conclude that the idea of her getting married was their idea, not hers.

On the following day, Tuesday, March 13, Cauchon arrived at Joan's prison cell for a fourth session, accompanied finally by Lemaistre. His fellow-friar Lapierre served as one of the two witnesses (the other being Nicolas de Hubent, a papal scribe). Lafontaine was also there, along with the same assessors, Midi and Feuillet. Lemaistre then produced two letters, one appointing Cauchon's promotor Jean d'Estivet as "promotor of causes of the Holy Inquisition," and the other appointing the urban dean Massieu as his summoner (as he was Cauchon's), and both letters were signed by the two notaries who had been appointed by Cauchon, namely, Guillaume Boisguillaume and Guillaume Manchon.[92]

We observe that Estivet's appointment was as a general promotor for Inquisition trials, and was not limited to Joan's case alone. In any case, however, he does not seem to have been present to acknowledge this assignment, or to do anything about starting the trial.

The only notice that the French Minute took of Lemaistre was to record that he asked the second question of the morning (Did she swear to St Catherine not to tell about the sign given to the king?), a point not acknowledged in Courcelles's version.[93]

From then on in Courcelles's text the narration usually changes from "we the bishop" to "we the bishop and vice-inquisitor." But we can assume that Cauchon was the spokesman for the two judges when they were said to speak in unison.

Questioning Joan together, then, they first asked her to say what the sign was that she gave to her king, and she replied, "Are you content that I perjure myself?" Then, they asked (or Lemaistre asked, according to the Minute) whether she swore to St Catherine that she would not reveal the sign, and she replied that it was her own doing that she swore it. But then she proceeded to say what the sign was, an angel bringing the king a crown. In the following long exchange on this topic, there was no further indication of Lemaistre's specific intervention.[94]

On the next day, Wednesday, March 14, in the fifth session, Lemaistre appointed another notary for the case, Nicolas Taquel, and then, with

[91] FM 126–27, LR 126–27.
[92] LR 129–33.
[93] FM 133, cf. LR 133.
[94] FM 133–40, LR 133–40.

Lafontaine standing in for Cauchon, he and the two assessors and two witnesses (and now the three notaries) went to question Joan in prison.[95] In asking her about her attempted escape from the tower at Beaurevoir, "the interrogator," as the Minute calls him,[96] that is, either Lemaistre or Lafontaine, said that according to the information they had obtained she cursed God and his saints. When she said that she never remembered doing such a thing there or anywhere, she was asked if she would like to consult the information received or to be received on this point, to which she declined, saying that she referred herself to God alone.[97] This would seem to be the first time that she was offered to see testimony against her, and perhaps we are to attribute it to Lemaistre's understanding of correct procedure.

Shortly afterwards, Joan interrupted the questioning by asking for a copy of the interrogations and her responses, so that if she were taken to Paris, she would be able to show them there how much she was interrogated and what her responses were, and not be vexed by so many questions (i.e., not be asked the same questions again).[98]

She was then asked what she meant by saying that Cauchon was in great danger for prosecuting her. She professed to repeat the words that she had spoken to him: "You say that you are my judge. I don't know if you are. But take care that you do not judge me wrongly, because you would put yourself in great danger. I give you warning, so that if God punishes you for it, I will have done my duty in telling you."[99] In expanding on what she said before—saying, "I don't know if you are"— she was in effect telling Lemaistre that she questioned whether Cauchon had the right to judge her.

In the afternoon session that same day, there is reference both in the French and in the Latin texts to *articles* ("this article," "the previous article"), doubtless referring to charges compiled in Estivet's preparatory libellus and shown to a few assessors but not revealed to Joan.[100] Questioning continued on sins that she might have committed, such as stealing the bishop of Senlis's horse and wearing men's clothes.[101]

[95] LR 142–43.
[96] FM 146 ("comme disoit l'interrogant").
[97] FM 143–46, LR 143–46.
[98] FM 147, LR 147.
[99] FM 147–48, LR 147–48.
[100] FM 149–50, LR 149–50.
[101] FM 150–54, LR 150–54.

On the next day, Thursday, in the seventh session, Cauchon was similarly absent, and questioning continued on her actions that appeared to be sinful (but still nothing said to do with the faith). The final question revealed how shamelessly they were invading the protected forum of conscience: "Did she know of any crime or failing for which she could or should die?" She answered, "No."[102]

In the eighth session, on Saturday, March 17, Cauchon was still absent, at least in the morning. Joan was asked whether she would submit to the Church. When it was explained that the Church Triumphant consisted of those in heaven, while the Church Militant consisted of the pope and cardinals and prelates and clergy and all good Catholic Christians—who could not err when gathered together—and then she was asked whether she would submit to the Church Militant, she responded that she certainly submitted to the Church Triumphant, and she would reply later about the Church Militant.[103] She undoubtedly picked up the suggestion that Cauchon himself represented that very Church Militant. They continued to pepper her with other questions weaving back and forth on various topics, including fairies, and most frequently her male clothing.[104]

In the afternoon session (the ninth and last), Cauchon joined the group, bringing with him Beaupère and Courcelles and the rest of the Paris Six, namely, Touraine and Maurice. Friar Lapierre was still a witness, but this time he was joined by John Grey, Joan's chief English guard.[105]

After lengthy questioning on the nature and purpose of her banner, they touched on one of the aftermaths of the tyrannicide affair, the assassination of the duke of Burgundy, now twelve years earlier (in 1419). She was asked if she thought that her king did right in killing him (+ or having him killed, FM). She responded that it was a great injury for the kingdom of France. But whatever was between them, God sent her to the aid of the king of France.[106]

Then Cauchon took up her statement that she would answer him in the same way that she would answer the pope. Would she refuse to answer the pope's questions as she refused to answer some of his, or would she answer

[102] FM 154–64, LR 154–64.
[103] FM 164–67, LR 164–67.
[104] FM 167–71, LR 167–71.
[105] FM 172, LR 172.
[106] FM 175, LR 175.

him more fully? She responded that she wished to be taken to the pope, and then she would answer everything that should be answered.[107]

Like the other prison interrogations, this last one ended without ceremony.[108]

4.6 Intervention of Jean Lohier, Papal Judge

According to witnesses deposed two decades later, a prominent jurist named Jean Lohier or Loyer (i.e., l'Oier)[109] arrived in Rouen at this time. He received his legal training not in Paris, where there was no Faculty of Civil Law, but to the south and west, in Angers. He received his bachelor's degree in canon law there in 1379, and was licensed as a doctor of both laws (JUD) by 1419.[110] He would eventually become dean of the Roman Rota or Apostolic Palace, the papal high court for civil cases.[111] According to the later inquisitor of France, Jean Bréhal, Lohier was already an auditor (judge) of the court, at the time of Joan's trial.[112] Bréhal was sent to Rome in 1454 to agitate for the reversal of Joan's condemnation,[113] and he may have found out about Lohier's career at that time.[114]

Lohier was probably traveling from his home town of Fécamp, on the coast north of Rouen, on his way back to Rome when he found himself in the middle of Joan's trial (or rather, not-yet-trial). He was summoned by Cauchon and ordered to give his opinion of the proceedings. Manchon was not present when Lohier, whom he calls "a solemn Norman cleric," gave his reply, but he encountered him in church the next day, and Lohier told him what he had said: that the proceedings were not valid and would not be upheld (i.e., on appeal), because they were held in the castle, a place not safe for judges, counselors, and practitioners; they concerned many persons who were not taking part, for they had not been summoned;

[107] FM 175–76, LR 175–76.

[108] FM 179; LR 179.

[109] The name means "goose-keeper."

[110] Heinrich Denifle and Emile Chatelain, *Auctarium Chartularii Universitatis Parisiensis*, vol. 2 (Paris 1897), col. 398 n. 2. There is a different Jean Lohier, an MA of Paris in 1403: see Denifle, *CUP* 4:107 (for n. "63" read "65"); p. 108 n. 65.

[111] He died, as dean, before March 2, 1450: see Charles de Beaurepaire, ["Éclaircissement sur Jean Lohier"], *Bulletins de la Société de l'Histoire de Normandie* 7 (1893–1895) 284–90. He was from Fécamp, and Beaurepaire traces his ongoing connections with his family there.

[112] NT 2:521.

[113] See Belon-Balme, *Jean Bréhal*, p. 68.

[114] We know that he is on record as a Rota auditor in May of 1433: Denifle, *CUP* 4:531 n. 6.

Joan had no counsel. There were many other reasons, he said. It seemed to him that they intended to put her to death. When he said he would stay in the city no longer, it was clear to Manchon that he was afraid of the English.[115]

In an earlier deposition, Manchon said that Lohier maintained that the proceedings should be held in a Church court and Joan kept in a Church prison; the case centrally affected the French king, but his cause was not represented. It was not a proper trial; no libellus or articles had been presented against her (*que libelle n'avoit point esté baillé, ne articles*); she had no one to advise her, a simple girl, in responding to difficult questions from learned masters. He told Manchon that it was clear that they were trying to ensnare her, especially in questioning her about her apparitions. She should be advised to answer not with certainty but tentatively, to evade their traps. They were clearly proceeding out of hatred for her.[116]

Courcelles also testified about Lohier. After the jurist arrived in Rouen, it was ordered (presumably by Cauchon) that some part of the proceedings be communicated to him. After reviewing it, Lohier told Courcelles personally that Joan should not have been proceeded against concerning the faith unless there had been information collected on her infamy in this regard, which was required by law.[117] That is, it had to be established that she was commonly believed to hold specific heretical beliefs or errors against the faith.

We can compare these objections against Cauchon's proceedings to Cauchon's objections at the Council of Constance against the "trial" of Jean Petit's *Justification of the Duke of Burgundy* held by the bishop of Paris and a deputy inquisitor in 1413, detailed in Chapter 3: it was not held in a safe place, it was a trial of faith concerning matters not condemned by the Church; the propositions allegedly held by Petit were distorted and had not in fact been held by him in that form; one of the

[115] NT 1:418-19.

[116] Doncoeur and Lanhers, *Réhabilitation 1450*, pp. 48–49. Manchon testified more briefly about Lohier's objections in 1452: NT 1:182, 216.

[117] NT 1:356: "Et postquam ipse Lohier hujusmodi processum vidit, ipse dixit loquenti quod sibi videbatur quod non debebat procedi contra eandem Johannam in materia fidei, nisi infomatione precedente super infamia, et quod de jure requirebatur talis informatio" (And after Lohier saw the proceedings record, he told the speaker [Courcelles] that it seemed to him that Joan should not have been proceeded against in the matter of faith unless there had been a preliminary investigation on her infamy, and this investigation was something that the law required).

judges, the bishop of Paris, was a mortal enemy of Burgundy and was plotting to kill him, confirmed by one of the hired assassins; Burgundy was an affected party, but had been allowed no part in the trial; masters from the University of Paris who were opposed to Burgundy participated in the trial, while independent masters were repelled, including the Picard Nation and the whole faculty of canon law.

If Joan had had a proper lawyer to advise her, he could have told her to object when being questioned without being charged, and, instead of answering, make a formal appeal against Cauchon to his immediate superior, the archbishop of Rheims, or to his ultimate superior, the pope. Counsel could also have told her to appeal because of the other grievances listed by Lohier, including recusal of Cauchon as a hostile judge. Of course, it was up to Cauchon himself as judge whether to accept an appeal and send it forward, and there was no likelihood that he would or could do that—for, as Lohier told Manchon, even the judges were intimidated by the threatening circumstances under which Joan was being prosecuted. In fact, as we just saw, Joan did in effect appeal to the pope in her last session: "She demanded to be led before him, our Lord Pope" (*Ipsa requirit quod ducatur ante ipsum dominum nostrum Papam*). But she was ignored.

The only hope for an appeal to be heard would be for an ally of Joan's to make the appeal directly to Rheims or Rome. The obvious person to do this was Charles himself. If Cauchon was at fault for not allowing Charles to be represented at the trial, Charles himself and his advisors were at fault for not doing something about it.

Lohier too could have arranged for the case to be appealed from Rouen. According to Manchon, he left Rouen immediately and returned to the Roman curia.[118] But, just a few months later, in October, he was co-opted to join the emissaries of the University of Paris to present their graduate lists to the pope, showing, Denifle says, that he forgot about Joan, and therefore that he deserves some blame. It shows also, he says, that the University did not harbor any resentment against him for his negative view of the proceedings in Rouen.[119]

[118] NT 1:216.

[119] Denifle, *CUP* 4:514, 531. For some reason, Denifle believes that Lohier started out from Paris on the October embassy, but he was probably already in Rome. He may have been back in France sometime during the fiscal year of 1432–1433 (September to September)—but in Rouen, not Paris—because of a payment made to Guillaume Erart (i.e., Erard, to be encountered below), acting as vicar-general for the absent archbishop Hugues d'Orges, for

Manchon testified also to Cauchon's reaction to Lohier's assessment: the bishop exclaimed, "Look here, Lohier wants us to decree some fine interlocutories in our process! He wants to calumniate everything, and he says that it's worth nothing. To believe him, we would have to begin all over, and everything that we have done would be worthless!"[120] In other words, Lohier considered everything done so far to be invalid, and that Cauchon would have to issue interlocutory decrees admitting judicial error and start over again.

Of course, it was out of the question that he would recuse himself and suggest that an unbiased judge take over. Cardinal Beaufort and the other English authorities would not stand for this. Nor would they allow Cauchon to summon French partisans, not to mention King Charles himself, to take part in the trial—and the French would not be likely to put themselves into their hands. Moreover, Cauchon was not about to reverse his policy of repressing experts who could advise her properly.

But one defect pointed out by Lohier, not presenting a libellus against Joan, could easily be repaired. He could do that now. Once in possession of her testimony against herself, he could properly charge her, as the law required. No matter that the testimony was illegally obtained; it was now irrefutable fact and could be used against her. There was no jury to be told that all of Joan's testimony was out of order and must be ignored.

There was, of course, a jury of sorts, the shifting panel of assessors, and they would have to be managed, if only by being cowed into agreement.

4.7 Marshalling Responses, Discussing Charges, March 18–24

On the next day after the last session, Passion Sunday, March 18, the Latin Record has Cauchon narrating a meeting that he and Lemaistre had with the six Paris theologians, Commissary Lafontaine, and five of Cauchon's original assessors (Fécamp, Longueville, Roussel, Venderès, and Coppequesne). Cauchon had various extracts of Joan's responses read to

obtaining an opinion from Master Jean Lohier on how to conduct a trial (Beaurepaire, "Éclaircissement," p. 287).

[120] Doncoeur and Lanhers, *Réhabilitation 1450*, p. 49: "Vela Lohier, qui nous veult bailler belles interlocutoyres in nostre proces! Il veut tout calompnier, et dit qu'il ne vault riens. Qui le vouldroit croire, il nous fauldroit tout commencer, et tout ce que nous avons fait ne vauldroit riens!"

them, and said that they would meet again on Thursday for further discussion. But meanwhile articles were ordered to be formulated to be used against Joan before the judges in the trial (*in judicio*).[121]

On first reading this, our natural assumption should be that they were now going to look for statements over the range of Joan's responses that could be turned into a libellus with articles to be used against her at trial. That was the way the inquisitors of old operated. And perhaps that is what they did. But nothing came of it, as such. Rather, as we will see, Estivet used his original libellus, with a few modifications made on the basis of the interrogations. Since he was not at this meeting of March 18, he was presumably consulted later.

At the Thursday meeting, March 22, there were ten additional consultants. Cauchon (together with Lemaistre, it seems) ordered the articles to be reduced in number and given to consultants to study.[122] This was the origin of the notorious Twelve Articles, worked up by Midi, undoubtedly with the other Paris theologians, and edited by Touraine.

On Saturday, March 24, Joan was again visited in prison. Lafontaine presided in place of Cauchon, along with Lemaistre, accompanied by five of the Six (minus Touraine), and a visitor, namely, the official of the diocese of Coutances, Enguerrand de Champrond. His master, Bishop Montjeu, together with Inquisitor Graverent, was prosecuting the heresy case against Montjeu's subject Jean Lecouvreur, which prevented Graverent from joining Cauchon against Joan. We saw that just a week before this, on March 15, Lecouvreur had staged a coup against his judges, and managed to send an appeal to the pope complaining about their violations of due process. Perhaps Champrond was sent to warn Cauchon to be on his guard against similar wiles on the part of Joan. If so, he would doubtless have been very impressed at how very unlikely Joan would be to escape the safeguards set in place against any such resorts to due process.

The purpose of the March 24 gathering was to have Joan authenticate the questions she had been asked, and the responses she had given, as Notary Manchon read them out. But since this task was accomplished during the course of just a single visit, it must have covered a drastically reduced selection of all the interrogating that had been accomplished during the sixteen sessions of the previous month.

[121] LR 179–80.
[122] LR 180.

After narrating this project, Courcelles in the Latin Record adds, almost as an afterthought, that before this reading began, the promotor appointed by the judges, who was also present, offered himself to prove the contents of the register, in case Joan should deny the truth of any of it.[123]

But how, we might ask, could Estivet prove what went on during the interrogations if he was never recorded by the notaries as having been present? Was he there surreptitiously? Or was there an understanding with the notaries that they would not mention him, just as the notaries did not mention themselves? Or was it only Courcelles here in the Latin Record who did not mention him—there being no French Minute concerning these events?

In the end, Courcelles reports, Joan accepted everything that Manchon read to her from the register, except for clarifying her surname, either *d'Arc* after her father or *Rommée* after her mother, and one other point, concerning her putting on a woman's garment. She would wear it outside of prison, to visit her mother's home. And once she was no longer in prison, she would take counsel about what to do.[124]

On the next day, Palm Sunday, March 25, Cauchon, together with Loiseleur and four of the Paris group—Courcelles, Beaupère, Maurice, and Midi—visited Joan in her cell to respond to her renewed request to attend mass and receive Communion. He insisted that she could not do so in men's clothes. Her final words were that wearing such clothing was neither against her conscience nor against Church law.[125] The lesson derivable from this visitation was inscribed on the margin of all three original copies of the Latin Record: "She chose not to hear mass rather than taking off her male garb."[126]

Then Estivet, not before this said to be present, asked for a copy of the foregoing, and three witnesses are named.[127]

On the day after Palm Sunday, March 26, Cauchon and Lemaistre met again with a dozen assessors, most of them the same as on March 18—Loiseleur being one of the new ones, and Chastillon and Marguerie the other two—to receive and review Estivet's libellus against Joan and to decide how to proceed. The judges called what had gone before the

[123] LR 181.
[124] LR 181–82.
[125] LR 182–83.
[126] LR 183: "Elegit non audire missam quam dimittere habitum virilem."
[127] LR 183.

"preparatory process," which proceeded *ex officio nostro*, and now he and Lemaistre decreed that Joan would be proceeded against in an ordinary process.

This at least was how Courcelles put it in the Latin Record. He was not a jurist or a judge, and may have garbled the notarial report that he was following. Presumably what Cauchon meant was that in the beginning he was proceeding *ex officio mero*, by himself, and now he and Lemaistre would proceed *ex officio promoto*, with a promotor.

The judges then declared the articles of the libellus to be well formed—presumably Estivet's original set of articles now somewhat modified, on the basis of the interrogations. They decreed that on the next day the promotor would propose them to Joan and she would be asked to respond to them. If she refused, she would be given a canonical warning, and, upon further refusal, the articles would be taken "as confessed" (*pro confessatis*).[128]

[128] LR 184–85.

CHAPTER 5

Trial Begun: Charges, Promises of Proof, Denials

5.1 Assessors Polled on Procedure; Judges Require Immediate Response

According to Courcelles's reconstruction of the proceedings, on the day that the actual trial began, after the attending assessors, thirty-eight of them, were listed, the judges proceeded to recount what happened. The assigned promotor, Jean d'Estivet, appeared before them in Joan's presence. He asserted that Joan was brought there, after certain informations and interrogations were effected by them, to answer any questions that he, as the judges' prosecutor, would ask of her touching the faith. He intended to prove, if need be (*et intendo probare, si opus sit*), the facts, laws, and reasons contained in article form in a book (*codex*) that he now exhibited and submitted to them. He requested that they make her swear to respond what she believed or disbelieved (*credit aut non credit*) concerning each article; or, if she refused, to hold her in contempt; and if she persisted in refusal, to excommunicate her.

Estivet asked that she be assigned a certain brief term within which to respond to the articles. She should be warned that if she failed to respond to any of the articles, the judges would consider them to be confessed by her (i.e., admitted to be true), as law and custom demanded (*sicut jura, stilus, usus, et communis observancia volunt et requirunt*).[1]

[1] LR 185–86.

H. A. Kelly, *The Trial and Retrial of Joan of Arc*, The New Middle Ages, https://doi.org/10.1007/978-3-032-07887-2_5

According to the French Minute, the judges then ordered the experts among the assessors to respond to the promotor's petition, and the results are given.[2] Courcelles omitted the whole process in the Latin Record.

Of the thirty-eight assessors named as present in Courcelles's text on that Tuesday, fourteen were stated to be licensed in theology, and sixteen as doctors or licensed in law, including Official Jean Basset. Courcelles failed to list himself as one of the theologians (perhaps because not yet licensed), but he was in fact polled on that day, according to the Minute. Four of the listed jurists (Raoul Roussel, Jean Alespée, Jean Colombel, and Nicolas Cavel) did not appear among the polled, while one who was not listed was polled, namely, Giles Deschamps.

The first to respond were eight of the jurists, beginning with Nicolas de Venderès, one of the confidential group that met on the day before. He agreed with the promotor that Joan should be sworn, and held in contempt and excommunicated for refusals. If she is excommunicated, she should be proceeded against according to law. He did not specify what that entailed, whether a standard judgment of contempt or Estivet's extreme and unjustified demand that silence should be treated as equivalent to a guilty plea.

The jurist Jean Pinchon, vicar-general of the diocese while the archiepiscopal see of Rouen was vacant, said that the articles should be read out, before she decided on her responses. Next to respond was Official Basset, who said the articles should be read out (i.e., repeated) before any excommunication was declared. Jean Guérin stated simply that the articles should be read out.

Commissary Lafontaine then agreed with Venderès, after which the civil lawyer Geoffroi de Crotay said that she should be given at least a threefold delay before she was excommunicated and convicted for refusing to swear, especially since even in civil matters a threefold delay is given before taking the oath on avoiding calumny. Two experts in both laws, Jean Ledoux and Robert Lebarbier, agreed, and the civil lawyer Giles Deschamps said that the articles should first be read to her and a day assigned for her to respond, after she had been advised. (We should remember that jurists in Roman civil law and JUDs could not have obtained their degrees from the University of Paris.)

The first of the theologians to speak was the abbot of Fécamp (Duremort), who thought that she was required to tell the truth about

[2] FM 187–88.

whatever was agreed to pertain to the trial. And if she had not taken advice on any particular matter, she should be given adequate time to do so, and respond on a future day. Jean de Chastillon, archdeacon of Evroux, agreed, as did Erard Emengart and Maurice Duquesnoy; and Guillaume Lebouchier said that she was required to tell the truth especially when it concerned her deeds.

The prior of Longueville (Miget) said that she should not be forced to state her belief on matters about which she had no knowledge. Paris theologian Jean Beaupère said that she was required to tell the truth on matters she was certain about which concerned deeds. But if she did not know what the truth was or what the law was, she should not be forced to state her belief. His Paris colleagues Jacques de Touraine and Nicolas Midi followed suit, with the latter adding that he left it up to the jurists to say precisely what oath she was required to make.

Beaupère did not show such concern for the rights of the defendant when he served as Cauchon's interrogator. The information secured during those freewheeling days was now safely in the hands of Midi and Touraine, who were busy shaping it into the Twelve Articles. They had what they needed, and could afford to take a by-the-letter stand for what followed—which they may have known would be a *pro forma* exercise.

Jean Lefèvre simply referred to the jurists. So did Jean de Nibat, at least concerning the articles; Joan's oath should be to tell the truth concerning the trial process and the faith, and if she asked for a delay on any difficult matter, it should be granted. Another of the Parisians, Pierre Maurice, said that she should respond concerning matters she had knowledge of. His fellow-professor Gérard Feuillet said only that she should respond under oath, as did Jacques Guesdon.

The last theologian to speak was the final Parisian, Courcelles, the ex-rector, who, as head of the University had complained about Cauchon's lack of diligence in instituting Joan's prosecution. Once again he spoke out against delay: she should respond during the reading of the articles. However, he allowed that on dubious matters pauses could be allowed.

Finally, four more jurists spoke. André Marguerie said she had to swear about what concerned the trial, and delays were to be given on doubtful questions. Denis Gastinel said that she should swear as the promotor demanded. On the question of how to proceed if she refused to swear, he would need to consult his books. Aubert Morel (Graverent's promotor against Ségueut) said she should swear, and so did Jean Duchemin, and both repeated what others said.

It is noteworthy that none of the assessors mentioned the need to establish *publica fama*, which Lohier had insisted on, which may indicate that it was customary to omit it. The way around this requirement in English tribunals was to end each article with a statement that it was widely known and even notorious. The French custom was to add a final article asserting that all of the previous articles were widely known.[3] As we will see, that was what Estivet did in his libellus (though there were also some allegations of notoriety in the articles themselves). But if the demand of the jurists that the articles be read beforehand had been followed, and if Joan had been given time to formulate responses, especially with the aid of adequate counsel, she could have insisted that Estivet prove his claim of *fama* for any article she wished. However, the subject would not come up at all in her responses.

While only the French Minute gives the result of the polling, only the Latin Record gives the decision of the judges, which coincided with Courcelles's opinion alone, against the more lenient opinion of others, of giving her a delay—which even Estivet advocated. Each article would be read in Latin, and then translated into French, and Joan would be required to respond then and there, according to what she knew. However, if she said that she needed time, it would be granted.[4]

5.2 Promotor Estivet's Presentation of His Libellus

That same morning, Tuesday, March 27, 1431, still in the presence of the thirty-eight assessors named, Promotor Estivet took an oath against calumny.[5] According to the French text, he swore that he put forward the articles against Joan in his libellus not out of favor, rancor, fear, or hatred, but out of zeal for the faith.[6]

Cauchon then told Joan that, since she was not instructed in scholarly matters, she could select one or more of the learned men there present to advise her, or, if she did not know whom to choose, they, the judges, could decide for her—since they were not seeking to punish her but rather to bring her to the way of truth and salvation if she should in any way be

[3] This too was a practice in England as well: Kelly, *Criminal-Inquisitorial Trials*, p. 126.
[4] LR 188.
[5] LR 189.
[6] FM 188.

deficient. The only qualification was that her counsel could not act as proctors and reply for her, in factual matters.[7]

It was, of course, out of the question that she should be allowed access to advisors from the French king's supporters, as Joan had specifically requested. She had good reason to doubt the sincerity of Bishop Cauchon, and she declined his offer. She thanked him for his solicitude for her welfare, but said that she would not separate herself from relying on God's counsel.[8]

If her treacherous confidant Loiseleur had been seated among the assessors that day (he was at the meeting the day before), she may well have chosen him. But he did not show up again for almost two months. He reappeared on the day when Joan was threatened with torture if she was not more forthcoming in her answers, and he was one of the very few who voted that she should be tortured.[9]

Joan agreed to take an oath to tell the truth regarding everything that concerned the proceedings. She then placed her hand on a copy of the four Gospels and swore accordingly.[10]

It is not clear that she was informed that this proceeding was any different from those that had gone before, in which she was required to take an oath and respond to questions. She had had different questioners before, and in varied circumstances. There were several differences this time, but we are not entirely clear on the format. According to Courcelles's Latin Record, Cauchon stated that each article was first read in Latin, and then translated into French. But the French text says instead that Courcelles himself at the judges' command began to expound the content in the libellus, that is, the articles.[11] This would be the first time that Courcelles took an active role in the proceedings. We remember that he deliberately omitted his name from the assessors attending on that day, and he did the same for the following day, Wednesday, March 28,[12] when the administering of charges continued.

[7] LR 189.
[8] FM 190, LR 190.
[9] FM 351.
[10] FM 190, LR 190.
[11] FM 190.
[12] LR 190–91.

Cauchon continues, in Courcelles's Latin Record, to say that the text of the articles of the libellus follows, together with Joan's responses, and including her responses given previously, to which she makes reference.[13]

These selections from her earlier responses were doubtless compiled either by Estivet or Courcelles, or both. But all of them would likely have been made after her responses to all of the articles. Estivet would collect what he could to counter Joan's denials, since he needed to prove whatever she denied.[14] He must have had some witnesses at the ready as well, to substantiate some of the less outrageous charges. But Cauchon would soon tell him that their services were no longer needed: no proofs would be required. Or perhaps what happened was that Estivet started the process of adding "proof-texts" to her responses, and he left off when Cauchon gave him the news, and Courcelles picked up later where he left off.

Estivet's libellus took the form of an opening address to the two judges, in which he summarized the crimes that she had committed, followed by seventy numbered articles, which were also addressed to the judges and not Joan.

His "opening statement" would not have been translated for Joan, and she would thereby have been kept unaware of what was in store for her.

This statement consisted of a single long sentence, to this effect: Before you, reverend judges, for the purpose that Joan "the Maid," who is manifoldly defamed of what follows, be pronounced by you a sorceress or sortileger (*sorceria sive sortilega*), invoker of evil spirits, a wrong thinker about the faith, a schismatic doubting and deviating from the article *Unam sanctam* (belief in "one holy Catholic and Apostolic Church") and other articles, an apostate from the faith, a blasphemer, cruelly bloodthirsty, a shameful wearer of men's clothes, allowing herself to be adored, a heretic or at least strongly suspect of heresy—and for all this to be punished and corrected by you—Jean d'Estivet, appointed as promotor of your office by you, proposes and intends to prove and to properly inform your minds, as plaintiff and accuser (*actor et delator*) against the said Joan as accused

[13] LR 191.

[14] Contra Hobbins, *Trial*, p. 236 n. 9, who thinks that Estivet put them in place in time for the presentation of his libellus in court on March 27. Hobbins says that the testimony from her depositions was inserted into the record at Cauchon's request, but he does not cite a source. See Tisset, 2:160 n. 2, who observes that testimony from Joan's later questioning, on March 31 and April 18, was added after earlier testimony, following article 60 (*recte* 61): see LR 280–81, treated below.

defendant (*delata rea*), all that follows, binding himself however to prove only what is necessary, and reserving the right to add, correct, change, and interpret matters of law and fact.[15]

This hard-charging approach on Estivet's part must have strained the belief of the assessors who were not part of Cauchon's inner circle intent on convicting her, and who had witnessed the weeks of interrogation, which had revealed her as scarcely the sort of hardened miscreant the promotor described. Here, for instance, are his words about her heretical activities: "...uttering, voicing, affirming, publishing, and engraving on the hearts of simple people false and lying propositions infected with heresy, and actually heretical, and contrary to the Catholic faith—propositions altogether scandalous, sacrilegious, contrary to good customs, and offensive to pious ears." How did this peasant girl, whose mother taught her the Paternoster, who did not learn to read and write, and who moved from rustic fields to leading armies, have the leisure to absorb such wicked doctrines and find the occasion to preach them so forcefully? And why were they not mentioned earlier? As it would turn out, he would provide no examples of her alleged outrageous preachings.

5.3 Article 1: Statement of Court Competency

The first article said that "you the judges" were competent judges, one (Cauchon) as ordinary of the diocese and the other (Lemaistre) as inquisitor of the faith, both fully authorized to expel heresies, sortileges, superstitions, and other crimes mentioned above from the said diocese and whole realm of France, and to prosecute these and other crimes, even those committed elsewhere.[16]

Let us picture the courtroom, the Castle chapel, where the assessors are once more gathered around the judges, and Joan is brought back in her always-present fetters, by Urban Dean Massieu. Now Estivet has finally taken on his role as prosecutor and plaintiff in this trial, which was assigned and claimed at the beginning, over a month earlier, revealing to Joan, who now at last is constituted as a formal defendant, exactly what he accuses her of.

Estivet has just delivered his very long opening statement, which I have greatly abbreviated. Joan understood nothing of it. She also understood

[15] LR 191–92.
[16] LR 192–93.

nothing of his first long article, which I have also abbreviated. But then, Thomas de Courcelles stepped forward, and translated the article into French, on the fly, presumably also abbreviating it, for her better comprehension. Then she was directed to say what she thought of it.

If Joan had been advised by proper counsel, she would doubtless have been advised to enter a formal recusation against Cauchon as her judge, since he was the formal enemy of her king, being a councilor and employee of Henry VI. Instead, she spoke of the clergy in general, not Cauchon and Lemaistre in particular. But, of course, Cauchon would have rejected the appeal. As it was, she responded only to the portion of the article that dealt with the Church. She stated that she certainly believed that the Roman pope and bishops and other churchmen were there to preserve the Catholic faith and to punish those deficient in faith. As for herself, she submitted herself only to the heavenly court of God and the Virgin Mary and the other saints, and she firmly believed herself not lacking in "our faith," and not wishing to be lacking in it.[17]

A fair auditor would have interpreted her reply to mean that, although she acknowledged that churchmen had the power to prosecute persons lacking in faith, she was not one, and she had no business here.

5.4 Articles 2–3: Omnibus Charges of Divination, Sortilege, Demonic Pacts, Fostering Idolatry, Lack of Faith, Denial of Doctrine, and Heretical Propositions

The first offenses that Estivet charged against Joan were rhetorically elaborated in article 2, citing no specific instances. The article was obviously formulated at a time when there was only one judge to address, namely, Bishop Cauchon:

> The said accused, not only in the present year, but from the time of her childhood, not only in your diocese and jurisdiction, but also in the neighboring and other parts of this kingdom, has performed, composed, mingled in, and commanded many charms and superstitions; she has been deified and permitted herself to be adored and venerated; she has called up demons and evil spirits, has consulted and frequented them, has had, made, and entered into pacts and treaties with them; she has similarly given counsel,

[17] LR 193.

> aid, and favor to others doing the same things, and has induced them to do the same or like things, saying, believing, maintaining, affirming that so to do, to believe in them, to use such charms, divinations, and superstitious proceedings was neither a sin nor a forbidden thing; but she has rather assured them that it is lawful, praiseworthy, and opportune, enticing into these evil ways and errors many people of different estate and of either sex, in whose heart she imprinted these and like things. And in the accomplishment and perpetration of these crimes the said Joan has been taken and captured in the boundaries and limits of your diocese of Beauvais.[18]

Joan denied it all, and added that if some people kissed her hands or garments, she did not encourage it:

> To this second article Joan answers that she denies the charms, superstitions, and divinations; and as for the adoration, if certain people have kissed her hands or garments it is not because of her or at her will; she kept herself from that as far as it was within her power. The rest of the article she denies.[19]

In a regular trial, after the defendant denied a charge, it would be up to the promotor to prove it, at least eventually, as Estivet promised to do, or else dismiss it. Or, if there was strong public conviction as to the defendant's guilt, the judge could order purgation with a set number of compurgators (which Joan would not be able to assemble, given the circumstances of her captivity). It would take a great many depositions of witnesses to even begin to prove this lavishly expanded set of accusations. But a beginning would be to bring Joan's own testimony about herself, collected over the previous many weeks, against her, to convict her out of her own mouth. What could be produced along this line? Let us look at what Estivet (or Courcelles) added to her reply in the Latin Record, namely, two of her statements. The first was a rather noncommittal comment:

> On Saturday, March 3rd, of this same year, in regard to the content of this article, when she was asked if she knew what was in the thoughts of the people of her party as they kissed her hands, her feet, and her garments, she answered that many people gladly saw her. And with that, she said that she

[18] LR 192–93 (Barrett 1932, 148).
[19] FM 194, LR 194 (Barrett 1932, 148).

> told them to kiss her garments as little as possible; but the poor came to her, so she did not disappoint them, but helped them as much as she could.[20]

The other was a response that she made to a question about whether she received a revelation to attack Compiègne:

> Again, on Saturday, March 10th, when asked if on making the sortie at Compiègne, where she was captured, she had been told by revelation or by her voice to make the sortie, she answered that on that day it had not announced her capture, and she was not counseled to go there; but she had often been told that she must be taken. Asked if when she made this sortie she passed over the bridge of Compiègne, she answered yes, and through the boulevard; that she went with the company of her men against the men of lord Jean de Luxembourg, that she twice drove them to the camp of the Burgundians, and a third time to the middle of the highway; and then the English cut off the road from her and her company, between her and the boulevard, so her men retreated; and she, falling back to the fields, on the Picardy side, was captured; and the river was between Compiègne and the place where she was taken, and between Compiègne and where she was taken there was only the river, and the boulevard with its ditch.[21]

In other words, the excerpts proved nothing—except the place where she was captured, namely, the diocese of Beauvais, therefore in the jurisdiction of Cauchon and Lemaistre (after Graverent licensed him for the diocese of Beauvais).

In Article 3, Estivet brought a solemn charge against Joan that she was guilty of promulgating heretical propositions:

> The accused is fallen into many divers errors of the worst kind, infected with heretical evil: she has said, uttered, voiced, affirmed, published, graven on the hearts of simple people certain false and lying propositions, infected with heresy and actually heretical, outside of and contrary to our Catholic faith, against the statutes made and approved by the general councils, as well as divine, canon, and civil laws: propositions scandalous, sacrilegious, contrary to good customs and offensive to pious ears; she has lent aid, counsel, and favor to those who have said, uttered, affirmed and promulgated these propositions.[22]

[20] LR 194 (Barrett 1932, 149), from FM 100, LR 100.
[21] LR 194–95 (Barrett 1932, 149), from FM 113, LR 113.
[22] LR 195 (Barrett 1932, 149–50).

Joan denied the charge outright, and asserted that she had stood with the Church as far as she could.[23]

Estivet could only have begun to prove such a charge by giving an example of a heretical statement that Joan had spoken, as supported by acceptable testimony. He obviously scoured the register of her earlier testimony to find some support for that florid accusation but he came up empty: nothing of what she had responded was found to support a charge of heresy.

A further conclusion can be drawn: that, even though at the end of his libellus Estivet would assert that everything in it was widely known, that is, that Joan was solidly believed to be guilty of all of the offenses listed against her, and that therefore a legitimate ecclesiastical judge, specifically, Bishop Cauchon, could legally institute an inquisition against her, charging her with these offenses, there was in fact no *publica fama* against Joan as a disseminator of heresies. Or, if there was, they should be challenged to prove it.

Let us recall Rota Auditor Lohier's judgment that no information had been collected on her infamy, which was required by law. There were only strong *assertions* of it, unsubstantiated by any witnesses, let alone by reliable and unbiased witnesses.

5.5 Further Articles (4–30) Presented on March 27, with Joan's Responses

Article 4, Estivet explained to the judges, was for their information, but it also contained injurious conclusions about Joan. The defendant came from the town of Greux, where she was only instructed in the basics of the faith by old women accustomed to using sortileges, divinations, and other superstitious works or magic arts, and she learned many pernicious things about fairies, and she confessed before the judges in court that she did not know that they were evil spirits.[24] She responded that the part about her birthplace and parents was true. As for fairies, she did not know what he was talking about. She was taught her creed and all else as a good child should be. Concerning her godmother, she referred them to what she had said earlier.[25] At this point, someone intervened, whether the promotor or

[23] FM 195, LR 195.
[24] LR 196.
[25] FM 196, LR 196.

one of the judges, and asked her to recite the creed; she replied that they should ask the confessor she recited it to.[26] (What she said about her godmother earlier was added to the next two articles.)

Estivet's statement in Article 4 that she had confessed to the judges in court that she did not know that fairies were evil spirits was denied by Joan and not backed up later by Estivet, or Courcelles, with any testimony from Joan's earlier answers.

Article 5 was a statement about a large tree near a spring at Domremy around which evil spirits called fairies were said to have interactions with those who practiced sortilege.[27] (We note that, instead of dismissing the reported fairies as figments of peasant imagination, it suited Estivet to assume them to be real, and therefore demons.) In response, Joan referred to her earlier statements about the tree and the spring, and denied the rest.[28]

Her earlier responses from February 24 and March 1 and 17 were later added here, but they were in no way incriminating: she had heard of cures there, but did not know whether they were true or not. She heard the voices of Saints Catherine and Margaret, but did not know what they said. Her godmother was an upright woman; she knew nothing about activities there, except that she had heard about goings-on on Thursdays that sounded like sortilege.[29]

Article 6 asserted that Joan used to perform incantations, sortileges, and other witcheries (*maleficia*) around the tree. She denied it, referring to her earlier testimony.[30] Estivet or Courcelles adds the continuation of her long response on February 24 here, where she spoke of joining in with children's songs and dances, and also mentioned that her godmother said she saw fairies there. Joan did not know whether it was true or not, but she herself never saw any.[31]

Article 7 asserted that she carried a mandrake for good fortune, which Joan denied, as she had done before.[32] Article 8 recounted what she did at Neufchâteau, "around the age of 20," tending sheep and learning to ride,

[26] FM 197, LR 197.
[27] LR 197.
[28] FM 197, LR 197.
[29] LR 197–98, LR 65, 85, 168, 169, 178.
[30] LR 198; FM 198, LR 198; LR 198–99.
[31] LR 199; FM 199, LR 199.
[32] LR 199, with testimony added from March 1, LR 200 (cf. LR 86).

hinting at bad company.[33] Article 9 recounted the story that at that time she sued a man for breach of promise.[34] Article 10 said she claimed that she had visions ever since that time, that is, for five years, and it related some of the things she claimed she heard from them; Joan referred to her previous answers.[35]

Article 11 recounted a reported conversation between Robert de Beaudricourt and Joan, and his repeated boasts, about her future three children. Joan referred to what she had responded elsewhere, and said she never said anything about having three children.[36] In fact, there was nothing in the earlier questions and responses about this. The article was obviously based on a point in their original arsenal which they did not get around to using during the interrogations. All that they would be able to find to back it up from her previous responses would be what she said to a question on March 12 about her voices, whether they called her daughter of God, daughter of the Church, or great-hearted daughter.[37]

Article 12 recounted her men's clothing and gear, with her assertion that she acted on God's command. As with all of the articles, this one was addressed to the judges; but after Joan referred to her previous statements, she was asked directly whether she acted on God's command, and she again referred to what she had said before.[38]

Article 13 charged Joan with currently holding and demonstrating in her actions the blasphemy that God and his angels and saints commanded what was against the purity of the female sex, prohibited in divine law, abominable to God and man, and prohibited by ecclesiastical laws under pain of excommunication, specifically, wearing men's clothes and armaments, including the dress of the most dissolute men. Joan simply commented that she had not blasphemed God or his saints.[39]

We note that the article itself did not establish the truth of its claim about the nature of Joan's alleged crime—say, by pointing to specific provisions of canon law. But the French Minute said that, after Joan's reply, it was "explained" to her that the sacred canons and Holy Scripture said that

[33] LR 200.
[34] LR 200–201.
[35] LR 201–02.
[36] LR 204.
[37] LR 205, cf. p. 126.
[38] LR 205. Testimony was gathered from February 22 and 27 and March 12 and 17 (LR 205–07).
[39] LR 207–08.

cross-dressing (women putting on men's clothes and men women's clothes) was a thing abominable to God. She was asked whether she took on those clothes at God's command, she replied that that question had already been sufficiently answered. If they wanted more, she asked them for a delay, and she would respond afterwards. She was then asked if she would put on women's clothes in order to receive Communion at Easter. She said that she would not change her clothes for any reason, saying that wearing male or female clothes made no difference for going to Communion, and that they should not refuse her because of her clothes. She was then asked "by one who spoke" (*par ung qui parloit*) whether she had any revelation or command to wear men's clothes; she replied that she answered this before, which they should read, and she would say more the next day. She added that she knew well who had her wear the clothes, but she did not know how she should reveal it.[40]

Courcelles does not include these French Minute exchanges in his version of the record, though he does add the third after the 14th article, as if it occurred then. He said that it was asked "by one of the two assessors" (*per alterum assistentium*).[41] Article 14 stated that Joan currently claimed that she did well in wearing the clothes of dissolute men, and would continue to do so until God revealed that she should not, which was blasphemy.[42] Joan responded that she did not do wrong in serving God, and said that she would say more the next day.[43]

Article 15 accused her of hardness of heart, disobedience to the church and contempt of the sacraments for not being willing to attend mass on condition that she wear women's garb.[44] She made it clear that it was God whom she was obeying (saying that she would rather die than revoke what she had done by God's command).[45] On being asked then and there whether she would give up male clothes to attend mass, she said that it was not the time for her to give up her clothing, and if the judges did not allow her to hear mass, God would be able to let her do so without them. As for the content of the article, she acknowledged the offer to change clothes,

[40] FM 208.
[41] LR 209–10.
[42] LR 209, FM 209.
[43] LR 209, FM 209.
[44] LR 210.
[45] FM 210.

but denied the accusations of irreverence and the rest.[46] Large excerpts from the questioning on March 15 and 17 were later added.[47]

Article 16 concluded the clothing-charges without specifying the crimes or sins involved. It said that when she was held at Beaurevoir and Arras she refused all offers of female clothing, preferring to act like a man rather than a woman, which was true to the present day.[48] Joan admitted her refusal of such clothing then and now; as for other activities of women, there were plenty of women to do them.[49] The testimony from March 3 follows in the Latin Record.[50] When all was said and done, even given that it was sinful to wear men's clothing, it was never explained how it could be a matter of faith or heresy. Of course, we saw that that was true even of eminent theologians like Cardinal d'Ailly in insisting that tyrannicide and associated crimes were heretical.

Moving on to another subject, Article 17 accused Joan of boasting about what she would do for her king, reinforcing it by the frequent use of divinations to reveal secret things about persons.[51] Estivet must have given the specific example of her recognition of Robert de Beaudricourt and the king, since Joan responded to it (alluding to her earlier testimony). She replied that she was acting as God's messenger when she spoke to Charles. She referred to her response about this, added in Courcelles's record from February 22 (she knew by her voices). Also added is her brusque dismissal on March 13 concerning rumors that she had revealed a concubinary priest and the whereabouts of a missing silver cup.[52]

According to Article 18, Joan constantly dissuaded Charles from making peace and urged him to bloodshed.[53] Joan responded by speaking of her own negotiations with Burgundy, declaring that the only possible peace with the English would be if they returned to England.[54] To support this accusation from Joan's interrogation, only one exchange can be adduced: why she did not agree to a treaty with the town of Jargeau (she responded that it was simply a matter of not allowing their request for a

[46] FM 211, LR 210–11.
[47] LR 210–12.
[48] LR 212.
[49] FM 213, LR 212–13.
[50] LR 213–14.
[51] LR 214.
[52] LR 214–15, cf. 49, 50–51, 140; Hobbins, p. 132.
[53] LR 215.
[54] FM 215–16.

fifteen-day delay; they had to evacuate immediately, or suffer the consequences).[55]

The next article, no. 19, presented an interesting alternative: either Joan committed the horrendous crime of consulting with demons using divinations to discover the sword hidden in the church at Fierbois, or she deceitfully hid it there herself beforehand.[56] Referring to her previous testimony, Joan denied both alternatives.[57] (The record supplies the testimony from February 27, when Joan said that she was acting under the direction of her voices.[58])

The prosecutor's assumption that Joan's voices were demonic was not proved or argued, but it did not have to be; the judges only needed to believe it. And it did fulfill one of the rules for discernment of spirits: Joan was evil, because she was on the opposing side in the current war.

Continuing the sortilege theme, Article 20 asserted that Joan placed "lots" or tokens (*sortes*) on a ring, on a banner, pennants, and other pieces of cloth that she and her crew wore. She performed many execrations and conjurations over them in many places, and publicly asserted that they would bring victory, especially at Compiègne before she was captured.[59] Joan responded that nothing that she did was sorcery or any wicked art (*sorcerie ne autre mauves art*), and the good fortune of her banner referred to the fortune sent by God.[60] Piled up in the record after this article were all the quizzings that had been done concerning banner and pennants, and concerning her ring with the inscription "Jesus Mary," which she wore when she touched St Catherine.[61]

There is nothing here to support the assertion of the article about her battle-cries at Compiègne. If it had come to gathering witnesses to support it, they would presumably be from the enemy side, and would have produced testimony like that of Lord Talbot in Shakespeare's play at the siege of Rouen: "Pucelle, that witch, that damned sorceress, Hath wrought this hellish mischief!"[62] Cauchon would doubtless be able to count on similar partisan conjectures among his assessors and on the English-

[55] LR 216, cf. 79.
[56] LR 216.
[57] FM 216.
[58] LR 216–17, cf. 76–77.
[59] LR 217–18.
[60] FM 218; LR 218: "non erat sortilegium nec alia mala ars."
[61] LR 218–20.
[62] Shakespeare, *1 Henry VI* 3.2.39–40. In the original text, "Pucelle" is spelled "Puzel."

favoring remnant in the faculties of Canon Law and Theology at the University of Paris.

In Article 21, Estivet charged Joan with acting out of rashness and presumption in sending letters to Henry VI and the duke of Bedford and other defenders of Orleans, containing much that was evil and pernicious and not consonant with the Catholic faith. He introduced one such letter into the record, labeling it as Article 22, namely, the letter of March 22, 1429, that she had been confronted with in her interrogations on February 22. In Article 23 he asserted that the letter showed either that she was deluded by evil spirits and that she frequently consulted them, or else that she perniciously and mendaciously made things up to deceive people.[63] Joan responded to no. 21 by saying that she did not act out of pride or presumption, but by the commandment of God. And she corrected some of the letter's contents,[64] as she had done before, in a response, added here, denying that she called herself a "chieftain of war."[65] To the next article, she said that the English would have been wise to believe her, and in a week's worth of years they would realize the truth of it.[66] To no. 23, she simply denied that she had acted by the advice of evil spirits.[67] Estivet neglected to point out just exactly what he found in the letter that was against the Catholic faith.

Article 24 was the bizarre charge that when she used the names of Jesus and Mary in her letters separated by a cross, it was code to her forces that she meant the opposite of what she wrote. Joan responded by referring to her earlier testimony. But all that would be found in interrogation testimony was what she said on March 17, when the judges asked her why she put the names in her letters, and she responded that it was her scribes who did it, and people told her that it was a fitting thing to do.[68]

A different crime was asserted in Article 25: Joan usurped the role of angels in claiming to be sent by God even when resorting to force (*ad viam facti*)[69] and bloodshed, which was contrary to holiness and an

[63] LR 220–22.
[64] FM 220.
[65] LR 221, cf. 51.
[66] LR 222.
[67] FM 222.
[68] LR 223, cf. 174.
[69] "To the way of deed," the opposite of *ad viam juris* (to the way of law).

abomination to the pious.[70] In response, Joan stated that she first sought for peace, but if that could not be had, she was prepared to fight.[71]

The final charge of the day, coming at the end of the cluster of Articles 26–30, was that in responding to the count of Armagnac on the three claimants to the papacy, she was presumptuous, setting herself above the authority of the Church in expecting to receive an answer directly from God.[72] Joan said to go back and review what she had said before on the subject.[73]

5.6 The Rest of the Seventy Articles, March 28

On the following day, according to the French Minute, Joan was required to swear again, which she did, as usual, limiting her oath to what concerned their proceedings, before listening to Article 31. Courcelles takes no notice of this in his version of the record, and, in fact, specifies Article 32 instead of 31 as the first one responded to by Joan on March 28.[74] Earlier on, he gave a list of the assessors who were present on that day (omitting his own name, as we saw). The commissary, Jean Lafontaine, appeared there for the last time in the proceedings—as did Official Basset,[75] but that story will be taken up later. According to Manchon's later testimony, Lafontaine was forced to flee for fear of the English. He had advised Joan to submit to the judgment of the Church (it was clear to all, he said, that she did not understand the implications of this demand).[76]

After taking her oath, Joan proceeded to make some further response to the articles about wearing men's clothes, specifically that she would not change them without God's leave.[77]

Article 31 is an example of a new charge that Estivet formulated after the interrogations of Joan began:

[70] LR 223.
[71] FM 223.
[72] LR 224–27.
[73] FM 224–26.
[74] LR 229.
[75] LR 190–91.
[76] NT 1:182. See Tisset, *Procès*, 2:406: Lapierre, Massieu, and Houppeville would also testify that Lafontaine drew ire by attempting to counsel Joan.
[77] FM 227.

> The said Joan, in and since the time of her youth, has boasted and daily boasts of having had many revelations and visions, and concerning these, in spite of being charitably admonished and lawfully and properly required upon legal oath (*debite ac juridice sub debito juramenti requisita*), she would not and will not swear; further, she refuses to declare them sufficiently by word or sign; but did and still does put off, contradict, and refuse. And when formally refusing to swear, on many and several occasions, she said and affirmed, in her examination and elsewhere, that she would not discover her visions and revelations to you [the judges], even if her head were cut off or her body were dismembered; that the sign would not be dragged from her lips which God showed her, by which she knew she came from God.[78]

Joan replied that she may well have said that she would not reveal the sign or other things referred to in this article. Her earlier statements on the sign should be understood to include that she would not reveal it without God's permission.[79]

We note that Estivet cites the language that Joan supposedly used in refusing Cauchon's request (who, of course, was in no way acting according to law in putting her under oath to respond to questions about unnamed suspicions against her). But this language is not contained in any of the excerpts from her previous testimony added by Estivet or Courcelles.[80] We will see that the same is true of Article 60, where Estivet again attributes to Joan the statement that she would rather have her head cut off than tell the judges everything, and even more abundant excerpts are added.[81]

The promotor followed up in Article 32 by urging, in effect, that the judges apply the rules of "the discernment of spirits" to Joan's revelations, rules stated prominently in the priest's manual, the *Rituale Romanum*, published in 1614, to determine whether evil spirits were present before the rite of exorcism should be used. Estivet skipped the first rule, which was to determine whether certain manifestations were natural or "above nature." Instead, he said that *if* Joan had the sort of revelations she claimed, they should be judged as coming not from good but from evil spirits, because of the evil deeds that she had committed, as specified in the

[78] LR 227 (cf. Barrett 1932, 181–82).
[79] FM 228.
[80] LR 228–29.
[81] LR 372–78.

preceding articles.[82] Joan rejected this judgment concerning her deeds, saying that what she did was by the revelation of Saints Catherine and Margaret. Then she clarified earlier responses, about being advised by others to put the names of Jesus and Mary in her letters. And where it says that "all she did" was by God's counsel, it should read "all the good that she did." She was then asked whether it was a good or bad thing that she went to La Charité; she responded that if it was bad, she would confess it. Asked about going to Paris, she said that her French companions were right in opposing their enemies.[83]

In Article 33, the promotor said that in claiming to know the future, Joan attributed to herself what belonged to God; she replied that God would reveal the future to whomever He chose, as He did to her.[84] According to Article 34, she was guilty of rashness in claiming to be able to recognize supernatural voices; she replied that she left that to God to judge.[85] Regarding her alleged boasting that she could tell whom God loved or hated (Article 35), she said she knew by revelation that God loved the king and the duke of Orleans more than her.[86] She referred to her earlier testimony when Estivet said that she claimed that she and others could hear a voice that should have been imperceptible to humans (Article 36).[87]

Estivet then claimed that, in admitting that she sometimes went against her voices, she showed that they were not from God, and when she admitted that she could not resist going against the command not to jump from the tower, she seemed to fall into the error of those who denied free will (Article 37); Joan again referred to earlier answers. To the follow-up question of whether she thought she sinned mortally in disobeying her commands, she left it up to God.[88]

Next, the promotor alleged, in spite of having committed many grave crimes and sins from her youth, Joan claimed that everything she had done was by God's will (Article 38), and she believed that she had never committed a mortal sin, even though Scripture says that the just man falls

[82] LR 229.
[83] FM 229–30.
[84] LR 230, FM 230.
[85] LR 233, FM 233.
[86] LR 235, FM 235.
[87] LR 236, FM 236.
[88] LR 237, FM 237.

seven times a day (Article 39); she referred to earlier answers.[89] In responding to the charge that she had many times received Communion dressed in male clothes, which was forbidden by the precept of God and Church (Article 40), she referred the latter assertion to God.[90] One could read this response to mean that she was not accepting the claim of the promotor and the judges that wearing male clothes was forbidden. In other words, let them prove that there was such a precept.

She again referred to earlier answers when Estivet said that it was by the Devil's instigation that she leaped from the tower, preferring to kill herself rather than end up in the hands of the English (Article 41).[91] She also had said enough about her supposed allegations that her saints had bodies (Article 42), spoke French (Article 43), and promised her heaven if she stayed a virgin (Article 44), and about her ability to distinguish among them (Article 45).[92] She similarly brushed off the charges that she had shown irreverence to God and the saints during the siege of Compiègne, and had blasphemed and denied them when recovering from her fall and after being imprisoned in Rouen (Articles 46–47).[93]

She readily admitted that she did not consult any bishop or parish priest about her belief in her saints (Article 48).[94] Her reverential treatment of such spirits, such as kissing the ground where they passed, smacked of idolatry and pacts with demons, Estivet claimed in Article 49. Joan referred herself to God on this point.[95] Estivet persisted in Article 50: she constantly invoked these spirits, asking them for advice, for instance in how to respond here in court. She replied that she had already spoken about this; she would continue to call her voices to her aid as long as she lived. When asked how she called on them, she replied that she called on God and Our Lady to give her counsel and comfort, and then they did. Asked to give an example, she did, and said a prayer to God to know how to answer these churchmen, and what to do about her male clothing. She added that her voices often told her news "about us, the bishop of Beauvais." Cauchon

[89] LR 238, 239, FM 238, 239.
[90] LR 241, FM 241.
[91] LR 242, FM 242.
[92] FM 243–45.
[93] FM 246.
[94] FM 247–48.
[95] LR 249, FM 249.

himself then asked her directly what they said about him, and Joan replied, "I will tell you privately."[96]

After some further questions about her voices, Estivet moved on to Article 51: what she said about St Michael's appearance to her must be judged presumptuous, rash, and fictitious, made up by the Devil's inspiration, or illusions produced by him. Joan referred to what she had said earlier. She denied having said what the promotor attributed to her, that a million angels would come at her bidding (and nothing of the sort appears in her earlier testimony later added after this article); she appealed to God concerning the promotor's judgments, which were contrary to the truth (*contre ses fais*, "against her deeds").[97]

Next, Estivet charged that Joan had so seduced the people that many worshipped her as a saint or an angel, which was scandalous and detrimental to religion (Article 52). Joan left the matter up to God.[98] She did the same when the promotor said that she put herself at the head of men in battle, contrary to God's precepts and out of presumption and pride (Article 53), and also when he said that she shamefully associated with men and avoided the company of women (Article 54). To the latter, she added that a woman was usually with her at night, and she took other precautions.[99] She similarly denied the charge that she abused her alleged revelations for worldly gain (Article 55).[100]

During the course of her long interrogation on March 3, Joan had been questioned about a certain Catherine of La Rochelle and her supposed revelations, which Joan's saints had dismissed as mere foolishness.[101] In Article 56, Estivet reveals that they were drawing on testimony that she said Catherine had given before the official of Paris (i.e., the judge of the bishop of Paris's consistory court). Among other things, she claimed that Joan would escape from prison by the Devil's help if she was not well guarded. Joan sarcastically responded that she certainly had not wished to have the Devil drag her out of prison.[102]

In Article 57, Estivet said that she made many predictions in her attacks on places which did not come true, but she denied making such

[96] LR 251–52, FM 251–52.
[97] LR 254–55, FM 255.
[98] LR 261, FM 261.
[99] LR 262–63, FM 262–63.
[100] LR 263–64, FM 264.
[101] LR 103–05, FM 103–05.
[102] LR 264–65, FM 264–65.

predictions "before you" (*coram vobis*: referring to her testimony before Cauchon or Cauchon and Lemaistre), even though "many reliable witnesses say that they were spoken and proclaimed by her" (*cum tamen multi fide digni referunt premissa esse dicta et publicata per ipsam*).[103] Perhaps the depositions of these witnesses were among those exhibited (or not!) before Cauchon's court on February 19. In this article there is another allegation that Joan spoke of a million angels. Joan responded that if she were further advised, she would willingly speak more about this. She explicitly denied the part of his article that claimed she had said that Jesus had failed her.[104]

Article 58 accused Joan of pride and vanity in exalting her banner and coat of arms, faults hardly punishable by law (and hardly connected with heresy), and Joan brushed them off. Article 59 accused her of similarly exalting herself by decorating her armor, and also of practicing sortilege by telling the future of children by candlewax, which she explicitly denied.[105]

Article 60 contained the perverse charge that Joan several times refused to swear to tell the truth in court, thus making herself suspect concerning the faith. In other words, because she refused to incriminate herself in illegal interrogations, she thereby made it likely that she was hiding something that she would be punished for if she revealed it! But, of course, as explained above, Joan had other reasons for not agreeing to answer all their questions, and she responded to this article by explaining some of them.[106]

Article 61 accused her of the error of misunderstanding the article of the mass creed, *Unam sanctam* ("I believe in one holy catholic and apostolic Church") in refusing to submit to the Church Militant, after it was explained to her. This is an example of a custom-made crime that resulted from pre-trial interrogations. Joan had obviously never heard of the Church Militant before; she had certainly never made a faulty statement about it that could be charged against her. As we saw above, she said that she would respond about this later, but Estivet took this as a refusal to submit to the Church, and he charged it against her. She replied to his article that she wished to defer to the Church Militant as much as she could, while referring herself to God. When pressed to say whether she

[103] LR 267.
[104] FM 267.
[105] LR 268, 271, FM 268–69, 271.
[106] LR 272, FM 272–73.

referred her actions to the Church Militant, she said that she would have an answer on the coming Saturday (i.e., three days hence).[107]

At this point, Estivet or Courcelles added not only her testimony from March 15 and March 17,[108] but also testimony from that coming Saturday, March 31,[109] and also testimony from three weeks beyond that, on April 18[110]—when, as we will see, Joan was deathly ill, and Estivet called her a whore.

In Article 62, Estivet said that Joan attempted to scandalize the people, setting herself above the Church, like the pseudo-prophets of old, and Joan said that she would also answer that on Saturday.[111] Article 63 was an unfavorable summary in the present tense of Joan's responses in court: she does not fear to tell lies, in violation of her oath, contradicting herself, and says many bad things about lords and a whole nation, and says many things not befitting a woman. In response, Joan simply held by what she said and referred herself to God.[112] She did the same for the following accusation, that she boasted that she knew she was forgiven for her sin of desperation of jumping from the tower, contradicting Scripture, which says that no one can be sure about such things (Article 64).[113] Next, she many times demanded revelations, for instance, about whether to tell the truth in court on certain points, which amounted to tempting God (Article 65). In her response, Joan gave these empty accusations more time than they deserved, saying in effect that she often prayed for needed enlightenment.[114]

In Article 66, Estivet summed up all of the foregoing: some of her offenses are violations of divine and human law; "some are sortileges, some divinations, some superstitions; and some savor of heresy formally or causatively or otherwise; many induce errors in faith and the favoring of heresy"; others are seditious, breaking the peace and inciting bloodshed; some are blasphemous and offensive to pious ears. Joan replied that she

[107] LR 278, FM 278–79.
[108] LR 279–80.
[109] LR 280–81.
[110] LR 281.
[111] LR 281, FM 281.
[112] LR 282, FM 282.
[113] LR 282–83, FM 283.
[114] LR 283, FM 283.

was a good Christian, and concerning all of the charges in the article she confided herself to the Lord.[115]

Article 67 said that she did all of the above repeatedly in various places, which Joan simply denied. Article 68 rehearsed to the judges that, when they heard of such things by *publica fama*, they found her vehemently suspect, and decreed that an inquisition was to be conducted against her by them, or one of them, and she was to be cited to respond concerning the above, which was done. Joan said that this article concerned the judges.[116]

Article 69 stated that Joan was indeed badly "infamed" about all of the above, and did nothing to correct herself but continued in her errors, in spite of many charitable efforts on the part of notable clerics and honorable persons. Joan replied that she had not committed the offenses alleged by the promotor, and had done nothing against the Christian faith. If she had been properly advised by counsel, she could have denied that there was any such *fama* about her on these matters, and insisted that they prove the existence of her criminal reputation before they proceed further, as provided for and actually demanded by law.

She was then asked, in case she had done anything against the Christian faith, if she would be willing to submit to the Church and to those to whom such correction pertained. She said that she would respond on Saturday after dinner.[117]

The final article, no. 70, stated that all of the above was true and publicly known, and the defendant had confessed it to be true before upright men. She denied the article, except concerning what she had admitted.[118]

Once again let me point out that Joan had the legal right to insist on a formal investigation to prove that there was general public consensus among respectable Christians that she was guilty of all these things. Judge Lohier even insisted that such an investigation was required by law.

Estivet concluded his libellus by protective boilerplate, once again using the vocabulary of civil litigation in calling himself the plaintiff (*actor*) and Joan the defendant (*rea*). He implored the judges to question the

[115] LR 283–84, FM 284. The central portion of the article reads: "quedam [predictorum] sortilega, quedam divinaciones, quedam supersticiones; et quedam formaliter, quedam causative et alias heresim sapiunt; errores in fide quamplura inducunt et fautoriam heretice pravitatis."

[116] LR 284, FM 284.

[117] LR 285, FM 285.

[118] LR 285, FM 285.

defendant on the above matters, duly enlarged and corrected, in the hope that it would be sufficient for them to produce a sentence.[119] We note that he did not repeat the phrases of his introduction about her being a schismatic and apostate; and whereas he had at first called her a heretic, and then modified it, "at least vehemently suspect of heresy," here he left her only on the verge of heresy.

5.7 Delayed Responses on the Church, March 31

Courcelles gives no account of what happened after Estivet finished presenting his libellus and obtaining Joan's responses on Tuesday and Wednesday, March 27 and 28, but simply moves to Saturday, March 31, telling of the visit of the two judges along with the Paris Six and the English theologian William Hatton, in the presence of the English guard John Grey and another, to question her on points for which she requested a delay. They were mainly concerned to make her commit herself further on the question of obedience to the Church, which she told Estivet and the judges that she would speak about on that day. They asked her if she was willing to submit ("refer herself") to the Church on earth, especially concerning crimes and everything that concerned her *processus*. (This, of course, must have sounded very much like submission to them as her judges.) She said that she willingly submitted to the Church Militant, as long as it did not require the impossible of her, such as disobeying God's commands. They asked, What if the Church Militant told her that her revelations were diabolical illusions? She said that she knew well that everything she had told them was commanded by God, and if the Church commanded the opposite, she would submit to no human but only to God. Did she believe that she was subject to the Church of God on earth, that is, the pope, cardinals, archbishops, bishops, and other prelates? Yes, as long as God was served. Did her voices tell her not to submit to the Church Militant on earth and its judgment? No, they said nothing other than to obey the Church, as long as God was served.[120]

Out of all of Joan's answers to Estivet's charges, it was these responses of Joan on the question of the Church Militant that were chiefly utilized by the judges later on, along with what she said on the charges of wearing male clothing.

[119] LR 286.
[120] LR 286–88, FM 286–88.

At the end of this prison session, the judges out of the blue asked Joan if she had had any metal files when she was being held in various places. She replied, "If any were found on me I have nothing more to say to you about it." The judges conclude (in the narration that Courcelles gives them): "When this was done, we left the place, to proceed further to what remained in the present cause of the faith."[121]

5.8 Upshot: What Now?

Cauchon had opened a cause of the faith, and invited in the vice-inquisitor of the faith, without having *publica fama* of offenses against the faith committed by Joan. He appointed a promotor immediately to formulate a libellus of charges against her, but instead of implementing it and starting a trial, he spent over a month forcing her to testify against herself. There were attempts to implicate her in a number of sinful or criminal activities, but nothing heretical or damaging to the faith. After this procedure was deemed invalid by Rota Judge Lohier, Cauchon emended this defect by having Estivet present his charges and requiring Joan to respond to them.

Estivet started out by claiming that she had propagated certain clearly heretical statements, but did not produce any examples in the course of elaborating her specific actions. The closest might be a supposed statement that was not preached by her in the open but elicited during her interrogations, that she would not submit to the Church Militant, which was somehow construed (it was not explained how) as a denial of the One True Church, and therefore as schismatic and/or heretical; but it did not seem very convincing in light of her insistence that she be taken to the pope.

At the end, Estivet summed up by resorting to the sort of broad statement that we saw used for Wyclif and Hus at the Council of Constance: some of their propositions were actually heretical, whereas others were simply scandalous or merely erroneous, without saying which. The same ploy would be used on Luther a hundred years later in the papal bull *Exsurge Domine*, over the objections of Cardinal Cajetan, who believed that Luther and the world deserved to know just exactly what was heretical about his positions.[122] But, as just noted, whereas Estivet originally said

[121] LR 288–89.

[122] See Henry Ansgar Kelly, "Luther at Augsburg, 1518: New Light on Papal Strategies," *Journal of Ecclesiastical History* 70 (2019) 804–22, pp. 817–18.

that some of Joan's propositions were actually heretical, at the end he said that they only "savored of heresy," which, if proved, could bring a conviction not of heresy itself, but only of "favoring heresy," or, technically, "vehement suspicion of heresy." This was what the Holy Inquisition wished to accuse her of to begin with.

Joan's responses can be easily summed up: she admitted no wrongdoing.

The next step that should have been taken in the trial was outlined by Estivet himself in his opening statement: he would set about proving what was necessary, which was everything. The way to do this would be, first of all, for each denied charge, to present a statement made by her during her interrogation, if he could find one that supported the charge; or by taking the depositions of witnesses who confirmed that she committed the crime in question or had spoken words that verified the charge. Then Joan should have been given the opportunity (with the help of competent and disinterested jurists) to offer rebuttals to Estivet's proofs. Then a summary of the trial should have been made and sent to assessors and consultants for comment.

In a legitimate trial, like Ségueut's, there would not have been the pretrial interrogations to draw upon, but there may have been admissions, *confessata*, as there were with Ségueut. The denied crimes were proved by testimony, *probata*, of witnesses, and the summary was taken from the *confessata* and *probata* together.

What Cauchon could have done, since he clearly did not want to use witnesses, was to have Estivet select for proving only those articles that he felt were provable by Joan's previous testimony and dismiss the others. What he did instead was to dismiss the whole libellus. In effect, he passed an interlocutory sentence throwing out the original indictment, and prepared a superseding indictment (the "Twelve Articles") based on the pretrial interrogation—an indictment that would be given to the "jury" without the defendant being charged with it.

In other words, he would proceed as if this *litis contestatio* had not occurred. But the exchanges between Estivet and Joan were on the record and could be drawn upon at will. Meanwhile, Estivet was no longer needed.

However, the greater body of assessors knew nothing of this, and the truth would not dawn on them until the next general meeting over a month later, on May 2.

CHAPTER 6

Back to the Interrogation Responses: The Twelve Articles

6.1 Joan's Initial "Confessions"

Doubtless Cauchon originally thought that the assignment of convicting Joan of Arc of heresy would be relatively easy. He saw the letter just days after her capture from the Holy Inquisition that she was vehemently suspect of heresy and they were ready to try her. Of course, he would have to reverse his Constance strategy of resisting heresy diagnoses at all costs and adopt his adversary Cardinal d'Ailly's policy of finding heresy under every rock. But he could call on his old colleague Master Jacques Tessier de Touraine and some of his other theology friends at the University to help him. He took on his trusted prosecutor Estivet from Beauvais to get up a strong case against her. However, when Touraine and Courcelles and the others arrived from Paris and looked over Estivet's draft-libellus, it seemed too exaggerated and unprovable, and they decided to try instead the old method of pre-trial interrogation and self-incrimination.

The trouble was, as time went on, Joan could not be made to admit anything serious, certainly nothing close to what their house-theologian Jean Petit wrote up in defending good Duke John, and some of the assessors seemed to be getting restless. The secret interrogations in prison were hardly more fruitful. Meanwhile, Lohier, under prodding from Cauchon (a mistake), gave voice to what others, like Basset, were undoubtedly thinking, that they were "picking" on Joan. They should at least get Estivet's libellus out of the way. But then what? Most of what he covered

H. A. Kelly, *The Trial and Retrial of Joan of Arc*, The New Middle Ages, https://doi.org/10.1007/978-3-032-07887-2_6

was useless, unprovable, except for what she said earlier, as Joan herself kept saying in her answers. They needed to start over.

After Joan was formally charged by Estivet on March 27 and 28, 1431, and the supplementary examinations were concluded on March 31, Cauchon and Lemaistre must have taken a break on the following day, April 1, which was Easter Sunday.

But on Easter Monday they were back at work. Courcelles in the Latin Record has them say that they and some other doctors and masters during this and the next two days compiled Twelve Articles summarizing Joan's testimony about herself. In the retrial in 1456 Courcelles distanced himself from the business, saying that the articles "seemed to have been compiled by Nicolas Midi."[1] This work was begun, we recall, over a week earlier, on March 22.[2]

6.1.1 The Twelve Articles

The assertions in the Twelve Articles are made in hypothetical form, attributed to "a certain woman" (*quedam femina*). Article 1 is the longest, and most of the other articles expand on its points. It tells what the woman had to say about seeing saints from the time she was thirteen, connected to "the fairy tree." She claimed that Saints Catherine and Margaret appeared to her and instructed her to assist a certain secular prince, and also to wear male clothes, and she was willing to refrain from going to mass rather than not wear them. She refused to submit to the Church Militant, in spite of many requests to do so. She affirms that she is sure that she will be saved.[3]

Article 2 recounts claims that she had made about the sign that convinced the prince about St Michael's coming to him, and of his being given a crown. Article 3: she could identify Saints Michael and Catherine and Margaret. Article 4: she claims to foretell the future. Article 5: she claims that God commanded her to wear male clothes; she often received Communion in them; she would not have given them up unless God commanded. Article 6: she admitted writing many letters under the sign of the

[1] NT 1:357.
[2] LR 180.
[3] LR 290–91.

cross—which was sometimes a code command to do the opposite of what was written. She threatened death to people who disobeyed her.[4]

Article 7 sums up her narrative about leaving her home and making her way to the foresaid prince, saying it was by God's command. According to Article 8, she admitted leaping from the tower against her saints' command; and though it was a sin to disobey them, she was forgiven. Article 9 says that she claimed her saints guaranteed her heaven if she remained a virgin; she believed that she had not committed any mortal sins, for otherwise her saints would not visit her. Article 10: her revelations said that God loved some persons more than her; and that He favored the French above the English and Burgundians.[5]

Article 11 states that the voices and spirits whom the woman called Michael and Catherine and Margaret were treated by her with reverence; that she embraced them, kissed their footsteps, and so on; and that she asked their help and obeyed them. She consulted no one about them, neither her parents nor any priest, and believed in them as much as in Christ's redemption. Finally, Article 12 says that if the Church ordered her to do something contrary to God's command, she would not obey. She would not submit to any human, even though the judges explained to her that the article *Unam sanctam Ecclesiam catholicam* meant that everyone had to submit to the Church Militant.[6]

The Articles were not authenticated by the notaries for their accuracy. A detailed analysis of the omissions, distortions, and falsities contained in them would be produced in 1449 by Guillaume Bouillé in the treatise that seems to have sparked the investigations that would result in the repudiation of her conviction.[7]

Still, even though the Articles make Joan confess to wrongdoing that she did not admit to during the interrogations, the offenses are still comparatively mild, compared to the line-up presented by Estivet. Nor do they come close to accusing her of heresy.

Even though Cauchon was violating canon law by forcing Joan to testify against herself during those weeks of February and March, since she did respond, her answers became fair game; and, because the Twelve

[4] LR 291–94.
[5] LR 294–95.
[6] LR 295–96.
[7] Bouillé's *Codicil* will be dealt with in Chapter 11.

Articles claimed to be based upon them, Cauchon could have made himself legal again by bringing them against her as charges. She could then respond and make any corrections or qualifications that she wished, and demonstrate where they had twisted her meaning. Instead, he sent them out to be commented upon as if the matter had already been adjudicated, a *res judicata*.

6.1.2 *Consult Letter and Model Report, April 5–12*

On Thursday, April 5, Cauchon and Lemaistre announced the form letter they were sending to doctors and experts whom they knew to be in Rouen to give their opinion by the following Tuesday on the enclosed assertions, especially whether any of them were against orthodox faith or Scripture or the Church or Church Fathers, or scandalous or rash, or involved in crimes and contrary to good morals. Especially important was the final clause: "…or what should be said about them in a trial of the faith" (*aut quid de predictis judicio fidei venit dicendum*).[8]

What they did first of all was to collect a group of two dozen or so theologians, which included Midi and his University colleagues, and ask them to formulate a joint comment; in other words, the authors were to gloss their own text. This statement then would be included in the requests that would be sent out to individual theologians and jurists.

Courcelles's record has the judges announce the deliberations concerning the Twelve Articles which they received on various days, and the joint letter is the first, notarized by the court notaries. The heading says that it is a statement of sixteen doctors of theology, including Midi, Beaupère, Touraine, Maurice, and Feuillet, and six licenciates or bachelors, including Isambart de Lapierre, no doubt there reluctantly with his superior Lemaistre, and Courcelles, who was not quite a doctor of theology. There was one master of arts, namely, Nicolas Loiseleur, who was not quite a bachelor of theology, but he was a long-time canon of Rouen.

First, they judged Joan's alleged revelations to be inventions of her imagination or else demonically inspired.[9] Then they threw the book at her, with charges ranging from the trivial to the grave:

[8] LR 289–90.
[9] LR 296–98.

> The said articles consist of and contain concocted lies; incredible ideas that she readily believed; also, superstitious divinations, scandalous and irreligious deeds, and rash and presumptuous utterances, full of boasting; blasphemy against God and female saints; impiety towards her parents; matters out of keeping with the command of love of neighbor; idolatry, or at least lying fictions; schismatic matters concerning the unity, authority, and power of the Church; ill-sounding matters; and matters vehemently suspect of heresy.[10]

They go on to give three justifications for a further lesser charge of "erroneous in faith," namely, (1) believing in her apparitions as firmly as she believed in Christian faith; (2) not receiving Communion at the set time (i.e., at Eastertime); and (3) saying that all she did was at the command of God.[11]

6.1.3 *Expectations of the Consultants*

Cauchon and Lemaistre then sent their request (or rather demand) for responses to other assessors or consultants, along with this model reply of the theologians.

It is important to put ourselves back into the minds of the recipients of these letters of solicitation, those that were not in Cauchon's inner circle. They would clearly recognize that the woman being spoken of was the notorious Joan of Arc, who had been interrogated by Bishop Cauchon in court during the first two weeks of Lent earlier that year, and then during Holy Week for two days had had heavy charges laid against her by the promotor with promises to prove them.

Whether or not the individual consultants attended any or all of the six interrogation sessions or the two days of delivering the charges, everyone would be likely to realize that the handful of offenses listed in the Twelve Articles were derived solely from the responses Joan gave to the interrogations, whether accurately or not, and did not cover most of the crimes

[10] LR 298–99: "In predictisque articulis esse et contineri mendacia conficta; aliqua non verisimilia, leviter credita ab ea; supersticiosas quoque divinaciones; scandalosa et irreligiosa facta; aliqua dicta temeraria, presumptuosa, plena jactantiis; blasphemiam in Deum et sanctas; impietatem erga parentes; aliqua non consona precepto de dileccione proximi; ydolatriam, aut ad minus conficcionem mendosam; scismatica de unitate, auctoritate, et potestate Ecclesie; male sapiencia ac de heresi vehementer suspecta."

[11] LR 299.

alleged by the promotor, which were denied by Joan but which he promised to prove. There is no reason for anyone to think that these charges had been dropped. Rather, the presumption must have been that when the trial reconvened, the promotor would have marshalled his witnesses to swear in and begin deposing.

6.2 The Local Consultations

6.2.1 Theological Condemnatory Agreements

One theological recipient of the request was de Duremort, abbot of Fécamp, a devoté of the proceedings from the beginning. He said he received the request from Cauchon on April 20, along with the joint opinion of the theologians, and responded on the next day that he could add nothing to what those learned masters had said.[12] Another theologian was Jean de Bouesque, the abbot's almoner, who had not attended any of the sessions. He cited much of the theologians' report and judged the woman to be an idolatress, and schismatic, and fallen into heresy, because of her obduracy and what she said about Saints Michael, Catherine, and Margaret, the Eucharist, and so on, and her assertions that she did everything by God's command.[13] The archdeacon of Evroux, Jean de Chastillon, was another theologian who expressed his agreement with the theologians, and even copied out their whole declaration, up to their specific "errors of faith."[14]

6.2.2 Other Theological Views

At the end of his main grouping of responses to the Twelve Articles, Courcelles placed two letters from other theologians. The first was a joint response of three divines, Pierre Minier, Jean Pigache, and Richard de Grouchet (Grouchet would testify in 1452 that he had attended the sessions out of fear and intimidation).[15] They apparently had written an unacceptable response earlier and were required to elaborate. They said now that everything depended on the origin of the alleged revelations. If they

[12] LR 302–03.
[13] LR 309–10.
[14] LR 309.
[15] Tisset, 2:403.

were demonic or just made up, there were bad things about them. But if they came from God or a good spirit, they could not be condemned.[16] The other letter was from an otherwise unknown bachelor of theology named Raoul Sauvage (Silvestris in Latin) giving a lengthy supplementary response to each of the articles. Many seemed bad, of course. But the knowledge about the future mentioned in the fourth article could be from God. And the wearing of men's clothes, in the fifth article, would be indecent, unless done to protect her virginity. He ended by saying that, for the judges' peace of conscience, it would be best to submit the assertions, with proper commentary, to the Holy See.[17]

6.2.3 *Juristic Condemnatory Agreements*

Ten jurists who were canons of Rouen replied separately that they agreed with the theologians. One was Jean Maugier, who held the position of cantor in the chapter.[18] Another was Jean Bruillot, who said that he conferred with many other jurists and fully agreed with them (without saying what they said).[19] The same was true of Jean Guarin.[20] A fourth jurist-canon in agreement was the familiar Archdeacon Nicolas de Venderès.[21] Two more were Nicolas Caval and Robert Lebarbier; the latter suggested sending her assertions to "their mother" the University of Paris, especially the Faculties of Theology and Canon Law.[22] Still another jurist-canon, Jean Alespée, asked for a delay, and was given until April 16. He then also agreed with the theologians and would willingly submit to the judgments of the University, the Holy Roman Church, and the general council.[23] Word would by now have circulated that Pope Martin V on February 1 had issued a call for a general council to assemble in Basel in Switzerland in March; but it was not until April that only a handful of delegates arrived, including those from the University of Paris.[24]

[16] LR 323–24.

[17] LR 324–27. For Raoul Sauvage, see Tisset, *Procès*, 2:412, "Le Sauvage." He is wrongly identified with Jean Savage, licentiate in theology, LR 297.

[18] LR 303–04.

[19] LR 304–05.

[20] LR 310–11.

[21] LR 305.

[22] LR 307–08.

[23] LR 308–09.

[24] A. Baudrillart, "Bâle (Concile de)," *DTC* 2:113–29, col. 115.

Another juristic canon of Rouen, Denis Gastinel, licensed in both laws, who had attended the first five public sessions of Joan's interrogations and the presenting of charges, gave an independent assessment of the articles. Condemnatory without referring to the theologians and without referring to Joan specifically, he judged that the material rendered any such perpetrator (*actor*) vehemently suspect in faith—erroneous, schismatic, and heretical—and, unless the erroneous doctrine and heretical stain were abjured, he—and he puts it in the masculine gender—should be turned over to secular judgment (i.e., death by fire), or, if abjuring, be put in prison to bewail his offenses and not commit them again.[25]

Gastinel was the only expert out of all the consultants, apart from Bouesque, who found heresy to be involved. Courcelles placed his assessment immediately after the model reply of the theologians. He put Official Basset's reply next.

6.2.4 *Hesitations of Official Basset*

We have recorded Basset's attendance at four of the six public interrogations and the two days of charging, and, just before the proceedings against Joan began, he presided over the trial of Jean Ségueut, jointly with the Inquisitor of France, Jean Graverent.

Basset stated that he could say little or nothing about such difficult matters of the faith, especially concerning such a woman's revelations. It is possible that they were genuine, but there was no reason to believe them in the absence of supporting miracles or testimony of Scripture, here quoting a passage from Innocent III's decretal *Cum ex injuncto*, sent to the diocese of Metz in 1199 (the passage was removed when the decretal was incorporated into the *Liber Extra*, i.e., it did not become law).[26]

[25] LR 300–01: "...in carcerem ad agendam penitentiam includatur, pane doloris et aqua angustie sustentandus, ut commissa defleat et flenda ulterius non committat," quoting Innocent III's decretal *Novimus*, X 5.40. 27 (CIC 2:924), on commuting a sentence of death (for forgery) to life imprisonment: "Pro illo vero falsario scelerato..., hoc tibi duximus consulendum, ut in perpetuum carcerem ad agendum penitentiam ipsum includas, pane doloris et aqua angustie sustentandum, ut commissa defleat, et flenda ulterius non committat." But notice that Gastinel does not specify life in prison but only prison.

[26] Innocent III, *Cum ex injuncto* (1199). See X 5.7.12, CIC 2:786, where Friedberg gives this *pars decisa* [removed passage] in italics: it reads: "Non est ergo credendum ei qui dicit se missum a Deo, cum non sit missus ab homine, nisi de se speciale proferat testimonium de Scripturis, vel evidens miraculum operetur" (One is not to believe him who claims to be sent from God rather than man, unless he can offer the special witness of Scripture concerning

Wearing male clothes would be unbecoming to a woman, if not divinely approved. Refusal to receive Communion once a year would, of course, go against Church law; and refusal to submit to the judgment of the Church Militant seemed to go against the article *Unam sanctam*. However, theologians should judge such matters. As for deliberating on the manner and form of the proceedings for this woman, if it were shown and explained to him (i.e., Basset himself) in terms of Pope Boniface VIII's decretal *Statuta* in his *Liber Sextus*, he would work as hard as he could to fulfill its provisions.[27]

We saw above that Basset and Graverent were acting on the main provision of *Statuta* in the Ségueut trial when they suppressed the names of the witnesses against Ségueut because of perceived danger. But if there was no such danger, the witnesses were to be publicly identified, as in other trials. The pope burdened the consciences of both bishops and heresy inquisitors not to declare danger to be present when there was none.[28]

In Courcelles's Latin Record, Cauchon claimed, perhaps falsely, to have read depositions of witnesses in court on February 19, before Joan's first appearance in court.

Presumably, Basset was saying that, since the charges had been made and denied by Joan, it was time to prove whatever accusations they could by swearing in witnesses in Joan's presence, recording their depositions, and then reading them in court for Joan to hear and respond to.

As we saw, the trial remained in a state of suspension. These anonymous articles that Basset and others were asked to opine about were not specifically tied to Joan's case. Insofar as she had been charged with committing them by the promotor, she had denied them, and she had not been proved to have committed them.

himself, or work a clear miracle). (The pope gives the example of John the Baptist as someone authorized by Scripture, when he said that Isaiah was speaking of him as "a voice in the wilderness.") This *pars decisa* was also cited by the Bishop of Lisieux in his response (LR 320; see below). Neither he nor Basset meant to invoke it as law, but merely as a statement concerning the difficulty of judging visions. Being predicted by the Bible many centuries after the Bible would be a very difficult criterion to fulfill.

[27] LR 301–02. The last phrase, "to fulfill its provisions," is my translation of *pro modulo sensus* (literally, "for the form of [its] sense").

[28] Boniface VIII, *Statuta*, *Liber Sextus* 5.2.20 (CIC 2:1078). Tisset, 3:124, mistakenly says that the decretal concerns the sending of a trial record to assessors for comment.

6.2.5 *Other Juristic Qualifications*

Further on among the reports, Courcelles includes the joint response of two advocates in Basset's court, Aubert Morel (Inquisitor Graverent's pro-tem promotor in the Ségueut trial) and Jean Duchemin, who had attended the public interrogations—Morel all of them, Duchemin the last four. They also responded to the poll on March 27 and heard the presentation of charges on that day and the next. Their opinion was an elaboration of Basset's. But instead of citing Boniface VIII's *Statuta* on publicizing witnesses, they quoted Innocent III's decretal *Novimus*, which recommended commuting death penalties to life imprisonment or sentencing an offender to prison rather than to death (in that particular case, for forgery).[29] In other words, perhaps they were saying, if Joan were convicted of any offenses, she should not be treated as a heretic! Gastinel had quoted the same language about imprisonment, but said that prison (and not life in prison) was to be imposed on anyone who abjured heresy.[30] In Morel's case, we must keep in mind that he had just convicted Advocate Ségueut of undoubted heresy, and the penalty that Basset and Graverent were contemplating for him was obviously well out of the range of burning at the stake or life imprisonment.

Next to their opinion Courcelles places the joint statement of eleven more advocates of the official court of Rouen. Three of them (Livet, Poustel, and Le Tavernier) had taken no part in the proceedings, three had attended all six public interrogations and the presentation of charges (Du Crotay, Ledoulx, and Colombel), and others had attended interrogations (Carré, Dessaulx, and Cormeilles two each, DuBusc four, and Anguy all six). They too followed the pattern of Basset, adding with regard to wearing men's clothes that she could be admonished to resume wearing women's clothes and excommunicated for refusing—unless, of course, she had a command from God (which was not to be presumed).[31]

The abbots of the monasteries of Jumièges and Cormeilles, Nicolas Leroux and Guillaume Bonnel, both doctors of canon law, writing on April 30, said that they originally replied that the whole matter should be submitted to the University of Paris, but, since the judges were not satisfied with that answer, they now responded, subject to the judgment of the general council, that the woman should be charitably admonished about

[29] LR 313–14. See Innocent III, *Novimus*, X 5.40.27 (CIC 2:924).

[30] See Tisset, 2:256 n. 1 and 269 n. 3.

[31] LR 314–16.

submitting to the Church, with the danger of refusal explained. Her claims to have revelations from God and a command from God to wear men's clothes cannot readily be believed. As for her not being in mortal sin, only God could know, since they could not judge secret matters, especially since they were not always present in examining the woman (giving away the pretense of anonymity).[32] They had both attended the public interrogations, but, of course, not the prison sessions.

A final jurist canon of Rouen, Raoul Roussel, who was also treasurer of the chapter, had attended most of the proceedings, but did not seem enthusiastic about the prosecution of Joan. We saw above that, even though he was listed as present on March 27, he did not respond to the poll conducted that day. Apparently the judges were not satisfied with his original response to the Twelve Articles, and he wrote again on April 30, saying that the assertions were false and mendacious, designed to further the goals of her and her allies. Beyond that, he agreed with the opinion submitted by the theologians.[33]

Cauchon and his close advisors must have been disappointed at the tepidity of the responses as they came in. Clearly, they should have made the original joint reply of the theologians more vigorous. Everything was too general, and nothing was said about the wearing of male clothes. It was all well and good to say that some of the actions in the Articles smacked of heresy and schism, but what were they? Obviously, more emphasis would have to be placed on Article 12, which spoke about the violation of *Unam Sanctam*.

[32] LR 321–22.
[33] LR 323.

CHAPTER 7

Three Confrontations: Pastoral, Pastoral, Coercive

7.1 Solicitous Appeal, Joan's Illness, April 18

Promotor Estivet's dramatic presentation of his libellus to the judges in the presence of Joan and the bank of assessors took place over two days, March 27 and 28, and, as far as the normal run of assessor went, they next expected to be called on to witness the presentation of witnesses who would be deposed to prove articles denied by Joan. Instead, around the middle of April, many of them began to receive demands to comment on a set of Twelve Articles, a thinly disguised summary of her answers to weeks of interrogation preceding the contestation of late March.

As for Joan, apart from the rump session of questions and responses conducted on March 31, she was kept to her cell, and nothing more was heard of her, as far as the court record was concerned, until replies to the questionnaire started to come in, and the judges supposedly decided that it was in her spiritual interest to visit her and tell her about the many bad things that were being said about her, stressing the pastoral role that Cauchon affected from the start, but now with even more emphasis on solicitude for the welfare of her soul and salvation. That, at least, is what Courcelles has them say in the Latin Record.

On April 18, therefore, Cauchon and Lemaistre visited Joan in her prison cell, accompanied by seven theologians, notably the three Paris theologians who in a week or so would go off to the University with the Twelve Articles, namely, Midi, Touraine, and Feuillet. The others were the

H. A. Kelly, *The Trial and Retrial of Joan of Arc*, The New Middle Ages, https://doi.org/10.1007/978-3-032-07887-2_7

Englishman Hatton, the regular attendants at the trial Guillaume Boucher and Maurice DuQuesay, and the Dominican Guillaume Adélie, who never appeared before or after this.

I follow the original Minute, which says that Cauchon first recounted to her that she had been examined for many days on difficult matters, and that learned clerics had found serious defects in her responses. And because she did not know what was against the faith, he wished her to choose one or more persons from among the assessors to advise her, or, if not, they would send some of their own choosing, both theologians and canonists. If she did not accept, she would be in great danger.[1]

Joan did not reply to these statements, but instead told them that she was ill and feared that she would die. She requested to go to confession and receive Communion, and to be buried in consecrated ground. She was told that if she wished to have the rites of the Church and the Eucharist, she would first have to submit to the Church, like a good Catholic (Courcelles inserts a comment from Cauchon that, of course, they were always ready to offer the sacrament of penance).[2]

She was then asked hypothetical questions about her revelations (e.g., What if God revealed something about her to someone else?). She was urged again to take and trust the counsel of the clerics and notable doctors there, and to submit herself to the Church. She merely referred to her earlier answers. Finally, the theologians accompanying the judges pressed her further to submit, and one of them, Midi (Courcelles suppresses his name), cited Matthew 18 on fraternal correction, about the offender who refused to listen to the Church. He applied it to her: if she would not submit to the Church and obey, she would be abandoned like a Saracen. She replied that she was a good baptized Christian and she would die like a good Christian.[3]

She was told that if she submitted to the Church Militant, she would be given Communion. She replied that she would add nothing for now about such submission. She loved and served God, she was a good Christian, and she aimed to serve and uphold the Holy Church with all her might.[4]

We learn from later testimony that one of the physicians who attended Joan in her illness was brought there by Estivet, who held one of the keys

[1] FM 327–29.
[2] FM 329–30; LR 330.
[3] FM 330–32; LR 332.
[4] FM 332–33.

to her cell.[5] When she said she became ill after eating a fish sent by Cauchon, Estivet called her a whore, and they traded insults.[6] The promotor obviously played a greater role in Joan's prosecution than the notarial records reveal.

In contrast, "Master Jacques" Touraine, Cauchon's Franciscan colleague from Constance, took a gentle approach to Joan. According to the same doctor, Touraine questioned her at times, and on one occasion he asked her if she had ever been in a place where Englishmen had been killed. She answered with some spirit: "In the name of God, yes, I have! How sweetly you speak! Why did they not go away from France, and go back to their own country?"[7]

7.2 Public Session, May 2: Trial Effectively Dismissed, Joan Exhorted

On May 2, a large assembly of clerics gathered in the *ad hoc* courtroom of Rouen Castle to hear Cauchon's summary of Joan's case thus far, and to witness further attempts to persuade Joan of the errors of her ways. Of the sixty-three clerics listed, nine were priests of Rouen with no qualifications, who made their first and last appearance on that day. Notably absent was Official Basset, who (at least in my interpretation) had agreed to participate if the procedure in heresy cases mandated in Pope Boniface's *Statuta* was being fulfilled, of publicly swearing in witnesses to prove charges denied by the defendant. It would have been too early to conclude anything on this point at this time. Besides, the two advocates of his court (Aubert Morel and Jean Duchemin) whose response was otherwise similar in its moderation to Basset's, were there, as were the other eleven advocates of his court who had given a joint opinion.[8] On the other hand, it may be that Cauchon did not want him there, and took steps to prevent

[5] NT 1:201 (others with keys were Cardinal Beaufort and Vice-Inquisitor Lemaistre).

[6] NT 1:349, testimony of Jean Tiphaine, Master of Arts and Medicine. Another physician there, Guillaume Lachambre, confirmed this, and said that when the Earl of Warwick was told of it, he prevented him from mistreating her further (NT 1:351). See also Boisguillaume's testimony, NT 1:437–38, who says that Estivet originally gained access to Joan in prison by pretending to be a prisoner himself, like Loiseleur.

[7] NT 1:448–49: Joan's response is partially recorded in French: "En nom Dieu, si, ay! Comme vous parlez doulcement! Quare non recedebant ipsi a Francia, et ibant ad suam patriam?"

[8] LR 333–34.

him from attending. That was Quicherat's assumption, when he found that Basset and his promotor Leroy were put into prison at this time. But Beaurepaire showed that their stay in prison, which lasted from May 9 to June 9, was in connection with another matter: they were imprisoned and fined by officers of Henry VI for claiming three clerics who had been arrested for treason, as under Church jurisdiction.[9] Nevertheless, Cauchon could have had a hand in the matter.

There was in fact a reason why Cauchon may not have wanted Basset in particular present among the assessors that day, because, before Joan was brought in, in a speech given in Courcelles's Latin Record alone, Cauchon sums up the entire proceedings that had been undertaken in her regard in one stunning sentence, which can be diagrammed thus:

[sub]**After she was fully interrogated,**
and
[sub]**After she responded to articles judicially proposed to her by the promotor,**

[main]**We summarized her confessions**
and
[main]**We sent them to experts.**[10]

Notice that only the presentation of articles was stated to have been done judicially, not the interrogations or the summarizing, both of which were illegal. She was interrogated without knowing charges. Her so-called confessions were not taken from the responses to the judicial articles, but from the responses to the interrogations. They were not presented to her as articles or charges. She was not given a chance to deny or qualify either the confessions or the summary articles, and the articles were first sent to a rigged committee. Cauchon makes no mention of her denials of all criminal actions charged against her. Finally, he lets it be assumed that the entire libellus of the promotor will be ignored, and there will be no attempt to prove any of the charges leveled therein through the deposition of witnesses.

[9] Beaurepaire, *Recherches*, pp. 126–28; cf. Tisset, 3:190 n. 4.

[10] LR 334: Literally: "Postquam ista mulier ad plenum interrogata fuerat et ad articulos sibi judicialiter ex parte promotoris proposita responderat, confessiones ejus in certam formam assercionum compendiose redactas transmisimus doctoribus et peritis" (After this woman had been fully interrogated and had responded to the articles judicially proposed on the part of the promotor, we transmitted her confessions compendiously redacted in the form of assertions to doctors and experts.)

Basset would no doubt have been highly critical of the way the trial was conducted.

Cauchon went on to say that, judging from the opinion of most of the consultants, he was well aware that Joan seemed to be defective in many ways, though he had not yet finally determined the matter.[11] Therefore, he continued, it seemed good to many conscientious men that they should labor to instruct her in the matter in which she was defective, in order to lead her to the truth. They first tried on several different days to bring notable doctors to her to persuade her, different ones on each day, to no avail. Finally, they decided to bring her before the assembled clergy on this day, so that by the exhortations of many of them she might be brought to humility and truth. They had deputed one person among them to deliver an admonishment, namely, the archdeacon of Evreux, Jean de Chastillon, a doctor of theology (who, we remember, had sent in a response to the Twelve Articles repeating the general opinion of the theologians). But, Cauchon concluded, if anyone else wished to give her salutary advice, he should please speak up.[12]

We recall that Cauchon twice urged her in her prison cell to take advantage of the learned men she had seen in the courtroom. We might suppose, then, that since she declined to do so, he arranged this meeting to do her the favor of having some of these experts instruct her on the implications of the crimes that she had committed, and was still committing.

When Joan was brought in, Cauchon urged her to listen to the archdeacon's admonitions, and then told him to proceed. Chastillon first gave her a general admonishment about the duty of every Christian to hold and believe the articles of faith. Joan's response was to tell him to first read the "book" that he was holding, and then she would reply. She relied above all on God, whom she loved with all her heart.[13]

There follows in the Latin Record, not the text of Chastillon's book, but rather Courcelles's summary of it. The booklet consisted of six articles. In the first, the archdeacon reminded Joan that she had said that she was willing to correct anything perverse in her conduct that clerics would

[11] LR 334: "Jamdudum, ex plurimorum sentencia et oppinionibus, satis cognovimus quod ista mulier in multis defectuosa esse videbatur, quanquam res non sit adhuc apud nos ultimate determinata" (We have long since been sufficiently aware, from the judgment and opinions of most of them, that this woman seemed to be defective in many things, even though the matter is not yet finally determined by us.)

[12] LR 334–35.

[13] FM 335–37, LR 335–37.

show her, and now many doctors and clerics have found great defects in her words and deeds. In the second article, he pointed out to her that she was wrong in saying that she would not submit herself to the Church Militant in the matter of her revelations and appearances. God did not want anyone to be subject to Him alone, because He gave power to ecclesiastical men to know and judge the deeds of the faithful, and whoever spurned them spurned God (*quos qui spernit, Deum spernit*). The Catholic Church could not err, nor judge anyone unjustly, and whoever did not believe this erred against the article *Unam sanctam*, which (Courcelles says) the archdeacon explained at great length; and one who stubbornly remained in this disbelief was to be judged a heretic. Not to subject oneself to the judgment of Holy Mother Church was to be schismatic and was also to think badly (*male sentire*) about the holiness of the Church and the infallible guidance of the Holy Ghost.[14]

In the next two articles, Chastillon went on to explain the evil of Joan's wearing of male clothes. On this subject, he could not say that the consultants were condemnatory, since they either totally neglected the point or at most considered her behavior an offense against feminine modesty. Deuteronomy forbade it, he said; St Paul ordered women to cover their heads; sacred general councils of the Church prohibited it (this was not true, but it might have been believed at the time). Her offense was exacerbated by her refusal to change clothes to perform her Easter duty of Communion. In all this it was clear that she gravely sinned. In the fourth article, he said that in constantly maintaining that it was no sin for her to dress as she did, she went against the doctrine of the saints and the precepts of God and the apostles and contemned the precept of the Church; this was an error in faith, and to hold it persistently would constitute a fall into heresy. And by attributing these sins to God and the saints she committed blasphemy. He urged her to stop.[15]

In the fifth article he told her that many clerics found that she told manifest lies about her apparitions and attributed unbecoming things to saints. Such things could lead to sedition and to the involvement of demons, and she should cease speaking of such matters. In the sixth and last article, he stated that these so-called revelations led to other crimes: claiming knowledge of the future, or of God's favor, or of forgiveness of her sins. This was divinatory, presumptuous, and rash. In adoring her

[14] LR 337–38.
[15] LR 339–40.

apparitions she was in danger of idolatry. She even said that she believed in them more than her Christian faith. It went against the precept of Christ and the Church to give ready credence to such apparitions.[16]

After the archdeacon finished reading his book, or explaining it in French, Joan was questioned on all of the points, presumably by him (both the original and Courcelles's accounts have the questions phrased in the passive: "Asked about...she replied"). She was first pressed to accept the article *Unam sanctam*. She said that she believed in the Church on earth and that the Church Militant could not err. On being told that if she did not believe in the article she would be a heretic and other judges would condemn her to fire, Joan replied that even if she were to see the threatened flames, she could say no more on the subject. On being pressed on whether she would submit to the pope and cardinals in a general council, she said that they would not extract anything further from her. What about the pope—would she submit to him? "Take me to him," she replied, "and I will answer him."[17]

The questioning then turned to the subject of male clothing. Joan may have instinctively realized the flagrant falsity of the archdeacon's assertion that general councils had forbidden such clothing to women. She said that she would willingly change into female clothing temporarily in order to go to Communion. Chastillon warned her to cease wearing male clothing and cease believing it was right for her, without returning to his assertion that persisting in her belief would result in heresy.[18]

On the subject of her revelations, she was first asked whether she would be willing to call on the archbishop of Rheims or others, who, she claimed, witnessed the angelic delivery of a crown. She said that she would tell them about the whole proceedings against her, if they would send a messenger.[19]

If Joan had been allowed an adviser, he could have told her that she could appeal the trial to the archbishop of Rheims, who was Cauchon's superior judge. He could also have reminded the court that it was the obligation of the prosecution to swear in witnesses to testify on points of contention. Basset might have raised this point from the floor, if he had been present.

[16] LR 340–41.
[17] FM 342–43, LR 341–43.
[18] FM 343–44, LR 343–44.
[19] FM 344, LR 344.

Chastillon raised the question of sympathetic advisors when he asked her if she would be willing to entrust the matter of her revelations and the other things in her trial to men from her side brought there under safe-conduct. She said to bring them, and then she would answer. Finally, she was asked whether she would submit to the church of Poitiers, where she was first examined. She responded, "Do you think that you can trap me in this way and get me to betray myself to you?"[20]

After this blunt statement of her awareness that their purpose was not to reform her wicked ways, as they pretended, but to get damaging admissions from her to condemn her with, "she was generally admonished" that if she did not submit to the Church, "other judges" would burn her body, and her soul would burn forever. She replied, obviously addressing everyone involved, that if they did to her what they threatened, they themselves would suffer for it in body and soul. She refused to answer the archdeacon's last demand, that she give one reason for not relying on the Church.[21]

Then, both records state, many doctors and learned men of all kinds there present tried to persuade her to submit to the Church Militant, the pope, and the general council, and she responded as before. Finally, Cauchon warned her to advise herself concerning these charitable urgings. She asked him how much time she had (the original account has her speaking Latin with this question: "Infra quod tempus me advisabo?"), and he responded that she must do so immediately and say what she wished.[22] Courcelles concludes with the judges' narrative statement: "And since she responded nothing further, we departed from that place and the said Joan was taken to her place of prison."[23]

This public session should not be seen as a continuation of the trial begun when the prosecutor, Estivet, formally charged Joan with crimes, and she formally replied. Here she was not "judicially constituted before the judges," and not put under oath. Chastillon did not accuse her of any crimes, but rather asserted her guilt as a given, and exhorted her to repent. He did not focus on alleged crimes of the past, such as her supposed violation of the commandment to honor her father and mother, or excessive bloodthirstiness in battle, but rather offenses that she was still committing, specifically attachment to and defense of wearing male clothing, reliance

[20] FM 346, LR 346.
[21] FM 346–47, LR 346–47.
[22] FM 347–48, LR 347–48.
[23] LR 348.

on her apparitions, and refusal to submit to the Church Militant. The last-named offense was not one that she committed in the past, but rather one that was generated from the questioning that she had undergone in court.

Chastillon's approach to two of these offenses, the refusal to submit to the Church and the insistence on the allowability of male dress, should have been of particular interest to Cauchon. Regarding the former, the archdeacon showed how the offenses of schism and errors of faith claimed by the group of theologians in their report could be converted into heresy and its punishment of death at the stake. He did the same thing for the latter, which the theologians had ignored: that a stubborn conviction on her part that God approved of male clothing for women was a heresy. There is nothing to indicate that Cauchon took this line of thought to heart. As we will see, no explanation will be forthcoming as to why Cauchon thought Joan was deserving of death as a heretic.

7.3 Further Evaluations Arrive

But Joan's apparent resistance that day did bear clear fruit immediately, in the form of late consultations submitted the very next day. The first of them was from a high-ranking canon of Rouen, a jurist named Gilles Deschamps, the chancellor of the diocese. After seeing how she resisted submitting her acts and sayings to the judgment of the universal Church, the pope, a general council, or four men from her party, or the Church of Poitiers, he stated that, unless he saw some correction in her statements or reasonable explanation, they were suspect in faith and contrary to morality and Church law.[24]

The next declaration came from the canons of Rouen as a body, that is, the whole chapter—which, as we recall, was the ruling ecclesiastical entity at the time, since there was currently no archbishop. They had delayed their collective response on the Twelve Articles, wishing first to consult the University of Paris theologians and canonists. But, after consulting others in the city, and witnessing the efforts on May 2 to get her to submit to the pope and others, which she completely refused to do, they now responded, judging that she should be considered a heretic.[25]

Another evaluation arrived a short time later, dated May 5, from a person familiar to us, namely, Philibert de Montjeu, bishop of Coutances,

[24] LR 305–06.
[25] LR 311–12.

addressed to Cauchon. As we saw above, he was the judge to whom Inquisitor Graverent had moved as co-judge after leaving after Official Basset's case against Advocate Jean Ségueut, which had prevented him from joining Cauchon in prosecuting Joan.

After Bishop Montjeu summed up the Twelve Articles against a "certain woman," he stated his assumption that their contents were properly obtained and accurately recorded:

> These are the points, Reverend Father, that I was able to draw out from the said articles extracted from the original proceedings, which I assume were produced in keeping with the law, since it is not to be presumed that Your Reverend Paternity and the very learned and expert doctors and masters summoned by you in this affair, especially dealing with such matters, would deviate in any way from the way of truth.[26]

This was doubly ironic. Jean Lecouvreur, the defendant whom Montjeu was currently prosecuting, was very determined to point out to the pope that Montjeu himself had not followed the proper procedures in the case against him, and he had succeeded in sending his appeal to the Holy See after Montjeu and Graverent had in effect denied it. To Montjeu's point here, however, he was right to be cautious. Even though he was very pro-English himself, perhaps he feared to lower himself to Cauchon's level. In fact, not only had Cauchon not properly obtained the contents of the Articles, but he had not even charged them against the woman. She was condemned without being heard.

Montjeu judges the woman (Joan), on the basis of the Articles, to have a spirit prone to evil, acted on by the Devil and void of the grace of the Holy Spirit. If she does not revoke her assertions, she should be treated like others who remain obstinately against the faith. But he ends by saying that his opinion should always give way to a more informed judgment.[27]

Finally, another bishop, namely, the Italian Zanon da Castiglione, head of the diocese of Lisieux, sent in a reply on May 15. He cites by name Innocent III's decretal *Cum ex injuncto*, the section excised from the

[26] LR 318: "Hec sunt que taliter qualiter, reverende pater, elicere valui ex jam dictis articulis extractis ex processu originali, juridice, ut existimo, facto, cum reverendam vestram paternitatem tamque doctos et expertos dominos et magistros, per eandem in hac materia accitos, a tramite veritatis, presertim in hac materia, deviasse usquequaque non sit presumendum."

[27] LR 316–19.

Liber Extra, on the difficulty of discerning spirits.[28] Given the circumstances of the woman in question—her low-class condition and fatuous and presumptuous assertions, and the ways in which she describes her visions and revelations—these latter would seem to be either demonically inspired or simply imaginary. If she refuses to submit to the pope of the Universal Church gathered in a general council or to other prelates having jurisdiction, she should be considered a schismatic and vehemently suspect in faith.[29]

We will see what the University of Paris had to say on the Twelve Articles when its opinion was read before the assessors on May 19.

7.4 Torture Chamber, May 9; Vote on Torture, May 12

A week after the judges' supposedly solicitous attempt to come to Joan's aid by encouraging her to revoke or modulate damaging statements that she had made, the judges threatened her with torture if she did not tell the truth on certain points.

Courcelles provides the judges with no explanation for this drastic reversal of approach. He simply has them narrate that Joan was brought before them in a great tower of the castle of Rouen, with nine assessors, namely, Archdeacon Chastillon, her earnest previous questioner, two other archdeacons (André Marguerie and Nicolas de Venderès), the theologian Guillaume Erard, and the English theologian William Hatton, who was a frequent participant from the beginning,[30] as well as an obscure abbot of Compiègne, not seen before or after, the urban dean Jean Massieu, the Rouen advocate in Official Basset's court, Aubert Morel, who was promotor for Inquisitor Graverent in the Ségueut trial, and, finally, Nicolas Loiseleur, her false friend and confessor—the first time that he had shown up in her sight since he was among the assessors in the last public interrogation on March 3.[31]

According to the Latin Record, Joan was admonished—but not put under oath—to tell the truth about many different points in her responses which she had denied and answered mendaciously, of which they had

[28] See n. 26 in the last chapter.

[29] LR 319–21.

[30] See Tisset, 2:404

[31] FM 348, LR 348.

knowledge because of "certain informations, proofs, and strong presumptions" (*certe informaciones, probaciones, et vehementes presumpciones*).[32] If they actually had such proofs, of course, they should have sworn in witnesses in Joan's presence in open court, and had their depositions read to her for her rebuttal, as Official Basset had indicated was proper procedure.

Instead, they simply read the sections of her responses that they claimed were lies (neither the Minute nor Courcelles's Record indicates precisely what sections these were), and told her that, if she did not tell the truth about them, she would be placed in torments, and they showed her the instruments of torture right there in that very room, and also the torturers who would inflict them upon her "at our command" (*jussu nostro*), "…to lead her back to the path and acknowledgment of truth, so that thereby they could procure for her the health of her body and soul, which she had put in grave peril through her lying fictions."[33] Courcelles here shows Cauchon keeping up his own fiction that he only had Joan's best interests in mind.

As in the previous session, Joan replied that even if she were shown the fire she was condemned to, she could answer no further than she had done before, and that, even if they had to tear her limbs and release her soul, she would say nothing more. And if she did say anything more, she would say that they made her say it by force (the Minute has only this response, with none of the references to torture or the judges' remarks).[34]

She volunteered that she had a visitation from St Gabriel on the feast of the Holy Cross (which was May 3, the day after her last time with them). She also said that she asked her voices whether she should submit to the Church, since churchmen urged it so strongly. The voices told her to rely on God. She stated further that she knew that God controlled all of her actions and that the Devil had no part in them. She asked her voices if she would be burned, and they again replied that she should rely on God and He would help her.[35]

They asked her once more whether she would count on the archbishop of Rheims in the matter of the crown, and she said to bring him there and

[32] LR 348.
[33] LR 348–49.
[34] FM 349, LR 349.
[35] FM 349–50, LR 349–50.

they would see what her answer would be. She added that he would in no way contradict her.[36]

Courcelles closed this session by having the judges narrate that, because of her stubbornness, they feared that torture could profit her little (*sibi parum proficere*); they decided to postpone any such action until they had further advice.[37]

Three days later, on May 12, in Cauchon's residence, the two judges met with a slightly larger group of assessors, twelve and then thirteen, to consult with them on whether to apply torture to Joan. The holdovers from the previous sessions were Archdeacons Venderès and Marguerie, Erard, Morel, Loiseleur, and, joining late, Hatton. The others now present were the Rouen treasurer Raoul Roussel, the lawyers Jean Ledoux, Robert Lebarbier, and Denis Gastinel, the theologians Nicolas Coppesquesne and Courcelles himself, and, finally, Lemaistre's brother-friar Isambart de Lapierre.[38]

For the benefit of those who were not in the torture-room on May 9, Cauchon recounted what had occurred there; and now he asked their counsel as to whether it was expedient to put Joan to torture. After hearing from each, and in view of Joan's previous disposition, the judges decided that it should not be done and that it was inexpedient.[39]

As with the previous poll on how to proceed, Courcelles did not include the results, which are detailed in the French Minute. The first to respond was Roussel: it seemed to him that she should not be tortured, lest the proceedings, which had been well conducted so far, could be maligned. The two archdeacons said no, it did not seem to be expedient at that time. Erard said that it would be a waste of time, since there was already enough material. Lebarbier agreed, and added that she should be once again charitably admonished to submit to the Church, and, if she refused, to continue the proceedings. Gastinel simply said no—probably because he also agreed that there was enough against her, since he had stated in his written response that she deserved to be burned as a heretic, or, if she abjured, to be imprisoned.

Morel surprisingly said yes, he thought she should be tortured, in order to find out the truth about her lies, even though he had said in his

[36] FM 350, LR 350.
[37] LR 350.
[38] FM 350–51, LR 350–51.
[39] FM 351, LR 352.

consultation that the punishment that she received should not be that of a heretic (burning), but only imprisonment. Then Courcelles also said he thought it good to torture her. He also said that she should be questioned—presumably under torture—about whether she was willing to submit to the judgment of the Church. But Coppesquesne said that it was not expedient for her to be tortured; rather, she should be charitably admonished to submit to the determination of the Church. Ledoux said the same, as did Lapierre, but the latter added that she should be admonished for a final time about submitting to the Church Militant.

Next, Loiseleur said he thought it would be good to torture her, as medicine for her soul; but then he stated that he relied on the opinions of the others. Lastly, Hatton, who came in late, voted against torture.[40]

Neither the Minute nor Courcelles's Record provides any clue as to what legal notions the judges or assessors had for when judicial torture could legitimately be used. The first respondent, Treasurer Roussel, may have hinted at a view that it was illegal in the present case, when he said that it would open the proceedings against Joan to a charge that they were not properly conducted. But most of the other assessors who voted against torture seem to have assumed that it would be allowable, but judged that it was not expedient or necessary in this case.

According to accepted procedure, an officially constituted defendant—like Joan, after Estivet had entered his libellus against her—could be legally tortured only when a charge was partially proved (e.g., by one witness instead of two), or when it was agreed that there were sufficient *indicia* (indications) or presumptions against him or her.[41] In Joan's case, no proofs had been established in court, except for a vague assumption that she had confessed to many crimes.

The purpose of judicial torture was to elicit the truth concerning the crime in question, in order to convict or acquit the defendant—not to provide for the defendant's spiritual welfare, which Joan's judges and their assessors professed to be interested in. The main crime they had in mind seems to have been her heterodox belief, which had been teased out of her, that she did not have to agree with the Church on earth about

[40] FM 351.

[41] Lyndwood, *Provinciale* 5.5.4 n. f (p. 305, end of note) states only the case of a single witness: "Et si probatio facta fuerit per unum testem solum bone opinionis et bone fame contra negantem crimen sibi impositum, tunc inquisitus potest torqueri, ut eruatur veritas" (And if proof was made solely through one witness of good opinion and reputation, then the person being tried by inquisition can be tortured, so that the truth might be drawn out.)

something or other that the Church determined. But it was never explained what points were at issue. And there also seemed to be the idea among the assessors that Joan could escape all censure if she would only agree hypothetically that "of course, everyone had to accept what the Church said, especially when the pope in a general council said so." But such agreement on her part was presumably not what Cauchon and his English masters were after.

At the end of the poll on torture, the Minute adds, seemingly as part of the poll, that Lemaistre said that she should be questioned again about whether she believed that she should submit to the Church Militant. The Minute identifies Lemaistre not as one of the judges but simply as *vicarius*, "vicar."[42] We are thereby given an important insight into the mind of the inquisitor, that he was most concerned about the charge dealing with her alleged refusal to recognize the authority of the Church.

[42] FM 351.

CHAPTER 8

University Advice Followed

8.1 Report of the University of Paris, May 19

The next event detailed in the proceedings occurred on May 19, 1431, when the judges appeared before a group of some four dozen assessors.[1] In addressing them, Cauchon made no mention of threatening Joan with torture on May 9 and polling a small group of consultants on May 12. Of the latter, all were present now except Guillaume Erard. This day he announced the results of consulting the Faculties of Theology and Canon Law of the University of Paris.

The consultation with the University was formally requested in the name of Henry VI, as was stated in the University's cover letter to the king, dated May 14.[2]

We saw above that sending the Twelve Articles of Joan's assertions to the University had been advised by two canons of Rouen, Robert Lebarbier and Jean Alespée, and the abbots of Jumièges and Cormeilles, in responses probably received by mid-April. Cauchon must have acted on the advice shortly after that, since the request was first presented to the whole University by the rector for that term, Pierre de Gouda, on April 29. As noted earlier, it seems that four of the crew of six Paris theologians helping

[1] FM 352–53 lists forty-four names, while LR 352–53 has fifty-one. Included in the first list but missing in the second are Lemaistre's fellow-friars Martin Ladvenu and Isambart de Lapierre.

[2] LR 354–56.

H. A. Kelly, *The Trial and Retrial of Joan of Arc*, The New Middle Ages, https://doi.org/10.1007/978-3-032-07887-2_8

Cauchon—namely, Beaupère, Midi, Touraine, and Feuillet, leaving only Courcelles and Maurice behind—were sent to present the Twelve Articles to the University, and to lobby the Faculties of Theology and Canon Law to take a severe view of them.

King Henry was told by the University that the proceedings against Joan were deemed to be "a holy and just process."[3] Similar praise was given in the University's separate letter of the same date to Cauchon: "In considering the well-known form of the proceedings, which conformed to the sacred laws, we approved it as the result of highly learned prudential undertakings of the greatest learning."[4] Their deliberations, concluded on May 14, were enclosed, undoubtedly brought back to Rouen by Beaupère and Midi (while Touraine and Feuillet stayed in Paris), in good time for Cauchon to impart the result to his assessors on May 19.

However, it was not expected to be a hard sell, since, after the English occupation of Paris by Henry V almost a decade earlier, the pro-Armagnac faculty had well and truly thinned out in the midst of the English and Burgundian rulers of the city and region. And the siege on Paris that Joan led two years before was naturally well remembered. A decade before the English advent, when Gerson and d'Ailly were easily able to find heresy in political assassination, there was a division of opinion between the Faculty of Theology and the Faculty of Canon Law, but now it will appear that there was only collegial harmony between the divines and canonists.

Recent-Rector Courcelles must have sent warm greetings to his successor-but-one Rector Gouda, with added good wishes from twice-Emeritus Rector Cauchon, which Gouda would have passed on to the meeting of the whole University that he called on April 29. After he presented the matter at hand, the four nations of the Faculty of Arts held separate discussions. When they returned, they all agreed that the question should be put to the two Faculties of Theology and Canon Law.[5]

8.1.1 *Conclusions of the Paris Theologians*

The University met again on May 14 to hear the two reports. First, the vice-dean of Theology read the text of the Twelve Articles of Joan's alleged

[3] LR 357: "…saincte et juste maniere de proceder."

[4] LR 356–58, at 357: "Formam insuper processuum celebrem sacrisque conformem juribus attendentes, maximis dissertissimisque prudenciis emanatam conprobavimus."

[5] LR 358–59.

assertions, followed by their judgment on each, which they submitted to the pope and the general council. I summarize their opinions as follows, giving their whole opinion only for the fifth article:[6]

1) Revelations, male clothes, Church Militant: The revelations were either lies or proceeded from malign and diabolical spirits: Belial, Satan and Behemoth.[7]
2) St Michael and the crown: Pernicious lying, denigrating angelic dignity.
3) Identifying her saints: Facile, rash, wrong, and erroneous belief.
4) Foretelling the future: Superstitious divination and inane boasting.
5) Male clothing: "The said woman is blasphemous against God and contemptuous of God in His sacraments, a transgressor of divine law and sacred doctrine and ecclesiastical sanctions, thinking badly and erring in faith, and inanely boasting; she should be held suspect of idolatry and of consecrating herself and her clothing to demons, imitating the rituals of the pagans."
6) Her letters: Treacherous, cruel, seditious.
7) Leaving home: Impious towards parents, erring in faith when promising victory.
8) Leaping from the tower: Pusillanimous verging on despair, rash, against free will.
9) Guaranteed salvation: Rash, pernicious; contradicts her previous assertions (in article 8); bad in faith.
10) God's love for some; against English: Superstitious divination; against command to love neighbor.
11) Venerating her saints: Idolatrous, invoking demons, erring in faith; false oath.
12) Not submitting to Church: Schismatic, wrong on unity of Church, apostate, obstinately erring in faith.[8]

We note that though there are errors in faith in this report there is no mention of heresy. This is in keeping with the elaborate condemnation of twenty-eight propositions in favor of magic rituals in 1398, which, as we

[6] LR 359–62.

[7] Satan, of course, *was* the Devil, and Belial was usually assumed to be another name for Satan. Behemoth was the land-monster of Job, paired with the sea-monster Leviathan.

[8] LR 361–62.

saw, the Faculty of Theology decreed was equivalent to the invoking of demons (though that was said to be accompanied with—unnamed—heresies).

The most significant aspect for subsequent decisions was, arguably, their exaggerated assessment of Joan's wearing of male clothing. This was matched, as we will now see, by the canonists, who did indeed take the desired step of finding heresy in her offenses.

8.1.2 Conclusions of the Paris Canonists

The canonists too prefaced their opinions by saying that they submitted them to the pope and the general council. But they included another significant preface: "If the said woman, in her right mind, should obstinately affirm the propositions set out in the above Twelve Articles, and should actually have committed the actions contained in them, it appears to the Faculty of Decrees, after diligently considering each of them, by way of counsel and instruction, speaking charitably,"[9] she is:

1) Schismatic, separating herself from the Church Militant.
2) Erroneous in faith by going against *Unam sanctam*, and heretical.
3) Apostate for cutting hair and wearing male clothes.
4) A lying diviner, claiming mission from God without miracle (like Moses) or Scripture justification (like John the Baptist).
5) Erring in faith by presumption of law: first, by remaining canonically anathema (excommunicated) for a long time; and second, by preferring male clothes to Church-ordered confession and Communion. Also, vehemently suspect of heresy: she should be interrogated on the articles of faith.
6) Erroneous in being certain of salvation.[10]

[9] LR 363: "Si dicta femina, compos sui, affirmaverit pernaciter proposiciones in duodecim articulis suprascriptis declaratas, et facta contenta in eisdem opera adimplerverit, visitatis diligenter proposicionibus supradictis, videtur Facultati Decretorum, per modum consilii vel doctrine, caritative loquendo...."

[10] LR 362–64.

8.1.3 *Judgment of the University of Paris*

There follows a conclusion which Denifle believes applies to both faculties: Therefore, if the said woman does not return to the faith and abjure her error, after admonishment by a competent judge, and perform fitting satisfaction, she should be left to secular judgment (that is, be burned to death).[11] That sentence, of course, should come only from the second conclusion of the canonists, where they found her actually heretical.

Thereupon, the rector directed the whole University to break into nations (which applied only to the Arts Faculty) to discuss the opinions of both faculties. When they returned, they signified their approval. Beaupère and the other delegates asked for a notarized instrument, which was produced.[12]

8.2 Assessors Polled

After the Paris judgment was read, the consultations that had been received locally were also read, according to the French Minute. Then Bishop Cauchon asked the assessors for their advice on how to proceed.[13] Courcelles omits this narration, and gives the impression that the assessors voluntarily weighed in with their opinions, on how to proceed, immediately after the University instrument was recited.[14] As could be seen immediately, the attitude of the group as a whole had taken a much more serious turn than that manifested in the previous assessments.

The first of the thirty-four assessors to speak was the Rouen chapter treasurer, Raoul Roussel, doctor of both laws, who, years later, would be archbishop when Joan's fortune would take a turn for the better. Now he forcefully moved it for the worse. He said that the case should proceed to sentence, and unless Joan returned to the way of truth, she should be condemned of heresy (without saying what the heresy was). Another juristic member of the chapter, Archdeacon Venderès, agreed with Roussel, and added that the trial could be concluded and sentence given in the same day (Courcelles has him say that consignment to the secular arm could also be done on that day).[15]

[11] LR 364; Denifle, *CUP* 4:526, no. 2385, n. 2.
[12] LR 364–67.
[13] FM 367.
[14] LR 367.
[15] FM 367, LR 367.

The theologian Abbot Duremort of Fécamp then spoke, giving a similar view. The promotor should ask Joan if she had any more to say, and, if she did not return to the truth, she should be declared a heretic and left to secular justice. Next was another theologian, her recent examiner, Archdeacon Chastillon. He was the first to bring up the University's opinion. He accepted it, as should all who have not studied the matter for themselves. As for the rest, he agreed with the Abbot of Fécamp.[16]

Abbot Bonnel of Cormeilles, a theologian, simply agreed with the University, as did the jurist Archdeacon Marguerie, adding that the trial could be concluded and sentence given at the same time.[17]

The theologian Erard Emengard said that she should be admonished to return to the way of truth, and, if she did not, he agreed with the Theology Faculty of the University (which, we recall, did not mention heresy, and had no sentencing recommendation). The theologian Guillaume Leboucher said that he stood with the general declaration that he participated in on April 9 (referring to the early theologians' report, which in fact was dated April 12). The University deliberation, which he agreed with, should be shown to Joan; and, if she was unwilling to "obey," the proceedings should be taken from there.[18] This opinion was supported by another theologian, Prior Miget of Longueville, and the vicar-general of Rouen, Jean Pinchon, a jurist, and another jurist, Pasquier de Vaux, canon of Rouen and Paris, who happened to be secretary and chaplain to the duke of Bedford.[19]

Then Beaupère, who had seen the Twelve Articles through the University and brought them back to Rouen, spoke: yes, the University was right; and, as regards the conduct of the trial, the judges should decide. The jurist Gastinel said that if she did not obey after being admonished, he stood with the University (probably the conclusion of the jurists, conviction as heretic, given his earlier dire recommendation).[20]

Then Midi, Beaupère's partner, who had composed the Twelve Articles, agreed that the conclusion and sentence could occur on the same day. For the rest he referred back to the April 12 deliberation. The theologian Maurice du Quesnay said that if Joan did not obey after admonishment,

[16] FM 367–68, LR 367–68.
[17] FM 368, LR 368.
[18] FM 368–69, LR 368–69.
[19] FM 369, LR 369.
[20] FM 369–70, LR 369–70.

he stood with the Theology Faculty of the University (which considered her guilty of various things, but made no recommendation).[21] Abbot Hautmont of Montemer said the same thing, and theologians Guesdon and Fouchier, speaking later, agreed with him.[22]

Theologian Pierre Houdenc said that if she did not return to the Church after charitable warning she would seem to be obstinate and heretical, and the judges should conclude as seemed best. Jean Lefèvre relied on the April 12 decision of the local theologians and the University theologians. Joan should be charitably admonished and a specific day set for her (to reply). Martin Ladvenu agreed with him.[23] Ladvenu was a friar at Lemaistre's Dominican convent in Rouen, who had accompanied Lemaistre on February 20, before the first public interrogation of Joan the next day,[24] but he made no more appearances until this day. He would serve as Joan's final confessor.

Then thirteen advocates of the Court of the Archbishop and Official of Rouen court, including Aubert Morel and Jean Duchemin, said that she was to be admonished to submit to the Church, and if she did not obey, the University jurists should be followed (i.e., conviction of heresy).[25] Basset himself, we recall, was currently in prison.

Two canons of Rouen, Maugier and Coppequesne, followed. The first said that unless she obeyed after being admonished, the case should proceed further. The other simply sided with the University.[26]

The theologian Raoul Sauvage referred to his lengthy previous statement (with its moderate positions, and a recommendation to send the case to the pope). He added that Joan should indeed be admonished, but it should be done publicly, in front of the people. If she did not turn to the truth, the judges should decide what to do.[27]

We recall that the theology trio Minier, Pigache, and Grouchet had submitted a clarified statement allowing for the possibility that Joan's revelations were genuine. Now Minier agreed with Sauvage, while Pigache

[21] FM 370, LR 370.
[22] FM 371–72, LR 371–72.
[23] FM 370–71, LR 370–71.
[24] FM 28, LR 28.
[25] FM 371, LR 371.
[26] FM 372, LR 372.
[27] FM 372, LR 372.

sided with the University, and Grouchet took a hard line: if she did not obey the Church after a warning, she should be declared a heretic.[28]

Next, Friar Isambart de Lapierre referred to the theologians' declaration of April 12, and then said that if Joan did not obey the Church after a warning, the judges should decide what to do.[29] One of the judges was, of course, his own convent superior, Jean Lemaistre.

The next consultant to vote was another of the Paris Six, Pierre Maurice, recently made canon of Rouen (we will hear much more of him soon); his response was like Lapierre's; Maurice's colleague Courcelles spoke next and agreed with him. Loiseleur followed, and agreed with both.[30] They seemed always to agree.

The last three consultants to speak were Jean Alespée, Bertrand Duchesne, and Guillaume Erard (the latter two are reported only in Courcelles's account). The first, another canon of Rouen, said simply that if she remained disobedient, she should be sentenced. Duchesne, a jurist, agreed with the jurists of the University (i.e., if she did not return to the unity of the Church, to be judged a heretic and delivered over to secular justice). Erard agreed with the recent chapter consultation of May 3 (which held for heresy) and the University.[31]

The judges thanked the reverend Fathers, and concluded that Joan would be admonished, and they would continue according to their advice.[32] According to Courcelles's version, Joan would be charitably admonished to return to the path of truth and salvation of body and soul, in accord with their sound advice. They would then conclude the case and set a date for rendering the law.[33]

8.3 Joan Privately Admonished, May 23

In carrying out the advice of many of the assessors that Joan should be charitably admonished, specifically concerning the judgments of the University of Paris on her case, Cauchon and Lemaistre did so in a private gathering on May 23, in a room of Rouen Castle near Joan's prison cell. This, of course, was contrary to Sauvage's recommendation that it be

[28] FM 372–73, LR 372–73.
[29] FM 373, LR 373.
[30] FM 373–74, LR 373–74.
[31] FM 374, LR 374.
[32] FM 374.
[33] LR 374.

done in a public session. The modest group of eight assessors included two high officials in the English government in France who were new to the proceedings: Louis of Luxemburg, Bishop of Thérouanne, who was Henry VI's chancellor, and Jean de Mailly, the young bishop of Noyon, a chief member of the English king's Council. The others were Beaupère, Midi, Erard, and Archdeacons Chastillon, Marguerie, and Venderès.[34]

As we know, all consultations that had been solicited were not on the charges that had actually been leveled against Joan and her pleas of not guilty, but rather on summaries of her answers to interrogations put to her before she was charged, marginally supplemented by her responses to the charges. These Twelve Articles of summaries were never shown to Joan to confirm their accuracy or inaccuracy.

The judges referred to these Twelve Articles (twelve sets of summaries) as "certain points" (*certa puncta*). Summaries of these summaries were now given to Joan, each followed by a summary of the defects it manifested in her as named by the theology and canon-law faculties of the University of Paris; these pronouncements of defects were taken to be admonitions to Joan to submit to the correction and determination of Holy Mother Church.[35]

In other words, only now, after Joan has been found guilty of heresy by the "jury," is she given a glimpse of the real charges against her, and a chance to reduce the sentence.

The lengthy first article was condensed into a single statement (*tu dixisti*, "you said") that Joan had made: that from the age of thirteen she had revelations and talked with Saints Catherine and Margaret. The clerics of the University and elsewhere considered the alleged revelations, on the basis of all of the circumstances, to be either lying fictions or produced by malignant spirits.[36] Left out were the specific names of the devils the theology professors had somehow come up with.

The second point concerned the crown borne by an angel and given to the king, or else first given to the archbishop of Rheims. The clerics said that this was not plausible: it was fabricated and against angelic honor. The third point dealt with the ways in which Joan said she could tell that she was talking with angels and saints. The clerics judged that she too readily

[34] FM 383, LR 374–75.

[35] LR 375. The "schedule" that follows and Pierre Maurice's exhortation appear only in LR (375–83).

[36] LR 375–76.

and rashly believed in them; and, in saying that she believed in them as strongly as she believed in Christ's passion and death, she erred in faith. The fourth point concerned her claims that through her saints she knew future or unknown things; the clerics judged this to be superstition, divination, presumption, and empty boasting.[37]

The fifth point took up her male garb, with greater detail supplied about her items of dress and armor; she received Communion in them, and wore them by the command of God. The clerics said that she thereby blasphemed God and had contempt for the sacraments, erred in faith, was suspect of idolatry, and desecrated herself and her clothing (leaving out "to demons"), imitating the rites of the gentiles.[38]

The sixth point took up her boasts in her letters, which the clerics said showed her to be various bad things, such as deceitful and cruel, and once again, blasphemous. They found her blasphemous again with regard to the seventh point, about her leaving home and joining the fight—which, as well as breaking the commandment about honoring parents, was erring in faith (the theologians were talking about her promises of victory as constituting an error in faith—also implausible, of course). Regarding the eighth point, her leap from the tower at Beaurevoir, they found that she verged on despair and suicide, and then was presumptuous in claiming that she was forgiven. She also had a wrong concept of human freedom. The next point, that she thought that she had not committed mortally sinful deeds, contradicted the previous point; and her certainty that she would go to heaven if she kept her vow of virginity showed her to be presumptuous, rash, mendacious, and thinking wrongly about Christian faith.[39]

The tenth point brought up the business about the saints not speaking English because they were not on the English side, and her dislike for the Burgundians when she found that the saints favored her king. This was blasphemous against the saints and broke the commandment to love one's neighbors. The next point dealt with the veneration she gave to her saints. The clerics concluded that, if she really had the visions she boasted of, she was an idolatress and invoker of demons, errant in faith, and guilty of making an unlawful oath in swearing not to reveal the sign given to her king unless she was ordered to do so by God. Finally, the twelfth point dealt

[37] LR 376–77.

[38] LR 377. Barrett, p. 302, and Hobbins, p. 185, translate the penultimate charge to mean "worship of yourself and your clothes." Tisset, 2:328, gives a correct rendering.

[39] LR 377–79.

with her position that she would not obey the Church if the Church told her to disobey the command she had from God, even though it was explained many times that everyone had to obey the Church Militant. The clerics found her schismatic in failing to understand the unity and authority of the Church, and also an apostate, and stubbornly erring from the faith.[40]

When we examine the clerical judgments reported in these summaries, we see that they follow only the responses of the theologians and not the canon lawyers. Specifically, unlike the canonists, the clerics cited did not associate any of her misdeeds with heresy, let alone judge her to be guilty of heresy.

All of this exposition may have been first done in Latin, which could have been only minimally or sporadically intelligible to Joan, and then explained in French. Courcelles's text says, at the end: "It was explained to the said Joan in French words by Master Pierre Maurice, canon of the church of Rouen, an outstanding doctor of sacred theology."[41]

Maurice, of course, was one of Courcelles's colleagues from the Theology Faculty of the University of Paris. Unlike Loiseleur, who had been a canon of Rouen for over ten years, Maurice was inducted only a year previously, but he was connected somehow with Bishop Luxembourg of Thérouanne, Henry VI's chancellor, there with them that day, and he had been chosen to welcome the young king to Rouen Cathedral last June.[42]

Speaking in French (given by Courcelles in Latin), Maurice begged Joan to think very carefully about her words and deeds, especially concerning the last article. Then he proceeded to address a long exhortation to her, calling her his dearest friend, and telling her that the two judges had admonished her four times and more, that harm to body and soul awaited her unless she corrected and emended her deeds and words and submitted herself and her deeds to the Church and accepted its judgment, but she took no notice. He appealed to her again in their name. "Although many could have been content with the facts of your case, the foresaid lord

[40] LR 379–80.
[41] LR 375.
[42] Tisset, *Procès*, 2:417.

judges" (Cauchon and Lemaistre), out of zeal for your welfare, sent your statements to the University of Paris.[43]

It appeared to this splendid institution, Maurice continued, referring to the University, which was the shining light of all branches of knowledge and the extirpator of errors, and to other doctors as well, that such apparitions as she spoke of were not to be credited without the express confirmation of Scripture or a miracle. She should have sought the advice of a prelate or other learned churchman, given her simple state of knowledge. She would surely agree that someone who claimed to be sent by the king should have proof that it was so. She should also agree that if a knight of her king should refuse allegiance to him, he should be condemned. Just so, she should agree that she, who was a child of the Church, owed obedience to its officials, that is, the prelates of the Church. God said to its prelates, "Who hears you, hears me, and who spurns you spurns me." As long as she refused to submit to the Church, she departed from it, and erred in the article *Unam sanctam*, which had been fully explained to her. He therefore begged her, on behalf of his masters the said bishop and vice-inquisitor, that she correct and emend all the above matters and return to the way of truth, by obeying the Church and submitting all to its judgment and determination. In so doing, she would save her soul and rescue her body, he believed, from death. But if she did not, her soul would be subjected to damnation, and her body, he feared, would be destroyed—from which fate may Jesus Christ deign to preserve her.[44] He made no reference to heresy, which alone would justify the death penalty.

The terse French Minute, after naming the attendees at this session, says merely: "To the first and other articles, to the qualifications solemnly explained by Master Pierre Maurice to the said Joan, and to the charitable admonishments and requests made to the said Joan, she responds," followed by her answer in French: she would remain satisfied with the

[43] LR 381. The quoted material reads in Latin (p. 381): "Et quamquam ex factis erga vos jam plurimi potuissent contentari, tamen domini judices predicti," etc. Barrett, p. 307 and Hobbins, p. 188, both mistranslate this to say that "although many of your judges would have been satisfied...they have submitted" (Barrett) or "although many of the judges thought the evidence against you was sufficient, they earnestly desired" (Hobbins), turning the assessors and consultants into judges in the case. Tisset, 2:331, gets it correct, interpreting *plurimi* simply as "others" or "other judges."

[44] LR 381–83.

responses she made in the proceedings.[45] She was then asked (it is not stated by whom) whether she believed that she was bound to submit what she said and did to the Church Militant or to someone else other than God. She replied similarly, and added that she would still say the same if she saw the fire to which she was condemned, and even in the fire, until death itself.[46]

8.4 Promotor Reappears, Case Closed

After Joan's final response, the French Minute stated: "And without delay, because the promotor and she did not wish to say anything, the case/cause was concluded."[47] Courcelles specifies that the judges asked the promotor and Joan whether they had anything more to say, and they both said that they did not. Cauchon thereupon read a "schedule" decreeing an end to the cause: the judges declared themselves competent, and since the parties renounced any further action, they were told to hear the sentence and any further proceedings on the following day.[48]

Courcelles notes that the whole session, beginning with the charitable admonition, was witnessed by Friar Isambart de Lapierre, and a priest from the diocese of London and a cleric from the diocese of Noyon.[49]

The promotor, of course, was Jean d'Estivet, who was the plaintiff-prosecutor in the case, appointed by Cauchon in January to be the prosecutor of the case against Joan, and appointed as such by Lemaistre as well when he joined Cauchon as co-judge, who had presented the charges against her. His role had been circumvented from the beginning. He had stated that it was at his request that Joan had been summoned to court to respond in matters of faith, on the basis of evidence he showed to Cauchon. But, instead of having her respond to charges against her, Cauchon made her swear to answer questions about herself. When, finally, under pressure from a passing papal auditor, Estivet was allowed to present his charges, nothing was heard from him again, until now.

[45] FM 383: "Ad primum et alios articulos, calificaciones per magistrum Petrum Mauricii eidem Johanne expositas, et moniciones et requisiciones caritativas eidem Johanne factas, respond" (etc.). Cf. LR 383: But after the said Joan was thus admonished and heard such exhortations, she subsequently replied in this way, etc.

[46] FM 383–84, LR 383–84.

[47] FM 384.

[48] FM 384, LR 384.

[49] LR 385.

But even now, neither the French Minute nor Courcelles's Latin Record registered his presence in this final private session of the proceedings. In the poll of the assessors taken four days earlier, the Abbot of Fécamp assumed that it was the promotor whose role it was to ask Joan if she had anything further to say, but, according to Courcelles, it was the judges who put this question to both the promotor and to Joan.

If Joan's trial had followed the rules of inquisitorial procedure, after she had denied the charges of crimes against her contained in the promotor's seventy articles, the next step should have been for the promotor to swear in witnesses in court in Joan's presence, and then have them deposed on the seventy articles, after which the depositions would be read in court, again in Joan's presence, along with any assertions that Joan had made herself that seemed to prove each charge. The promotor would then argue that specific testimony was sufficient to prove Joan's guilt of specific charges in the articles. Next, Joan would have been given the opportunity to rebut the witnesses with arguments and witnesses of her own, and with the advice of counsel. Then the judges would have consulted their assessors for their advice on how to weigh the evidence, before coming to a conclusion. The trial would have lasted a long time. Or perhaps just a short time. It would have been of specific interest to know exactly what heresy it was of which she was vehemently suspect.

CHAPTER 9

The Court at the Scaffold, May 24

9.1 Appeal to Pope Rejected

On the next day, May 24, Courcelles presents the judges as narrating that they arrived at a public place, in the precincts of the abbey of Saint Ouen in Rouen, where Joan was on a scaffold before a large crowd of people, along with twenty-seven named assessors "and many others." First listed among the assessors was "the cardinal of England," Henry Beaufort, Bishop of Winchester, half-brother of Henry IV and therefore great-uncle of Henry VI. He was followed by the two bishops who had attended the conclusion of the trial (Thérouanne and Noyon), and another English bishop, William Alnwich of Norwich; then eight abbots, including the abbot of Saint-Ouen for the first time, Fécamp, and other regulars; the prior of Longueville and another prior; then the doctors of theology Beaupère, Midi, and Maurice (three of the remaining Paris Six), Chastillon, du Quesnay, Leboucher, Lefèvre, Houdenc, and Fouchier; the bachelors of theology, Courcelles (the last of the remaining Paris Six), Hatton, Coppequesne, Sauvage, Grouchet, Minier, and Pigache; and then the jurists: Roussel the treasurer, Guérin, Venderès, Pinchon, Ledoulx, Lebarbier, Marguerie, Alespée, Morel, Colombel, and Duchemin.[1] Promotor Estivet, who had only studied canon law at Paris, was so far not said to be present.

[1] LR 385–86; FM 385–86 lists only sixteen names.

H. A. Kelly, *The Trial and Retrial of Joan of Arc*, The New Middle Ages, https://doi.org/10.1007/978-3-032-07887-2_9

Guillaume Erard, licensed in theology, was there: he gave a sermon allegedly for Joan's benefit as well as for the public audience, on the theme of John 15.4 (a vine branch must stay connected to the vine to bear fruit); he labored to show that Joan through many errors and grave crimes had separated herself from Holy Mother Church and scandalized the Christian people.[2]

Then Erard addressed Joan directly, saying that the judges there present had many times "summoned" her and required her to submit all of her words and deeds to Holy Mother Church. He pointed out to her that many of her words and deeds had been considered by clergymen to be bad and erroneous. Joan replied,

> I will answer you. As far as submission to the Church is concerned, I have responded to them: I have told them that all of the things that I have done and said should be sent to Rome, before our Holy Father the Pope, to whom, and to God first of all, I submit myself. As for the words and deeds that I have done, I did them on God's behalf.[3]

Asked whether she would revoke all the words and deeds that had been reproved by the clergy, she said, "I refer them to God and to our Holy Father the Pope." She was told that this was not sufficient, and that there could be no resort to the pope, who was such a long distance away. Besides, ordinaries were judges in their own dioceses, and therefore she was bound to submit to them. Therefore, it was necessary that she refer herself to Holy Mother Church (at this point there is a marginal note in the main manuscript of the Latin Record: *Joanna dicit se velle obedire Ecclesie* [Joan says she wants to obey the Church]), and to agree with clerics and with men who knew about such things and with what they determined about her words and deeds. And she was given this admonishment three times.[4]

Orders or admonitions were often repeated three times in judicial proceedings in order to make them appeal-proof. Thus, after Joan clarified her previous answers concerning the pope, that she was willing to submit her case to the pope, she now actually insisted that her case be taken to the pope, an unequivocal appeal from the present tribunal; the judges rejected the appeal on the spot, on the grounds that the pope was too far away. He

[2] LR 386.

[3] FM 386–87, LR 386–87.

[4] FM 387–88, LR 387–88; Tisset, 1:388 n. 1.

was only a few days away by courier. Just two months earlier, in the diocese of Coutances, we saw an appeal being made to the pope from Inquisitor Graverent in the Lecouveur case. It was standard procedure that when such an appealed grievance was found to be meritorious, the pope would commission geographically local judges to try the case.

9.2 First Sentence, to Secular Justice

Then Cauchon, speaking both for himself and Lemaistre, began to read the sentence of death against Joan. As will be seen below, it was not completely delivered, being interrupted by Joan. The text of it is included in Courcelles's Latin Record later on, as a kind of appendix.[5] I will analyze the whole of it here, in order to see what the judges intended to convict her of and how they justified it.

After an introduction on the importance of opposing erroneous doctrines that could seduce the faithful, Cauchon addressed Joan directly: she had been delated to him and the vice-inquisitor, who were her competent judges, for many pernicious crimes, and was summoned by them to a trial of the faith. And they, having examined everything in her proceedings, especially the responses, confessions, and assertions she made, and considering the deliberations of the Faculties of Theology and Canon Law of the University of Paris, and indeed, of the whole University, and the opinions of many other experts, declared her a lying concocter of apparitions, a diviner, blasphemer against God and His sacraments, seditious, cruel, apostate, schismatic, and erring in the faith in multiple ways. Although many times urged to emend herself and to submit to Holy Mother Church, she obstinately refused to do so, and many times refused to submit to the pope and the general council. Hence it was that they declared her automatically excommunicated and a heretic, because of being pertinacious and obstinate in the aforesaid sins, excesses, and errors (*te tamquam pertinacem et obstinatam in predictis delictis, excessibus, et erroribus ipso jure excommunicatam et hereticam declaramus*), and, lest she spread the leprosy of heresy to others, she was to be left to secular justice, but allowed to go to confession, if she showed signs of penitence.[6]

[5] LR 413–14.

[6] LR 388, 413–14; Hobbins, pp 192, 202. The crimes alleged in this sentence are analyzed in Duparc, *Nullité*, 5:92–106.

Even though the judges did not name heresy among the crimes they found her guilty of, they seem to have found it in the "fact" that she stubbornly persisted in these offenses, which were not heretical in themselves. This was in keeping with the argument of Archdeacon Chastillon on May 2 regarding two of Joan's crimes, refusal to accept the article *Unam sanctam* and asserting that the wearing of male clothing was morally acceptable. It is noteworthy that in this sentence, the judges encompassed the first offense as her refusal to submit to the Church, but did not mention the male clothing, which would very soon figure so largely in her case.

They also failed to include the alternative possibility to falsifying her apparitions, which many of the consultations had broached, namely, that they were the work of demons. Nor did they include the charge that her divining of the future was effected by consulting demons.

None of the participants in the long process against Joan manifested any awareness of the possibility of connecting the charges of divination (telling the future) and sortilege (finding and interpreting portents) with heresy. This possibility came to the fore with Boniface VIII's *Liber Sextus* of 1298. It included the decretal *Accusatus de heresi* of Alexander IV (1254–1261), which had admonished heresy inquisitors of the time not to concern themselves with divinations or sortileges unless there was a manifest connection with heresy.[7] The *Ordinary Gloss* of John Andrew, produced shortly afterwards (1300), gave some examples of such a connection, the first of which would prove the most important: uttering nefarious prayers around the altars of idols, offering sacrifices, consulting demons, and receiving their responses. He cites two passages of St Augustine for this example, collected by Gratian in his extensive treatment of the offense of sortilege-divination.[8]

[7] Alexander IV (1254–61), *Accusatus de heresi*, *Sext* 5.2 (*De hereticis*), c. 8 §4 (CIC 2:1071–72).

[8] Johannes Andreae, *Glossa ordinaria in Librum Sextum* 5.2.8 §4 ad v. *saperent*, n. q (CJC 3:1:622) ad v. *saperent*: "...sicut est circa aras idolorum nefarias preces emittere, sacrificia offerre, demones consulere, eorum responsa suscipere"; Andrew draws on Gratian's *Decretum*, Cause 26, qq. 1–5, dealing with a priest convicted of being a sortileger and diviner (CIC 1:1019–360); he cites the canons *Hi qui* (q. 2, cap. 3, col. 1021), in which St Augustine says he dislikes the finding of *sortes* in the pages of the Gospels, but it is preferable to consulting demons, and *Igitur* (q. 4, cap. 1, § 3, col. 1024), where Augustine (really Rabanus Maurus) describes *arioli* (*harioli*) as those who "utter nefarious prayers around the altars of idols, and by means of these celebrations receive the responses of demons." Andrew's other examples of divination that clearly savor of heresy are: 2) associating with heretics in order to

Earlier on, the Catalan heresy inquisitor Nicolau Eymeric had gone even further in his *Directorium inquisitorum*, which he finished in Avignon in 1376.[9] He concluded that the mere invoking of demons savored of heresy, and that those who did so should be considered heretics.[10] Theories of demonic magic were being elaborated at the time of Joan's prosecution,[11] which would culminate with the publication of the *Malleus Maleficarum* by two Dominican heresy inquisitors in 1486.[12] In fact, as we will see in the next chapter, one of their notable predecessors, another Dominican, Johannes Nider, famous for the sorcery anecdotes in his *Formicarius* (1437–1438), will say that Joan was burned as a magician (*maga*), who had an evil spirit as her familiar.[13] But so far no one who had been connected with Joan's prosecution had come up with any such ideas.

Nor had anyone thus far in the proceedings made any mention of abjuration, which could save a person from death, after a first-time conviction of heresy. According to the text of Cauchon's half-finished sentence, once she was handed over to secular judgment, it would seem that it was too late to recant, too late to avoid the ultimate judgment of death. She could only be allowed to go to confession if she repented. But it was, of course, implied. And prepared for.

9.3 Capitulation, Abjuration

In the event, after the reading of the sentence had begun, according to the French Minute, Joan interrupted Cauchon and said that she wished to go along with everything the judges and the Church "would say and sentence," and obey all their commands. She then made the following revocation, in the presence of the large multitude of people there: she said several times that, since the people of the Church had said that her revelations were not to be upheld or believed, she did not wish to uphold them. Then

practice it; 3) making predictions by means of the body and blood of Christ; and 4) getting responses by re-baptizing a boy.

[9] Nicolau Eymeric, *Directorium inquisitorum* [1376], ed. Francisco Peña [1578]); I use the Venice 1595 edition (Hathi Trust online).

[10] Ibid. 2.43.14, p. 343aD.

[11] Michael D. Bailey, "From Sorcery to Witchcraft: Clerical Conceptions of Magic in the Later Middle Ages," *Speculum* 67 (2001) 960–90.

[12] Henricus Institoris (Kramer) and Jacobus Sprenger, *Malleus Maleficarum*, ed. and tr. Christopher S. Mackay, 2 vols. (Cambridge 2006).

[13] See Chapter 11.

the alternative sentence, which was held ready, was taken out and read through from the beginning.[14]

According to Courcelles's Latin Record, she began to speak after a great part of the sentence had been gone through, saying that she wished to hold everything that the Church ordained and which the judges said and sentenced, and to obey their every command and will. Since the churchmen had said that her revelations should not be upheld or believed in, she no longer wished to uphold them, but subjected herself completely to Holy Mother Church and to the judges. She then recited a long abjuration written in French, which would have had to be first read to her, since she could not read at all.[15] Courcelles gives both the French and the Latin forms of this extensive text. The beginning is based on the canon *Quociens* in Gratian, a formula recited by a schismatic bishop who returned to the Church.[16] She was first made to confess that she lyingly fabricated apparitions and rashly believed in them, superstitiously divining the unknown, and blaspheming God; she transgressed divine law, Holy Scripture, and canonical sanctions; she wore dissolute, malformed, dishonorable clothing, against the decency of nature, and cut her hair in male fashion, and took up arms, cruelly desiring human bloodshed, saying she did all through God's command, showing contempt for God in His sacraments, creating seditions, idolizing and invoking demons, incurring the crime of schism, and multiply erring in the faith.[17]

(We see that the wearing of bad clothes, not mentioned in Cauchon's discarded sentence, was now included, but only as a crime of indecency, unless it was to be read with the previously mentioned offenses of breaking divine, scriptural, and canonical law. Omitted was her constantly repeated large offense of refusing to submit herself to the Church Militant.)

The formula continued: she hereby abjured and receded from all these crimes and submitted herself to Holy Mother Church for emendation, and vowed and swore to St Peter, to the pope and his successors, and to her two judges that she would never return to these things from which she had been freed by the Redeemer's grace.[18]

[14] FM 388.

[15] On Joan's lack of learning, see Marina Warner, *Joan of Arc: The Image of Female Heroism* (New York 1981), p. 94.

[16] Gratian, *Decretum* C. 1 q. 7 c. 9, *Quociens* (CIC 1:431).

[17] LR 389–90, in French; in Latin, LR 390–91.

[18] LR 390, 391.

Having Joan specify that she abjured *all* heresy put her under a provision of Alexander IV's decretal *Accusatus*, namely, that a future commission of *any* heresy would constitute a relapse into heresy.[19]

At the Nullity Trial, Courcelles said that Archdeacon Venderès compiled this version of the abjuration. Tisset says that it seems certain that it was not the version that Joan read (or rather repeated). There were many witnesses that said that the actual version was only six or eight lines long.[20] One of them was Urban Dean Massieu, who added that it was certainly not the one that was in the record. Massieu in fact read the original text out loud from the scaffold, in preparation for Joan's signature, but when he finished his reading, he said, there was a flurry of consternation and murmuring. Cauchon himself was much upset, and insisted that it be emended before they proceeded. Massieu perceived that Joan did not understand what it said, and he warned her about the danger of signing it. Joan replied that if the clerics and Church, into whose hands she ought to place herself, thought she should sign it, then she would willingly do it. Master Erard then said, "Do it now! Otherwise, you'll end your days in fire here today." The people standing around were causing a great ruckus, and many stones were thrown, it was not clear by whom. Once she signed it, she asked the promotor (neither record acknowledged Estivet's presence there that day) where she would be taken afterwards, and he told her that she would go back to Rouen Castle, dressed in women's clothes.[21]

The notaries must have thought that the invented longer formula was "good enough" in reflecting the substance of the actual formula, since they gave it their endorsement.[22]

9.4 Alternative Sentence, Life in Prison

Cauchon obviously accepted that it would not do to delay the proceedings to emend the text of the abjuration, so he proceeded to read the alternative sentence. It was mainly identical to the earlier one, up to the point that they, the judges, found her to be erring in multiple ways from the Catholic faith.[23] Now they said that, seeing that she had revoked her

[19] Alexander III, *Accusatus de heresi*, §1.
[20] Tisset, *Procès*, 3:136–43.
[21] Duparc, *Procès*, 1:433–34.
[22] See Tisset, *Procès*, 3:134–43; Duparc, *Procès*, 5:87–88, 109–15.
[23] LR 392–93.

errors—genuinely, they believed—and abjured them "along with all heresy" (*cum omni heresi*), they absolved her from the excommunication with which she had been bound, as long as she sincerely returned to the Church and obeyed what they would impose upon her. But because she had rashly offended against God and the Church, as aforesaid, they definitively condemned her to do salutary penance in perpetual prison "with the bread of pain and water of sadness," to weep over the things that she had done and to commit them again no more, with the possibility of moderating this sentence always reserved.[24]

This language of the salutary punishment of prison, taken from a decretal of Innocent III on the punishment for a counterfeiter, had been used by Denis Gastinel, who had concluded that Joan was guilty of heresy and should be sentenced to prison if she abjured. However, Gastinel did not specify perpetual prison, as did the pope. Perpetual prison was specified by two other jurists of Rouen, Morel and Duchemin, who specifically cited Innocent's decretal. And it was specified here, though with the possibility of commutation.

As for Joan's excommunication, there was no previous reference to it throughout the proceedings, except that some of the assessors mentioned that it might be incurred by Joan if she refused to take the oaths imposed on her. Now Cauchon and Lemaistre were asserting that she had been in an excommunicated state all along, and that she was hereby absolved of it, as long as her abjuration (which included a willingness to submit to the Church) was sincere. If it was not, she was still excommunicated. Furthermore, the wording of the sentence clearly implied that if she were to violate any of the terms of her absolution, the excommunication would again take effect. But, as we will see below, Cauchon did not adhere to this position, since he allowed Joan to receive Communion. True, this was after he was assured by Martin Ladvenu that she had made a good confession; but being absolved in the forum of conscience would have had no effect upon a judgment of excommunication made in the judicial forum, without a formal lifting of the sanction by the judge (or by *some* judge, in the case of *ipso facto* excommunication).

[24] LR 393.

9.5 Inquisitor's Visit

In the afternoon of the same day, Vice-Inquisitor Lemaistre made a rare appearance on his own. The French Minute speaks of him in the third person, but Courcelles's reconstruction has him speaking in the first person. He went with Midi, Loiseleur, and Courcelles, and some others (Courcelles names the inquisitor's fellow friar, Isambart de Lapierre), to speak to Joan in her prison room, and told her that it behooved her humbly to obey the sentence of her judges, and also to resume female clothes and put away male clothing, as had been ordained by her judges. Female clothes were brought to her, and, when she saw them, she said that she would willingly take them, and obey all the judges and ecclesiastics, and accordingly she immediately took the female clothing and put aside the male clothes, and also wished and permitted her hair to be cut.[25] In Courcelles's version, Lemaistre adds a warning about the consequences of relapse: "...she was also required to completely abandon her errors and former exhortations (or fabrications)[26] and in no way return to them, explaining to her that in case there were a return to such, from then on the Church would not receive her but abandon her entirely." The exchange about the clothes was not much altered, except that now it was the command of the Church rather than that of the judges, and Lemaistre had Joan agree to take female clothes before they were shown to her. And the agreement to have her hair cut turned out to be having it completely shaved off.[27]

The business about female clothing may have been a part of setting up the justification for accusing Joan of relapse. But the exchange between Joan and Estivet on the scaffold reported by Massieu shows that Joan's rejection of male clothing had always been part of the planned regimen in case she should submit herself to the judges' determinations at this point.

[25] FM 393–94, LR 393–94. It is not clear how her short male hairstyle could be cut to the longer female style.

[26] LR 394. The A text reads *adjuraciones* (threats?) instead of *adinvenciones* (fabrications); Tisset accepts the latter without noting the variant.

[27] LR 394.

CHAPTER 10

Sentenced as Relapsed, Without Trial

10.1 Interrogation on Clothes and Visions

The previous momentous events had taken place on Thursday May 24. Four days later, on Monday May 28, according to the French Minute, Joan was constituted before the two judges. Because she was dressed in male clothing, which she had recently put away on order of the judges, they asked her when and why she had put them on again.[1]

Tisset gives this part of the proceedings the bracketed title of "[CAUSA RELAPSUS],"[2] which is more appropriate for the French Minute than for the Latin Record, since Courcelles strips away the judicial setting of the encounter, minimal as it was (no locale was specified; Joan was not put under oath; and the attendees were not listed as assessors, being mentioned only after the conclusion of the encounter). Instead, he has the judges narrate that they went to Joan's prison, accompanied by Venderès, Hatton, Courcelles, Lapierre, and four others, to observe her status and disposition, and they found her wearing male clothing.[3]

In response to their first questions, as to why she had re-assumed the male clothing and who induced her to do it, she said that she did it of her own accord. When she was told that she had promised and sworn not to

[1] FM 395.
[2] Tisset, 1:395.
[3] LR 395.

H. A. Kelly, *The Trial and Retrial of Joan of Arc*, The New Middle Ages, https://doi.org/10.1007/978-3-032-07887-2_10

do it, she replied that she never understood that she had taken an oath. Asked again why she did it, she replied that it was more lawful and appropriate to do so when she was among men. Another reason was that the promise that she would be allowed to go to mass and receive Communion and be freed of her fetters had not been kept. She did not respond to the next question, whether male clothes had been emphasized in her abjuration. Instead, she continued her complaints about being in fetters. She added that if her prison conditions were better (according to the French Minute she also asked for a female attendant), she would be good and do what the Church wished.[4]

It seems clear that she did not regard the wearing of male clothes an offense against God or Church that figured in her abjuration, but a practical matter of the life that she had chosen and later the life in prison that she was being forced to lead. We recall that the subject of her clothing did not appear in the sentences, and it was given no particular emphasis in the long abjuration that was substituted for her original formula that she signed.

The judges then told her that they had heard from some persons that she still adhered to the illusions of her pretensed revelations, which she had renounced, and accordingly they asked her if she had heard the voices of Saints Catherine and Margaret since last Thursday. She replied yes, that they had told her what a great pity it was that she had betrayed herself, making her abjuration to save her life and thereby condemning herself. She said that before that Thursday her voices had told her what to do on the scaffold, and she had done it, answering boldly to what the preacher had said against her. He had falsely claimed that she had done things that she had not done. If she said that God had not sent her, she condemned herself, because God truly did send her. Her voices told her later that she did a great wrong to herself by confessing that what she had done was not good. Whatever she revoked on Thursday she did because of fear of the fire.

The judges told her that one of the things she said in her abjuration was that she had falsely boasted that the voices were Saints Catherine and Margaret. She denied that she had done this, but admitted that what she had revoked was done out of fear. Now she would prefer to suffer the one punishment, death, than to stay longer in prison. She concluded by saying that she had never done anything against God or the faith, no matter what

[4] FM 395–97, LR 395–97.

it was ordered her to abjure. She did not understand what was written in the schedule of abjuration. She did not intend to revoke anything unless it pleased God that she should do so. In the matter of her clothes, she would take on women's dress, if the judges wished it, but she would do nothing else concerning the rest.[5]

The French Minute ended this session simply by listing the persons in attendance, while Courcelles has the judges narrate that they departed from Joan, to proceed as law and reason demanded.[6]

This short session, which could not have lasted more than half an hour, would turn out to be the entirety of evidence for relapse.

10.2 Assessors' Call for Review Ignored

On the next day, Tuesday May 29, the judges assembled a group of assessors, thirty-nine of whom are named by Courcelles,[7] and Cauchon put them in the picture. He recounted that after the last public session, on the vigil of Pentecost, May 19, on their advice they admonished Joan about the faults that the University of Paris had found in her. And when she refused to acquiesce, and when neither she nor the promotor had anything further to say, they concluded and set Thursday May 24 for the sentence. Two versions of the sentence were prepared, in case she recanted (Courcelles omits this latter point).[8]

According to the French Minute, Cauchon then recounted that, on that day, after a solemn sermon was preached, she was admonished to obey what the Church said; and, because she was unwilling to obey, the reading of the sentence began. But then she asked to speak, and she submitted herself to the Church and the judges. She abjured her errors vocally, in accord with the text read to her, which she signed. She was absolved then and there, on condition that her contrition was genuine and not feigned, and penance was enjoined.[9] In contrast, the Latin Record has Cauchon narrate that he told the assembly that, after the sermon and admonitions, she abjured her errors and signed the abjuration, "as is more

[5] FM 397–99, LR 397–99.
[6] FM 399, LR 399.
[7] LR 399–400; FM 400 simply speaks of "a solemn congregation."
[8] FM 400–01, LR 401.
[9] FM 401.

fully narrated in the preceding"—referring to the account in the Latin Record, according to which Joan interrupted the sentence.[10]

According to the Minute, the vice-inquisitor with others visited her on the same day, warning her to obey the Church's mandates, and they induced her (*induxerunt*) to put on female clothes, which she did.[11] Courcelles instead has Lemaistre narrate that on the afternoon of that Thursday, after dinner, Joan was charitably admonished by him and others assisting him to persist in her good intention and to guard against relapse. At that time she also abandoned her male clothes, in accord with the precepts of the Church.[12]

However, at the persuasion of the Devil, that night and over several days, Joan told various persons that her spirits and voices had returned to her and told her many things. Likewise, not content with female clothes, as soon as she could get and keep male clothing, she put it on. And just yesterday, hearing the outcry (*clamor*) about this, the judges went to her and found her in male clothes. The report of what then happened was recited by the notaries, as was the text of her previous abjuration.[13]

The judges then requested the counsels and deliberations of the assessors present. The first to respond was one of the handful of persons who had attended the session in Joan's prison cell the day before: the jurist Archdeacon Venderès. He only tacitly referred to her relapsed state, saying that Joan should be judged a heretic and sentenced to secular justice, while recommending mild treatment (the standard formula, meaning that she should be burned to death). The theologian Abbot Duremort of Fécamp said that it seemed to him that she had relapsed. The word of God should be proposed to her, and the schedule just read should be read again in her presence and explained to her, setting forth to her the word of God. Then the judges should declare her a heretic, and she should be delivered to secular justice, as Venderès said. Courcelles then spoke, putting the abbot's points differently: he judged that Joan was relapsed; but it was a good idea for the previous day's record to be read again in her presence and explained by proposing to her the word of God. Once this was done, the judges could proceed.[14]

[10] LR 401–02.

[11] FM 401–02.

[12] LR 402.

[13] FM 402. LR 402 leaves out "that night and over several days," and gives a shorter account, referring to the details given earlier in LR.

[14] FM 402–03, LR 402–03.

Unlike Venderès, the Abbot of Fécamp obviously felt that something more was needed before Joan was convicted. He named some procedures but did not explain their purpose. What these masters should have recommended, since they believed that her actions constituted a relapse into heresy, was that she should be put on trial for this crime. She should be summoned by Cauchon and Lemaistre, put under oath, and charged with two counts of relapse into heresy, and required to plead guilty or not guilty. If she was unable to deny or refute the charges, she should be condemned as a relapsed heretic and handed over to the secular arm. If the judges maintained that the offenses were notorious, having been committed before them, and in need of no proof, they should explain just how her words and deeds constituted heresy and a relapse into heresy. To condemn her without a trial would be equivalent to their having condemned her earlier for her responses to their interrogations without having the promotor present his seventy articles and obtain Joan's pleas.

The forty-some other assessors who responded had little different to suggest. Archdeacon Jean Pinchon, a jurist, said that she was relapsed, and referred to the theologians for the rest. Erard, the scaffold preacher, referred to the Abbot of Fécamp, and an English doctor of theology, Robert Gilbert, present for the first time in these proceedings, agreed with Erard. The Abbot of Saint-Ouen, Archdeacon Chastillon, and theologians Emengart and Boucher agreed with Fécamp.[15]

The theologian Pierre Miget, Prior of Longueville, made an important point: the procedures recommend by Fécamp should be done *cessante passione*, "with suffering ceasing," that is, I take it, Joan should be released from fetters and all other constraints. Then, he said, if the woman should confess what was in the report, they should proceed as suggested.[16] This looks like an effort toward giving her due process.

The English theologian Hatton and three jurists, Marguerie, Alespée, and Garin, simply agreed with Fécamp, but the jurist Denis Gastinel wanted her delivered as a relapsed heretic, but without adding the *pro forma* plea for mercy. The jurist Pasquier de Vaux followed him in this harsh condition, after voting with Fécamp.[17]

[15] FM 403–04, LR 403–04.

[16] FM 404, LR 404. Tisset 2:351 and n. 1 translates *cessante passione* as "after the period of the Passion," taking it as a time for deliberation on Joan's part, while admitting that it makes no sense, since Passiontide was long over.

[17] FM 404–05, LR 404–05.

The next three assessors, all theologians, agreed with Fécamp, after making comments: Pierre de Houdenc thought she always was a heretic and now was relapsed; Jean de Nibat said she was relapsed and impenitent; and Jean Lefèvre said that she was pertinacious, contumacious, and disobedient.[18]

The remaining assessors, nos. 20–42, all agreed with Fécamp, including Maurice (24), Loiseleur (27), Morel (35), Ladvenu (36), Courcelles (40), Lapierre (41), and Maugier (42), with only Lapierre making a comment: the woman should be charitably admonished about the salvation of her soul and told that she had nothing to hope for in this temporal life.[19]

According to the French Minute, the judges concluded that it should be done as the assessors recommended. Then the sentence that was to be delivered was read out.[20] Courcelles, however, simply says that the judges thanked the assessors and concluded to proceed against Joan as a relapsed heretic as law and reason demanded.[21] There was no reference to the Fécamp provision that received so much support from the other assessors, including Courcelles, of formally taking her through the final questioning that supposedly established her relapse into heresy. It would have given the proceedings some semblance of due process.

10.3 To the Scaffold

That there was to be no review, and certainly no trial, was demonstrated by the recitation of the pre-prepared sentence. It was confirmed by the citation signed that same day, May 29. The citation was addressed by the judges to all the priests of the city and diocese of Rouen, and ordered each one of them, without waiting for any other, to cite before the judges at 8:00 in the morning in the Old Market Place of Rouen on May 30 a woman named Joan who had relapsed into several errors against the orthodox faith which she had previously abjured, as was and is duly and sufficiently clear from her confessions and assertions and otherwise.[22]

[18] FM 405–06, LR 405–06.
[19] FM 406–08, LR 406–08.
[20] FM 408.
[21] LR 408.
[22] LR 408–09.

Jean Massieu, the city dean, submitted a document to the judges, dated 7:00 a.m., May 30, attesting that he had personally cited Joan to appear before them at 8:00 on that day.[23]

The judges themselves were in the prison with Joan around the time that the citation was served. We know this from testimony that they collected *ex officio* a week later, on June 7, telling of their presence there. They did not take the notaries with them; otherwise Courcelles would have had the judges relate the event on a page signed by them. He added this unratified testimony to the Latin Record as an appendix.[24] The first witness, Archdeacon Venderès, the composer of her spurious abjuration, testified that Joan early on May 30 said that she was deceived by her apparitions—which were real. Venderès asserted that she said this in the presence of the judges (*Ad hec presentes erant, scilicet, nos, predicti judices,* etc.), and of Pierre Maurice (her examiner on May 23), Courcelles himself, the spy Nicolas Loiseleur, a pair of Dominican friars from Lemaistre's Rouen house, namely, Martin Ladvenu and Jean Toutmouillé, a canon of Rouen named Jacques Lecamus, and some others.[25] Venderès's testimony and the depositions that follow are the only witness-testimonies appearing in Courcelles's entire Latin Record.

The second witness, Friar Ladvenu, said that only his companion Friar Toutmouillé was present when he and Maurice and Loiseleur solicitously urged Joan to think on her soul's salvation and asked her about her apparitions. He said that she was disillusioned about her voices, and she revealed other things that contradicted her previous accounts.[26] Ladvenu was the one who heard her confession that morning and gave her Communion, as he testified in 1452, and he asserted then that she had never lost confidence in her voices and their divine connection.[27] The friar may well have felt coerced when he gave his testimony to the contrary a week after her execution.

Next, Maurice testified that Joan admitted to him that she was the angel who brought the crown, but she insisted that her other apparitions really did occur, whether they were good or evil spirits. When Maurice told her he thought they were evil spirits, Joan agreed that she had been

[23] LR 409.
[24] LR 416–22 (appendix).
[25] LR 416 (appendix).
[26] LR 416–18 (appendix).
[27] Duparc, 1:442–44.

deceived by them, but she would leave it up to the ecclesiastics to decide whether they were good or evil.[28]

Friar Toutmouillé testified that when he arrived that morning with Ladvenu, Maurice was already there, and he told him about Joan's disillusionment with her voices. Toutmouillé said that he witnessed Cauchon telling her that her voices deceived her, and that she agreed with him—but then Toutmouillé said that he was there before the judges, when Joan was being asked about her voices.[29] Canon Lecamus said that he accompanied Cauchon to Joan's cell and heard her say that she was deceived by the voices. He testified to her going to confession to Ladvenu and being given Communion by him.[30] Courcelles himself was also there and testified that Joan said that she was deceived, and that Cauchon told her that they were not good spirits and did not come from God.[31]

Finally, Loiseleur said that he had accompanied Maurice to Joan's prison to urge her to save her soul, and he reported her statements about the angel and the crown, and her loss of belief in her spirits. Loiseleur said that he himself urged her to confess publicly that she had been deceived. She asked forgiveness from the English and the Burgundians for what she had done to them.[32]

10.4 Relapsed and Heretical, Without Heresy

In the Latin Report proper, Courcelles has the judges relate that they were present in the square around 9:00 on Wednesday, May 30, assisted by the two bishops of Thérouanne and Noyon, Archdeacons Chastillon, Marguerie, and Venderès, along with Roussel, Gastinel, Boucher, Alespée, Houdenc, Hatton, the prior of Longueville, and Pierre Maurice, and many others, when the foresaid Joan was brought before them, in the sight of a great multitude of people there, and placed upon a scaffold.[33] The French Minute says that Courcelles himself was there, and so was the Englishman, Robert Gilbert, Dean of the Chapel Royal, and that it was

[28] LR 418–19 (appendix).
[29] LR 419–20 (appendix).
[30] LR 420 (appendix).
[31] LR 420–21 (appendix).
[32] LR 421–22 (appendix).
[33] LR 410.

Gilbert who conducted Joan to the scaffold.[34] She was also accompanied by two of the Rouen Dominican friars (who must have been Martin Ladvenu and Jean Toutmouillé),[35] colleagues and subordinates of Inquisitor Lemaistre, whom he and Cauchon had appointed to give her spiritual counsel.

It was now finally obvious to all the assessors present that Cauchon had no intention of conducting a trial against Joan. He and the token other judge Lemaistre were there for the sole purpose of sentencing her as already condemned. The first order of the day that he announced was that there would be a sermon delivered by the distinguished theologian Nicolas Midi, to serve as a salutary admonition to Joan and as edification to the crowd. The sermon was on St Paul's statement to the Corinthians that if one part of the body suffers, so does the rest of the body (1 Cor. 12.26). It is not readily evident how the text was relevant to Joan's predicament.

After the sermon ended, the judges—presumably meaning Cauchon, speaking for himself and Lemaistre—admonished Joan to take care for her soul and salvation, repenting with true contrition, and to confide in the advice of the notable clerics who instructed her on matters of salvation, and especially the two friars they had appointed to advise her and who were there with her then.[36]

That done, Cauchon relates, it was clear from the foregoing that the said woman had never truly receded from her errors, obstinate rashness, and unspeakable crimes. Rather, the diabolical malice of her obstinacy had shown her to be in many ways more worthy of condemnation, in fallaciously simulating contrition, repentance, and amendment, with perjury in the Lord's name and blasphemy to His ineffable majesty, and thereby thoroughly undeserving of the grace and Communion offered by them, the judges, in the previous sentence, being obstinate, incorrigible, and heretical, and relapsed into heresy. They therefore pronounced a definitive sentence over her.[37]

[34] FM 410. Gilbert, the future bishop of London, was a friend of Cardinal Beaufort, and had been involved in the campaign against Wycliffite heresy. See Irene Zadnik, "Gilbert, Robert," *Oxford Dictionary of National Biography Online*, https://www.oxforddnb.com/view/10.1093/ref:odnb/9780198614128.001.0001/odnb-9780198614128-e-47839?rskey=t0ym4V&result=1.

[35] Tisset, 2:356 n. 2, 407, says that Ladvenu's companion was Isambart de Lapierre, but he cites no evidence.

[36] LR 410–11.

[37] LR 411.

The sentence began with a sentiment opposite to Midi's theme: when the poison of heresy infects one member, care must be taken lest it infect other members. The judges then addressed Joan: they had by a just judgment declared that she had fallen into many errors and various crimes of schism, idolatry, invocation of demons, and others; but they thought that she had receded from them, when she renounced them and publicly swore, vowed, and promised that she would not return to those errors, or to heresy of any kind, as stated in the text signed by her.[38] However, it was sufficiently and manifestly clear afterwards that her heart was seduced by the author of schism and heresy (i.e., the Devil) and she fell into the same errors and aforesaid crimes, and by the clearest possible judgments (*clarissimis judiciis*) they had proved that she had only falsely denied her erroneous fictions. Therefore, declaring her to be bound by the sentences of excommunication which she had previously incurred and fallen into the original errors, they judged her to be relapsed and heretical, and they committed her to the secular power, requesting it to moderate its judgment short of death and mutilation. If signs of true penitence should appear in her, the sacrament of penance was to be administered to her.[39]

We note that in this strangely brief statement of their case against Joan, the judges asserted that they had convicted her of errors and crimes, but they named no error, did not mention heresy, and listed only three crimes (schism, idolatry, invoking demons). She promised not to return to those errors or to any heresy, but she had not been said to have held any heresy beforehand. Nevertheless, they said that they had rigorously proved that she was a heretic, and had relapsed into heresy.

Once Joan was delivered to the secular authority, her fate was considered to be out of the ken of the ecclesiastical court, so it was not recorded either in the French Minute or the Latin Record. Our knowledge of what happened comes largely from the later litigation to overturn the verdicts of the courts that condemned her.

Courcelles did add a document to his record that told of Cauchon's action against one of the Rouen Dominicans who dared to object against the prosecution of Joan on the day of her execution. It consists of the confession of the friar, Pierre Bosquier, addressed to Bishop Cauchon, admitting his wrongdoing for saying on May 30 that Joan had been badly judged. The sentence issued by Cauchon and Lemaistre follows, dated

[38] The crimes listed here are analyzed in Duparc, *Procès*, 5:106–19.
[39] LR 411–12.

August 8, 1431, telling of the friar's delation to them concerning his words, "which seemed to make him a favorer of Joan," or, as Bosquier said in his confession, "a favorer of heretical depravity." They condemned him to prison until Easter the next year.[40] Whether Cauchon had jurisdiction over the friar is not clear, but Lemaistre, as prior of the Rouen house, clearly did.

[40] LR 430–33.

CHAPTER 11

Interim Assessments of the Prosecution of Joan of Arc

11.1 Letters

No chronicler gave a surviving account of Joan's trial and burning to death at the stake and the reactions in Rouen and elsewhere. But appearing after the disciplining of Friar Bosquier in the Latin Record are documents justifying Joan's death, undoubtedly added by Courcelles, including letters of Henry VI and the University of Paris.

11.1.1 Henry VI, June 8, 1431

The king wrote to the emperor and various kings and princes, telling of the very famous judicial processus (*processus celeberrimus*) conducted concerning her, but with no details, except that she was interrogated, and that her answers were sent to the University of Paris and elsewhere. The judges found her to be a diviner, idolater, invoker of demons, blasphemer, and schismatic, who erred in the faith in many ways. (There was nothing about the fact that she had been a very successful military commander in battles waged on behalf of the French claimant to the realm of France.) She was urged to return to the right path, but she refused to submit to the pope, general council, or Church Militant. She finally submitted to the ordination of the Church and abjured her errors. But because of her pride she returned to the errors and false follies (*insanias*) that she had vomited out. She was left to the judgment of the secular power, which determined that

H. A. Kelly, *The Trial and Retrial of Joan of Arc*, The New Middle Ages, https://doi.org/10.1007/978-3-032-07887-2_11

she should be burned. When she saw her miserable end approaching, she admitted that her spirits were evil and that she had been deluded by them.[1]

On the last point the letter was doubtless drawing on the depositions that the judges collected the day before, June 7, added to the Latin Record. There was, of course, no judgment made by any secular tribunal before Joan was burned to death.

11.1.2 Henry VI, June 12, 1431

Another missive in the king's name, dated June 12, this one an open letter ("To all who read this") was not included by Courcelles in the trial record. It survives only as an exhibit submitted at the end of Joan's retrial in 1456.[2] It seems to have been hastily drafted, and may not have been sent. I summarize it as follows:

> Because the woman Joan, vehemently suspected of having publicly proclaimed many great errors and committed very enormous crimes against our Catholic faith, as we were urgently informed by the University of Paris, was arrested in the diocese of Beauvais, the bishop of that diocese requested us, King Henry, to deliver her to him to judge her. And the said bishop, along with the vice-inquisitor of the Holy Inquisition, convicted her and left her to our hands and to secular justice, as can be more fully seen in the record of the proceeding. But because some persons may accuse these judges and their assistants for having taken part in this prosecution before the pope or general council, we wish to defend them, being assured by the University and other consultants and observers that the proceeding was canonically done. We promise to defend the said judges in any trial, and order our subjects to participate in their defense.

We observe that there is no reference to hostilities between the warring factions and the arrested woman's connection to such hostilities; rather it is set forth simply as a matter of public-spirited protection and enforcement of religion. It may have been the intention of the drafters to have the University request that she be delivered to the Inquisition, housed in the University, and to have the king explain that the bishop would join the Inquisition to his prosecution. There is only the slightest hint in the letter that Joan was engaged in warfare against the king; the motive indicated for

[1] LR 423–26 (appendix).
[2] NT 1:503–07.

her arrest is the laudable desire to take action against her dreadful unnamed crimes against the faith.

The letter reveals the fear on the English side (completely unfounded, it turned out) that the French party, which owed so much to Joan, would immediately protest against the trial before the pope and general council. It explains the elaborate employment of assessors at the proceeding and consultation with the University, as well as the production of the Latin Record for use in rebutting objections to it.

In 1456, Bishop Mailly of Noyon, who, as we saw above, attended the admonition of Joan on May 23—and who was also present at her abjuration and her execution—was asked about his presence when this letter was granted to Cauchon and others who participated in the proceedings against Joan. He admitted that he was there, but did not remember much about it.[3]

11.1.3 *Henry VI, June 28, 1431*

At the end of the month, on June 28, a third letter was sent out in the king's name, this one in French, which Courcelles did include in the trial dossier. It was addressed to prelates, nobles, and cities of his realm of France, and it did describe Joan's military activities. She demanded to wear the coat of arms of France and she led great companies of armed men and inflicted great cruelties and shed much blood, while spreading rebellions, superstitions, and false belief. After she was captured, she was tried and convicted. At the end, the king encouraged sermons to be preached against Joan.[4]

Although the shamefulness of wearing male clothes was mentioned at the beginning of both this letter and the letter to the emperor, it was not said to figure in the judgment of crimes against her. We note that she is nowhere in the three letters said to have been found guilty of heresy.

[3] NT 1:355. See Tisset, *Procès*, 2:414–15. He was about seventy when he testified in 1456, having become bishop in 1425. He died in 1472 at the age of around 96. He represented the Duke of Burgundy at the Congress of Arras in 1435.

[4] LR 426–30 (appendix).

11.1.4 *The University of Paris, ca. July 1431*

Courcelles then included in his register a letter by the University of Paris to the pope, telling of Joan's case. It is undated, but it was sent some time before the end of 1431, since it found a place in Courcelles's Latin Record, and was thus written in time for inclusion in the record, which was completed before the end of 1431, and addressed to Pope Eugene IV—elected in March, during Joan's prosecution. The letter begins by speaking of the dangers of pseudo-prophets, and goes on to say that the bishop of Beauvais and the vicar of the heresy inquisitor of France were much to be commended for their diligence in protecting Christian religion. For when a woman wearing male clothes was judicially accused before them of fictional revelations and grave crimes against orthodox faith, they took care to examine her and prove the truth of her actions. And, because the judges communicated the proceedings to them at the University for their deliberation over articles asserted by her, they now thought it good to impart their advice to the pope as well. For the said judges informed them that the said woman, who called herself Joan the Maid, had spontaneously confessed many things in court (*quamplurima in judicio sponte confessa est*), by which they found it established, after consultations, that she should be judged to be superstitious, a prophetess, an invoker of evil spirits, an idolater, a blasphemer of God and His saints, a schismatic, and multiply erring in faith. Despite many charitable exhortations to submit to the judgment of Holy Mother Church, she would long submit to no man living on earth (the pope is not mentioned), or the sacred general council.

Finally, she revoked her errors and signed an abjuration. But only a few days later, the unhappy woman had fallen back into her original follies (*insanias*). For this reason, the said judges in a definitive sentence condemned her as relapsed and heretical and left her to the judgment of the secular power. But as she saw the death of her body approach, she confessed that she had been deceived by those spirits in whom she had believed, and, as it seemed, she repented her sins before her death, and, asking forgiveness from all, passed from this life.[5]

Another letter to the college of cardinals followed, incorporating in it this letter to the pope.[6]

[5] LR 433–35 (appendix).

[6] LR 435–36 (appendix).

11.2 Latin Record: Public or Not?

What about the record of the trial that Cauchon ordered Courcelles to prepare? We saw at the beginning that the traditional view of time of the register's compilation, repeated by Tisset in his edition of the trial records, is that Courcelles produced it for Cauchon some four years after the trial, around 1435. But Jean Fraikin in 1973 demonstrated that Cauchon could not have sealed the court book as bishop of Beauvais after August 8, 1432, when he took over his new appointment as bishop of Lisieux. He pointed out further that Cauchon put his seals to the copies of the record on November 30, 1431. This was the date specified by Cauchon in his expense account to the English authorities for arranging Joan's heresy trial, for which he was on a ten-pound per diem salary.[7]

According to one of the two main notaries, Guillaume Manchon, testifying at the nullity trial in 1455, one copy of the register was for Cauchon himself, another for "the Lord Inquisitor" (either Jean Lemaistre, the vice-inquisitor for Rouen, Cauchon's co-judge, or his superior, Jean Graverent, inquisitor of heresy for France), and a third was for Henry VI.[8] Cauchon's copy survives in the Library of the Parlement de Paris, and it has been reproduced in facsimile.[9] Manchon's co-notary Guillaume Boscguillaume said that two more copies were made.[10] One of them was intended for the pope, and Manchon kept the other; he exhibited it at the nullity trial, and it was ceremoniously destroyed at the end of the proceedings.[11]

Daniel Hobbins points out that the register was framed as an open letter, addressed "to all who will read the present letter or public instrument"; he concludes from this that it was meant for public distribution, and as such was "a text consciously looking for a public and attempting to justify the trial."[12] In other words, it was a "conscious attempt at self-justification" on Cauchon's part which would constitute "a powerful

[7] Fraikin, "Date de la redaction."

[8] NT 1:416.

[9] See *Le procès de condamnation de Jeanne d'Arc: Reproduction en facsimile du manuscript authentique, sur velin no. 1119, de la Bibliothèque de l'Assemblée Nationale*, intro. Jean Marchand, 2 vols. (Paris 1955), 1:xx–xxi: MS A. The trial is titled in the original *Processus in causa fidei contra quondam quandam mulierem Johannam, vulgariter dictam La Pucelle.*

[10] NT 1:436.

[11] Marchand, *Procès de condemnation*, p. ix.

[12] Hobbins, *Trial*, pp. 5–6.

argument for the correctness of the trial" intended to "reach a select international audience."[13]

But open letters by the judges were the standard format for trial records, as we have seen. Such format by itself was not a guarantee of circulation. According to a statement addressed to the judges in the trial of rehabilitation in 1455, Isabelle Rommée d'Arc and her son Pierre and their counsel informed the judges that that deceitful, violent, and wicked proceeding was long hidden (*diutius occultatus*) and not brought to light until Rouen and the whole of Normandy were delivered from the English.[14] Rouen was reconquered only in November of 1449 and the rest of Normandy only in 1450. The first verifiable citing of it was by the theologian Guillaume Bouillé in 1449 (see below).

However, it may well be the case that Cauchon ordered the record, not only for the standard purpose of recording all such procedures, but also to defend himself against any possible or expected judicial assaults, of the sort suggested above when discussing Henry VI's letter of June 12. Surely, Cauchon must have thought, his metropolitan superior, Archbishop Regnault de Chartres of Rheims, Charles VII's chancellor, would call the case to his tribunal! Surely, the king and his allies would bring it before the pope! But nothing of the sort happened, either before Cauchon became the bishop of Lisieux in 1432 or later.

11.3 Propaganda at Paris

11.3.1 A Bourgeois Report, June 1431

An anonymous journal-keeper of Paris, the so-called Bourgeois,[15] recounted a long sermon (*preschment*) that he says was given against Joan in Rouen on May 30. His account gives so many details that it was probably taken from a poster like the Ségueut trial-letter, placed on the doors of the cathedral in Paris.

Joan was said to be standing on a scaffold, so that she could be seen by all, dressed in men's clothes; and a long rehearsal of her crimes followed.

[13] Ibid., p. 9.

[14] NT 1:9–10.

[15] *Journal d'un Bourgeois de Paris, 1405-1449* (Paris 1881), ed. Alexandre Tuetey; trans. Janet Shirley, *A Parisian Journal, 1405-1449* (Oxford 1968). For the relevant excerpts, see Quicherat, *Procès*, 4:460–74.

She caused simple folk to idolize her; she told the King of France she was sent from God, and was ordered to kill without mercy those who disobeyed her; she carried a great club to beat persons with; she was sure that she would go to paradise; she received Communion dressed as a man.[16] "Such and worse were the false errors that Lady Joan held, and the people were horrified to hear the great errors against our faith that she had held and still did hold." She replied boldly to the articles that were put to her, like one fully on the Devil's side.[17]

The judges or prosecutors who were putting these articles to her were none other than masters of their own university in Paris (*les clers de l'Université de Paris*), who stood before her, humbly begging her to repent and revoke "that evil error" (*celle malle erreur*), so that all would be forgiven through penitence; otherwise, she would be burned right there and go to hell. She cried for mercy, recanted, and changed clothes, but then changed back again and took up her error as before. She was condemned by all to die. She was burned part-way and then shown to the people to see that she was really a woman. When she was burned to ashes, many people there and elsewhere said she was a martyr, but others denied it, saying that whoever supported her for such a long time had done wrong.[18]

11.3.2 Graverent's Sermon, July 1431

On July 4, the feast day of St Martin in Summer, the Inquisitor of France, Jean Graverent, OP, gave a sermon in Paris at the church of St Martin-in-the-Fields, concerning Joan of Arc. As we know, he had been absent in Coutances during the time of Joan's trial in Rouen, and authorized Jean Lemaistre to serve as judge of the Holy Inquisition alongside Cauchon in Rouen. We saw that Graverent himself had served as co-judge in the elaborate heresy trial of Jean Ségueut just before Joan was delivered to Rouen Castle to begin her trial. Graverent would clearly have been very interested in Joan, but his information about her was all second hand.

He stated that her humble parents were morally offended by her insistence, from the age of fourteen or so, on dressing in men's clothing, so much so that they would have put her to death if they could have done so in good conscience. As a result, she left them, going off with the Devil of

[16] *Journal d'un Bourgeois*, pp. 266–68 (cf. *Parisian Journal*, pp. 260–63).
[17] Ibid., pp. 268–69 (cf. *PJ*, p. 263).
[18] Ibid., pp. 269–70 (cf. *PJ*, pp. 263–64).

Hell, filled with blood and fire, ever after a killer of Christian people, until she was finally burned to death. First, however, she recanted and was given a sentence of four years of imprisonment on bread and water—though she spent her time in prison living the life of a lady. But then the three devils who appeared to her in the form of Saints Michael, Catherine, and Margaret, who were much afraid of losing her, rebuked her for changing out of her male clothes. They told her not to be afraid; they would protect her. So she retrieved the riding gear she had hidden in the straw of her bed, and put it on again. When the University, or those around her, saw that she was being so obstinate, they handed her over to the secular court to be put to death. She appealed to those devils who had appeared to her as saints, but they did not appear. She changed her mind again, but it was too late. He says nothing about her military life, leading the armies of France against the forces of England and Burgundy.

Graverent concludes by saying that Joan was one of four women who were followers of the itinerant Franciscan preacher Friar Richard, along with Pieronne of Brittany, and her companion, and Catherine of La Rochelle, and that all had been taken (*prinses*), except for Catherine, who was at large with the Armagnacs. The great offense committed by Joan, which he denounces in his sermon, was that on a Christmas Day at Jargeau she had received Communion from the friar three times (presumably at each of the three masses that he, like all priests, was allowed to say on that day), while Pieronne had done so twice, as both had admitted in their confessions, and as witnesses who were there had testified. (No such confession or charge appears in Joan's trial.)

All this is recorded by the Bourgeois of Paris.[19] The points that he remembered from the sermon show either that Graverent's informants were very ignorant, or that the Inquisitor himself was unscrupulous in twisting the facts in order to accommodate the lessons he wished to teach.

In the previous year, the Bourgeois had reported that Pieronne and another woman had been captured at Corbeil, just south of Paris, and that a sermon was preached upon them in Paris on September 3 (1430). The other woman was set free for the time being, but Pieronne was consigned to the flames that day for maintaining that she had visions of God dressed in white with a red tunic underneath. She furthermore held that Joan was

[19] Ibid., pp. 270–72 (cf. *PJ*, pp. 264–65).

sent by God to do what she did, and also admitted receiving Communion twice in one day.[20]

In one of the articles that Estivet had lodged against Joan in her trial, he said that in the "confession" that Catherine of La Rochelle made before the Official of Paris, she warned that Joan would escape from prison with the Devil's help, if she were not carefully guarded.[21] It may be that Catherine was testifying as a witness in the trial against Pieronne. This trial may have been conducted by the Official alone, since only he was mentioned. Perhaps Graverent was already co-judge in the trial of Jean Ségueut in Rouen when the trials against Pieronne began.

11.4 Basel, Arras, and Pio Eneo

The humanist Eneo Silvio Piccolomini, who became Pope Pius II (1458–1464), in his posthumously published *Commentaries*, portrayed Joan as a heroine like the classical Camilla, "whether divinely or only humanly inspired."[22] Jules Quicherat suggested that he received information (or opinions) about her, reflected specifically in his account of her trial and death, from the Norman clerics who attended the Council of Basel.[23] Piccolomini spent a year or so early on at the council, not long after Joan was executed, as a secretary of Cardinal Domenico Capranica; later on he became a key player, serving as secretary to the council's pope, Felix V. But after leaving Basel the first time, he wound up as a secretary to Cardinal Niccolò Albergati, Pope Eugene IV's delegate to the Congress of Arras in 1435.[24] There too he would find an abundance of Norman clergy, including, very prominently, Cauchon and Courcelles.

Cauchon, who attended the Council of Basel from the fall of 1434 as counsellor of Henry VI, returned to France in July of 1435 to represent

[20] Ibid., pp. 259–60 (cf. *PJ*, pp. 253–54).

[21] LR 264, Estivet's Article 56.

[22] See Pius II, *Commentarii rerum memorabilium que temporibus suis contigerunt*, ed. Adrianus van Heck, 2 vols. (Vatican City 1984), Book 6 chapter 10, pp. 381–88; *The Commentaries of Pius II*, trans. Florence Alden Gragg, introduction and notes by Leona C. Gabel (Northampton MA 1937–1957), pp. 436–43.

[23] Jules Quicherat, *Procès de condemnation et réhabilitation de Jeanne d'Arc*, 5 vols. (Paris 1841–1849), 4:517 n. 3, speaking specifically of the trap laid for her by stealing her clothes). Quicherat reproduces Pius's full account on pp. 507–18.

[24] See Arthur White, *Plague and Pleasure: The Renaissance World of Pius II* (Washington 2014), pp. 65–69.

the English king at Arras: he was not only the leader of the English-French delegation, but also served as the spokesman for the main English delegation when its leader, John Kemp, Archbishop of York, was ill, before the arrival of Cardinal Beaufort.[25]

Courcelles, a world-class opportunist like Cauchon, also went from Basel to attend at Arras, as one of the four emissaries chosen by the University of Paris: he represented the Faculty of Theology (another was Robert Ciboule, for the Faculty of Arts).[26] In his pleas on behalf of the city of Paris, Courcelles was judged by a prominent churchman in the audience to have "the voice of an angel."[27] Courcelles was also an extremely important participant of the Council of Basel. From 1437 onward he authored most of its decrees. He was named a cardinal by Pope Felix.[28]

At Arras, Cauchon was actually pitted against Regnault de Chartres, Archbishop of Rheims, spokesman for the French side, who as Cauchon's metropolitan superior could have called him to account for malfeasance in convicting Joan of heresy and relapse into heresy (the latter without trial), or taken the matter to Rome, whether directly or through the papal delegate Cardinal Albergati. But, just as the archbishop did nothing to aid Joan before, so too he did nothing at Arras.

At Basel, although there were many occasions when participants like Cauchon, Courcelles, Beaupère, and others were the target of Council Fathers loyal to Charles VII, according to Heribert Müller, there is no sign that they were attacked for what they did to Joan of Arc. However, that leads Müller to the wholly unwarranted conclusion that there was general agreement that she received a good trial![29]

Pius's account of Joan's fate goes like this: after she was captured, she was sold to the English and brought to Rouen, where she was diligently examined to see if she used sorcery or a demon, or whether there was some depravity in what she believed about the faith. Nothing worthy of correction could be found except for the male clothing that she wore, but this was not thought worthy of the death penalty. She was thrust into

[25] Joycelyne G. Dickinson Russell, "The Congress of Arras," *History* 40:1 (1955) 31–41, p. 32.

[26] Joycelyne G. Dickinson (Russell), *The Congress of Arras, 1435* (Oxford 1955), p. 17.

[27] Heribert Müller, "'Et sembloit qu'on oyst parler un angèle de Dieu': Thomas de Courcelles et le Councile de Bâle; ou, Le secret d'une belle ressuscitéeréussite?" *Comptes rendus des séances de l'Académie des Insciptions et Belles-Lettres* 147 (2003) 461–84, at pp. 461, 466–68.

[28] Ibid., pp. 462, 469–77.

[29] Ibid., p. 465.

prison under threat of death if she were to resume such garb. She was tempted by the guards, who brought her various pieces of armor, and she incautiously put them on, not realizing that she was putting on her death.[30]

It is credible, Pius adds, that the English after capturing her did not think themselves safe, fearing her escape, and therefore sought a reason for her death. At any rate, her judges, upon her resumption of male attire, condemned her to the flames as relapsed. "Thus died Joan," he concludes, "that astonishing and marvelous maid" (*Sic Johanna obiit, mirabilis et stupenda virgo*).[31] He does not implicate Church authorities in any way. He did nothing later to qualify this simple-minded account of her fate when editing his histories.

Cauchon divided the rest of his life between Lisieux and the Lisieux episcopal residence in Rouen, and it was there in Rouen, the scene of the crime, that he died on December 18, 1442. Whether his conscience ever troubled him about what he had done to Joan of Arc is not known. He was buried in Lisieux, where his body was discovered in 1931 in the chapel of the Blessed Virgin.[32]

11.5 Joan Judged a Demonic Sorceress

The Dominican heresy inquisitor Johannes Nider (d. 1438) included a number of accounts of demonic sorcery, including that of Joan of Arc, in his dialogue-treatise *Formicarius*, completed in Vienna in 1437–1438. He had been prior of the Dominicans in Basel when the Council opened there in 1431, and he stayed to attend it until late 1434 or early 1435.[33] It was there that he learned about Joan.

In response to the student-interlocutor's question whether good men had been deceived by sorceresses in their own day, the master (Nider himself) replied that he would repeat some cases he had heard by public report, concerning which he withheld his own judgment.[34] He began with a woman in Cologne who, just in the past year, claimed to be Joan of Arc, resurrected by God. After performing magic feats (tearing up a napkin and breaking a glass and restoring them), she was summoned by the heresy

[30] Pius, *Commentarii* 6.10, p. 387; Quicherat 4:517; Gragg, p. 442.

[31] Ibid.

[32] Favier, *Pierre Cauchon*, pp. 553–54.

[33] See Michael D. Bailey and Edward Peters, "A Sabbat of Demonologists: Basel, 1431–1440," *The Historian* 63 (2003) 375–96, pp. 382–83.

[34] Johannes Nider, *Formicarius* [1438] (Strasbourg 1517), book 5, chapter 8, fol. 81vb.

inquisitor, but refused to appear and escaped his judgment but not his excommunication. She wound up living as a priest's concubine in Metz, thereby showing by what spirit she was led.[35]

As for Joan of Arc herself, who was active less than ten years before this; she was famed for her prophetic spirit and the power of her miracles. She dressed in male clothes, in token that she was sent by God to assist King Charles in securing his kingdom. After many feats, she finally even sent threatening letters to the Bohemians, among whom were many heretics. Thenceforward, all sorts of layfolk and ecclesiastics began to wonder what spirit she followed, whether it was diabolical or divine. Great men wrote treatises about her, expressing opinions about her not only diverse but also adverse.[36]

"But after she had helped and strengthened King Charles in his realm in many ways for a number of years, finally—by God's will, it is believed—through an army of Englishmen she was captured and imprisoned."[37]

"But then professors of both divine and human law were invited and summoned in a great multitude, and she was examined for many days. And, as I heard from Master Nicolas L'Ami, licentiate in theology, who was the emissary of the University of Paris, she finally confessed that she had a familiar angel of God—who, in the judgment of the most learned men, was judged to be an evil spirit, by means of many conjectures and proofs. By this spirit she had become, as it were, a sorceress (*velut maga*), and they permitted her to be consumed in flames by secular authority."[38]

Nicolas L'Ami was a canon of Beauvais, who had attended Cauchon's proceedings as an assessor only once, on March 3, at the last public session of interrogation,[39] after which he departed to Basel for the council.[40] In the questioning that occurred on March 3, there was only a brief

[35] Ibid.

[36] Ibid.

[37] Ibid., fols 81vb–82ra: "Postquam autem regem Carolum in multis juvisset et firmasset regno annis quibusdam, demum, nutu ut creditur divino, per Anglicorum armatum capta est et incinerata [*lege* incarcerata]."

[38] Ibid., fol. 82ra: "Accersitis autem et vocatis in magna multitudine magistris tam divini quam humani juris, multis diebus examinata est. Et, prout a magistro Nycholao Amici, licentiato in theologia, audivi, qui ambasiator fuit Universitatis Parisiensis, tandem ipsa fassa est se habere familiarem Dei angelum, qui, judicio literatissimorum virorum, judicatus est esse malignus spiritus, ex multis conjecturis et probationibus; per quem spiritum velut magam effectam, ipsam ignibus per publicam justiciam consumi permiserunt."

[39] LR 90.

[40] Tisset, 2:406.

discussion of how Saints Michael, Gabriel, Catherine, and Margaret looked when Joan saw them.[41] But, of course, L'Ami could have been informed by other assessors joining the council later, notably Nicolas Midi, who arrived in 1434,[42] like Cauchon. Loiseleur arrived in 1435.[43]

Nider says that L'Ami also told him of two women in Paris who claimed to have been sent by God to help Joan, whereupon they were arrested as sorceresses by the heresy inquisitor of France. After being examined by many doctors of theology, they were found to have been deceived by the evil spirit. One of them agreed and abjured, but the other did not, and she was burned.[44] So perhaps it was L'Ami who had sorcery on the brain and distorted the account of Joan's trial. However, since Nider says that the letter that the king of England sent to the emperor gave a similar account, the distortion more likely lay with Nider.[45]

11.6 First Investigations Into Joan's Trial

It was not for almost twenty years, until the French recovery of Rouen, that there were serious attempts to overturn Joan's conviction. King Charles has been blamed by historians for his lack of zeal, both for not rescuing her after her capture, and for delaying any action against her conviction and execution. Pierre Duparc argues in the king's exoneration that, just as a rescue from Rouen would have had little chance of success, so too a "retrial" would have been severely hampered while Rouen was still in English hands and its pro-English clergy still in power, and necessary documents and witnesses unavailable.[46] But that hardly justifies the nearly two decades of failure to speak out against the injustice that was done to Joan.

11.6.1 Professor Bouillé's Codicil, *1449*

Once Rouen was captured, Charles did move quickly, but only at the urging of a pro-French theologian named Guillaume Bouillé, dean of the

[41] FM 91–92, LR 91–92.
[42] Tisset, 2:417–18.
[43] Ibid., 2:414.
[44] Nider, fol. 82ra.
[45] Ibid. "...et prout de hac historia rex Anglie nostro imperatori Sigismondo satis late scriptotenus historiam innotuit."
[46] Duparc, *Procès*, 5:3–5.

cathedral chapter of Noyon, a prominent master at the University of Paris, in his written defense of Joan. Bouillé called his treatise a *codicillus* (i.e., a small *codex* or book),[47] and it was probably composed around the time that the English withdrew from Rouen on October 19, 1449; it must have resulted in Charles's commissioning him on February 15 in the following year to undertake an investigation of Joan's trial. In the commission, Charles calls Bouillé his beloved and faithful counselor,[48] and, in fact, Bouillé was in residence at the king's court in Tours, serving as the University's emissary, at the very time of the capture of Rouen.[49]

Bouillé composed his *Codicillus*, which he dedicated to the exaltation of the house of France, with the express intention of urging jurists to investigate the iniquitous judgment of the deceased Pierre Cauchon, then bishop of Beauvais, which convicted Joan as a heretic and invoker of demons.[50] He added that the royal silence on this matter created a stain on the king's honor, as if he had actively supported a heretic and invoker of demons. Therefore, the king should proclaim her innocence by having the trial examined by experts and its sentence against her denounced as iniquitous.[51]

Leaving it to legal experts to determine whether or not the *ordo judiciarius* was followed in the trial, Bouillé instead demonstrated by precise citations from the trial record, which he had in his hands, that there was no way in which Joan should have been found guilty of invoking demons, or wrongly wearing male clothing and taking up arms, or refusing to

[47] Guillaume Bouillé, *Codicillus…continens brevia…avisamenta ex originali processu…contra Johannam…Puellam…recollecta*, ed. NT 2:317–48 (I form the title from his first sentence). The *Codicillus* is also edited and translated (with subdivisions added) by Doncoeur and Lanhers, *Réhabilitation 1450*, pp. 65–122, as part of the Nullity dossier.

[48] Charles VII to Guillaume Bouillé, 15 February 1550, ed. Doncoeur and Lanhers, *Réhabilitation 1450*, pp. 33–34.

[49] Denifle, *Auctarium*, 2:778–79: on October 4, 1449, while Bouillé was at Tours, the University sent a message him to present their grievances to the king. Earlier on, according to the *Auctarium*, Bouillé had served three months as rector of the University (elected December 16, 1437) (col. 499 n. 3). His major benefice was the deanship of Noyon, petitioned in 1447 (col. 600 n. 7). He served several times as emissary of the University: to the king in 1446 (col. 667), to the duke of Orleans in 1448 (col. 748), and to the patriarch of Antioch/bishop of Poitiers, Jacques Jouvenal des Ursins, in September of 1449 (col. 775). Note that Jacques Jouvenal was succeeded by his brother Jean (future judge at Joan's retrial) as archbishop of Rheims in March of 1449. See Eubel, *Hierarchia*, 2:222.

[50] Bouillé, *Codicillus*, NT 2:317–18.

[51] Ibid., 2:318–19.

submit to the Church Militant.[52] He then detailed the falsity of the Twelve Articles concocted against her.[53] He ended by proving that she could not be judged as relapsed into heresy, since she had never fallen into heresy in the first place and had not even been suspected of heresy.[54]

11.6.2 Bouillé's Seven Depositions, 1450

Charles issued his commission to Bouillé in Rouen on February 15, 1450. All that survives from the inquest are the depositions of seven witnesses, taken in Rouen on March 4 and 5: four Dominican friars, namely, Isambart de Lapierre, Jean Toutmouillé, Martin Ladvenu, and Guillaume Duval, the notary Guillaume Manchon, the urban dean Jean Massieu, and Cauchon's first assistant interrogator, Jean Beaupère, one of the Paris Six, who was also a canon of Rouen.[55]

Duval is listed in the Latin Record as having attended only once, on March 27 1431, the day on which the formal trial began with Estivet presenting his charges against Joan.[56] Duval recounts how his colleague Lapierre attempted to coach Joan in her answers, and how Lapierre was furiously reproached for it later that day by the earl of Warwick.[57]

Manchon tells of another time when two of the other friars, Lapierre and Ladvenu, incurred Warwick's wrath, and Cauchon's, too: one time when Jean Lafontaine was substituting for Cauchon, and, accompanied by Lemaistre as judge, asked Joan about submitting to the Church. The friars explained the general council to her, and advised her to submit to it, and she agreed. When Cauchon found out, he was furious not only with Lapierre and Ladvenu, but also with Lafontaine and Lemaistre for being complicit. Lafontaine fled the city, and Lemaistre had to intercede for the friars. Cauchon thereafter made it a policy never to let Lemaistre see Joan without accompanying him.[58]

[52] Ibid., 2:319–36. On p. 334, he invokes the principle that the Church does not judge hidden things (*cum Ecclesia maxime de occultis non judicet*).

[53] Ibid., 2:336–47.

[54] Ibid., 2:348.

[55] Ed. Doncoeur and Lanhers, *Réhabilitation 1450: L'enquête ordonnée par Charles VIII in 1450*, pp. 31–57.

[56] LR 185. Courcelles gives his name as Johannes Valée. See Tisset, 2:398.

[57] Doncoeur and Lanhers, *Réhabilitation 1450*, p. 47.

[58] Ibid., p. 50.

Earlier in his deposition Manchon gives the first of his accounts of Auditor Lohier's objections against the validity of the proceedings.[59]

A main theme in the depositions of Lapierre, Toutmouillé, and Ladvenu concerns the reasons for Joan's condemnation as relapsed into heresy and sentenced to death, namely her resumption of male clothes. Joan blamed it all on Cauchon for committing her back to a secular instead of church prison. She had put the male clothes on to protect herself from an English magnate who was threatening to violate her.[60] Cauchon bragged to Warwick that it was all over when he left the prison that day. It is interesting the way that Ladvenu phrases it: "…the day in which she was judged to be relapsed by the said bishop *and many others* because she was found in prison *to have taken on men's clothes* again."[61] The only other judge was Friar Lemaistre. But the assessors, who included Lapierre and Ladvenu himself, participated in the judgment, because they lacked the courage to protest against it, and he confirmed that the declaration of heresy was only for the paltry reason of cross-dressing, and not for the other trumped up reason of communicating with infernal spirits.

The Bouillé hearings, for some reason, halted after only two days, and nothing more was forthcoming from the king's side, or even from Bouillé.

The most valuable witness at this time would have been Lemaistre himself. Whether he was on Bouillé's list of future witnesses will never be known. He will last be heard of just before the next inquest begins. Perhaps by that time the investigators will be thinking of him as a defendant!

11.6.3 Estouteville-Bréhal Hearings, 1452

Two years later, Cardinal Guillaume d'Estouteville, who at the time was serving as papal legate to France (sent by Pope Nicholas V, who succeeded Eugene IV in 1447), conducted a "field inquisition" into Joan's trial and condemnation, in conjunction with Jean Bréhal, OP, Inquisitor of Heretical Depravity for Northern France. This latter position, of course, had been held in Joan's time, by Jean Graverent, who had deputized the reluctant Jean Lemaistre to serve as vice-inquisitor in the diocese of

[59] Ibid., pp. 48–49.

[60] Ibid., p. 37 (Lapierre), cf. 38–39 (Toutmouillé), 43 (Ladvenu).

[61] Ibid. p. 43: "…illa die in qua pro relapsa ab episcopo prefato et aliis multis judicabatur propterea quia in carceribus habitum virilem resumpsisse invenerant…." The French version on p. 42 is similar.

Beauvais, hence as co-judge with Cauchon. Bréhal, like Graverent, was a theologian, and prior of the Dominicans of Paris. His appointment as inquisitor had probably taken place only a short time before he was commissioned with Estouteville to investigate the trial that had convicted Joan.[62] The resulting investigative process in 1452, which was truncated, would be incorporated into the Trial of Nullity in 1456, and it was thereby preserved for our inspection.[63]

The current archbishop of Rouen, in place since 1444, was Raoul Roussel, an old ally of the English occupiers. As we recall, his participation in Joan's prosecution was somewhat ambiguous; but he became more decisive against her at the end: he led the way to her execution in saying that she should be convicted of heresy if she did not repent. After the liberation of the city from the English, he swore allegiance to Charles VII (in 1450), and he received Cardinal d'Estouteville when he arrived in the city in 1452, but he took no part in the investigation into her condemnation.[64]

The cardinal and inquisitor issued a citation in Rouen dated May 4, 1452, naming twenty persons to be summoned and deposed on articles formulated by their promotor, later identified as Guillaume Prévosteau. Prévosteau, who will appear prominently later, was not a canon lawyer, but licensed in civil law.[65] The articles can be summarized as follows:

1) Bishop Pierre Cauchon held a trial against Joan, whom he hated because she fought against the English, and he sought her death by all the means he could.
2) Cauchon purchased Joan, a prisoner of war, for the English for a great sum.
3) The English feared Joan greatly and desired her death.
4) Cauchon promised the English that Joan would be kept in their prison in Rouen Castle, not in a Church prison.
5) Cauchon was not a legitimate judge against Joan, and she frequently protested against him.
6) Joan was known to be a good Catholic, frequently going to confession and hearing mass.

[62] Belon-Balme, *Jean Bréhal*, p. 12.
[63] NT 2:176–244.
[64] Tisset, 2:422.
[65] NT 1:179–80, 191; see p. 167: Prévosteau was *licenciatus in jure civili.*

7) Joan frequently submitted her deeds to the judgment of the Church and to the pope, and her words seemed to come from a good rather than bad spirit.
8) When Joan was questioned about submitting to the Church, she understood her interrogators to mean the clergy favoring the English.
9) She was condemned as relapsed even though she was willing to submit to the Church.
10) After she was condemned to recant and to put on female dress, she was forced to put on male clothing, whereupon her judges declared her relapsed, for they wished her death, not her return to the Church.
11) Even though the judges knew that she submitted herself to the judgment of the Church and that she was a faithful Catholic, they condemned her as a heretic to death by fire, whether because they favored the English or because they were intimidated by them.
12) All of the above, concerning the condemnation of Joan by the hatred and disfavor of the judges, was and is common and notorious knowledge in Rouen and in the whole of France.[66]

Five persons had already been questioned on these articles on May 2 and May 3.

On May 6, Cardinal Estouteville announced that he was leaving Rouen, and he appointed as his substitute in these proceedings Philip de Larose, treasurer of Rouen.[67] Thereupon Promotor Prévosteau "added other articles"—or, rather, he substituted a new set of twenty-seven articles. Thirteen additional witnesses were interviewed upon them, as well as four of the five original witnesses, including Guillaume Manchon and Martin Ladvenu, beginning on May 8. I sum up the articles as follows:

1) The English hated Joan and thirsted after her death.
2) They feared her and sought to deliver her to death.
3) They took her here to Rouen, put her in prison, and instituted a trial of faith against her.
4) All participants in the trial, including judges, confessors, consultants, and the promotor, acted under extreme fear of the English.

[66] NT 1:177–79.
[67] NT 1:190–91.

5) The notaries too acted in fear and could not record Joan's responses truthfully.
6) They were compelled to omit things favorable to her and add contrary statements that she did not make.
7) No one dared to counsel or defend her; some who spoke in her favor were threatened.
8) She was kept chained in a lay prison and forbidden all counsel.
9) Even though she was a simple girl of nineteen and not knowledgeable in the law, she ably defended herself.
10) Some English, pretending to counsel her, urged her not to submit to the judgment of the Church, in order to avoid death.
11) To catch her in her words, examiners asked her difficult questions to which she did not know the answers.
12) They fatigued her with long questioning in order to catch out something sinister in her answers.
13) She often asserted that she wished to hold nothing against the Catholic faith and to renounce anything in her words and deeds against faith.
14) She many times said that she submitted herself to the judgment of Church and pope.
15) The English did not permit such words of submission to be recorded.
16) Joan never said that she was unwilling to submit to Holy Mother Church, or the Church Militant.
17) If she did say something about not submitting to the Church, the promotor himself admitted that she understood the Church spoken of to be the clergy favoring the English.
18) The original French record of the proceedings was greatly distorted and falsified when translated into Latin.
19) The proceedings were held and sentence given under duress and intimidation.
20) As a result, the proceedings were vitiated and mendacious in many ways.
21) The proceedings and sentence were invalid and unjust, because the *ordo juris* was not followed and the judges had no jurisdiction over Joan.
22) They were also invalid because Joan was denied all means of defense.
23) Although the judges knew that she had submitted herself to the Church and was a faithful Catholic, and allowed her to go to

Communion, they condemned her as a heretic to be burned because of their favor toward the English or out of fear of them.

24) With no further sentence by a secular judge, the English led her to execution.
25) Joan breathed the name of Jesus to the last and moved everyone to tears.
26) The English procured all this because they feared Joan, and also to defame the French king.
27) All of the above was held by public fame and was notorious in the diocese of Rouen and in the whole of France.[68]

The garrulous and repetitive new articles notably reduced Cauchon's blame and increased that of the English, with emphasis upon their intimidation of the participants. Only one crime alleged against Joan was referred to, refusal to submit to the Church. In the first set, the issue of male clothing was at least mentioned as the excuse for the judgment of relapse, whereas in the new set it was not named at all, nor were the charges of invoking demons or idolatry or anything else, and the relapse-judgment itself went unnoticed. Article 21 stated that the *ordo juris* was not followed but no specifics of violated rules were given, except the general ones of not allowing defenses and not disallowing enemies.

One of the new interviewees was the Augustinian friar Jean Lefèvre, licensed in theology, who had been an assiduous attendee at the proceedings against Joan, beginning with her first appearance on February 21 (in 1441 he was consecrated as an auxiliary bishop for the diocese of Rouen).

The interviews were completed on May 10, 1452,[69] and on May 22 Estouteville wrote to Charles VII that Inquisitor Bréhal and Dean Bouillé would report the results to him.[70] According to the modern Dominican scholars who documented Bréhal's career, Marie-Joseph Belon and François Balme, the king expressed his great satisfaction, but thought it necessary to put the matter in the hands of the pope; and after Estouteville went on to Bourges, in early July, he advised Bréhal to continue his efforts and collect opinions from leading theologians and canonists.[71] But they offer no documentation, except to show that the king contributed £100

[68] NT 1: 192–96.
[69] NT 1:250.
[70] Belon-Balme, *Jean Bréhal*, p. 24.
[71] Ibid., p. 25.

then to the cause, and another £27 in August, when Estouteville and the king were in Bourges. They conjecture that Bréhal did not return to Paris but stayed on with the cardinal in Bourges and wrote his *Summarium* there (see next chapter).[72] In December 1542, Bréhal was with Estouteville in Lyons, and in that month another royal grant (of £37.17) was given to Bréhal for investigating Joan's trial of faith.[73]

The cardinal must have soon departed for Rome, where he is recorded as present on January 3, 1453.[74] Just days earlier, on December 31, Archbishop Roussel of Rouen died. Because of a dispute among the canons in electing his successor, Pope Nicholas appointed Estouteville on April 20. He took the post on July 9 through his proctor, the archbishop of Narbonne, over the objections of the canons. The pope mollified the canons by promising them on November 16 of that year that they could elect whomever they wished when the cardinal died (but that did not happen until thirty years later, in 1483). The cardinal made a solemn entry in person on July 28 (presumably in the year following, 1454).[75] Perhaps the canons who survived from the time of Joan's conviction and burning were fearful that with the cardinal as their archbishop their shameful role in the affair would be more likely to be held against them and retribution sought. However, even though the trial would be held in Rouen in 1455 and 1456, Estouteville does not seem to have taken part in the proceedings, which never referred to him under his present title of Archbishop of Rouen. All the signs are that he abandoned Joan.

Fortunately, however, the representative of the Holy Inquisition this time proved to be a stalwart on the side of righteousness. Jean Bréhal would prove to be a tireless champion on Joan's behalf until he achieved victory.

[72] Ibid., pp. 25–26.
[73] Ibid., p. 51
[74] Ibid., p. 50.
[75] *Gallia christiana* 11 (Paris 1759), col. 90.

CHAPTER 12

Expert Opinions on Joan's Conviction Produced, 1452–1454

12.1 Inquisitor Bréhal's Summary to Friar Leonard of Vienna

On the very day that Archbishop Roussel died, December 31, 1452, Jean Bréhal wrote from Lyons to another Dominican friar named Leonard, professor of theology at the University of Vienna, asking his advice in the name of the king on the nature of the trial in which Joan was convicted.[1] He states the case thus: "His majesty believes that his honor was gravely damaged in the past by his enemies, the English, because [they captured] a certain simple girl, a virgin, who first waged war for his side under God's guidance—as is proved by almost irrefutable evidence—[and] they proceeded against her in a trial of faith, to the ultimate extent of hostilely burning her to death under a judgment of the faith, to the slander of the king and his realm; therefore His Royal Majesty very much wishes to determine the truth of this sentence and judgment."[2] He commissioned

[1] The letter is edited by Quicherat, *Procès*, 2:70–71, and also by Belon and Balme, *Jean Bréhal*, pp. 55–56. The latter authors correct the year from 1453 to 1452 (pp. 57–58), and identify the recipient as Leonard Huntpüchler de Brixenthal (pp. 52–55). For a French translation see Jean-Baptiste-Joseph Ayroles, *La vraie Jeanne d'Arc*, 5 vols. (Paris 1890–1902), 1:238–29.

[2] Belon and Balme, *Jean Brehal*, pp. 55–56: "Nam Majestatis sue decus per hostes suos Anglicos in eo permaxime ab olim per enormiter lesum existimat, quia quamdam simplicem puellam et virginem, que divino nutu, ut prope irrefragabili comprobatur evidentia, rem

H. A. Kelly, *The Trial and Retrial of Joan of Arc*, The New Middle Ages, https://doi.org/10.1007/978-3-032-07887-2_12

him, the inquisitor of France, to send "legitimate documents on the trial and faithful extracts" to learned persons everywhere, especially outside of France, to exclude all partisanship. He urges Friar Leonard, for the honor of their Order and the commendation of his own royal worthiness, to write and decide something in the matter. Doubtless this was just one of several such letters that Bréhal wrote to scholars, presumably experts in law as well as in theology.

By "faithful extracts," Bréhal may have meant nothing more than his own *Summarium*,[3] which comprised six principal articles that needed to be discussed, each consisting of a fact or seeming fact derivable from her statements, or pertinent sample of such statements, and a question as to whether they justified conviction on the charges stated in the sentence. I summarize the articles as follows:

1) She said that she saw apparitions and corporal visions. Should she thereby have been found guilty of being a lying confabulator, pernicious seducer, presumptuous, light of belief, superstitious, invoker of demons, diviner, and blasphemer against God and saints, as stated in the sentence?
2) She predicted some events. Are the above charges justified because of this?
3) She showed reverence to her apparitions. Does this justify the charges of invoking demons and idolatry?
4) She wore male clothing and engaged in war. Does this justify finding her guilty of contempt of the sacraments, violator of divine law and ecclesiastical law and sanctions, an apostate, seditious, and cruel?
5) She seemed to refuse to submit herself to the judgment of the Church Militant concerning her deeds and statements. Do her actual statements (including her frequent wish to be taken to the pope) show that she was schismatic, multiply erring in faith, rashly delinquent toward Holy Church, expressly and obstinately refusing with a hardened mind to submit herself to the correction and judgment of Holy Mother Church, excommunicated and heretical?

bellicam pro ejus sorte pridem gessit, [ceperunt, et] sub causa fidei adversus eam processerunt, quin imo ad extremum sub ipso fidei judicio, in regis et regni vituperium, istam hostiliter incendio exstinxerunt; quocirca regia Majestas summopere cupit ipsius sententie et rei judicate comperire veritatem."

[3] Bréhal's *Summarium* is edited and annotated by Belon and Balme, *Jean Bréhal*, pp. 28–46.

6) After her abjuration, or revocation, she resumed male clothing and again adhered to the apparitions which she had publicly renounced. From her statement, was she rightly considered pertinacious and truly relapsed, and condemned as an incorrigible heretic and delivered to the secular arm?

12.2 Lelli and Pontano to Friar Leonard

We see that there is nothing in Bréhal's summary about who the judges were—notably that one of them was a fellow Dominican friar, exercising the position of inquisitor of heretical depravity. He may well have considered that such matters were more suitably put to experts in law rather than in theology. He did, however, include with his letter and *Summarium* the treatments made by the two canonists that Cardinal Estouteville had brought with him from Rome, namely, Teodoro dei Lelli (or de Leliis or Lellis), an auditor or judge of the Rota (like Jean Lohier, who objected to Cauchon's procedures at the time of Joan's trial), and Paolo Pontano, an advocate in the papal consistory.[4]

The proper title of Lelli's treatise, according to Belon and Balme, was *A Consultation in Favor of Joan, Commonly Called the Maid, and a Defense of Her Concerning the Charges Contained in the Trial Produced Against Her.*[5] Like Bréhal's summary, it deals mainly with her alleged wrongdoings, though this time with the Twelve Articles concocted against her and sent out to the University theologians and canonists and other consultants. He says at the beginning that even a cursory reading shows that they were not fairly and sincerely constructed, and that therefore the consultant who relied on them was deceived.[6]

It is only at the end that he lists, very briefly, the legal considerations for nullity, but only as topics for discussion, not opinions of his own.[7] I summarize:

[4] Belon and Balme, *Jean Bréhal*, p. 51 n. 3. I follow their account of the treatises given on pp. 46–50. According to Beaurepaire, "Recherches," pp. 417–18, Lelli and Pontano were sent to Rouen to adjudicate an appeal to the pope by Observant Franciscans (Cordeliers) in Rouen who had been excommunicated and imprisoned in 1450 by Archbishop Raoul Roussel.

[5] Ibid., p. 47: *Consultatio ad favorem Johanne vulgo dicte la Pucelle ejusque defensio super capita contenta in processu contra ipsam efformato*. It is printed by Quicherat, *Procès*, 2:22–58.

[6] Lelli, *Consultatio*, p. 22.

[7] Ibid., pp. 56–58.

1) Whether the bishop of Beauvais, who favored the English, was a competent judge of Joan, just because she was taken captive in his diocese.
2) If so, whether he should have been replaced, seeing that at many points she seemed to recuse him, and given that, before she began to respond, she asked for prelates on her side to be present.
3) Whether the case should have been remitted to the pope by the judges, seeing that she said she submitted to him and insistently asked to be sent to him, in a cause of faith, of major import.
4) Whether the proceedings were nullified when, after the bishop said that he would conduct them with the inquisitor, he proceeded instead with his vicar for over two months, during which time Joan was examined.
5) If the proceedings were null for this reason, whether the vice-inquisitor could ratify them.
6) Whether calumny and iniquity openly appear in the proceedings, seeing that Joan was handed over for punishment by illicit pacts and a sum of money sent by the bishop, the judge, to the king of England himself, with Joan protesting; furthermore, she was kept in a secular jail, as noted throughout the proceedings, guarded by armed soldiers, continuously shackled and injured (*macerata*) in prison, refused defense opportunities, regularly accused with a multitude of perplexing questions, as seen in the *Summarium*:[8] Does all this show the calumny and injustice of those judging her?
7) Whether Joan should be considered relapsed, since she said that she understood nothing of the text of abjuration, and seeing that the advice of a majority of the assessors was not followed, i.e., that the text be read again to her and explained with admonitions; instead she was hurried to judgment, or, rather, execution; and seeing that she had asked before to be sent to the pope, which the judges refused to allow; also her reassumption of male clothing was more proper when among men, and the promise was not kept that she would be allowed to go to mass with her chains removed; also she offered to wear female clothing if put in a better prison. Lelli adds at the end, referring to witnesses in the field inquisition initiated by Cardinal Estouteville in Rouen in May of 1452, that witnesses

[8] Quicherat says that this *Summarium* is to Lelli's second treatise, which Belon and Baume believe to have been produced and given to Bréhal only in 1454 in Rome (*Jean Bréhal*, p. 68).

testified that she did take on female dress, but that it was taken from her so that she would be declared relapsed.

Lelli also cites the Rouen depositions when defending Joan's use of male clothing.[9] He adds that, according to relevant law, male clothing was prohibited for women only when superstitious or indecent, not when worn for good reason or necessity.[10] He does not raise objections to giving weight to a mundane practice like this in a heresy trial that results in executing the defendant by fire.

In his own *Summarium*, Lelli sums up the proceedings and occasionally raises doubts of the sort mentioned in his *Consultatio*, for instance, Cauchon's alleged jurisdiction over Joan as bishop of Beauvais,[11] the seemingly fraudulent failure to include the preliminary investigation in the record,[12] the missing inquisitor and vice-inquisitor,[13] as well as Joan's warnings to Cauchon, which seem to reject his jurisdiction.[14] On the original day of judgment, May 24, Joan says that she had previously responded that all of her words and deeds should be taken to Rome to the pope; but since this previous response is not in the record, one may justly suspect that it was fraudulently omitted. When she repeated then and there that she wished to be sent to the pope, the answer, about ordinary judges in their dioceses, was perhaps deceitful, and contrary to the authority of the Holy See.[15] Lelli is astonished that the counsel of the majority of the assessors—that the text of the abjuration, which Joan said she did not understand, be reviewed before her—was not followed; rather, without further ado she was hurried to judgment and to the cruel death of fire. This should be noted as impugning the trial.[16]

Unlike his predecessor at the Rota, Jean Lohier, Lelli took no notice of the failure of the promotor to charge Joan before she was interrogated.

[9] Lelli, *Consultatio*, p. 30.

[10] Ibid., p. 33.

[11] Lelli, *Summarium*, ed. Pierre Lanéry d'Arc, *Mémoires et consultations en faveur de Jeanne d'Arc par les juges du procès deehabilitation* (Paris 1889), pp. 17–33, at p. 17.

[12] Ibid., p. 19.

[13] Ibid., pp. 19–20, 21, 28.

[14] Ibid., p. 25.

[15] Ibid., p. 30.

[16] Ibid., p. 33.

Paolo Pontano's *Consultatio*[17] resembles Lelli's, in that most of it dealt with the Twelve Articles that were sent to consultors before adding brief legal objections. He spends the most time on the question of submitting to the Church,[18] and cites deponents from both sessions of the field inquisition set up by Cardinal Estouteville and Inquisitor Bréhal in May of 1452; and, like Lelli, he completed his treatise in time for Bréhal to send it to Vienna to Friar Leonard von Brixenthal at the end of the year.

At the end, he briefly expresses legal doubts and raises questions as to whether the proceedings against Joan were null and void, as follows:

1) Cauchon had no jurisdiction?
2) The inquisitor's power of delegation was doubtful?
3) Cauchon proceeded alone through important acts?
4) Cauchon often used deputies to examine Joan in a grave criminal trial?
5) As proved in the second session of the recent proceedings, great fear was brought to bear upon the vice-inquisitor and others?
6) Joan recused Cauchon as not competent, suspect, and her capital enemy?
7) Joan submitted to the pope and the general council?
8) A case of such gravity, concerning apparitions, and its doubtfulness as a cause of faith, was reserved to the Holy See, especially since Joan appealed to the pope?
9) Joan was kept in a secular prison and inhumanely treated by armed capital enemies?
10) She was denied counsel, and was under age?
11) Her young age exempted her from heresy (which was dubious here), at least for relaxing the penalty?
12) The terrorizing and banishing of persons who wished to counsel her?
13) Her request to see and discuss the articles of abjuration was denied?
14) The notaries were prohibited from recording her excuses?
15) The articles sent to consultors were mendacious?

[17] *Consultatio domini Pauli Pontani*, ed. Lanéry d'Arc, *Memoires*, pp. 55–71. Lanéry, like Quicherat, takes it to be later than Pontano's *Opinio*, whereas Belon and Balme, *Jean Bréhal*, p. 49, judge it to be earlier.

[18] Pontano, *Consultatio*, pp. 62–67.

16) Difficult questions, captious interrogations, with counsel denied?
17) Spies urged her not to submit to the Church, and her female clothes were stolen?
18) There was no preliminary inquiry about her infamy?
19) The characterization of her in the abjuration text and the sentence of condemnation, namely, as "a mendacious simulator of divine revelations and apparitions, a pernicious seducer, presumptuous, superficial in belief, superstitious, a diviner, blasphemous against God and His saints, contemptuous of His sacraments, a violator of divine law and the sacred doctrines and sanctions of the Church; seditious, cruel, an apostate and schismatic, multiply erring in our faith, offending against God and Holy Church in many ways; expressly, with hardened mind, obstinately, and pertinaciously refusing to submit herself to the Church, the pope, and the general Council; pertinacious, obstinate, excommunicated, and heretical,"[19] is not justified from the contents of her trial?

Pontano's other treatise, his *Opinio*,[20] follows a similar pattern, and also draws on the May inquest. However, it is abundantly argued through juristic citations, and it begins each of the topics scholastically, first arguing superficially for Joan's guilt and then heavily for her innocence. For instance, regarding the opening topic of her apparitions, Pontano states that at first sight they seem to have come from evil spirits, for they were authenticated by no miracle or scriptural reference; they urged warfare and bloodshed, in keeping with the Devil; and waging is forbidden to women. However, he continues, the opposite seems truer, and then argues that private revelations are not judged by the Church, and there were many signs that her visions came from good spirits; moreover, Joan was a virgin, very humble and devout; the messages she was given were virtuous; and she died a good Catholic death, crying out the name of Jesus in the midst of the flames. She even performed miracles, by accurately foretelling the future; and, in fact, her very military success as an eighteen-year-old peasant girl was itself a miracle. The war she fought in was a just one. Private

[19] The sentence that Pontano quotes from here is the one that was interrupted by Joan and not actually delivered, recorded by Courcelles later (LR 313–34); the one actually given ends the list of crimes at "multiply erring in our faith" (LR 393).

[20] *Opinio Pauli Pontani, JUD et Advocati in Consistorio Sacro*, ed. Lanéry d'Arc, *Mémoires*, pp. 35–54.

revelations supersede other laws—for instance, excusing Jacob's lie or Samson's suicide—especially when, as in Joan's case, her pursuits were licit. Even granted that she was a victim of Satan transformed into an angel of light, she venerated her apparitions as good, as St Michael and Saints Catherine and Margaret. Finally, she was not pertinacious about the visions but submitted all to the judgment of the Church, as will be proved in the fifth doubt.[21]

He proceeds the same way in the matter of male clothing. In the third doubt he takes up her other deeds, while in the fourth he examines her words (most of her alleged crimes on this score, of course, were "committed" during the questioning before she was charged, which Pontano, like Lelli, does not point out). After a long defense of Joan on the fifth doubt, the question of submitting to the Church, Pontano takes up the sixth and last doubt, whether the trial was invalid because the *ordo juris* was not followed. Here he goes through most of the juridical deficiencies outlined in his *Consultatio*, with some citations listed for the first eight.

12.3 The Treatise of the New Chancellor of Paris, Robert Ciboule, January 2, 1453

Two days after Bréhal signed his letter to Laurence von Brixenthal and enclosed his summary of the trial, together with the treatises of the theologians Lelli and Pontano, a very important personage, the theologian, Master Robert Ciboule, signed his short treatise, *De Puella quadam Johanna*, that is, on January 2, 1453. Just two years before, in 1451, Ciboule had become the first person to hold the position of the chancellor of the Cathedral and University since Jean Gerson died in exile from Paris in 1429. Ciboule had aided Cardinal d'Estouteville in 1452 in reforming the University.[22] His treatise could be seen as an effort to undo the University's part in Joan's destruction.

Importantly, like Courcelles, Ciboule had been in his studies in the faculty of theology at the University of Paris at the time of Joan's trial (Ciboule started in 1430). But unlike Courcelles, he did not participate in the proceedings—Courcelles being the only non-doctored theologian from Paris to do so[23]—and, of course, neither were voting members when

[21] Ibid., pp. 35–42.
[22] Belon and Balme, *Jean Bréhal*, p. 59 n. 1.
[23] Müller, "Courcelles et Bâle," p. 464.

the theology faculty made its adverse conclusion in Joan's case. As we saw above, Ciboule represented the Faculty of Arts when Courcelles represented the theologians at the Congress of Arras in 1435. Rector of the University in 1437, Ciboule received his doctorate of theology in 1438. He undertook important missions for Charles VII in the years following. From 1447, he served as penitentiary for the Paris chapter, until he was appointed chancellor by the bishop, Guillaume Chartier (who would be one of the bishops in the Nullity Trial).[24]

In the dossier of official records that he compiled of the trial of 1455–1456, Bréhal included a collection of consultations, placing first the 1429 treatise of one of Ciboule's predecessors as chancellor of Paris, Jean Gerson,[25] and Ciboule's last,[26] before the verifications of all instruments and his own giant treatise. Like Lelli and Pontano, he drew on the entire record of the trial (presumably the Latin Record of Courcelles).

Ciboule's work is particularly significant because he is the first to analyze the trials held against Joan as an actual "cause of the faith," which should be limited to offenses against the faith—the only crimes heresy inquisitors, "inquisitors of the faith," have jurisdiction over. He says that he was ordered "to say something" about the trial by an irrefragable authority which he could not refuse. He limits himself to examining the final sentence, to see if it conforms to Joan's confessions and the convictions in the record, insofar as they concern infidelity and heresy, and also whether the trial was properly juridical.[27]

In concentrating on the sentence, it is as if Ciboule took up Pontano's final point of discussion.[28] He breaks it into fourteen separate charges. Most of them, he says, concern moral allegations, and have nothing to do with faith. For instance, fornication would not concern faith, unless one held that fornication was not a mortal sin.[29] The first name Joan is called in the sentence is a "mendacious inventor of visions," which, if true, would not automatically be connected with faith. The same with the second, a

[24] Philippe Contamine, "La réhabilitation de la Pucelle vue au prisme des *Tractatus super materia processus*: une propédeutique," in *De l'hérétique à la sainte: Les procès de Jeanne d'Arc revisités* (Acts 2009 Cerisy conference), ed. François Neveux (Caen 2016), pp. 177–96, n. 16.

[25] Jean Gerson, *Opusculum super facto Puelle*, NT 2:32–39.

[26] Robert Ciboule, *De Puella quadam Johanna*, NT 2:348–400.

[27] Ibid., p. 359.

[28] Ciboule, however, uses the sentence actually read on May 24, where the list of crimes ends with "multiply erring in our faith."

[29] Ibid., pp. 350–51.

"pernicious seducer," or the third, being "presumptuous." What about "light of faith"? That is usually a good thing, unless it means "easily believing things against the faith," which was not demonstrated in the case of Joan. Number 5, being "rash," is not against the faith. The sixth, "presumptuous diviner," implicates her with evil spirits, which can be eliminated through the discernment of spirits. Next, "blasphemy," is opposed to the confession of faith, or derogates from faith, but there is nothing in the trial record to justify this claim—a clear case where the sentence seems to be at odds with the truth. Number 8, "contemptuous of the sacraments," is contradicted throughout the record. The ninth, "violator of laws," is true of every sin, and is not specific to faith. Next, "being seditious," does not concern faith, nor does the next, being "cruel"—and certainly not verified in Joan.[30]

The last three charges, "apostate," schismatic," and "multiply erring from the faith," are obviously pertinent to a trial of the faith, and will be taken up. But, to begin with, no specifics are given of her alleged multiple errors, and none are deducible from her words and deeds. Any moral failings alleged in her do not count. The same would be true of any made-up visions. If they were true, they were not against faith.[31]

Her supposed refusal to submit to the Church is one of the strongest charges against her, but it has little merit. The questions on this point were captious and confusing. A simple person is not required to know all of the implications; besides, experts are divided on the subject. It is not surprising that contradiction can be found in her responses. But in spite of all this, her answers, it seems to Ciboule, show that she was led by a higher spirit than just by her natural intelligence.[32]

Secret things in general do not have to be submitted to the Church, and the Church does not pass public judgment on what is not public; but Joan did agree to submit everything.[33] Her answers did not violate the credal statement about "the Holy Catholic Church" (Ciboule here follows the Apostles' Creed, whereas it was the Nicene statement of "One Holy Catholic and Apostolic Church" that was always pressed against Joan). This statement does not require a belief in everything about the

[30] Ibid., pp. 351–58.
[31] Ibid., pp. 358–61.
[32] Ibid., pp. 384–85.
[33] Ibid., pp. 387–88.

Church, including its power of judging, but only that it exists.[34] When asked whether she believed that she was subject to the Church, she answered, "Yes, but to God first." Her faith was firm regarding this article, and it certainly cannot be said that she denied it with a hardened heart, as the Twelve Articles and the sentence untruly stated.[35]

What of the judgment of the Faculties of Theology and Canon Law of the University of Paris? According to Ciboule, all of the circumstances about their responses need to be carefully considered, but at least in the point about submission to the Church the notorious discrepancies between the Twelve Articles and Joan's responses is important.[36]

When she interrupted the sentence, she stated that she wished to hold what the Church held. Much of what was in the abjuration she was not convicted of. She did not swear off male clothes. As for the so-called relapse into infidelity, it was not possible, since there was no original lapse into infidelity established. Ciboule's conclusion is that she was not unfaithful, not schismatic, and not heretical, heresy being an error of the intellect that is obstinately held. In addition, of course, the trial was bad in both matter and form, notably because the judges were her enemies, and she was kept in an abusive prison.[37]

12.4 Critique of Canonist Jean de Montigny

Bréhal placed Bouillé's manifesto, which sparked the whole nullity effort, before Ciboule's treatise. Then, before that, he put the very important *Opinio* of the canon lawyer Jean de Montigny which best summed up the canonical deficiencies of the trial held against Joan.[38]

Montigny was a canon of the Paris cathedral chapter and a counselor of the secular high court, the Parlement de Paris. In addition to giving him his own *Summarium*, Bréhal let him have the whole trial record, but for scarcely four or five days. He also gave him Pontano's *Consultatio*, and asked him to respond to the first eighteen of Pontano's final questions.[39]

His first major point is that for a heresy trial there needs to be a heresy, something directly opposed to what a Catholic is bound to hold. Narrowly

[34] Ibid., pp. 388–90.
[35] Ibid., pp. 390–91.
[36] Ibid., p. 391.
[37] Ibid., pp. 394–99.
[38] *Opinio domini Johannis de Montigny, decretorum doctoris*, NT 2:266–317.
[39] Benon et Balme, *Jean Bréhal*, pp. 63–64. See Montigny, *Opinio*, p. 297.

speaking, according to the Archdeacon's *Rosarium*, Christian faith is what is affirmed at baptism, namely, the articles of the Apostles' Creed.[40] More generally, it refers to definitions made by the pope or councils on questions of faith. Most broadly, it refers to anything connected with such faith, whether defined or not. It is, of course, licit to express doubts about what is not defined. As for what is defined, he refers to the expanded creed of Innocent III in the Fourth Lateran Council, which stands at the beginning of the *Liber Extra*.[41] Therefore, assent or non-assent to revelations is not a matter for a heresy inquisition.[42] One reason for believing in such manifestations occurs if they are accompanied by outstanding salubrious works, such as Joan performed in raising the siege at Orleans and making true predictions. The visions most certainly should not have been the reason for dragging her into a trial of faith and for judging her to be a heretic.[43]

We must always keep in mind the primary meaning of the term: according to St Augustine, a heretic is one who for temporal good or vainglory or power invents or follows false new-fangled opinions.[44] If one wrongly believes that the Church holds something it does not, there is no heresy, as long as the error is not defended. Joan did not confess any error against the faith, and there was no proof against her, since no other proofs were presented apart from her confessions. And she expressly said that if she had ever said anything against the faith, she did not wish to maintain it, and asked clerics to show her in what way she had knowingly erred.[45]

Next, changing from long garments into short, that is, from female to male dress, cannot be the basis of a trial of faith. In Joan's case her garb was dictated by her mission to raise the siege of Orleans. According to legal maxim, "When one thing is allowed, so is everything necessary for it." Getting rid of female skirts was a *sine qua non* for soldiering.[46]

[40] Guido da Baisio's *Rosarium* (1300), widely used supplement to the Ordinary Gloss to Gratian's *Decretum* (I use the unfoliated edition of Strasbourg ca. 1475). Montigny is citing his comment on the canon *Canones*, D. 15 c.1 (CIC 1:34), where the first four general councils are discussed.

[41] Innocent III, *Firmiter credimus*, X 1.1.1 (CIC 2:5–6).

[42] Montigny, *Opinio*, pp. 267–69.

[43] Ibid., p. 272.

[44] Ibid., p. 273, citing the canon *Hereticus*: Gratian, *Decretum* C. 24 q. 3 c. 28 (CIC 1:998).

[45] Ibid., p. 279.

[46] Ibid., p. 280. He states the maxim thus: "Aliquo concesso, conceduntur omnia sine quibus" (With one thing conceded, all things are conceded without which [it is impossible].)

Similarly, Montigny continues, taking up arms in a just cause can hardly be seen to be a matter of heresy. Nor can the marks of veneration shown to her by the populace. If they praised her because they recognized the grace of God in her, it was all to the good.[47]

Now, then, even supposing that Joan was a heretic, was the trial conducted properly? To begin with, no matter concerning heresy had been turned up. Joan frequently recused Cauchon. His refusal to admit clerics on her side was also grounds for recusal. She often asked to consult the Holy See; and he should have submitted the case to the Holy See on his own. Besides, the Church does not judge secret matters.[48]

Joan had legitimate grievances in the proceedings which constituted matter for appeal, but she was young and did not understand the law; even if she had she would not have been able to exercise her rights, for she was constantly incarcerated and deprived of counsel. There was no preliminary proceeding to establish infamy of suspicion, which was grounds for appeal at the beginning. Montigny asserts that this was especially necessary in this case, for there was never any suspicion among respectable persons of any hint of heresy, but rather Joan was reputed to be faithful and Catholic.[49] He cites the legislation of Innocent III, the decretal *Cum oporteat*, which specifies that there is to be no inquiry into the truth of crimes until the defendant's infamy has been established, that is, reputable witnesses testifying that he is widely believed to be guilty of those crimes.[50]

He also cites Boniface VIII's two constitutions on the subject in his *Liber Sextus*, though it is not clear why he does so. The first, *Postquam*, says in effect that if a defendant spontaneously confesses a crime in court without first having his infamy established about it, he cannot complain that he was wrongly treated and appeal the case.[51] (Joan, of course, far from volunteering anything, was forced to say all sorts of things under oath which would be turned against her as crimes.) It confirms that the crimes being tried in inquisitions should first be shown to be publicly blamed on the defendant—which means, of course, that the crimes have to be specified at the beginning, before any questioning is undertaken. Boniface's second constitution, *Si is*, says that if a judge starts to inquire

[47] Ibid., pp. 284–85.
[48] Ibid., pp. 290–93.
[49] Ibid., pp. 293–94.
[50] Innocent III, *Cum oporteat*, X 5.1.19 (CIC 2:740–41).
[51] Boniface VIII, *Postquam*, *Sext* 5.1.1 (CIC 2:1069).

into a defendant's guilt of certain crimes without first establishing infamy, and the defendant makes no objection, there can be no appeal later.[52] Joan was not directly asked about any crimes for a long time, since Cauchon was fishing for evidence about unmentioned crimes, and also hoping for admissions that could be construed as crimes of erroneous belief. She repeatedly objected to the irrelevance of the questions, telling the interrogator to "pass on," and asking whether a question concerned the proceedings.[53]

Pope Boniface's main point in these two laws was that, if a guilty defendant unguardedly admits his own crime before he is properly accused of it, he has nobody but himself to blame. In bringing them up in connection with Joan, Montigny could have made the point that, even though Joan did not know the law, and did not have learned counsel, she instinctively knew that Cauchon's procedure was wrong and biased against her, and she abundantly fulfilled Pope Boniface's requirement that the defendant object against what the judge was doing, when she kept asking, "Is this part of your process?"

Montigny goes on to say that Joan was wrongly forced to answer all sorts of questions, whereas by law she should have been asked only about the crimes concerning the faith (*in fide*) that she had been "defamed" about, that is, suspected by the general populace to be guilty of.[54] According to Montigny, this was grounds for appeal, citing Innocent III's decree *Qualiter et quando*, from the Fourth Lateran Council, the Magna Carta of rules on inquisitorial procedure. The specific section of the decree noted by Montigny, *Debet*, reads thus: "The person against whom an

[52] Boniface VIII, *Si is*, *Sext* 5.1.2 (CIC 2:1069).

[53] See, for instance, the questioning of February 27, LR 69–70, and on March 1, LR 85–86, where, after three times rejecting questions as not pertinent to the process, she told them to ask the assessors on their oath whether it was pertinent, and they said that it was. Bréhal in his summary found it particularly shocking that their favor of the English could make them descend to such villainy. See Jean Bréhal, *Recollectio*, NT 2:405–600, p. 574.

[54] Montigny, *Opinio*, p. 294: "Cogebatur ad omnia inquisita, etiam quecumque et quantumcumque occulta, per juramentum respondere, et de respondendo generaliter et absolute quibuscumque interrogandis compellebatur, cum tamen de eis tantum debuisset per juramentum cogi ad respondendum de quibus erat diffamata, seu in fide suspecta aut notata." (She was forced to respond by oath to everything that was asked, even whatsoever was secret and insofar as it was secret, and compelled to reply in general and absolutely to all things that were to be asked of her, whereas she should have been forced to respond by oath only about those things concerning which she had been defamed, that is, suspected or blamed, in the faith.)

inquisition is to be conducted should be present, unless he should absent himself through contempt, and the articles of inquiry are to be explained to him, so that he may be able to defend himself."[55] Montigny therefore implies Lohier's basic objection, even though he does not phrase it in the same way, that Joan should have had the charges explained to her before she was questioned.

Montigny does note that there were appealable grievances in the way in which she was put under oath and compelled to respond to all sorts of questions, even about private and secret matters, and was constantly made to repeat her oaths.[56]

Montigny goes on to mention other grievances, namely, the biased summary of her confessions sent out for consultation with experts, denial of hearing mass (her male clothing was no excuse, he says, since the masses could have been held in private), and the command that she could speak to no one without Cauchon's specific permission. He returns to the point of abusive interrogation: there should not be repeated interrogation concerning one crime (*de delicto unius sepius inquiri non debet*), but in Joan's case there was constant doubled questioning of her to the very end. Although she repeatedly asked for copies of her replies and for advice in modifying them, all her requests were denied, including her desire to be taken to the pope. And through it all she was kept in a harsh secular prison.[57]

He takes up separately the questionable claim that Joan refused to submit to the Church. She sometimes understood the judges, whom she had rejected, to say that they were the Church to whom she was bound to submit. Such submission would entail a renunciation of the defenses belonging to defendants in virtue of natural law, as stated by the Clementine constitution *Pastoralis*.[58] Such a requirement by the judges to submit to the public judgment of the Church was completely fraudulent. The Church does not require submission in all things. Specifically, the Church

[55] Innocent III, *Qualiter et quando*, constitution 8 of the Fourth Lateran Council (CIC 2:745–47), §*Debet*: "Debet igitur esse presens is, contra quem facienda est inquisitio, nisi se per contumaciam absentaverit, et exponenda sunt ei illa capitula, de quibus fuerit inquirendum, ut facultatem habeat defendendi se ipsum." It goes on to say that the names of all witnesses are to be revealed, to reduce the possibility of slander, and the defendant is to be given the opportunity to rebut all charges.

[56] Ibid., pp. 294–95.

[57] Ibid., pp. 295–97.

[58] Clement V, *Pastoralis*, *Clem.* 2.11. 2 (CIC 2:1151–53), section *Ceterum* (fol.1153).

never judges secret matters in its public court. Another point: heresy inquisitors and bishops who falsely charge innocent persons with offenses against the faith are automatically excommunicated in virtue of the Clementine *Multorum*.[59] Again: even if there is vehement suspicion that a person is guilty of heresy (which was not true in Joan's case), it is not sufficient for a conviction of heresy itself.[60]

He proves that Joan in no way erred concerning the article *Unam sanctam Catholicam Ecclesiam*,[61] and argues that the sentences and abjuration were invalid in both matter and form. She did not understand the crimes named in the abjuration, and had admitted none of them. The final sentence of relapse was similarly not valid. There was no heresy to begin with, so there could not be a lapse into heresy. The whole trial was based on evident trickery and open calumny, especially in the matter of the fabricated articles.[62] Montigny then proceeds to answer specifically the eighteen questions posed by Pontano, though he begins by saying that they have all been answered by what he has already said.[63]

12.5 Basin, Bochard, Bourdeilles

Another jurist, Thomas Basin, was also asked to respond to Pontano's points. On becoming bishop of Lisieux in 1448, the second successor of Cauchon himself, Basin had taken an oath of allegiance to Henry VI at Windsor Castle, on February 3, 1448,[64] but then changed over to Charles VII when the city was captured in 1449. He performed the duty in a straightforward way, arguing first that the proceeding against Joan should not be annulled or nullified, as if it were originally valid, but rather declared ipso facto null and void, never having had any legitimacy. However, he adds further considerations to show that nullification is also in order (in case it is not found null from the beginning); and then he refutes specific

[59] Clement V, *Multorum*, *Clem.* 5.3.1 (CIC 2:1181–82).

[60] Montigny, *Opinio*, pp. 297–300. The last point is proved by citing Innocent III, *Litteras*, X 2.23.14 (CIC 2:357).

[61] Ibid., pp. 300–04.

[62] Ibid., pp. 304–07.

[63] Ibid., pp. 307–11.

[64] Document published in Thomas Basin, *Histoire des règnes de Charles VII et Louis XI par Thomas Basin*, ed. Jules Quicherat, 4 vols. (Paris 1455–1459), 4:158–60.

allegations against her. His treatise was included in the dossier in 1456.[65] Years later, he summed up her life and trials, as well as her exoneration, in the course of his history of Charles VII, as we will see below.

Jean Bochard, Bishop of Avranches, was likewise asked, by the judges, to contribute a comment, and was given Pontano's summary.[66] In defending her revelations, he mentions that one of his predecessors as bishop in his diocese received a revelation from St Michael, and in consequence a church was built in his honor in the place indicated by the archangel.[67]

Yet another prelate, Elie de Bourdeilles, Bishop of Périgueux, contributed a very lengthy defense, which was also added to the dossier.[68] He says that he was asked to do so by the king. He had access to a summary of the trial and the sentence, and he distinguished twenty different charges against Joan, all of which he argues were unfounded. He proceeds in the manner of scholastic theologians, first giving reasons why each charge seems plausible, and then decisively arguing against it. But he seems equally capable in his juristic as in his theological citations.

12.6 Montigny on Reversing Joan's Trial

At the end of his treatise, Montigny takes up the question of how to retract or revoke the trial that condemned Joan. Just as it is possible for persons reputed to be Catholic during their lifetimes to be declared heretics after they die, so too the reverse: persons declared heretics can be posthumously declared Catholic. It should take place in the Roman curia, to which Joan repeatedly submitted herself. There would thereby be no grounds for objecting to the venue.[69]

What form should the proceedings take? Surely the same sort of *ex officio* inquisition that was used against Joan should now be turned against Cauchon? Think of the trial of John Wyclif at the Council of Constance. The problem of dealing with a deceased defendant was handled by summoning, by means of citations posted on doors of Constance churches, persons to come forward and say why the memory and teachings of Wyclif should not be condemned. Since no one showed up, the council

[65] Thomas Basin, *Consulendo in materia condemnationis Johanne Puelle*, NT 2:157–219. He sets forth his rationale on pp. 157–58.

[66] *Opinio domini Johannis Bochardi Abrincensis episcopi*, NT 2:257–65.

[67] NT 2:262.

[68] Elie Bourdeilles, *Opus reverendi patris domini ElieHelie*, NT 2:40–156.

[69] Montigny, *Opinio*, pp. 311–12.

promotor accused all such persons of contempt of court. Then propositions culled from Wyclif's works were presented to the council and condemned. Next, witness depositions attesting to Wyclif's impenitent death were heard, and a final sentence of condemnation was passed, on May 4, 1415, declaring him to have been a pertinacious heretic who died in heresy, and ordering his body removed from consecrated ground.[70]

But instead, Montigny envisions Joan's case as a civil suit for damages, with plaintiffs and defendants (*agentes* and *defendentes*). Although there are many possible interested parties and all are to be heard, both in particular and in common, nevertheless for the present, it seems that those closest to Joan should be put before all others and admitted to such a trial, as prosecuting their injury in her miserable death.

As for the defendants, those to be summoned (*evocandi*), it should be the "judgers" (Montigny never refers to Cauchon and Lemaistre as judges, *judices*, since they were not legitimate, but rather as judgers, *judicantes*), especially the bishop, if they are still alive, or their successors in office or their heirs, who seem obliged to make restitution.[71] But in the case of their successors in office, it should be with the clause "if they believe it concerns them" (*si sua crederent interesse*).

There should be a narration of the iniquity of the trial and its defects aimed at a declaration of its nullity, or nullification or revocation, and, as a consequence, to declare Joan a Catholic and to have lived in a Catholic way and faithfully up to the day of her death, and to be held and reputed as such. Those who are summoned as defendants are to be condemned to make reparation for such great wickedness. If none appear, it would be suitable to summon a proctor of the king of England, even from the beginning, to be condemned along with them (*procuratorem regis Anglie non immerito etiam a principio processus vocandum, aut eumdem procuratorem, una cum ipsis, ad reparationem tante iniquitatis condemnandum*).

[70] Kelly, "Trial Procedures Against Wyclif," p. 21; Mansi, *Sacrorum conciliorum*, 27:629–36.

[71] Montigny, *Opinio*, p. 312. Here is his sentence, which I cannot make good sense of: "Quo vero ad vocandos, viderentur debere vocari judicantes, si superstites sint, aut eorum successores in dignitatibus et officiis, et heredes, si quos habent, presertim episcopus, qui anulum habuit, qui ad restitutionem eorum que habuit his—a quo causam habent—teneri videntur." (As for those to be summoned, it seems that the judgers should be called, if they are alive, or their successors in their dignities and offices, and their heirs, if they have any—especially the bishop, who had the ring—who seem to be bound to the restitution to them of those things that he had, for by him they have cause.)

There should also be some memorial (*signum*) for Joan, since nothing else can be done, but he leaves it, and what he has said above, to the judgment of the consistorial advocates of the Sacred Palace.[72] Pontano, of course, was one such.

At the end, he returns to some points that might be taken to derogate from her faith, and concludes that, whatever is to be said on these points, it can be concluded that she was not a heretic, and should not have been condemned as a heretic.[73]

[72] Ibid., pp. 312–13.
[73] Ibid., pp. 313–17.

CHAPTER 13

The Arc Family Sues at the Papal Court, 1455

13.1 Delayed Action

As will be seen, Montigny's plan of action was eventually followed, with important modifications. But nothing was done for some time. Cardinal Estouteville was back in Rome by the beginning of 1453, as we saw in Chapter 11, and doubtless his legal experts, Lelli and Pontano, returned with him. We just saw that Montigny suggested that Pontano and his colleagues in the papal consistory discuss what form the reversal of Joan's conviction should take. So what happened? Nothing is heard of the matter for over a year, and then only that, in May of 1454, a payment was made from the king to Bréhal of £100 for the business of Joan's trial of faith.[1]

13.2 Promotor Estivet as Prime Villain

No further action seems to have been taken by anyone until 1455, when a petition was submitted to the pope in the name of the surviving immediate members of Joan's family, namely, her mother Isabelle, and her brothers Pierre and Jean, as well as other relatives and neighbors in the diocese of Toul. The petition may have been intended for Nicholas V, but he died on March 24 of that year, so it was Nicholas's successor, Calixtus III (who was elected on April 8 and consecrated on April 20), who issued a

[1] Belon-Balme, *Jean Bréhal*, p. 66 n. 1.

H. A. Kelly, *The Trial and Retrial of Joan of Arc*, The New Middle Ages, https://doi.org/10.1007/978-3-032-07887-2_13

favorable response, or rescript, namely, the bull *Humilibus supplicum votis*, dated June 11, 1445 (mistake for 1455), preserved in the Nullity dossier.[2]

The tenor of the Arc family supplication can be gathered from the *narratio* portion of Calixtus's bull. The pope says that they recounted that Joan of Arc, sister of Pierre and Jean and daughter of Isabelle, even though she hated all heresy, was falsely reported as stained with the crime of heresy and as having committed other crimes contrary to the Catholic faith, at a time when she was established (*constituta*) in the diocese of Beauvais. The false report was made by Guillaume (not Jean) d'Estivet, the promotor of cases in the diocese of Beauvais, or by someone else exercising that office then, who likely was suborned by persons jealous (*emuli*) of Joan and the Arc family. He made the report to Pierre, Bishop of Beauvais, "of good memory," and to Jean Lemaistre, a former professor of the Order of Preachers, who claimed to be the deputy of the inquisitor of heretical depravity in those parts. The bishop by his ordinary authority and Lemaistre acting on his own alleged powers, on the basis of the false report, instituted an inquisition against her, which the promotor prosecuted. Without any actual evidence or strong suspicion or clamor of *fama*, they put her in prison; and eventually, even though their inquisition did not establish it, they concluded that she was besmirched with heresy or had committed other things contrary to the faith or excesses and crimes of such sort, or had adhered to errors against the faith, even though such things were neither notorious nor true, and though Joan had requested that, if they alleged that she had said or was saying anything that savored of heresy, they should send it to the Apostolic See, whose judgment she was prepared to accept.[3] Instead, they proceeded with their inquisition, in which Joan was deprived of every way to defend her innocence, and the *ordo juris* was set aside, and they issued an unjust definitive sentence in which they judged her guilty of being a heretic and having committed other crimes and excesses of the same kind. In consequence she was handed over to the secular authority and put to death.[4]

All this redounded to the ignominy and opprobrium of the said mother and brothers and other kinfolk and neighbors of Joan. But, since the records of this inquisition clearly showed that it was null and void, the

[2] Calixtus III, *Humilibus supplicum votis*, 11 June 14[5]5, NT 1:18–20 (the date reads *quadragesimo quinto* instead of *quinquagesimo quinto*).

[3] Ibid., pp. 18–19.

[4] Ibid., pp. 19–20.

petitioners, in order to recover their honor, and Joan's honor, requested of the pope that the stain of infamy that accrued to them be removed by his commissioning judges in those regions to carry out a trial of nullity and purgation of falsehood from Joan, and bring it to a just end.[5]

One wonders how the circumstances and motivations surrounding the prosecution of Joan could have been so distorted in the vital step of securing a papally sanctioned retrial of her condemnation. Perhaps the complete silence concerning the role of the occupying English forces was deliberate, so as not to have to identify any English defendants—for instance, Henry VI— in the commissioned proceedings. It was in keeping, of course, with the letters sent out under Henry's name immediately after Joan's execution in order to justify the trial, the motivation for which was obvious.

The emphasis on Cauchon is understandable, less so that on Lemaistre, while that on Estivet is completely unprepared for. Estivet was the promotor of causes in Cauchon's diocese, whom Cauchon employed as promotor in Joan's trial, and Lemaistre followed suit when he finally joined Cauchon as co-judge. He was given no importance by any of the experts examined in the last chapter. Bouillé does not mention him, and neither do Lelli, Pontano, Montigny and others. In the depositions of 1452, he is mentioned only in connection with Joan in her prison, as we saw above, in telling of Joan's illness in prison on April 18, and in Isambart de Lapierre's statement that he threatened the bishop of Avranches (Jean de Saint-Avit, d. 1442) when he refused to give an opinion of the proceedings against Joan.[6] In all of these cases, Estivet is referred to only under his alternate name of Jean Benedicite.

The pope responded to this petition of the Arc family by addressing his bull to three prelates to serve on such a commission, namely, the archbishop of Rheims and the bishops of Paris and Coutances (without giving the names of the current holders of these sees), commanding all three of them, or only two or even only one, along with the appointed inquisitor of heretical depravity for France, to decree what they would deem to be just in this matter, after summoning the current (*modernus*) sub-inquisitor of heresy in the diocese of Beauvais and the current promotor of criminal

[5] Ibid., p. 20.
[6] NT 1:221–22.

cases in the diocesan court of Beauvais, and others who should be summoned, and hearing everything proposed concerning these matters.[7]

In specifying the current sub-inquisitor and promotor of Beauvais, the pope may have implied that the accused culprits, Estivet and Lemaistre, were no longer living. The petitioners had made it clear that Bishop Cauchon was dead (ironically calling him "of good memory"), but perhaps they did not know of the status or whereabouts of the other two. One of the notaries of Joan's original trial, Boisguillaume, would testify in 1456 that he believed that Estivet had come to a bad end, like the bad man that he was, for he had been found dead in some pigeon-house outside the gates of Rouen.[8] As for Lemaistre, he was still alive in January of 1452, when he was assigned to preach in the Rouen cathedral. But he was not summoned to testify in the investigations of March 1450 or May 1452, and he would be referred to as dead in the later proceedings.[9]

It is noteworthy that one of the addressees of the bull, namely, the archbishop of Rheims, Jean Jouvenal des Ursins, was Cauchon's immediate successor as bishop of Beauvais, having held the see from 1433 to 1444, which may have been one of the reasons he was chosen to judge the matter. But it has been noticed that in the year that he was appointed, when talking of the wonders of God performed for Charles VII and the recovery of part of his lands, including the raising of the siege at Orleans, he makes no mention of Joan. Instead, he attributes it to the courage that God gave to a small band of valiant men at the request and prayer of the king.[10] Heinrich Denifle rejects the explanation that his silence was out of fear of offending the king. Jouvenal was not timid, he says. It must be that he and others had changed their attitude toward her after she was burned, as some, like Archbishop Regnault de Chartres of Rheims, had already done; God forbid that we should say that they were embarrassed to talk about her.[11]

[7] Ibid.

[8] NT 1:438. Tisset, 2:400, says that Boisguillaume testified that he died in a *bourbier* (scandal) outside Rouen on October 20, 1438.

[9] Tisset, 2:410; 3:50–52; NT 1:152, 158, 315–16; 2:5.

[10] Jean Jouvenal des Ursins, *Epistre faicte pour envoyer aux trois Estas tenus à Blois l'an mil iiij^c xxxiii*, ed. Henri Denifle, *La désolation des églises, monastères, et hopitaux en France pendant la guerre des cent ans*, vol. 1 (Paris 1897), pp. 497–501, at pp. 500–01.

[11] Denifle, ibid. p. 500 n. 2. Sébastien Cazalas, *Jean Juvénal des Ursins (1388-1473): Étude des épîtres politiques* (Paris 2020), notes that in his only reference to Joan, Jouvenal is very

Of course, it would not occur to the pope (or his curial officials) to suggest summoning persons from the diocese of Rouen, where the trial actually took place, because the Arc supplication failed to mention this circumstance.

13.3 The Papal Commissioners in Paris (Before Rouen)

After the pope signed off on his bull, a copy must have been sent to each of the three addressees, and they must have agreed to convene a tribunal to investigate the case, after inviting Jean Bréhal, the heresy inquisitor for northern France, to join them. Indeed, we find that two of the three commissioned judges, namely, Archbishop Jouvenal and Bishop Guillaume Chartier of Paris, did appear with Inquisitor Bréhal in the cathedral of Paris on November 7, 1455, for this purpose.[12] However, they pretended that they knew nothing of the reason why they were there, but rather were informed of it by Joan's mother. She, along with one of her sons, Pierre, came before them to explain Calixtus's commission to them and presented them with "the apostolic mandate and rescript" addressed to them. We know this because it is recounted at the beginning of the record of the resulting proceedings, which took the form of a large letter addressed by its two notaries "to all who will inspect it," dated July 7, 1456.[13]

The widow Isabelle d'Arc, through certain assistants, proceeded to explain that, after she gave birth to her daughter and reared her properly in the faith, Joan often went to confession and Communion, and never thought anything against the faith. However, certain adversaries and persons envious of her and her kinfolk as well as of their princes and local residents dragged her to a trial of the faith. Whereupon, acting with no legitimate authority, removing all defenses from her, in spite of tacit and explicit recusals and appeals, by a deceitful, violent, and iniquitous trial in which the *ordo juris* was set aside, falsely attributing many crimes to her, they condemned her and cruelly burned her to death, to the infamy of

matter-of-fact (p. 337 n. 254). See *Écrites politiques de Jean Juvénal des Ursins*, Peter Shervey Lewis and Anne-Marie Hayez, eds., 4 vols. (Paris 1978–), 2:420.

[12] Inquisitor Bréhal was also there, but Richard Olivier de Longueil, bishop of Coutances since 1453, was absent. See Duparc, *Procès*, 5:21. Chartier was the brother of the poet Alain Chartier and the chronicler Jean Chartier: see Quicherat, *Procès*, 4:51. Quicherat gives Jean Chartier's inexact history of Joan written between 1440 and 1450, here, 4:52–93.

[13] NT 1:8; 2:611–12.

Isabelle herself and her irreparable detriment. But eventually, after Rouen and the whole of Normandy were brought back to the control of the French, that deceitful, violent, and wicked trial, which had long lain hidden, was brought to light, and its iniquity was evident through examination and reliable report. Therefore, Isabelle and her kin, on the advice of many upright persons, applied to the Holy See—to which Joan herself had often submitted herself and begged to be brought—and asked for timely remedies. Pope Calixtus graciously commissioned Archbishop Jean and Bishop Guillaume there present, and also Bishop Richard of Coutances, as well as one of the inquisitors of faith in the realm of France, to take cognizance concerning the nullity and iniquity of the said trial, and to declare its nullity by their sentence and by purging Joan and all her relatives of every stain of infamy, thus granting to Isabelle herself opportune remedies of law.[14]

Then, falling at the knees of the two prelates and the inquisitor, Isabelle begged them with many groans and sighs to receive the pope's rescript from her and to carry out its provisions. Among her assistants there with her were many learned men who spoke of the defects of the trial (mentioning no names), including the prejudice of the judges, the harshness of her manacles, "the unusual and extraordinary mode of questioning," the threats, the falsification of articles, the fictitious relapse, and Joan's simplicity and integrity. They urged the delegated judges to accede to the widow's request.[15]

The delegates took Isabelle and her assistants aside into the sacristy away from the crowd (there were as yet no notaries present), and offered condolences to her and asked many questions concerning herself and Joan. They took the papal rescript and read it, and then the archbishop, speaking for himself and the bishop, agreed to receive it and set it in motion, summoning notaries and counselors, and, after due summoning of parties, put it into effect and did not deny the widow her due of justice.[16]

But since the widow was not learned in the law, they wished her to choose prudent advisors, lest she be misled by emotion or unwise advice, and, instead of reparation and purgation, aggravate the harm, and instead of annulling the trial held against Joan, end up confirming it. For, since she was condemned a long time ago in a cause of faith by learned and

[14] NT 1:8–10.
[15] NT 1:10–12.
[16] NT 1:12–13.

grave judges, there was a presumption in favor of their sentence, and the extraordinary course of retracting the sentence should not be undertaken without a great abundance of documents. St Augustine notes that litigants, even when reasonably convicted, invariably say that the judges were bad and their judgment null and void. If it was important to hold God and justice in view in the first instance of such judgments, it was even more important in the second instance.[17]

They therefore assigned another day, November 17, for a more formal reception of the papal mandate. Isabelle accepted the day and departed, having left the delegates an authentic copy of the bill and various fuller explanations in Latin and French of the foregoing, while the delegates arranged for further consultations with experts. This day's events were recorded by local notaries.[18]

13.4 Obscuring English Villainy, Exculpating Assessors and Consultants

On November 17, when the official notaries were in place, a spokesman for Isabelle, Pierre Maugier, doctor of canon law (he was in fact the dean of the Faculty of Canon Law at the University of Paris),[19] identified later as the lawyer (*advocatus*) of Isabelle, Pierre, and Jean d'Arc,[20] spoke first. He summed up the previous session's events, presented the original sealed papal bull, and requested that the mandate be carried out quickly. The delegates received it reverently, and, since they had already read it during the previous meeting and consulted with learned men on how to execute it, concerning the citing of parties and the location and time, and, since they desired to impart its contents to all concerned, they ordered it to be read publicly by the scribe of the Paris diocesan court.[21]

When this was completed, and as the delegates were retiring with advisors to discuss their response and the parties to be summoned, Maugier requested leave to speak. Perhaps he was concerned that the oddity of presentation of the case in the bull was brought forcefully to the fore, but

[17] NT 1:13–14.
[18] NT 1:14–16.
[19] Duparc, *Procès*, 5:26–27. He is to be distinguished from the canon of Rouen Jean Maugier, who took part in Joan's trial.
[20] NT 1:53.
[21] NT 1:16–18.

he maintained that he was being urged by the widow and her relatives and all people there to explain to them in French the injustice of the judges and the innocence of Joan. The delegates did not think it necessary or useful, but because of the insistence of the widow and others present, after consulting with prelates and doctors and jurists, they agreed, but admonished him to keep it brief.[22]

Maugier first insisted that he meant to speak only against the judges and the promotor mentioned in the rescript. As for those who had given opinions against Joan, they should be held excusable because of the false articles they were given to evaluate.[23] This, of course, was not true. The Twelve Articles sent to the University of Paris and other assessors who did not attend the trial were not so manipulated as to excuse the unjustified conclusions that most of them came to, especially Maugier's own faculty's final judgment of heresy (unless she repented, she deserved to be burned at the stake).

In the discourse that he proceeded to give in French, Maugier likened the malice of Bishop Cauchon, Guillaume d'Estivet (keeping the erroneous first name of the rescript), and Jean Lemaistre, sub-inquisitor for Beauvais, and their colleagues and accomplices, to that of the two old judges who accused Susanna in the Book of Daniel. He asserted at length that they fostered capital enmities against her (not mentioning that it was because of their favor toward the English claimant and occupiers, against whom Joan had fought). They put her in a harsh prison in the secular power (again not mentioning the English), vexed her with subtle questions on difficult matters and twisted her answers, extorted abjurations with threats, invented relapses, and wickedly destroyed her by burning her in public. He addressed the learned judges before him, saying that her innocent blood cried out to heaven, and it fell to them to decree just reparations.[24]

Joan was a good Catholic, he insisted, with no suspicion of heresy about her. When accused of wearing men's clothing or bearing arms for a time, she gave Catholic answers that excused her actions, on grounds of public necessity and utility, and the divine impulse behind them. She should therefore be held blameless of any such faults attributed to her,

[22] NT 1:21.
[23] NT 1:21–22.
[24] NT 1:21–24.

especially any that would merit a trial of the faith.[25] Once again he refrained from speaking of the armed combat against the English—which, of course, was likewise not named in the papal mandate.

These judges, Maugier continued, do seem to have conducted an investigation into infamy against her in her native regions, as was required by law; however, they did not record it but rather deceitfully suppressed it, because it revealed only her virtuous life. Such deceit, according to doctors of the law, nullified any subsequent sentence. Further, a criminal sentence could not be passed except when a defendant spontaneously confessed in court or was convicted. This girl, a minor, thrown into a severe prison, in fear and terror of guards and deadly enemies and afflicted by the constant vexations of the judges, should not be considered confessed or convicted or condemned in any way, especially by judges whom she had repeatedly recused, and against whom she had appealed to the pope.[26]

Joan constantly said that she had revelations from God and the saints and was helped by them. She did not refuse the judgment of Church concerning them, but embraced it. Such revelations should be judged only favorably, or, if there be doubt about them, left to God. She should not have been called an idolater or diviner because of them, or falsifier of such revelations, and not be deemed a seducer of the people for her efforts to bring subjected inhabitants back to the obedience of their natural king and lord. She expressed belief only in God and invoked only the saints of God, with no question whatsoever of any adoration or invocation of evil spirits.[27] That is the closest that Maugier came to referring to the military and political struggles that lay at the heart of the enmity that brought Joan to her judicial conviction and execution.

Maugier asked the delegated judges to review the record of her trial, to see that she was falsely asserted to have confessed to crimes, and was wrongly convicted as erring in faith and relapsed into heresy, and, accordingly, to retract those condemnations. As for the opinions against her in the record of many experts in divine and human law, he repeated what he had already said in Latin, that they were based on falsifications of her

[25] NT 1:24–25.
[26] NT 1:25–26.
[27] NT 1:26.

responses, which the delegates could see by comparing the articles to her actual testimony about herself.[28]

Overcome by threats and fear, Joan was compelled to submit to a short abjuration, which was then deceitfully replaced by a much longer formula that she could not even understand. Throughout the trial she often said that she submitted herself and her deeds to the pope of the Roman Church, whereby she showed that she was not schismatic but a true Catholic, not a heretic but obedient and faithful, who had made a valid appeal to the pope. The mendacious sentence against her should be declared null, and the parties named in Pope Calixtus's mandate should be summoned and justice declared for the widow and her kin.[29]

Unlike Prévosteau's presentation in 1452, which indicted the English for intimidating not only Joan but also Cauchon and the assessors of the trial, Maugier laid all the blame of malice and intimidation upon the three persons named in the papal bull, Promotor Estivet and Judges Cauchon and Lemaistre, and even omitted reference to the alleged jealous instigators of the prosecution that Isabelle and her sons had first named, which the pope repeated.

13.5 Summoning Concerned and Unconcerned Parties

Maugier's presentation may have been longer than Archbishop Jouvenal and Bishop Chartier wished, since they seem to have changed their minds about retiring for deliberation. Instead, they immediately set about fulfilling the pope's mandate. First, they formally added Inquisitor Bréhal to the bench. Then, considering that a proceeding like this could not go forward without summoning parties, they cautioned Isabelle and her two sons (now both present) about the difficulties of a trial (*super difficultatibus processus*), and then questioned them under solemn oath about their zeal in the matter. They replied that they intended to pursue their injury and seek justice. They asked for the pope's mandate to be executed, and for summonses to be issued.[30]

One of the difficulties, of course, was that at least one of the denounced offenders, Bishop Cauchon, was deceased. In such cases it was necessary

[28] NT 1:26–27.
[29] NT 1:27–28.
[30] NT 1:28–29.

to put out a call for other defenders to come forward, or at least those who had some stake in the matter. In Wyclif's posthumous trial at the Council of Constance, mentioned above, summonses were posted calling for persons to come forward to say why the memory and teachings of Wyclif should not be condemned. Because no one responded to this summons, the promotor accused all such potential defenders of contempt of court. (Of course, if anyone had shown up to defend Wyclif, he would have received a fate much worse than a contempt conviction.) The promotor then introduced Wyclif's offending propositions, and witnesses to his final impenitence, which was declared "proved by the *ordo juris*" (i.e., saying that the rules for condemning an absent or deceased defendant had been followed).[31] Another posthumous trial held at the same council, we recall, was that of Jean Petit, where defenders did appear, among them Cauchon. Something similar might have played out this time if it had been decided to attack the memory of Cauchon for his criminal acts of injustice. Instead, as we saw, he was said to be "of good memory."

The delegates and their advisors then stepped aside and ordered the persons named in the mandate to be cited specifically, and others generally, to Rouen, where the trial took place, to speak against the rescript and relevant persons and to proceed further as justice demanded. They then called Isabelle and her sons over and gave them letters of citation.[32]

Two more citations were prepared and signed on that day, November 17, one for the diocese of Beauvais and the other for the diocese of Rouen. The one for Beauvais (which appears second in the dossier) was addressed to all clergy in the city and diocese of Beauvais (except the bishop, but including the promotor of criminal cases). The judges-delegate narrated that the illustrious Master Maugier presented the bull of Pope Calixtus to them, while the noble knight Pierre d'Arc and his mother Isabelle were standing by. After the text of the bull was recited, they said, they were requested by the said Pierre and Isabelle to cite, in accordance with the bull, the bishop of Beauvais, the sub-inquisitor of heresy for the diocese, and the promotor of criminal cases, and all others concerned in the case.[33] The bull in fact did not order the summoning of the bishop of Beauvais,

[31] Kelly, "Trial Procedures Against Wyclif," p. 21. See Mansi, *Sacrorum conciliorum*, 27:629–36.

[32] NT 1:29.

[33] NT 1:43–44. The last part reads, "omnes alios et singulos communiter vel divisim interesse credentes." The same idiom (ablative *sua* with *interesse*) appears elsewhere in these citations, but in the Rouen version on p. 37 there is a mistake: "*seu* quomodolibet interesse

but only the "modern" sub-inquisitor and promotor, and other persons at the discretion of the judges.

In the odd fiction of such citations, the judges ordered the execution of the letter, under pain of excommunication: they were to cite all to appear in Rouen on December 12. If they could not find the three specific individuals personally, they were to seek them in their residences, if they could safely go there. Otherwise, they were to attach the citation to the doors of the cathedral. If the citees did not appear, the judges would proceed at the instance (petition) of the parties that did appear. The recipients of the citation would have to report back what they had done to implement the citation.[34]

The other citation of November 17, for the diocese of Rouen, was addressed to all the clergy to whom it came, or who were concerned in the trial described below. The delegated judges tell of the mandate from Pope Calixtus which the members of the Arc family presented to them, complaining bitterly about the damaged reputation of Joan and themselves caused by the violence of certain persons jealous of them or of the republic where they were accustomed to live. Joan was falsely denounced by the promotor of Pierre Cauchon, bishop of Beauvais, and a trial was held against her by the bishop and the vice-inquisitor of heresy. She was convicted on the basis of falsely fabricated articles and cruelly put to death. Under pain of excommunication, the recipients of the citation were to affix the document to the doors of the cathedral in Rouen, and in due course were to report back the results.[35]

The citation called for all interested parties, specifically those who had denounced or accused Joan, or who had defended the proceedings against her, to appear in the archbishop's hall in Rouen on December 20, to say what they wished against the papal mandate, and to respond to the complainants and to the delegated judges' promotor.[36]

The promotor of the judges mentioned in the citations was the canon lawyer Simon Chapitault, who would be appointed only after the court re-opened in Rouen on December 12.[37] Chapitault first appeared on November 18, as one of the witnesses (along with Guillaume Bouillé) to

credentes" should be "*sua* quomodolibet interesse credentes" (those believing themselves to be in any way concerned).

[34] NT 1:43–47.

[35] NT 1:33–39; it is followed by the certifications of four notaries, pp. 39–41.

[36] NT 1:33–39.

[37] NT 1:65–66.

the appointment by Isabelle and Pierre d'Arc of sixteen proctors to prosecute the nullity of proceedings against Joan and to appear before the papal commissioners. On November 24 Jean d'Arc appointed the same proctors.[38] The most important Arc proctor will prove to be Guillaume Prévosteau, who, we remember, was the promotor for Cardinal d'Estouteville in 1452.

The Beauvais citation was received only on November 29, a Saturday, at the hour of vespers, by the notary Jean de Frocourt, a canon of Beauvais. In his report, which he wrote that very day, he characterizes the citation as "for and on behalf of" the Arc family. He says that he brought it immediately to the presence of the bishop of Beauvais, Guillaume de Hellande, whom he found in the ambulatory of his residence. With the bishop there happened to be Regnault Brédoulle, promotor of cases (or fiscal procurator) of the bishop's court, as well as Germer Morlaines, prior of the Dominican friars of Beauvais. The notary read the citation letter to all three, and cited the bishop and the promotor to appear in court in Rouen on December 12, to respond to the Arcs and to the promotor of the judges-delegate. He also asked the prior if there was a sub-inquisitor of heresy in the vicinity, and he replied that he did not know of one, but said that he would notify the inquisitor himself in Paris about the case.[39] This inquisitor, of course, was none other than Jean Bréhal, who had already been co-opted to investigate the flaws of the original trial, and who would soon be appointed co-judge in the "trial of the trial," or, what I call in the title of the present book the "retrial" of Joan.

Bishop Hellande replied to Frocourt that he did not think that the case concerned him, but he sent his respects to the delegates. Promotor Brédoulle similarly replied that he had nothing to do with the case. Frocourt then stood before the major church in Beauvais (the cathedral) while services were in progress and cited all persons who believed themselves to be concerned with the case, and then attached the citation to the church doors. He named some persons who witnessed these actions, as well as witnesses to his earlier encounter with the bishop, promotor, and prior.[40]

The two notaries who received the Rouen citation, which summoned all concerned persons to appear on December 20, attached it to the

[38] NT 1:29–33.
[39] NT 1:48–50.
[40] NT 1:50–51.

cathedral doors of Rouen only on December 11, which was the day before the cited parties from Beauvais were due to appear in court in the hall of the archbishop of Rouen. On this later due date, December 20, the notaries reported that, even though the citation had been read by many, no one appeared in response to it.[41]

[41] NT 1:41–43.

CHAPTER 14

The Trial of Nullity Opens in Rouen, December 1455

14.1 Joan's Wrongs Vigorously but Vaguely Rehearsed

On December 12, 1455, Archbishop Jouvenal and Bishop Chartier were sitting in tribunal in the palace or major hall of the archbishop of Rouen. The archbishop of Rouen himself, Cardinal Estouteville, surprisingly played no role in these proceedings. A proctor for the Arcs, a canon of Rouen, noted that the bishop of Beauvais, the promotor of criminal cases in Beauvais, and the sub-inquisitor of heresy in the diocese had been cited to appear on that day, and, since they did not appear, he requested that they be held in contempt. The judges instead extended the time for their arrival until December 15.[1]

On December 15, a different proctor appeared for the Arcs, namely, Guillaume Prévosteau, and assisting him as their advocate was Pierre Maugier. After Prévosteau reviewed the citations, Maugier gave an oration in French (recorded only in Latin), reviewing the sad complaint of the plaintiffs, namely, that Joan of Arc, a humble and innocent virgin, who, coming to the aid of our king for the good of his realm (otherwise undefined), presumably inspired by God, was wickedly and unjustly imprisoned and falsely put through a pretensed trial of the faith, under the pretensed judges Pierre Cauchon, then bishop of Beauvais, and Jean Lemaistre,

[1] NT 1:52–53.

H. A. Kelly, *The Trial and Retrial of Joan of Arc*, The New Middle Ages, https://doi.org/10.1007/978-3-032-07887-2_14

pretensed sub-inquisitor of the faith for Beauvais, at the instance of Jean d'Estivet (now with the correct first name), asserted to be Cauchon's promotor, and other accomplices. This inexperienced girl, many times harshly and subtly interrogated, detained in shackles by her capital enemies (not identified as the English captors), was decreed by the judges, against all truth and justice, to have deviated and erred from the faith and from the doctrine and traditions of the Church. She was twice most iniquitously condemned: first, to perpetual prison after making an abjuration whose content she did not understand, and, secondly, as having fallen back into errors of the faith. She was then cruelly burned to death. The result was great infamy both to Joan and to her kinfolk.[2]

Maugier appealed to the present papally commissioned judges, running through a dozen or so biblical and juristic quotations, then saying that it remained to bring the nullity and deceits of the proceedings and sentences into the open. He first told in detail of Joan's admirable upbringing, and then made short work of the revelations by which she was led to militate with great honor in France, winning many usurped cities and locales from the enemy and predicting their final extirpation (coming close to the military context of the affair). And, finally, when she was in the hands of her capital enemies and iniquitous trial, she frequently asked the judgment of the Holy See, a sign of her Catholic person.[3] He proceeded to list twelve reasons why the trial against her was null and void:

1) No jurisdiction; she had no domicile and committed no offense of the faith in the pretensed jurisdiction of the judges.
2) Intimidation against the vice-inquisitor co-judge.
3) Joan's recusal of Cauchon as her capital enemy.
4) Joan's express appeals to the pope and the general council.
5) The difficult subject matter of private revelations, which should be sent to the Holy See.
6) The horrors and terrors of prison, equivalent to torture.
7) Denial of counsel.
8) Her minor age of nineteen (trials and sentences against undefended persons under twenty-five are invalid).
9) Unjustified severity of the sentences.

[2] NT 1:54–56.
[3] NT 1:56–59.

10) Scribes forbidden to record her excuses and appeals to the Holy See.
11) False compilation of Twelve Articles on which expert opinions were taken.
12) False advisors (not to submit to the church); removal of female clothing (forcing her to resume prohibited male clothes).

He implored the judges to do justice by the plaintiffs and restore their fame and honor by declaring the nullity and iniquity of the trial and sentences against Joan.[4]

We see that Maugier now introduced the element of fear into the invalidating circumstances of the trial, but only regarding Lemaistre, while continuing to remain silent about the English, who were the ultimate source of that fear. He did not mention the similar fear brought to bear upon the assessors, as Prévosteau had done, but once again deflected blame from them on the grounds that they were deceived by the falsified articles. To his eleventh point, he added that those who were thus seduced by them should be excused, for only the guilty should be punished.[5]

14.2 More Pretrial Procedures, December 15–16

After Maugier finished his presentation, Archbishop Jouvenal and Bishop Chartier continued to await the appearance of cited parties for some time. Then, after having been assured by public fame and the report of various persons that some of those mentioned in the trial in question and in the papal rescript had passed away, they offered to hear their heirs or successors or acquaintances defend the fairness of Joan's trial, which, *prima facie*, was to be presumed; and they would also listen benignly to anything

[4] NT 1:60–63.

[5] NT 1:61–62: "Unde et sic seductis deliberantibus non est eis imputandum, sed excusandi sunt. 'Pene' enim 'suos tenere debent actores'" (Whence also those deliberating upon them who were thus misled are not to be blamed, but rather they should be excused, for "Punishments should bind their exactors.") The legal maxim he cites here, *Poenae suos tenere debent actores*, means that only those whose evil deeds exact (call for) punishments should undergo such punishments. See *Black's Law Dictionary*, ed. 7, ed. Brian Garner (St Paul 1999), p. 1674. Duparc misses this point in his translation (3:55).

that they could or should say to justify or excuse the cited parties, living or dead.[6]

We recall that the papal letter noted that Cauchon was dead, and may have implied that Estivet and Lemaistre were also deceased by directing the delegates to cite the "modern" sub-inquisitor and promotor. Their letter of citation simply specified that the bishop, the sub-inquisitor, and the promotor should be cited, without elaboration. They would later have read Notary Frocourt's report filed on November 29 and seen that Estivet was no longer the Beauvais promotor, and that there was no longer a sub-inquisitor for the diocese.

In the "offer" just quoted, the judges made it clear that they considered some deceased as well as living persons to have been cited, and they now invited other persons to come, and to exonerate them and their accomplices (mentioned in the papal letter) in any way, if possible. Which means, apparently, that they considered the cited persons to have been implicated in the wrongdoing complained of by the Arc family. The papal mandate and the Beauvais citation were rather noncommittal on this point.

After more waiting and more no-shows, Proctor Prévosteau accused the cited persons who did not appear of contempt of court, requested a declaration from the judges to that effect, and asked further that the opportunity to object to the papal mandate be formally ended.[7] Instead of acceding to these requests immediately, the judges appointed two notaries who were also canon lawyers, Denis Lecomte and François Ferrebouc, to record the proceedings, and then appointed Simon Chapitault as their

[6] NT 1:63. The last part of this sentence is mispunctuated by Duparc and misconstrued in his translation (3:57). I give it as follows: "Obtulerunt prefati domini omnibus heredibus aut successoribus in officiis vel beneficiis, executoribus, consanguineis, servitoribus, et amicis, eos libenter et ad plenum semper, quandocumque deceret, audire, ymo et quemcumque, pro justicia processus agitati, pro quo, prima facie, dicebant presumendum esse; et ab eis omnibus quecumque ad justificationem vel excusationem facere possent et deberent cum benignitate recipere." I translate as follows: "The said lord delegates offered to all their heirs, or successors to their offices or benefices, or their executors, relatives, servants, and friends, to hear them willingly and fully, at all times, whenever it would be fitting, and, indeed, to hear anyone whomsoever, in favor of the justice of the trial that was held; and they said that the presumption was, *prima facie*, in favor of the trial. And they also offered to benignly receive from all of them anything whatsoever that they could and should say that made for the justification or excusing of the said cited parties, whether living or dead." Duparc interprets the *processus agitatus* to refer to the proceedings now under way, rather than to the original trial.

[7] NT 1:64.

promotor.[8] At Prévosteau's repeated request, they decreed all those persons cited who had failed to appear—even though it was not clear who they were—to be in contempt from that day forward. Then they cited them again to appear on December 20, when all interested persons in the diocese of Rouen were to appear after being cited at the entrance of the cathedral (posted only the previous day, December 11). If the cited persons now in contempt did not appear on December 20, they would be precluded from objecting to the papal mandate or to the citation. Finally, the plaintiffs were ordered in the meantime, before that day, to present their petition, in the form of a libellus or summary.[9]

I noted that when the judge-appointed promotor Estivet called himself a plaintiff (*actor*) and presented a libellus in the *ex officio* inquisition against Joan, he was using the terminology of a civil suit. In the present case, the trial seems to be regarded both as a civil suit for damages, with the Arc family as plaintiffs, and an *ex officio* inquisition ordered by the pope, with a promotor appointed by the judges.[10] The judges could have seen the family and their proctor as denouncers of alleged miscreants and external promotors in a promoted inquisition, but they did not say so.

Next, Proctor Prévosteau and Promotor Chapitault, working together as joint prosecutors, with the proctor petitioning (*instante*) and the promotor requesting (*requirente*), asked if the notaries of the original trial, especially Manchon, wished to speak in its favor. When they responded that they did not wish to accept any responsibility for the trial, by way of defending or justifying it, the judges asked them to turn in any records that they had. Whereupon Manchon showed them a paper codex recording the trial in French, made by him, from which the Latin codex, which he also exhibited, was made.[11] The two prosecutors then requested the record of the 1452 depositions be accepted.[12]

On December 16, the promotor and proctor asked the judges (now including Inquisitor Bréhal) to order the summoning of witnesses to be deposed in Rouen, which they did, in a citation dated that day, addressed to the clergy of Rouen, to summon, on behalf of the promotor and the

[8] NT 1:64–66.

[9] NT 1:66–67.

[10] Duparc suggests that the trial was a combination of *ex officio* inquisition and an *accusatio*, the older form of criminal trial (5:17), but the terminology does not indicate this interpretation.

[11] NT 1:67–68.

[12] NT 1:68–70.

Arcs, specific witnesses, who included Massieu and Manchon, Isambart de Lapierre and Martin Ladvenu, and Nicolas de Houppeville.[13]

14.3 The Plaintiffs' Libellus Presented, December 18

On December 18, Proctor Prévosteau, obeying the order of the judges (for the plaintiffs to present a petition in the form of a libellus before December 20), "delivered his petition before the same oft-mentioned lord delegates, or their notaries, in this fashion."[14] What follows is doubtless a scribal account of his oral delivery of his libellus, since, as we will see, he will submit his articles in writing on December 20.

In it, the proctor addresses the judges, in the name of the plaintiffs, *contra dictos reos*, "against the said defendants,"[15] using the standard ambiguous term *reus*, which meant not only "defendant" but also "guilty person," so that there was always in all trials the unavoidable suggestion that the accused was guilty until proven innocent. Prévosteau is saying here that the defendants have already been identified, whereas they have not. He soon states that his clients' action is against the current bishop of Beauvais, Guillaume Hellande, the sub-inquisitor of heresy for Beauvais, the current promotor of cases for Beauvais, and all others who believe themselves to be concerned in the case and to be legitimately intervening defendants in the trial (*in judicio legitime intervenientes reos*).[16] He goes on to summarize the events of November 22 (actually November 17), when the delegated judges appointed a promotor and issued citations against the persons mentioned in the papal mandate and others with interest in the case to appear as defendants (*reos comparituros*).[17]

Actually, of course, neither the pope nor the judges in their citations identified anyone as actual defendants. Furthermore, as we have seen, the notary Jean de Frocourt on November 29 had reported to the court that both Bishop Hellande and Promotor Brédoulle had informed him that

[13] NT 1:70–72.

[14] NT 1:73: "...suam petitionem penes eosdem sepedictos dominos delegatos, seu eorundum notarios, tradidit in scriptis in hunc modum."

[15] NT 1:73.

[16] NT 1:73–74.

[17] NT 1:74–75.

they did not believe that they had any involvement in the case. He was also informed that there was no current sub-inquisitor for the diocese.[18]

14.3.1 *Defects of the Trial*

Prévosteau proceeds: Since the defendants (*rei*) did not appear on the day assigned, he asks them to be declared in contempt, and he renews the plaintiffs' petition, now presented in writing, as follows. In spite of the fact that Joan was a good Catholic girl, and with no valid information to the contrary to begin a trial of the faith against her, the defendants presumed to charge her with error, idolatry, and various invented crimes against the faith and the Church, keeping her in harsh chains and prison and subjected to threats and terror, plagued her with difficult questions, uneducated as she was and unused to deceit, being suspended by the then bishop of Beauvais, and excommunicated by the vice-inquisitor Jean Lemaistre, by reason of falsely imputed matter of heresy and questions of the faith.[19]

These pretensed judges had her guarded in a secular prison by armed English guards, her capital enemies. They kept the test of virginity that she had undergone from the trial, and, when she fell ill under the vexations that they visited upon her, they took care to cure her, not out of mercy, but because they wished to preserve her for the extermination that they had premeditated for her. They continued to plague her with hard questions, to which she gave good answers—directed, it would seem, by the Lord. They put a sinister interpretation on the visions that she experienced. They refused her requests to submit her responses to clergy not her enemies and to take them to the pope, in effect recusing them as judges. They created false articles from her responses to solicit judgments against her (those who gave such judgments should be excused, unless they had sinister motives). Moreover, in addition to the honest notaries who recorded the trial, dishonest and hidden scribes added false material to the register.[20]

Finally, the said defendants (*dicti rei*), especially the bishop of Beauvais and the inquisitor (the current bishop and nonexistent sub-inquisitor have shifted to Cauchon and Lemaistre), blinded by perverse motives, did not hesitate to declare Joan guilty (*rea*) of offenses against the faith and the

[18] NT 1:48–51.
[19] NT 1:75–77.
[20] NT 1:77–78.

Church, namely, idolatry, error, superstition, rashness, invocation of demons, and heresy, and they extorted an abjuration of these crimes from her on a paper that she did not understand, by fear and fraud, and condemned her to perpetual prison; and then a few days later declared her relapsed into heresy, and turned her over to the secular branch, whereupon she was burned to death while calling upon her Redeemer Jesus Christ. The reputation of Joan and of the plaintiffs was badly damaged as a consequence.[21]

We observe that the jealous slanderers of the Arcs have been left out of the narrative, along with Promotor Estivet. The background setting of the war against the English is only rapidly alluded to in describing Joan's prison guards.

Prévosteau continues by detailing seven ways in which the trial was null and void. First, there was no jurisdiction over the "litigants" (using the awkward vocabulary of civil suits): Joan was not a resident of the diocese of Beauvais, and the offenses falsely imputed to her were not said to have been committed there, and therefore the bishop of Beauvais was not a competent judge. Second, the two judges were automatically excommunicated for falsely imposing the crime of heresy upon her. Third, Joan had recused the bishop as her capital enemy. Fourth, the vice-inquisitor was acting under extreme fear of the English, who were assisting in the trial. Fifth, Joan appealed to the pope. Sixth, important cases of heresy needed to be sent to the Holy See. Seventh, the violent circumstances—a young girl kept in chains in prison under constant threat, forced to "confess" by torturous conditions—nullified everything.[22]

The proctor continues: she was also denied counsel, and one person who wished to help her was driven away by threats. No accommodation was made for her young age. Her responses were truncated, with exonerating details omitted, and a set of Twelve Articles was concocted that falsified her deeds, and they omitted her wish to submit to the Holy See. Spies with the judges' approval went to her cell to seduce her, as the serpent did with Eve, claiming to be on the side of the French king, telling her not to submit to the Church, and to resume male clothing, while female garments were removed. All this fraud nullified any sentences that were passed.[23]

[21] NT 1:78–79.
[22] NT 1:79–82.
[23] NT 1:82–84.

14.3.2 Refutation of the Charges Against Joan

Furthermore, Prévosteau says, the trial was invalid because of false charges. The visions that Joan experienced were interpreted by the defendants, seduced by *affectio sinistra*, as coming from evil spirits. But even though the source of such phenomena is known to God alone, and the Church does not judge hidden things (*De occultis penitus Ecclesia non judicat*), the indications were overwhelming that they came from good spirits in Joan's case.[24] Joan should not be blamed for engaging in war, for it had all of the elements of a just war, and was sanctioned by God, who ordered the English to go home.[25] Finally the conflict with England was brought to the fore!

Instead of refuting the notion that there was a valid general law against women wearing men's clothing, as he could have done, Prévosteau admits that there was a canon against it (*prohibitum a canone*), but he argues that there were many reasons why Joan's use was legitimate, and it certainly should not have been taken as evidence of relapse into heresy.[26]

Leaving her parents in obedience to a call from God was not a sin. Her leap from the tower was not an act of desperation but an effort to escape captivity. She did not lie about the angel with the sign for the king. It is licit sometimes to hide the truth by appropriate feigning or wordplay (*fictione bona aut verborum circumlocutione*). There was nothing blameworthy in saying that she was sure of salvation if she kept her virtue, or in claiming to know the future. Even the prophets do not always prophesy. She did not say that Saints Catherine and Margaret hated the English, but that they loved whom God loved and hated whom He hated. Nor did she say that she had committed no sin.[27]

The defendants falsely claimed that she refused to submit to the Church. To begin with, there is no obligation to submit to the judgment of the Church, apart from doctrinal articles of the faith. As noted, the Church does not judge private matters, like the sort of visions that Joan had. The Church gives us the liberty of holding what we wish. However, once Joan understood what was meant by submitting to the Church, she agreed to do so. She asked to be sent to the pope, and in denying this it was the defendants, not Joan, who refused to submit to the judgment of the

[24] NT 1:84–87.
[25] NT 1:87.
[26] NT 1:87–88.
[27] NT 1:88–89.

Church. The bishop expressly forbade the notaries from recording her submission. Moreover, she was allowed to go to Communion just before she died, which the defendants would not have allowed if she had not submitted.[28]

Furthermore, she could not be declared relapsed into heresy, because she had not lapsed into any heresy in the first place. She did not understand what was read from the pretensed schedule of abjuration. In the deliberation that followed, almost everyone agreed with the Abbot of Fécamp, that she should be questioned as to whether she understood it. If this had happened, she would never have said that she was suspect of heresy, or mendacious, or that she had committed such crimes, or that she abjured them. The prolix abjuration later read publicly was not the same, which further invalidated the trial. What Joan said about her abjuration was that, out of fear of death, she falsely confessed herself a heretic. She did not intend to revoke anything except what was pleasing to God.[29]

Prévosteau concludes by returning to the falsely constructed Twelve Articles that were submitted to the University of Paris. The defendants constructed their sentences against Joan on the basis of the resulting opinions. If the opinion-givers were genuinely deceived, they may be legitimately excused, but the sentences and their results must be declared altogether fraudulent, iniquitous, and invalid. The plaintiffs ask the judges to declare the whole process held against Joan by Bishop Cauchon and Vice-Inquisitor Lemaistre to be null and void, Joan herself innocent of all charges of heresy and error, and the plaintiffs free of any stain of infamy. Joan's innocence should be publicly proclaimed at the place where she was burned to death, and crosses, memorials, and epitaphs erected there and throughout the realm. Their judgment should be inserted in the chronicles of France, and the defendants fined great sums to be given to the plaintiffs. Or, he says at the end, the plaintiffs ask the judges to come to such conclusions, and order such reparations as are called for by canon law. He ends by offering to prove anything of the above that needs to be proved.[30]

[28] NT 1:89–92.
[29] NT 1:92–93.
[30] NT 1:93–96.

14.4 Cauchon's Grandnephew Renounces and Denounces Joan's Trial, December 20

At the end of Prévosteau's libellus, awkwardly sandwiched between the requested sanctions and the suggestion that the judges come to their own conclusions, is the plaintiffs' insistent plea that the delegates' promotor be joined to them.[31] Presumably this had already been done by the time the libellus was submitted on December 18.

On December 19, Chapitault and Prévosteau showed up in court with nine "old and sick" witnesses summoned to appear on that day, who were sworn in before the judges. The summoner, vicar of the current urban dean, reported that he summoned six of them to appear on the 19th and the other three on the 20th, to testify to the truth in a trial concerning a trial of the faith held against Joan by a certain bishop of Beauvais and sub-inquisitor at the instance of their promotor, "Guillaume" Estivet, and its nullity and the exoneration of Joan. The witnesses included Friar/Bishop Jean Lefèvre, Nicolas de Houppeville, Manchon, Massieu, Ladvenu, and Archdeacon Marguerie.[32] We will see later that they, or most of them, were not only deposed now but brought back in the following May for further testimony.

On December 20, the day appointed for all interested persons in the Rouen diocese to come to court, only one person appeared, Jean de Gouys, a canon of Rouen representing Jacques de Rinel, Master of Arts, Cauchon's grandnephew (his father's mother was the bishop's sister),[33] and his other relatives. He submitted a document disclaiming any interest in the trial, which gave the most honest account of the trial against Joan so far heard in these proceedings. Rinel said that he saw the summons from the judges in a case of nullity of a trial of the faith held by Cauchon and the inquisitor of the faith at the instance of the promotor of the same

[31] NT 1:96: "…requirentes instanter ipsi actores vestri promotoris adjunctionem sibi impartiendam per vos decerni" (the said plaintiffs instantly requesting that the joining of your promotor to them be decreed).

[32] NT 1:96–98. One of the witnesses, Jean Riquier, was only forty-seven years old (NT 1:459).

[33] His father was Jean de Rinel, Cauchon's nephew; see Philippe Contamine, "Maître Jean de Rinel (vers 1380–1449), notaire et secretaire de Charles VI puis de Henry VI pour son royaume de France, l'une des 'plumes' de l'union des deux couronnes," in *De part et d'autre de la Normandie médiévale: Recueil d'études en hommage à François Neveux* (Caen 2009), pp. 115–34.

faith (an interesting deduction) against Joan the Maid, during the time of the English and the recent wars—even though Joan was considered by the grandees of this realm to be of a holy, honest, and Catholic life. The summons was for those who believed themselves to have an interest in the original proceedings. Rinel and the rest of his kin had no such interest, he said. But, instead of simply saying that he therefore had no obligation to respond to the summons, he explained his lack of connection, and why he had no intention of defending Joan's trial as valid. First, he himself was only four or five years old at the time. Second, he heard from others later that Joan was subjected to a trial of the faith by the wish ("the envy and suggestion") of the king's enemies, because she was inflicting such heavy damage upon them by warring on the king's behalf. If she had been on the enemy side, she would never have been dragged into such a trial.[34]

It then turned out that he had a further purpose for his response: he wished the judges to agree that their sentence should have no adverse effect upon him and his co-heirs, and others "having the cause" of the said bishop, because of the amnesty that the king had granted to the people of Normandy when it was regained and returned to his rule.[35] In other words, they should not be liable to damages for offenses committed by the bishop.

After Rinel's petition was read, the judges gave their commitment that they had no intention of doing anything against the assurances given by the king to the inhabitants of Normandy. One of the witnesses in attendance that day was Guillaume Bouillé.[36]

Also on December 20, Prévosteau and Chapitault instituted a new request that the named persons who were cited and failed to appear on that day be declared in contempt, and that the proceedings continue in their absence. We will see later that the judges issued a new citation for them to appear on the following February 16. Then Prévosteau exhibited *articuli concludentes*, "concluding articles," to be accepted, and to be opposed by any persons concerned enough to do so.[37] These are taken up in the next chapter.

[34] NT 1:98–100.
[35] NT 1:100.
[36] NT 1:99.
[37] NT 1:101–02.

14.5 Search for Cauchon's Original Investigations

We recall that in the introduction to the Latin Record, Cauchon speaks of the investigations he ordered to be undertaken and which, he said, he had recited in open court in the presence of assessors.[38] The present judges-delegate were anxious to find this alleged body of testimony. After receiving the Latin Record, which was compiled by Thomas de Courcelles and signed and verified on each page by each of the three notaries, Manchon, Boisguillaume, and Taquel, the judges first interviewed the notaries, and they said that they had not seen any such informations during the course of the proceedings, even though by order of the judges (Cauchon and Lemaistre) they were referred to in the record. The delegated judges, with Archbishop Jouvenal presiding, set up many commissions of inquiry and made multiple requests in word and writing, that if anyone knew of the whereabouts of said informations they were to come forward, especially those connected with the bishop of Beauvais and the Dominican house in Beauvais.[39]

Because they could find nothing, they interviewed many witnesses, and re-deposed the notaries. Manchon especially deposed again that he had seen nothing, and if he had seen them, or witnessed their exhibition to the assessors, he would have recorded it. Similarly, Thomas de Courcelles, one of the assessors said to have been shown the informations, said he did not remember any such thing. He also said that Master Lohier later said that the process could not legally proceed for that reason, that the preliminary informations either did not exist or were not displayed, as by law they should have been. The only witness they record is a merchant from Joan's area who encountered one of Cauchon's commissioned investigators, who said that his report was rejected because it contained nothing unfavorable about her.[40]

It was obvious, of course, from the questions that were asked of Joan and from Estivet's libellus that Cauchon's agents had collected a great deal of malicious gossip about her. But presumably it was not the sort of

[38] The pertinent passages, LR 22–23 and 25–26, are copied here: NT 1:247–48. The second passage is also preserved in the original record, FM 25–26.

[39] NT 1:245–46.

[40] NT 1:246–47. Courcelles was interrogated in the following year (January and April of 1456, NT 1:355–56), but must also have been interviewed earlier, for his testimony to be cited here.

testimony that would have passed muster even among the core group of clergy whom Cauchon had chosen to be his original assessors. But because the judges could find nothing, on December 20, 1455, they ordered new informations to be collected in Joan's home region, and they set out articles for witnesses to be deposed upon.[41]

At least fourteen witnesses were interviewed at this time, between December 16 and 19, including Manchon, Massieu, and Ladvenu, who would later be recalled to testify again.[42]

[41] NT 1:247–51.
[42] NT 1:411–61.

CHAPTER 15

The Arc Family's Case Against Joan's Trial in 101 Articles

Prévosteau's libellus containing his "concluding articles," submitted to the court on December 20, 1455, on behalf of the plaintiffs, is introduced by a supposed quotation from canon law (the "sacred sanctions"): "He is to be blamed who neglects fame and does not defend the innocence of his kin oppressed by cunning fraud."[1]

15.1 Preliminary Remarks

Prévosteau addresses the archbishop of Rheims, the bishop of Paris, and Inquisitor Bréhal, commissioned by the pope to judge the suit of Isabelle d'Arc, mother of Joan the Maid, and her two sons against the subinquisitor of heresy in the diocese of Beauvais and the promotor of criminal cases of the episcopal court of Beauvais, along with a certain Guillaume d'Estivet and the reverend, formerly, Pierre Cauchon, Bishop of Beauvais, and Jean Lemaistre, pretensed inquisitor or vice-inquisitor, in the said diocese, if they are still living, or their heirs and responsible persons (*habentes causam*) if necessary and concerning them, and against the reverend Guillaume de Hellande, present bishop of Beauvais, and all others who believe themselves to be concerned, jointly and individually, defendants (*reos*).[2]

[1] NT 1:111.
[2] NT 1:111–12.

H. A. Kelly, *The Trial and Retrial of Joan of Arc*, The New Middle Ages, https://doi.org/10.1007/978-3-032-07887-2_15

The action concerns reparation for the injuries to Joan from her trial and execution, brought about through the malevolent deeds of the said defendants or their accomplices, by a declaration of nullity, and by a proclamation of her innocence, in accord with the following articles.[3]

First of all, the plaintiffs wish to harm no one maliciously but only to seek the truth, and specifically they do not intend to say anything against those who participated in the malicious extraction of articles against Joan, "except for the said judges and promotor" (*demptis tamen dictis judicibus et promotore*) (art. 1).[4] (He gets ahead of himself in saying that the defendants have already been "said" to be "judges.")

15.2 Narrative of the Defendants' Criminal Actions

Prévosteau proceeds: the plaintiffs and Joan enjoyed good fame (art. 2). Joan detested all heresy (art. 3), she was devout (art. 4), there was no infamy of heresy or error of faith concerning her, and therefore a trial of faith should not have been begun against her (art. 5). Nevertheless, the said judges and promotor, led by passion and hatred or favor of the king's enemies, following no *ordo juris*, with no legitimate inquisition preceding, subjected her to a trial of faith and falsely imposed crimes and errors against the faith and the Church upon her (art. 6).[5] At this point he introduced the crucial point that Cauchon and the rest were enemies of Charles VII, which had been missing in the pope's commission.

When Joan asked for counsel from the king's side and attendance at mass, the aforesaid (Bishop Cauchon) denied the latter request and remained silent about the first (art. 7). Both Lemaistre and Cauchon were automatically excommunicated for falsely accusing her of heresy and holding an inquisition against her, which nullified the inquisition (art. 8). They put her in a harsh secular prison guarded by her enemies (art. 9). They had her examined, and when she was found to be a virgin, they bound themselves by oath not to reveal it (art. 10).

In this prison, the said defendants (*rei*) put difficult questions to her, accompanied by threats, causing her to fall deathly ill—all over the objections of Joan and of many of the assessors, some of whom left and others

[3] NT 1:112.
[4] NT 1:112.
[5] NT 1:113–14.

were expelled (art. 11). They did this questioning with only a few counsellors present whom they switched in each examination, to the exclusion of honest consultants, which caused no little discussion (art. 12).[6]

(We see that Prévosteau ignores the multiple public sessions with scores of assessors present, who showed no signs of objecting to the questioning, as detailed in the French Minute and Courcelles's Latin Record, which he had before him. And he presents no objection against the illegal form of the whole proceeding: instead of bringing charges against her at once, Cauchon interrogated her for weeks, in order to gather already-confessed offenses for charges. Prévosteau also mistakenly attributes Joan's illness, which occurred later, just before the judges visited her on April 18, to the earlier prison interrogations.)

He goes on to say that, to prevent her from dying a natural death and to preserve her for an immortal departure full of public infamy, the defen dants had many physicians tend to her (art. 13). Then, and when she was recovering from her illness, they vexed her with questions about certain apparitions of good spirits and about the Church, which she answered well (art. 14).[7]

Joan repeatedly rejected the judges' jurisdiction over her. She recused them as her capital enemies, which, because it was not taken up and discussed, automatically nullified all that followed; and she often required the pope's judgment, which was a legitimate appeal (art. 15).[8]

Joan gave good responses concerning her visions (art. 16), and also concerning the Church, to which she submitted and often requested everything to be brought to the judgment of the pope and the general council (art. 17). When some clergy wished to tell Joan to submit to the council, Cauchon silenced them, and frightened off or expelled other learned men (art. 18).[9]

The said accusers (*actores*), wishing for a judgment of death, continued the iniquitous trial after her illness, with the promotor of Beauvais prosecuting (the Seventy Articles) (art. 19). The defendants concocted articles allegedly from her responses (the Twelve Articles) and obtained many opinions concerning them (art. 20). The articles were distortions of her answers, and those who were misled by them should not be blamed (art.

[6] NT 1:114–16.
[7] NT 1:116–17.
[8] NT 1:117.
[9] NT 1:118.

21). Apart from the good notaries who compiled the French record, others produced falsities, and it is believed that the articles were based on their entries. Moreover, "a certain other person" (*quidam alius*) produced a so-called authentic record, much different from the French one (art. 22).[10]

(Prévosteau doubtless knew from Manchon that the author of the Latin Record was Courcelles, but he did not name him; he was set to be a witness in the coming investigations.)

After Joan was cured of her illness, the two judges passed two iniquitous sentences against her, even though no heresy or other crime had been proved against her, contrary to all law (art. 23). By these means the said defendants proceeded to a prepared abjuration, which, as noted, had no matter of the faith in it. After this was read, which Joan did not understand, they sentenced her to perpetual prison, even though they said that she was returning to the bosom of the Church (art. 24). Then, contrary to their promise to put her in the company of honest women, these wicked judges sent her to be chained among her capital enemies, the English (art. 25). During the night these defendants or their accomplices removed her women's clothes from where she had them ready to put on and replaced them with only men's clothes, which she would have to put on when she tended to the call of nature (art. 26). What is worse, someone came to her in her bed and tried to rape her, and to protect herself she had to put on the male clothes (art. 27).[11]

The defendants then falsely accused her of relapse into heresy, even though she had not fallen into any heresy in the first place, for, having understood nothing of the text of abjuration read to her, she had effectively abjured nothing (art. 28). Even though this conclusion was not reached by a majority of the consultants, the defendants decreed that she would be condemned as relapsed (art. 29). Then, only six or eight days after the first sentence, they iniquitously passed the second sentence condemning her of relapse and delivered her to the secular arm, and a sermon slanderously defamed her of heresy (art. 30).[12]

Prévosteau could have been specific: the first sentence was delivered on May 24, and it was exactly six days later, May 30, that the second sentence was pronounced. He could also have revealed that it was Nicolas Midi

[10] NT 1:118–19.
[11] NT 1: 119–21.
[12] NT 1:121–22.

who preached the slanderous sermon, but he has so far avoided naming names of conspirators. Perhaps he knew that Midi was dead. Thomas de Courcelles would testify in the following month, January, 1456, that he believed that the deceased Nicolas Midi was the one who had formulated the much denounced Twelve Articles.[13]

Joan was put to the flames with no further judicial action after being delivered by the defendants, her capital enemies (art. 31). She died with admirable patience and piety (art. 32), and therefore it is to be concluded that Joan lived and died without stain of heresy as a good Christian (art. 33).[14]

Because many believe that Joan's innocence was besmirched and her kinfolk's reputation damaged, the latter rightly obtained a rescript from the pope, directed to the present honorable judges, to declare Joan's innocence and to restore their good standing (art. 34).[15]

15.3 Formal Objections Against the Trial

However, even though the above, and the depositions to follow, is enough to establish the case, some more should be said to elucidate the nullity and iniquity of the proceedings (art. 35), both in form and matter (art. 36). The nullity follows from the rule of law that no impediment comes from what is not lawful (art. 36),[16] and the plaintiffs follow canonical authorities in asserting that the trials and sentences of the said defendants are null (art. 38). Citing both canon law[17] and civil law, Prévosteau says that Joan was not under the jurisdiction of the bishop of Beauvais: she had no domicile there, and none of the crimes ascribed to her were said to be committed there (art. 39).[18] This last article expanded on the first reason given for nullity by Dean Maugier on December 15.

[13] NT 1:357.

[14] NT 1:122–23.

[15] NT 1:122.

[16] Referring to *Sext* 5.[13].52 (CIC 2:1123).

[17] He cites X 2.2 (*De foro competenti*) though a wrong chapter (*At si clericus*), which comes from the previous title, *De judiciis* (2.1.4, CIC 2:240), but it has the statement "A sentence passed by someone not one's judge does not hold"). However, he goes on to cite the last chapter in title 2, *Licet ratione* (X 2.2.20, CIC 2:255), which speaks of cases before a bishop "by reason of crime, contract, or domicile."

[18] NT 1:123–25.

Since Cauchon was automatically suspended and Lemaistre excommunicated for falsely charging Joan with heresy, in virtue of the Clementine constitution *Multorum*,[19] their sentences were not valid (art. 40). Cauchon lost any competency when Joan recused him as a capital enemy (art. 41). Lemaistre's actions were null because he acted from force and fear of the English (art. 42). Joan clearly appealed to the pope, which nullified further proceedings (art. 43). Major cases were to be sent to the pope (art. 44). The harsh conditions, especially considering her age and sex, were a cause of nullity (art. 45). These conditions amounted to torture, so that anything that seems incriminating in her responses can be discounted as produced under torture (art. 46).[20]

Joan was denied counsel in spite of her young age (art. 47), and trials against undefended persons under twenty-five are null (art. 48). The law commends mercy and moderation for young offenders, not shown by the defendants (art. 49). Records of trials are to be accurate, but these judges, especially Cauchon, falsified the record (art. 50). Articles were falsely formed, omitting her justifications and submissions to Church and Holy See, and given to consultants (art. 51). False consultants claiming to be true Frenchmen urged her not to submit to the Church (art. 52). For all these defects of form, the proceedings should be declared null and void by the delegated judges (art. 53).[21]

Like other defenders of Joan, Prévosteau neglects to impugn Cauchon for failing to bring charges against Joan immediately, in the form of the promotor's libellus, which allowed him, first alone, and then, in Joan's prison cell, in the company of Lemaistre, to interrogate Joan without indicating what crimes they were going to accuse her of. It was only when the Rota Judge Lohier pointed out this defect in the proceedings that Estivet finally ran through his list of seventy articles, and was able to expand on them from Joan's enforced answers, especially with regard to the manufactured crime of failing to submit to the Church Militant. But by that time, they already had enough to concoct the Twelve Articles to send to the University and other consultants.

[19] Clement V, *Multorum*, *Clem.* 5.2.1 §4 (CIC 2:1182),

[20] NT 1:125–28. He cites the chapter *Cum in contemplatione* from the title *De regulis juris* (X 5.41.6, CIC 2:928), stipulating that cases are not to begin with torture. Duparc mistakenly refers to Justinian, *Digest* 50.17.

[21] NT 1:128–32.

Even though this illegal method of making defendants incriminate themselves put them at a terrific disadvantage, once they did it, their admissions were fair game, which Prévosteau must have known: although Joan's responses were coerced, once she responded in court everything that she said was automatically "notorious," and would have to be dealt with unless it could be impugned in some way, for instance, as something false admitted by a defendant under torture in order to stop the torture. This was the purport of Prévosteau's article 46. In the articles that follow, he takes up the accusations manufactured from her "confessions."

15.4 The False Accusations

Prévosteau will argue that the recorded responses to the interrogations in no way justify any of the charges or conclusions that were expressed against her. Rather her responses show her never to have deviated from the Catholic faith (art. 54). First, regarding her visions of spirits: her adversaries call them evil, and charged her with being an idolater, erring, heretical, and an invoker of demons. The plaintiffs contend that they cannot and should not be judged as other than good (art. 55). Such determinations should be left to God, for the Church does not judge secret matters (art. 56). The plaintiffs argue that they were good spirits, because Joan was a good and simple girl, a confirmed virgin (art. 57). She lived a devout life (art. 58), and the spirits urged her to good deeds (art. 59). She also died piously in the midst of the flames (art. 60). She often predicted true things, notably the victory of our king and the expulsion of the English (art. 61). Such pre-announced truths should be judged to come not from the Spirit of Evil but from God, who is Truth; and we should see her military feats as done by divine not malign aid (art. 62).[22]

Joan should be excused for fighting on behalf of her king, first, because the war was just, and second, because she was commanded by God, for the law of inspiration surpasses all laws; it excused Samson from homicide, Jacob from lying, Abraham from adultery, and David from having many wives, as pointed out in the decretal *Gaudemus* (art. 63).[23] (Adding these

[22] NT 1:132–36.

[23] NT 1:136, citing Innocent III, *Gaudemus*, X 4.19.8 (CIC 2:723–24), who says that by divine revelation Jacob was excused from lying, the Israelites from theft, Samson from homicide, and the patriarchs with their many wives from adultery.

examples of what would ordinarily be sinful behavior hardly strengthened Prévosteau's argument that Joan was sinless in participating in a just war.)

Even if her apparitions came from evil spirits, Joan should be excused: because she honored them, deeming them saints. This can in no way be considered idolatry, as Gratian points out in his discourse on kinds of error—in this case mistakes of person, as when the Devil appears as an angel of light (art. 64).[24]

Joan's adversaries also try to blame her for wearing men's clothing, forbidden by the canon *Si qua mulier* in Gratian's Distinction 30, and also in Deuteronomy, chapter 22. But Joan did this licitly, for reasons given in the next article (art. 65).[25]

As his first justification, Prévosteau asserts that Joan had a reasonable cause for wearing the clothes that she did, and that what is done by divine inspiration is not culpable, for where the Spirit of God is there is liberty, as St Paul says (2 Cor. 3.17). Secondly, the laws cited mean that women should not wear male clothes for purposes of lust, as explained by the scholars. Joan, on the contrary, wore them to prevent lust and avoid provoking men to lust. Moreover, clerics are allowed to change from clerical clothes, as Innocent III says in the decretal *Clerici* (i.e., the Fourth Lateran canon mandating proper garb for clerics, "unless a just cause of fear necessitates a change of habit").[26] Joan used male clothes to preserve her virginity and to defend her virtue, which the English sometimes attempted to violate, as is established through her confessions and legitimate proofs, and will be established further (art. 66). Furthermore, Joan offered to wear women's clothing if she were put among women and in a Church prison, and not imprisoned among her enemies. She also put on women's clothing in obedience to her pretensed judges, and only resumed male clothes out of necessity and to protect herself, as detailed above (art. 67). Nor is it true that Joan refused to hear mass if she had to wear female clothes (art. 68). Nor did she deserve to be called relapsed for resuming her clothes, as also explained above (art. 69).[27]

As for going off without parental permission, a divine command superseded such authority, and, besides, she asked and received her parents'

[24] NT 1:136–37, citing Gratian, *Decretum*, C. 29 q. 1, §4 (CIC 1:1092). St Paul warns about Satan sometimes appearing as an angel of light, 2 Cor. 11.4.

[25] NT 1:137.

[26] Innocent III, *Clerici*, X 3.1.15 (Fourth Lateran c. 16, CIC 2:453): "…nisi justa causa timoris exegerit habitum transformari."

[27] NT 1:137–38.

pardon (art. 70). He brushes off her use of the name of Jesus in her letters (art. 71), and the accusation of "desperation" in leaping from the tower (art. 72). As for the angel and crown, she did not lie about them but lawfully concealed the truth (art. 73).[28] He explains away the allegations about her confidence in salvation (art. 74), predictions of the future (art. 75), statements about saints hating the English, and supposedly saying she never sinned (art. 76).[29]

Next, Prévosteau devotes a series of articles to the false and deceitful accusation that she did not wish to submit to the Church. Although she was not obliged to do so, in fact she did. On the first point, one acting under divine inspiration is exempt from the common law; and one cannot act against one's conscience (art. 78). Moreover, the Church does not and cannot judge secret matters. We are bound to believe certain doctrines, but are free to follow our own view on other things; Fathers like Gregory and Augustine disagree on some points. Joan did not err in holding her own opinion (art. 78).[30]

Being a simple girl, Joan at first did not understand what was meant by "the Church," but, after it was explained to her, she always expressed her submission (art. 79). Learned men who wished to clarify the deliberately obscure questions of the judges and tell Joan that the universal Church was meeting at the time in Basel and that she could submit herself to it there were hounded out of the city by Cauchon and others, among them Houppeville, Lohier, and Lafontaine, who were forced to return home (*ad propria*) (art. 80).[31]

It will be proved that men disguised as her partisans came to her in prison and urged her never to submit to the judgment of the Church if she ever wished to get out of prison; therefore, if she said anything wrong, they should bear the blame (art. 81). However, if her responses are carefully studied, they will all be found to be without any offense to the faith or the Church (art. 82). Moreover, granted her simplicity and sincerity, it will be seen that she always implicitly and explicitly submitted to the judgment of the Church (art. 83).[32]

[28] NT 1:138–40.
[29] NT 1:140–41.
[30] NT 1:141–42.
[31] NT 1:142–43.
[32] NT 1:143–44.

In fact, Joan explicitly submitted herself to the Church, for she repeatedly asked to be sent to the pope, to whom major cases are to be referred, as we see in the decretal *Majores* (Pope Innocent III's assertion before his instruction on baptism) and the canon *Hec est fides* in Gratian (St Jerome writing to Pope Damasus) (art. 84).[33] Earlier, Prévosteau had spoken of Joan's requests to be taken to the pope as judicial appeals. Here he is invoking them as an indication of her willingness to subject herself to the Church.

Furthermore, Joan submitted to the general council, and she wanted the Church to review the articles before she abjured, which her judges refused. Thus, it was the judges rather than Joan who refused to submit to the Church (art. 85).[34]

(We see that this article is in keeping with the general tenor of the articles, aimed at exculpating Joan and just proving her judges at fault in finding her guilty, whereas the plaintiffs should have been bringing explicit charges against the judges for violating the laws of judicial procedure.)

Shortly before her end, Joan was allowed by the judges to receive Communion, which means that they acknowledged that she had submitted to the Church (art. 86).[35] (It might have been retorted that it was only after she repented her sins that she was allowed Communion. But in fact no public statement was recorded of her repentance. Cauchon merely said from the scaffold that he had appointed two friars to urge her to repentance).[36]

Joan could not be said to be relapsed into heresy, because nothing that she had said before her conviction showed that she had fallen into any heresy in the first place (art. 87).[37]

She understood nothing of the schedule of abjuration that was read to her, and therefore she did not understand what she abjured. The Abbot of Fécamp and others said that she should be questioned about what she understood, which was not done. She could never have confessed that she was suspect of heresy or had committed the crimes stated there. Therefore: not relapsed (art. 88).[38]

[33] NT 1:144, citing X 3.42.3, *Majores* (CIC 2:644), and Gratian, *Decretum*, C. 24 q. 1 c. 14, *Hec est fides* (CIC 1:970).

[34] NT 1:144.

[35] NT 1:144–45.

[36] LR 411.

[37] NT 1:145.

[38] NT 1:145.

Moreover, it will be abundantly proved that the abjuration contained in the record is not the one that was shown and read to Joan when the judges made her abjure, for that was small in size with little content (art. 89). And, if the words in Joan's confession as relapsed (i.e., referring to her interrogation by the judges on March 28)[39] are rightly understood, she cannot be taken for relapsed. Joan said that she condemned herself to save her life. In other words, she called herself a heretic even though she was not a heretic, only to save her life; she also said that she understood nothing of the abjuration, and that she condemned herself because of her voices, unjustly and ignorantly; and she concluded that she did not intend to revoke anything that was not pleasing to God (she did not say "unless it was pleasing to her revelations or voices"). Therefore, since this was not what was in the abjuration, she could say it without being relapsed (art. 90).[40]

The judges formulated a set of twelve biased articles claiming to sum up Joan's admissions, which were sent to the University of Paris; the rest of the trial and the sentences depended upon them, which makes the proceedings null (art. 91). The consultations held in Rouen and vicinity were similarly based on these fabricated articles, with a presumption of deception (art. 92); all opinions were meant to be formed according to the articles (art. 93).[41] If therefore the consultors had God and conscience before their eyes, as is to be supposed, they are free from all blame, giving just conclusions about a false case. Therefore, the plaintiffs do not wish to make conclusions against them, apart from those who were complicit with the defendants (art. 94).

(The truth was, of course, that even though the Twelve Articles did indeed distort many of Joan's positions, they did not amount to more than an account of a strong-headed girl who claimed to have special revelations from God and the saints. They came nowhere near to constituting the dossier of a heretic. As a result, the great majority of those clerics who submitted comments on them and urged her conviction in a trial of faith deserved to be condemned as accomplices to her murder.)

Prévosteau brings his case to a conclusion by saying that, because the unjust sentences emanated from these false proceedings, they should be nullified (art. 95), and their cruel execution of the sentences, resulting in

[39] LR 395–99.
[40] NT 1:145–46.
[41] NT 1:146–47.

Joan's burning, should be publicly condemned and reparations made (art. 96). In keeping with the present judges' apostolic mandate, Joan's innocence should be made known and her reputation restored to her and her relatives (art. 97).[42]

The plaintiffs ask the judges to decree these conclusions immediately (art. 98), especially since they are formulated in articles, which they offer to them (art. 99), and they renew their request to have their promotor joined to them against the defendants (art. 100). Finally, they assert that all of the above articles are true and publicly known (art. 101).[43]

Prévosteau ends with a long supplication to the judges, the oral version of which he gave on December 18: that they, for the foregoing reasons, declare the trial of pretensed inquisition or matter of faith against Joan of Arc to have been based on invalidity, deceit, falsities, lies, and manifest violence and wickedness, should find it null and void, and declare it of no effect and revoked; moreover they should vindicate Joan's innocence with a definitive sentence, declaring her free of any stain of heresy or guilt of crime, with all infamy removed from her and hers, and that this sentence should be posted publicly in her place of execution and elsewhere, with epitaphs erected in her honor in Rouen and other suitable places. He urges that her vindication be recorded in the chronicles of France, and that the guilty defendants be assessed heavy pecuniary fines to be paid to the plaintiffs.[44]

[42] NT 1:147–48.
[43] NT 1:148.
[44] NT 1:148–50.

CHAPTER 16

Proving the Charges

16.1 Charges Accepted and Inquests Ordered, February 1456

The written form of Prévosteau's libellus, summarized in the last chapter, was handed in on December 20, 1455, after having been delivered in summary *viva voce* on December 18. Another thing that supposedly happened on December 20 was the promulgation of a citation with that date, summoning the current bishop of Beauvais, Guillaume de Hellande, to appear at the court in Rouen on February 16, as well as the promotor of causes for the diocese and the sub-inquisitor of heresy of the diocese, in accord with the papal commission.[1] It is noteworthy that both Cauchon and Lemaistre are said to be deceased in this citation, and the same is true in the Lorraine inquest authorized on that date, taken up below.[2]

A note following says that the citation was executed on Monday, February 9, 1456, by being posted on the doors of Rouen Cathedral, and a copy left for a week.[3] Another note, by the notary Gérard Toussaint, follows, rehearsing that on February 12, in virtue of the citation and representing the Arc family, Toussaint went to the bishop of Beauvais and the promotor and served them. They told him that they had no interest in the

[1] NT 1:157–63, at p. 158.
[2] NT 1:248.
[3] NT 1:163.

H. A. Kelly, *The Trial and Retrial of Joan of Arc*, The New Middle Ages, https://doi.org/10.1007/978-3-032-07887-2_16

matter, as they had stated before. At the time of the trial, Pierre Cauchon was bishop ("whom you, most reverend Father, Archbishop of Rheims, succeeded"), and he held the trial in a different jurisdiction. Nevertheless, Toussaint gave them a copy of the summons and of the plaintiffs' articles, which they were unwilling to accept. He then went to the Dominican church and asked Prior Morlaines if there was a sub-inquisitor there; even though no one there knew any such, he nevertheless left the citation and articles with the unwilling prior and convent.[4]

On the scheduled day of the court's resumption, February 16, only two of the judges appeared, namely, Bishop Chartier of Paris and Bréhal.[5] Prévosteau was also there, but a proctor appeared in Chapitault's place, a canon lawyer named Jean Rebours or Le Rebours, who presented his letter of authorization, dated February 13.[6] The promotor of the diocese of Beauvais, Regnault Brédoulle, also showed up, for himself and as proctor of Bishop Hellande.

The court adjourned and resumed on the next day, February 17, when Prévosteau and Rebours asked that the submitted libellus be accepted, and the defendants be required to contest the case, if need be. The articles, first turned in on December 20, but postponed for consideration until that day (February 17), were read and accepted, and Prévosteau and Rebours were admitted to prove them. Brédoulle first said that he did not believe that the contents of the articles were true, or that Bishop Cauchon did what he was said to have done. He left all defense to the judicial process that Cauchon produced. He consented to having witnesses sworn in, but did not intend to appear further in the matter, saying it was of no concern to him, and he did not wish to respond further to the articles. This could be considered a contesting of the case (*litis contestatio*),[7] which sufficed for the beginning of the trial. The proctor for the Beauvais Dominicans also appeared. He ignored the articles and insisted that there was no sub-inquisitor in their priory, and requested that no more citations be sent to them.

After considering these allegations and excuses and also those of Cauchon's heirs, instead of saying that they were accepted, the bishop of

[4] NT 1:163–65.

[5] NT 1:150–51.

[6] NT 1:152.

[7] *Pace* Philippe Contamine, "Le procès en revision de la condemnation de Jeanne d'Arc (1450–1456): raisons, obstacles, procedure, résultats," *Histoire de la Justice* 30 (2020, no. 1) 17–36, who says that there was no *litis contestatio* in this trial (p. 30).

Paris, in the name of all the judges, simply declared that "all others who were cited and did not appear" were in contempt.[8]

Bishop Chartier then set the beginning of the inquest to prove the articles on February 25 in Paris and its completion on April 5 in Rouen,[9] and Bréhal appointed another Dominican to take his place in examining witnesses.[10] But on March 31, less than a week before the deadline, Chartier and Bréhal agreed to an extension to April 21; but on April 18, another extension was sought and granted, namely, May 12.[11]

16.2 Completed Inquests Received, May 13, 1456

Chartier and Bréhal sat in tribunal on May 12; Prévosteau and a different stand-in for Chapitault, namely Jean Levieux, appeared before them to present the completed inquests.[12] Court was adjourned until the next day, and the depositions were received, with orders to cite adverse parties to reply to them on June 1.[13] The texts of the accumulated inquests follow.

But first the "information" organized by Cardinal Estouteville in 1452 was presented.[14] However, the aborted investigation ordered by Charles VII in 1450 was not included.

There follows the report of the inquest authorized by the judges on December 20, 1455, to be held in Joan's place of origin, as described above. The inquest was assigned to two local clerics, the dean of the church in Vaucouleurs and a canon of Toul. The Twelve Articles for deposing witnesses included two about Joan's attendance at church and her going to confession, but nothing about her receiving Communion. One question was whether any inquests had been made in Lorraine earlier, after Joan was captured at Compiègne and held by the English.[15] The commissioners received their instructions on January 26, 1456, and completed their task on February 13, having interviewed thirty-four witnesses, only three of whom reported inquests conducted on behalf of the English king.[16]

[8] NT 1:154–56.
[9] NT 1:156–57.
[10] NT 1:165–66.
[11] NT 1:167–70.
[12] NT 1:170–71. He appeared earlier as a proctor for the Arc family (1:30).
[13] NT 1:173–75.
[14] NT 1:176–244.
[15] NT 1:248–51.
[16] NT 1:251–315. Testimony about earlier inquests is on pp. 293, 303, and 310–11.

Next follows the inquest at Orleans. The commission is not given, but the first and sixth depositions were conducted by Guillaume Bouillé, dean of Noyon, familiar from the events of 1449–1450, and a sub- or vice-inquisitor. The longest deposition is the first, that of the count of Dunois, taken on February 22, and the next five are dated later, namely, February 25, March 7, two on March 8, and the next on March 16.[17] The remainder, nos. 7–40, with mainly minimal responses, are undated and the examiners not noted.[18]

As for the Paris inquest, there was a citation of witnesses sent out on January 10, 1456: five, including Courcelles were named, and others would be supplied by the bearer of the citation.[19] On February 17, there was a citation of all potential defendants to appear in the episcopal court in Paris on February 25 to see witnesses sworn in to prove articles against Cauchon, Lemaistre, and Estivet.[20] There follow lengthy depositions on articles that are not supplied. The first two, examined on April 2, are physicians who attended Joan when she was ill in prison.[21] Also testifying on April 2 was Jean de Mailly, bishop of Noyon, who did not attend the trial but was present at the abjuration. The next is Courcelles, who was first deposed on January 15, and now is being interrogated again, probably on April 2 or April 3.[22] The date is not given, but the next witness, Jean Monnet, who acted as a scribe for Beaupère, was deposed on April 3, and following him is a squire who testified on April 5.[23] The next is another squire, who was interviewed later in the month, on April 20, before the judges themselves, Archbishop Jouvenal, Bishop Chartier, and Bréhal's substitute, Friar Verel, as were the next three, on April 30, and the duke of Alençon on May 3,[24] and the rest of the witnesses through May 11.[25]

The date of the citation of witnesses in Rouen is not given,[26] but many of them were recalled on May 11 to testify again on May 12.[27] The monk

[17] NT 1:316–32.
[18] NT 1:333–40.
[19] NT 1:345.
[20] NT 1:41–44.
[21] NT 1:347–49.
[22] NT 1:355.
[23] NT 1:359, 362, 367.
[24] NT 1:370–80.
[25] NT 1:388–410.
[26] NT 1:344.
[27] NT 1:346.

Miget, Prior of Longueville, was first examined on December 16, and the notary Manchon on December 17, and now both were re-examined on May 12, the latter at great length.[28] The next ten, notably, Urban Dean Massieu, the second notary Boisguillaume, Friar Ladvenu, Nicolas de Houppeville, Friar/Bishop Lefèvre, and Archdeacon Marguerie, were similarly recalled from December.[29] The final seven, including the third notary, Nicolas Taquel, seem to have been first interviewed now, in May of 1456.[30]

Finally, there was a single deposition taken at Lyons on May 28, 1456, that of Jean d'Aulon, seneschal of Beaucaire.[31]

16.3 Testimony of Thomas de Courcelles, ca. April 1456

Since Courcelles played such an important role in Joan's trial in preparing the official record, his testimony deserves a close look. Note that when we last saw him, he was deeply involved with the schismatic Council of Basel and its new pope, Felix V, who wished to make him a cardinal. Later on, he adroitly changed sides and was instrumental in putting an end to the schism he fomented. In 1447 he suddenly appeared as Charles VII's theologian on the committee of conciliation headed by Archbishop Jouvenal, which the king had set up the previous year, and he helped to compose the bull of retraction published by Pope Nicholas V on January 18, 1449. He was appointed a canon of Paris in that year, and succeeded Ciboule as penitentiary in 1451, a position he still held. He was now about fifty-six years old when he was sworn and examined.[32] His testimony could have been much more informative than it was, but he constantly pleaded a faulty memory. I conjecture the content of the articled questions.

Q 1–4 (Joan's youth): Courcelles testifies that the only *fama* then and there about the young Joan was that she said that she experienced voices from God.

[28] NT 1:411–28.

[29] NT 1:428–58.

[30] NT 1:458–73. Taquel of course also testified in 1452 (1:196–200). This time (p. 465), he says that the Latin Record was made "a great time (*magnum spatium*) after Joan's death," but he can't remember exactly when.

[31] NT 1:473–88.

[32] NT 1:355.

Q 5 (Cauchon and Lemaistre as judges): He supposes that Cauchon accepted the task of proceeding against Joan because he was a counsellor of the king of England, and Joan was captured in his diocese. He heard that the inquisitor was given a gift to participate, but he heard nothing of the sort about the bishop.

Q 6 (Courcelles's participation): He was at Paris at the time and was ordered by the bishop to come to Rouen to participate in the process. He came with Midi and others, some of whom he could not recall. He did not know whether any preliminary investigations were made in Rouen or in Joan's place of origin; he never saw any, and did not recall that any informations were read in court.[33] After Master Jean Lohier arrived in Rouen, it was ordered that the proceedings thus far be communicated with him in some way. After he had read the record, he told Courcelles that he did not think that Joan should be proceeded against in matters of faith unless there had first been an investigation on infamy, which was required as a matter of law. Courcelles well remembered that in the first deliberation he himself did not conclude that Joan was a heretic unless she should pertinaciously maintain that she should not submit to the Church. In the third and last deliberation, as far as his conscience could bear witness, before God, he stated that she was as before, and if she was a heretic earlier, she was one then; but he never positively considered her a heretic.

Q 7 (threats against assessors): He remembers nothing.

Q 8 (zeal of the English against Joan): He remembers nothing.

Q 9 (Joan in custody): She was in the Rouen Castle prison, in iron fetters (whether always so or not, he did not know); many assessors believed that she should be in the Church prison, but he does not recall whether it was brought up in the formal deliberations.

Q 10 (Joan as virgin): Cauchon said that she was found to be a virgin, and she undoubtedly was, since otherwise the trial would not have remained silent about it.

Q 11–13, 18) She underwent several interrogations, but he does not remember what she was asked about, except, once, whether people on her side kissed her hands. Nor does he remember that Joan complained about being interrogated. He does recall that at one point it was decreed that she would henceforth be questioned in the presence of only a few

[33] NT 1:355–56.

persons, but does not know why, and also that Master Jean Lafontaine was one of those appointed to do the questioning.

Q 14 (Joan's illness, attending physicians): [not mentioned]

Q 15 (Joan's rejection of her judges): [not mentioned]

Q 16 (submission to the Church): She was asked about submitting herself and her deeds to the determination of the Church, to which she gave several answers, as can be found in the record, to which he refers.[34] (If Courcelles was able on this occasion to refer to the record, which he himself compiled, surely it could have been consulted at many points to assist his faulty memory. Perhaps his questioners did not have the text available.)

Q 20–21 (the Twelve Articles): It was reasonably conjectured that they were compiled by Master Nicolas Midi, now deceased. But whether there was any deliberation for the purpose of correcting them and whether they were ever corrected, he does not know.[35]

Q 22 (spies on Joan): He was told more than once by Master Nicolas Loiseleur that he spoke several times with Joan while in disguise, but does not know what he said to her. He did tell her that he was a priest, and he thinks he heard her in confession.[36]

Q 23–25 (on the scaffold at Saint Ouen): A little before the first sermon, Master Jean Chastillon exhorted her several times, in his presence; and he heard that Master Pierre Maurice exhorted her fraternally about submitting to the Church, but he remembers nothing more.

He does not know who wrote the text of the abjuration beginning "You, Joan," nor does he know what was read or explained to her. While he himself was seated in the scaffolding behind the prelates, Master Erard gave a sermon, but he does not remember what he said, except that he referred to "the pride of this woman." After Cauchon started reading the sentence, something was said to Joan and she responded, he knows not what. But he does remember that Master Nicolas de Venderès produced a sheet of writing beginning with the words *Quotiens cordis oculus* (As often as the eye of the heart), but whether it is in the record or not he does not know, and whether he was holding it before or after Joan's abjuration he is not sure, but thinks it was before. He did hear some of the assessors

[34] NT 1:357–57.
[35] NT 1:357–58.
[36] NT 1:358.

speaking with Cauchon, telling him that he should not finish the sentence but receive her to recant, but does not remember the exact words.[37]

Q 26 (resumption of male clothing): Word came to Cauchon that Joan had put on male clothing again, and he went to see her. Courcelles went with him. When she was asked why, she said that it was more fitting to wear male clothes when in the company of men, rather than women's dress.

Q 27–28 (on the scaffold in the Old Market): He was present at the sermon and the reading of the sentence, but left before she was burned. He thinks that she went to Communion. That is all he knows.

The most telling thing he said about any heresy on her part focused on whether she submitted to the Church or not. He should have remembered that when she was on the scaffold the first time and was once again urged to submit to Holy Mother Church, she repeated her demand to be taken before the pope in Rome. Doubtless this was a sore point with Courcelles, since he had recently gone through a long phase in which he himself refused to submit to the pope of Rome.

16.4 Old Assessor Jean Lefèvre, Then Witness, Now Judge, June 1, 1456

On June 1, two substitute judges took the place of Archbishop Jouvenal and Bishop Chartier. One was the canonist Hector de Coquerel, Official of Rouen, and the other the theologian, Jean Lefèvre, since 1441 an auxiliary bishop serving in Rouen.[38]

Lefèvre had been an assiduous assessor at the proceedings against Joan, beginning with her first appearance on February 21, 1431. When polled on how to proceed on March 27, the first day of Joan's actual trial, Lefèvre simply referred to the jurists.[39] As to procedure after the consultations were in, on May 19, he aligned with the harsh theologians of Rouen and Paris, but voted that she should be charitably admonished and given time to respond.[40] In the final poll, on May 29, after Joan had been found again

[37] NT 1:358.
[38] NT 1:489–90.
[39] FM 188.
[40] LR 370.

in male clothes and confiding in her voices, he agreed that she should be declared a relapsed heretic; he added that she was "pertinacious, contumacious, and disobedient."[41]

When he was first interviewed as a witness, in the Estouteville inquiry of 1452, he testified that at one point he had tried to intervene on her behalf: when she was being pressed on whether she was in the state of grace, he objected that it was not a proper thing to ask of her. But Cauchon told him that it would be better for him to keep quiet. He was very positive in his report about Joan, saying that she seemed inspired in her responses over three weeks, when answering questions designed to make her contradict herself. He never heard her refuse to submit to the Church. He said that her pious end moved even the judges to tears.[42]

Lefèvre was one of the "old and sick" witnesses interviewed in December 1455,[43] who were called again in May 1456. Only the later deposition was recorded, when it was said that he was around seventy years of age.[44] He repeated that he thought that her answers were inspired, though he believed that she depended too much on her revelations. He thought that the English proceeded against her out of hate and fear, but whether the judges hated her he could not say. But he knew that the proceedings were being paid for by the English, and all were afraid to say what they thought—and here he repeated his earlier testimony about being silenced by Cauchon. He did not repeat his statement that the judges were moved to tears.[45] His claim that he tried to intervene on Joan's behalf was confirmed by the testimony of Dean Massieu.[46]

We may agree that he was probably induced by fear to go along with the other assessors in recommending Joan's conviction as a relapsed heretic. But his additional judgment about her insubordination and disobedience does not put him in a good light.

[41] FM/LR 405–06 (cf. 402–03).
[42] NT 1:237–38.
[43] NT 1:96–98.
[44] NT 1:447.
[45] NT 1:447–50.
[46] NT 1:430.

16.5 Vacuous Contempt Proceedings and Productions of Evidence, Ending July 2, 1456

On May 30, 1456, Jouvenal and Chartier wrote a letter to Lefèvre and Coquerel appointing them to serve in their place alongside Bréhal in a case pending between the Arc plaintiffs and the current bishop of Beauvais and the promotor of cases of the diocese of Beauvais, as well as the (nonexistent) sub-inquisitor of the same diocese. They stated that "for certain reasons" they could not be present to continue the proceedings.[47] It will turn out that they were in Paris reviewing the evidence in the case.

On June 1, Promotor Prévosteau and Chapitault's substitute Levieux appeared before Lefèvre, Coquerel, and Bréhal, and announced that this was the day on which the bishop of Beauvais and the other two designated defendants were cited to appear, to speak against the evidence which they had submitted for the Arc side (in the case of Prévosteau) and for the judges (on Levieux's part), and which had been published by the judges Chartier and Bréhal. Then, because Jouvenal and Chartier were absent (the record mistakenly says that it was Chartier and Bréhal who were absent), Lefèvre and Coquerel, deputed by them, presented their letter of deputation to one of the notaries. Thereupon the court was adjourned until the next day. Three nondescript persons and the notary Boisguillaume were witnesses at the session.[48]

Boisguillaume and three other random witnesses attended the session on June 2, in which the two proctors appeared before Lefèvre, Coquerel, and Bréhal, and asked for the defendants to be declared in contempt. It was so ordered, and June 4 was assigned to the parties for further productions.[49] The two proctors appeared on that day, accusing the defendants of contempt, as is the custom (*ut est moris*), only to be continued to the next day.[50] They did the same thing on June 5 (mistakenly called "25"), on which day another day was assigned, namely June 9.[51]

Two citations for the so-called defendants had been prepared by the judges, Jouvenal, Chartier, and Bréhal, on May 10, one for June 1[52] and

[47] NT 1:490–92.
[48] NT 1:489–90.
[49] NT 1:492–93.
[50] NT 1:493.
[51] NT 1:498–99.
[52] NT 1:494–95.

the other for "two days after being served."[53] It was served (by being posted) on June 1,[54] before the defendants were condemned for contempt in not obeying the June 1 citation, which was decreed on June 2.

Various productions were made by the proctors on June 5, notably a page of Manchon's corrections to the original trial record.[55]Also produced was Henry VI's important open letter of June 12, 1431, summarized in Chapter 11, offering to defend anyone accused before the pope or general council of prosecuting Joan,[56] and the record of the inquest conducted by Cardinal Estouteville.[57]

There follows in the record the citation for June 9 by the substitute judges, dated June 5, 1456, of the usual alleged defendants (*rei*), namely, the bishop, promotor, and nonexistent sub-inquisitor of Beauvais, with only Cauchon of the original trial said to be dead.[58] On that day, business was continued until June 10, when the non-appearing defendants were again declared in contempt, and Lefèvre and Coquerel left the setting of the date for concluding the trial to the actual delegated judges and Inquisitor Bréhal.[59]

On June 18, 1456, there appeared for the first time in the Rouen courtroom, along with Archbishop Jouvenal, Bishop Chartier, and Inquisitor Bréhal, the third commissioner, the Bishop of Coutances, Richard Olivier de Longueil.[60] He was a Norman, a jurist, who had been serving as the Official of Rouen in 1449 when King Charles VII was welcomed into the city after the withdrawal of the English occupiers. He was an important personage, on the king's council and entrusted with various missions. The pope would make him a cardinal at the end of this current year.[61] We will see below that Olivier had already joined the other judges in Paris for their deliberations.

[53] NT 1:499–500.
[54] NT 1:500–01.
[55] NT 1:496–97, 501–03.
[56] NT 1:503–07.
[57] NT 1:510.
[58] NT 1:510–13.
[59] NT 1:513–15.
[60] NT 1:515–16.
[61] Duparc, *Procès*, 5:21. He became cardinal in the consistory of December 17, 1456, as did Eneo Silvio Piccolomini, who would become the next pope, Pius II, less than two years later.

The judges assigned July 1 for the conclusion of the case.[62] (In the citation this time both Cauchon and Lemaistre were said to be dead.[63]) On that day, Prévosteau appeared with Chapitault himself before the four judges and accused the no-shows of contempt, but the judges continued the case to the next day.[64]

On July 2, before the four judges, there appeared, along with the judges' promotor, Chapitault, one of the Arc brothers, Jean, speaking for himself, over the protests of Prévosteau, who still represented his mother Isabelle and brother Pierre. The usual suspects were declared in contempt, and cited again for July 7.[65]

Then Simon Chapitault, the promotor appointed by the judges to help conduct the case, presented in writing his concluding summary, called *motiva juris*, "reasons of law,"[66] produced below in the record.[67] Guillaume Prévosteau, formerly the proctor of the whole Arc family, must have done the same, with the *motiva juris* of the plaintiffs.[68]

16.6 Promotor Chapitault's Concluding Statement

Since this trial was set up as a civil suit by the Arc family seeking damages from defendants, the judges should by right have been neutral between the parties, and the same should have been true of their appointed proctor. But, as has been evident, Chapitault obviously threw in with the proctor of the plaintiffs, and there was no defendant or defendant's proctor to object, since the real *rei*, accused guilty persons, were dead or unfindable, and only "dummy" defendants were put in their place.

[62] NT 1:516.

[63] NT 2:4–7.

[64] NT 1:516–17. In the brief summary of July 1 that follows, pp. 517–18, the Bishop of Paris is omitted from the list of judges, and "Guillelmus" Prévosteau is called "Johannes."

[65] NT 2:1. At this point Duparc gives two versions of the court record on each page, the top (A) from London, British Museum MS Stowe 84 and Paris, Bibl. Nat. MS lat. 5970 (followed by Quicherat), and the bottom (B) from Paris, Bibl. Nat. MS lat. 17013 (see Duparc, *Procès*, 1:xx–xi). I cite the A text unless otherwise indicated. In this case, the B text omits Prévosteau's protest.

[66] NT 2:2.

[67] NT 2:7–15.

[68] NT 2:15–32.

We have seen Chapitault's views before the new witnesses were interviewed. Now we can expect to examine his assessment of the case after all of the evidence was presented, notably the testimony of a great number of witnesses. However, since he addresses only the delegated judges, without name or number, without mentioning the added judge, Inquisitor Jean Bréhal, and refers to no recent event, it may have been prepared some time before.

He tells the judges that the evidence forces him to show the iniquity of the sentence that the judges in the original trial passed against Joan, and to adhere to the plaintiffs' side. He now wishes to add something further by way of an exhortation.[69]

He runs through the highlights of objections to her prosecution, the judges as capital enemies, the harsh prison, the irrelevance of her male clothing to a trial of the faith, the suppressed investigation into her *fama*, her unswerving rectitude, her status as a minor, her recusal and appeals, the mendacious twisting of her responses in articles sent to consultants, the fabricated abjuration, and the false testimony added after her death.[70]

Added to these are the collected testimonies and the treatises by learned men, which should lead the judges to enforce the strictures of the Clementine constitution *Multorum* and the decretals in the title *De hereticis* in the *Liber Sextus* to correct and punish those who maliciously presume to impose charges of heretical depravity upon the innocent.[71] He approves and praises the case put forward by the plaintiffs and petitions that the suit be canonically concluded.[72]

16.7 Final Presentation of the Plaintiffs

The concluding *motiva juris* of the plaintiffs is similarly framed as a hortatory address to the judges delegated by the pope; however, the pope is named as Nicholas V, from whom the commission had originally been sought, before his death on March 24, 1455—which may mean that the oration's prologue was taken from an early draft.[73] But the judges' promotor is said to be standing with the plaintiffs, and the name of the Beauvais

[69] NT 2:7–8.

[70] NT 2:9–13.

[71] NT 2:14, referring to *Clem.* 5.3.1, *Multorum* §4 (CIC 2:1182) and to *Sext* 5.2 in general (CIC 2:1069–78).

[72] NT 2:14–15.

[73] The mistake is discussed by Belon-Balme, *Jean Bréhal*, pp. 68–69.

promotor is correctly given, *Johannes Estiveti dictus Benedicite*, as one of the three *rei* or defendants.[74]

The opening of this proceeding on December 7, 1455 is recited,[75] and it is stated that there was a valid citation of the opposing parties, with postings in Rouen and Beauvais (but without mention of who the opposing parties were), so that, as a result, every honest person could be aware of it and not remain ignorant of this just proceeding.[76] It was properly held in Rouen, where the wicked proceeding that condemned Joan had been enacted, and all the stages required by law had been decreed, and the deceits and contumacies of the adverse parties accused, and articles, witnesses, and proofs received, and a legitimate comparison of Joan's responses with the pretended excerpts of the Twelve Articles, along with consultations of outstanding doctors, especially over Joan's Catholic responses and visions of good spirits, and the iniquity of those judging her in the original proceeding.[77]

The formal defects of that proceeding were quickly run down: no reason for a trial of faith, Joan was not in the Beauvais jurisdiction, had not committed heresy, Cauchon proceeded without the vice-inquisitor, who, witnesses testified, was threatened; Joan recused Cauchon as a capital enemy, and appealed to the pope; she was harshly imprisoned, allowed no counsel, not referred to the General Council, and articles were falsely extracted.[78]

The rest of the lengthy address deals with the faults against her compiled in that proceeding from that self-testimony compelled from her (no objection to its being compelled before any charges were leveled). Only rarely is there a reference to the deposition of the witnesses. Once, for instance, it is stated that witnesses deposed that Cauchon forbade the notaries to record the multiple times she submitted to the Church.[79]

The theologians and jurists who judged her were excused of blame because they based their opinions on the Twelve Articles—except, of course, for those who were aware of the deception. (In fact, of course, the adverse judgment went far beyond what was warranted even by those articles. The reluctance to seek out and punish Cauchon's willing

[74] NT 2:15–16.
[75] NT 2:16–17.
[76] NT 2:18.
[77] NT 2:18–19.
[78] NT 2:20–21.
[79] NT 2:27.

collaborators has been noteworthy throughout.) The notaries and other witnesses testified to the extent to which the articles were falsified.[80]

Joan was convicted on nothing but wearing male clothes, which had nothing heretical about it; there was no sin of faith, no heresy, no relapse. The sentences accused her of general and vague crimes.[81] It remains for the learned judges to delete the stain of heresy that was put upon her, accompanied with "solemn sermons, representations, images, crosses, and other public signs of perpetual reparation and memory."[82]

16.8 Submission of Treatises, Including a New One by Martin Berruyer, Bishop of Le Mans

According to the dossier, after the above-mentioned motives of law were submitted, consultations in defense of Joan were presented,[83] the first one being the short assessment written by Jean Gerson in the wake of the examination at Poitiers, dated May 14, 1429, giving her his stamp of approval.[84] There follows the long treatise of Élie de Bourdeilles, Bishop of Périgueux,[85] followed by the shorter one of Thomas Basin, Bishop of Lisieux,[86] both spoken of in an earlier chapter, and then that of Martin Berruyer, Bishop of Le Mans, completed only a couple of months earlier, on April 7, 1456.[87]

Berruyer begins by briefly noting that the trial against Joan was invalid because Cauchon as Bishop of Beauvais had no jurisdiction over her, he and his assistants were her capital enemies, and she recused him as her judge, and appealed the trial to the pope.[88]

Then, addressing the substance of the charges, he first argues that Joan's was not a human endeavor but was supernaturally based, and, in a second chapter, that she was clearly motivated not by the Devil but by God, because of her age and character. Regarding the first, he says, her young age would indicate that she was not involved in divination,

[80] NT 2:27–28.
[81] NT 2:30, cf. 23–24.
[82] NT 2:31–32.
[83] NT 2:33.
[84] NT 2:33–39.
[85] NT 2:40–156.
[86] NT 2:157–219.
[87] NT 2:219–57.
[88] NT 2:220.

sortilege, or tacit or explicit pacts with the Devil; it was usually old women, because of lack of faith or some sin, whom God permitted to be deceived by demons.[89] He then shows that she was not guilty of the crimes stated in the sentence against her, lying confectrix of revelations, pernicious seductrix, presumptuous, light of belief, superstitious, divinatrix, and so on.[90]

Regarding her wearing of male clothing, she did not break any laws, and therefore could not be called a *prevaricatrix* of laws.[91] Later, he cites Thomas Aquinas at length on the licitness of such garb for women, and cites Vincent of Beauvais for examples of holy women doing so.[92]

After her so-called abjuration Joan was sentenced and left to the secular arm for two reasons, her male clothes and her revelations, neither of which had anything to do with faith and neither of which were in the abjuration.[93] The injustice of her conviction and execution is abundantly clear. Not only was no error found in her action or words, but all who examine her responses to the most complex and subtle questions will say he believes that it was not she who was speaking but the Holy Spirit speaking in her.[94]

There follow in the dossier the brief treatise of Bishop Bochard of Avranches,[95] the extensive and expert legal opinion of Jean de Montigny,[96] and then the treatise of Guillaume Bouillé, the one who started the whole process with his manifesto to the king in 1449,[97] and finally the tract of the chancellor of Paris, Robert Ciboule, produced at the beginning of 1453.[98]

But then we learn that these submissions were already in the hands of the judges, and that they started their deliberations over them and all other materials a month earlier.

[89] NT 2:225. Favier, *Pierre Cauchon*, p. 629, paraphrases him as saying that Joan was not a sorceress because she was a virgin.

[90] NT 2:37–44; he is using the sentence that was interrupted by her abjuration: see LR 238.

[91] NT 2:240.

[92] NT 2:248–49.

[93] NT 2:256.

[94] NT 2:257.

[95] NT 2:257–65.

[96] NT 2:266–317.

[97] NT 2:317–48.

[98] NT 2:348–400.

CHAPTER 17

The Trial Ends

17.1 The Judges Begin Deliberations in Paris, June 1456

We saw above that on May 30, the delegated judges, Archbishop Jouvenal and Bishop Chartier, appointed two clerics to act in their place because they were away on unstated business.

After the texts of the submitted treatises, the notaries give an account of what the judges were occupied with. They do not date their account, but say that not only Jouvenal and Chartier but also Bishop Olivier and Inquisitor Bréhal were in Paris "through June,"[1] going through the evidence and arguments of the case, until they broke off to continue with a fuller examination in Rouen.[2] We also saw that they were all said to be in court in Rouen on June 18.[3]

In the summary that the notaries give of the judges' review in Paris, they do not mention any concern about juridical irregularities of the proceeding against Joan, or her judges or individual assessors, except to refer to the articles that her judges pretended to extract from her confessions.[4] They speak specifically of the page of corrections that Manchon intended

[1] NT 2:400.
[2] NT 2:402–03.
[3] NT 1:515–16.
[4] NT 2:401.

H. A. Kelly, *The Trial and Retrial of Joan of Arc*, The New Middle Ages, https://doi.org/10.1007/978-3-032-07887-2_17

for the record, which were never made,[5] which we saw submitted to the court in Rouen on June 5.[6]

They considered the crimes alleged against her, and contained in the abjuration, which, according to witnesses in the inquests, she did not understand, and which was extorted from her by force and fear.[7] Together with consultants they reviewed the opinions given in the original proceeding, the allegations of their own promotor and those of the plaintiffs, and pre-inserted treatises on the early trial, and considerations of prelates and doctors on questions of law; and they intended to communicate further with many counsellors, who were also present at the first proceeding. They related all this to the notaries and ordered everything inserted in the record, intending further consideration when they returned to Rouen, until they finally decided to issue their sentence. But it was decided that much of the discussion would not go into the record, because of its abundance.[8]

Therefore, all of the material having been read and reviewed, especially the opinions given in the early proceeding, because these opinions were based on the said distorted Twelve Articles, and because the consultants did not agree among themselves, with some wishing to see the whole record, others wanting it to go to the Holy See, others referring to constraints of force and fear, and most of them saying that Joan should be admonished once again to submit to the Church (as in fact she had submitted tacitly and expressly to the Holy See and demanded that she and her actions be submitted), therefore the delegated judges and the advisors summoned by them decided that those opinions threw little light on the facts and were for the most part completely irrelevant.[9]

The delegates then ordered that Master Jean Bréhal, whom they had appointed co-judge and co-delegate with them, should make a *Recollectio* or assessment of all the relevant material. The text of the resulting treatise followed.[10]

The treatise is so massive that the delegates had either made this assignment long before, or else Bréhal had anticipated it and worked on it for many months.

[5] NT 2:401.
[6] NT 1:496–97, with text given on 501–03.
[7] NT 2:401–02.
[8] NT 2:402–03.
[9] NT 2:403–04.
[10] NT 2:404. The treatise covers pp. 405–600.

17.2 Bréhal's Concluding Treatise

17.2.1 Pulling Some Punches

As discussed above, Bréhal by training was a theologian, but he was a judge in his profession of heresy inquisitor, and so would be familiar with many aspects of procedural law (including any distortions of canon law traditionally practiced in France).

He divides his treatise into two parts, dealing with matter and form: the first with nine chapters, and the second with twelve.

The "matter" concerns what he considers the main accusations that were laid against Joan. The *Summary* he made back in 1452 (see Chapter 12) dealt with similar subjects. The first four concerned her apparitions, the consolations she received from them, her predictions of the future, and the reverence she showed to the spirits who appeared to her. The fifth took up her departure from home without obtaining her parents' leave, and the sixth her dressing in male garb. The seventh concerned her reported rash statements and boasting, the eighth her refusal to submit to the Church, and the last her reversion to male clothing and resumption of revelations after her abjuration.[11]

None of these topics make any mention of heresy or any other offenses against the faith, although at the seventh chapter he adds that some of her statements were held to be "perilous in faith," or, as he puts it in the text, "reprehensible in faith,"[12] which he proceeds to refute. He concedes that, although Joan may not be excusable in everything, he is not concerned to find her innocent of all blame, but specifically blameless of the crime of heresy, with which she is principally charged.[13]

The twelve chapters on the defective form of the proceedings against Joan are then listed. The first two concern Cauchon: his lack of legitimate competence (jurisdiction) and his bias. It is very telling that he did not

[11] NT 2:407.

[12] NT 2:475.

[13] NT 2:486. This is the sort of statement from Joan's defenders seized upon by the Devil's advocates in her canonization proceedings, which were indeed about her overall "heroic virtue." See Henry Ansgar Kelly, "Joan of Arc's Last Trial: The Attack of the Devil's Advocates," in *Fresh Verdicts on Joan of Arc*, Bonnie Wheeler and Charles T. Wood, eds. (New York 1996), pp. 205–38; repr. in *Inquisitions* (2001), article IV. See specifically *Sacrae Rituum Congregatione, Aureliensis: Beatificationis et Canonizationis Ioannae de Arc: Positio super introductione causae* (Rome 1883), part 3: *Summarium additionale: Excerptum ex processu Aureliae condito anno 1885 super dubio "An sit signanda"* (1885), section 1, p. 37.

reproach Cauchon for interrogating Joan before charging her, in order to get material for charging her, which was against the law of inquisition—presumably because this was precisely what inquisitors of heretical depravity had been doing in France for 200 years, whenever it suited them.

The third chapter concerns the circumstances of Joan's imprisonment, the fourth her recusing of "the judge" and appeal to the pope. The next deals with the sub-inquisitor, Lemaistre, and his efforts at evading the appointment as co-judge, and the intimidation to which he was subjected. The sixth takes up the distortions in the Twelve Articles, the seventh her abjuration, the eighth "the pretensed relapse." Then, in the ninth chapter, he discusses her interrogators and their difficult questions, and in the tenth the assessors, defenders, exhorters, preachers, and others partaking in the proceedings. The last two chapters deal with the consultations received and the definitive sentence.[14]

Bréhal begins by saying that it is not enough for him to show that there was insufficient material to hold a trial of faith against Joan, without touching upon the defects of the proceedings, even though it is out of his area of expertise, and others more learned have treated it.[15]

He has no trouble elaborating at great length on the wrongdoing of Cauchon and the illegitimate conditions he forced on Joan. As for Sub-Inquisitor Lemaistre and the role played by the Holy Inquisition, which he now supervised in northern France, he must have been highly embarrassed. He does not mention the eagerness of Inquisitor Graverent's vicar-general Billorin at the University of Paris to try Joan as soon as she was captured as vehemently suspect of heresy. His letter to that effect was included in the register of the proceedings.

Bréhal was aware that Graverent readily assigned Lemaistre full powers to exercise jurisdiction in the temporary exclave of the Beauvais diocese, so that he could participate in Joan's trial. He begins his brief Chapter 5 on Lemaistre by saying that he leaves it to those who are expert in the law to decide whether he functioned as Joan's legitimate judge. He notes that he concurred with Cauchon in great part in the actions of the proceeding, but adds that evidence gathered from the register and witnesses concerning his fearfulness and involuntary cooperation render his actions suspect and therefore null or at least nullifiable.[16]

[14] NT 2:510–11.
[15] NT 2:511.
[16] NT 2:541–44.

Bréhal then has a compact chapter on the prevarications of the Twelve Articles, turning Joan's innocent answers into offenses or at least suspect actions, starting with her apparitions, her male clothes (not going to Communion at Easter if it meant changing from male clothes), refusing to submit deeds and words to the Church Militant, and so on. All false. Therefore the consultors were deceived, and had no way of finding out the truth. Especially in a trial of the faith, consultants are to see the whole process.[17]

In his rehearsal of falsified offenses against Joan in cause of faith, he does not observe that there was no mention of errors against the faith, much less heresy. Furthermore, he does not at this point find fault with the experts consulted. He will do so later, in Chapter 11, limiting himself to the University professors.

17.2.2 On Being "caught in heresy" and the Role of **publica fama**

Now he moves on, in Chapter 7, to address the fact that Joan was induced or compelled to make an abjuration. He specifies, first of all, just when an abjuration should be made. An abjuration should happen when a person holds an error against Church faith and practice and is caught promoting it. He cites Pope Lucius III's decree *Ad abolendam* of 1183 from the *Liber Extra*.[18] But not every error or sin is an error in faith, and not every error in faith contains heresy. If one mistakenly believes something false about the faith, it is a defect rather than a fault. A deliberate error is heresy, and, if one holds it persistently, one is rightly called a heretic.[19]

On what it means to be caught in heresy, he cites the Ordinary Gloss to *Ad abolendam*, and says it must be by evidence of word or deed, for instance by manifestly dogmatizing heresy, or else by legal proof. (Bréhal does not cite the Gloss's explanation of legal proof: "...for instance, by

[17] NT 2:544–49.

[18] NT 2:551, citing Lucius III, *Ad abolendam*, X 5.7.9 (CIC 2:780–82). For the words on being caught in heresy, see top of col. 781: "...quicuncunque manifeste in heresi deprehensus..."

[19] NT 2:551–52.

witnesses, or by one's own confession.")[20] This is confirmed, Bréhal says, by a canon in Gratian, *Si quis diaconus* (actually, it is irrelevant).[21]

Bréhal goes on to say that light or strong (*levis aut vehemens*) suspicion does not constitute proof, but only violent suspicion constitutes proof. To back up this statement, he cites the canon *Fraternitatem* from Gratian[22] and the law *Si inter* from Justinian's *Digest*,[23] both of which are completely irrelevant, and in between, the decretal *Litteras* from the *Liber Extra*. This latter law does indeed say that even vehement suspicion is insufficient for conviction, but says nothing about violent suspicion being sufficient.[24] However, he continues, not even violent suspicion suffices, when the contrary can be proved or is proved. Here he cites the canon *Nec aliqua*, about virgins who indulge in sexual activity (kisses, embraces) but remain intact,[25] and the decretal *Proposuisti*, on not believing the husband who swears he had sex with his wife if she is found to be intact.[26] Therefore, since Joan did not fall into any condemned error or pertinaciously adhere to any such error (as he abundantly demonstrated in the first part of his overview), it is clear that she was wrongly forced to abjure.[27]

But perhaps some will say that she labored under *publica fama*, which induced violent presumption, as could be argued from Innocent III's 1199 decretal *Inter sollicitudines*, in the title *De purgatione canonica*.[28] Doubtless Bréhal was thinking of the passage in which the pope said that he did not blame the archbishop of Sens, in the absence of an accuser, for proceeding to make inquisition into the truth (*inquirere veritatem*) against a suspect, on the report of public fame (*fama publica deferente*).[29] This was an early statement on Pope Innocent's part of the inquisitorial trial,[30]

[20] NT 2:553, citing Ordinary Gloss to *Ad abolendam*, v. *deprehensi* (CJC 2:1673, gloss c, lines 67–69).

[21] Gratian, *Si quis diaconus*, D. 50 c. 29 (CIC 1:190–91), only speaks of clerics caught in adultery and demoted.

[22] Gratian, D. 54 c. 15, *Fraternitatem* (CIC 1:911–12), deals with freeing converted slaves.

[23] Justinian, *Digest*, 34.5.8, *Si inter* (on return of dower/dowry).

[24] Innocent III, *Litteras*, X 2.23 (*De presumptionibus*).14 (CIC 2:357): no condemnation for such a grave crime only on suspicion, even though vehement.

[25] Gratian, C. 27 Q. 1 c. 14, *Nec aliqua* (CIC 1:1048–49): Cyprian of Carthage speaking about virgins who have become unchaste while remaining intact.

[26] X 2.19 (*De probationibus*). 4, *Proposuisti* (CIC 2:307).

[27] NT 2:553.

[28] NT 2:553, citing Innocent III, *Inter sollicitudines*, X 5.34.10 (CIC 2:872–74).

[29] *Inter sollicitudines*, col. 873.

[30] Kelly, *Criminal-Inquisitorial Trials*, p. 14.

which he would bring to perfection in the decree *Qualiter et quando* at the Fourth Lateran Council (as we saw Montigny explain in his treatise). *Fama publica* was to serve as probable cause for starting an inquisition.

Bréhal is silent about this function of *fama publica*—doubtless because French heresy inquisitors had a long tradition of violating the rules of inquisitorial trials. Instead, he says that there are two kinds of *fama*, one referring to a person's general reputation, concerning which, if there is doubt about it, an inquiry is made; and here he cites three decretals from the title *De electione* in the *Liber Extra*.[31] Against a life well lived, he says, presumptions are not easily made, citing Innocent III's *Cum in juventute* from the title on purgation.[32]

The other kind of public fame, he continues, is "a rumored attribution (*famosa insinuatio*) and widespread acknowledgement arising from suspicion alone, with an uncertain author." He cites only a canon in Gratian for this definition, tracking its final phrase, *incerto auctore*.[33] He noticeably refrains from citing the scriptural references of Pope Innocent in *Qualiter et quando*: the *clamor et fama* of the unjust steward and of Sodom and Gomorrah. He could also have pointed out that Cauchon's opening statement in the Latin Record stated that it was the *fama* of Joan's immodesty in wearing male clothing and statements against the faith that induced him to begin an inquisition against her, adding that the University of Paris and the Holy Inquisition found her similarly defamed.[34]

Instead, he takes this kind of *fama* as something that might come up as evidence in a trial. He says that it proves nothing in itself: hence the saying that "fame is fleeting"; and therefore it should not easily be believed in court, as it says in the canon *Si quid de quocumque*,[35] since, as it says in *Cum in juventute*, the multitude easily follows what one person says.[36]

[31] NT 2:553–54, citing X 1.6.3, *Postquam* (CIC 2:49), c. 20, *Innotuit*, §*Multa* (2:62–63), and c. 40, *Scriptum est* (2:84–88, at 88).

[32] NT 2:554, citing Innocent III, *Cum in juventute*, X 5.34.12 (CIC 2:874); he also cites two chapters from the title on presumptions, X 2.23.3, 6 (CIC 2:353–54).

[33] Gratian, *Decretum*, part 3, *De consecratione*, D. 4 c. 36, *Sanctum est* (CIC 1:1374): St Augustine says of a shipwreck account that it was commended not by the authority of Scripture but by *fama*, with an uncertain author.

[34] LR 1–2.

[35] Gratian, D. 86 c. 23, *Si vero quid de quocumque clerico* (CIC 1:303), a warning of Pope Gregory the Great to a bishop that, if he should hear of something about a cleric that could offend him, he should not readily believe it, but rather investigate the truth of the matter in the presence of his church elders.

[36] Innocent III, *Cum in juventute*, X 5.34.12, col. 874.

Therefore, since Joan was commended for her life in her home region and everywhere else, what they say about her ill-fame is not true.[37]

It also says in *Cum in juventute* that when a person finds himself wrongly defamed, he can insist on purgation.[38] Bréhal could have cited this for what he goes on to state: when a person's infamy causes scandal to upstanding people, purgation is called for, not abjuration.[39] He again cites *Litteras*, which says that there should be no condemnation on the basis of suspicion alone, but only purgation.[40]

A bit later Bréhal anticipates an objection from *Inter sollicitudines*, which, in addition to purgation, has the suspect indeed undergo an abjuration. The abjuration was for something else, Bréhal says: not heresy, but keeping company with heretics.[41] (There is no mention of how the latter crime—favoring heretics—was established.)

After appealing to *Litteras*, Bréhal also draws once more on *Ad abolendam*, which has only purgation as a way of dealing judicially with suspected heretics.[42] Then he cites Innocent III's decree at the Fourth Lateran Council in 1215, *Excommunicamus*, which incorporated the language of *Ad abolendam*,[43] before setting forth the decree *Qualiter et quando*, which established the new trial of *inquisitio* on the basis of *fama* (here intended for crimes other than heresy).[44] After Gregory IX started the practice of authorizing special judges to prosecute heresy suspects, they quickly adopted the inquisitorial trial, and became known as heresy inquisitors, *inquisitores heretice pravitatis*, and they eventually did away with the rules set forth in *Qualiter et quando*, even though these rules remained the law of the Church, as I point out in Chapter 1.

The chief violation of the heresy inquisitors was that, even though they might claim (out of the hearing of the suspect) to be basing their prosecution on legitimate *publica fama*, as Cauchon did, they did not say it to the suspect, so that it could be open to challenge; they did not reveal what suspicions they might have, or level charges and explain them (as required by the law). Rather, they forced the suspect to testify against himself under

[37] NT 2:554.

[38] Innocent III, *Cum in juventute*, col. 874.

[39] NT 2:554.

[40] NT 2:554, citing Innocent III, *Litteras*, X 2.23.14 (CIC 2:357).

[41] NT 2:555, citing Innocent III, *Inter sollicitudines*, X 5.34.10 (CIC 2:872–74).

[42] Lucius III, *Ad abolendam* (1184), X 5.7.9 (CIC 2:780–82).

[43] Innocent III, *Excommunicamus*, Fourth Lateran c. 3, X 5.7.12 (CIC 2:787–89).

[44] *Qualiter et quando* no. 2, Fourth Lateran c. 8, X 5.1.24 (CIC 2:745–47).

oath, hoping that they could draw admissions that would verify their suspicions; or, if in fact there was no *fama* or actual suspicion of offenses, that he would be manipulated into confessing some; or, in the case of heresy, of saying something against sound doctrine, even though he had never said anything like it before. It would still be an actionable confession of a crime.

Of course, a morally and legally scrupulous heresy inquisitor would take care to be fair, but a paid assassin like Cauchon could exploit the illegal short-cuts that the heresy inquisitors used when it suited them and when they were in control, and it would be awkward for a heresy inquisitor like Bréhal to offer the sort of criticisms that Lohier did, without inculpating the Holy Inquisition itself. Bréhal solves it by avoiding all mention of *fama* as triggering an *inquisitio.* He concludes safely by pointing out that infamy generated by enemies, as in Joan's case, who was slandered by her capital enemies, the English, was deserving of no rebuttal, and did not call even for purgation, let alone abjuration.[45] He finishes the chapter by stressing the elements of Joan's lack of knowledge of what was in the abjuration she agreed to, as well as being affected by coercion and fear.[46]

He disposes of Joan's alleged relapse easily: it did not meet the requirements of a relapse, either formally (there was no preceding lapse) or materially (her clothing and apparitions had nothing to do with faith).[47]

17.2.3 On the Interrogators and Exhorters of Joan

In Chapter 9, Bréhal takes up the interrogations to which Joan was submitted before she was charged. As noted, this practice was against canon law, but Bréhal could hardly have impugned Cauchon for the practice, since it was standard operating procedure of the heresy inquisitors. Instead, he focuses on the unfairness of the questioning, which aimed at entrapping Joan into admissions that could be charged against her. In other words, they were being too illegal, maliciously so. Questions were appropriate when charges were leveled. We saw some follow-up questions to Joan's answers when Estivet presented his seventy articles against Joan.

[45] NT 2:554–55.
[46] NT 2:555–59.
[47] NT 2:560–64.

Bréhal cites canon law to say that when questioning was done on spiritual matters, it should be kept simple and not overly subtle.[48] When done in good faith (*cum de bona fide agitur*), it should not deal with the fine points of the law. To do so "greatly detracts from the work of the Holy Inquisition" (*maxime derogat negotio Sancte Inquisitionis*). According to Thomas Aquinas, simple persons should not be examined on the subtleties of faith except where there is suspicion that they have been depraved by heretics.[49] He goes on to say that, according to Thomas, when simple persons accused of heresy are examined on the articles of faith, they are not expected to explicitly believe all of the articles of faith.[50] Here Bréhal (perhaps deliberately) misses the opportunity of pointing out that when Joan was questioned she was not yet accused of anything; and that, when she was finally accused by Estivet, he did not accuse her of heresy, except in his vague first article, where he said that she had made heretical propositions; this was not verified in the remaining articles; and in his summary Article 66, he only said that some of her offenses savored of heresy.

Bréhal concludes by saying that, unless there is a vehement presumption that a simple person has been corrupted by heretics, there is no call for such close questioning. This was certainly the case with Joan, when she was questioned on the above matters, most of which had nothing to do with the articles of faith; he goes on to give examples of questions put to her, for instance, as to whether the spirits spoke French or English, whether God hated the English, and the like.[51] A wicked and malicious judge will readily take the responses of simple souls to ambiguous questions for errors of impiety and cruelly condemn them, something that is strictly forbidden under penalties in the Clementine constitution *Multorum*, which he returns to again at the end of his chapter.[52]

In Chapter 10, he argues forcefully that defendants should have defenders in their trials, especially when they are young and not knowledgeable in the "rites" of judicial procedure.[53] He rejects the argument that defenses

[48] NT 2:566, citing a decretal from the twelfth century (so, before *inquisitio* was established), namely, Alexander III's *Dilecti*, X 2.1.6 (CIC 2:241).

[49] NT 2:566, quoting Thomas, *Summa Theologiae*, 2–2, q. 2, a. 6, resp. to obj. 2. See his *Opera omnia*, Leonine edition (Rome 1882 ff.), vol. 8, p. 33.

[50] NT 2:566; he does not cite where Thomas says this.

[51] NT 2:566–67.

[52] NT 2:567–68, 569, citing *Clem.* 5.3.1 §4 (CIC 2:1182).

[53] NT 2:569.

and appeals are forbidden to heretics: that holds true only after they are convicted.[54]

Bréhal refers to the offer made to Joan on March 27 (by Cauchon) to choose advisors from among the attending assessors.[55] He reads her response not as a refusal but as accepting it with thanks, while not receding from God's counsel. In any case, he says, the record shows that she never did receive counsel, and witnesses say that no one dared to help her, for fear of death. She did, however, receive false counsel from persons out to betray her.[56] Of similar import were the exhortations directed at her, "charitably" advising her to repent for the things that she was falsely accused of. They were intended to confuse her by their prolixity.[57]

As for the assessors, who were there in their forties and fifties, and rarely less than thirty, doctors and persons of various distinctions, invited from Paris and other places under English control (he recalls the fifty philosophers summoned to dispute with Catherine of Alexandria), they were there more for show than for justice. He notes that when Joan challenged the relevance of certain points to a trial of faith (such as the sign given to the king, or knowing when she would be freed from prison), most of them said they were relevant, when they obviously were not. He applies to them what Remigius of Auxerre says of the high priests and elders who condemned Christ: they themselves are to be condemned, both because they assembled together and because they were leaders and priests. For the more persons who come together to commit an evil deed, and the wiser and more exalted and noble they are, so much the worse is the evil they commit, and the greater punishment they deserve.[58] He did not, however, take any steps to see to it that they, those who were still alive, were punished in this life, even if only by publishing their names.

[54] NT 2:570.

[55] LR 189–90.

[56] NT 2:570–71.

[57] NT 2:571–73.

[58] NT 2:573–74. Bréhal probably found this text in Aquinas's *Catena Aurea* 26.1; see https://www.corpusthomisticum.org/cmt26.html.

17.2.4 On the Role of the University of Paris

In taking up the consultants in Chapter 11, he expressly says that he speaks short of blaming anyone in particular.[59] He limits himself to the two faculties of the University of Paris, and to the two subjects of Joan's apparitions and her submission to the Church.[60] He marvels that theologians, professors of the divine Scriptures and heralds of celestial wisdom, could find evil rather than good in a young woman of her background, in whom only her manifest enemies saw any faults, against *fama publica*.[61] He shows that it was presumptuous in the extreme to judge such apparitions as she had, and declare them either fabricated or diabolical.[62]

As for their conclusion that she was schismatic, against the unity of the Church, an apostate, and pertinaciously erroneous in faith, even if the articles against her were true, it seems hard (*durum tamen videtur*) that they could say such things about her, since, if she refused to submit, she stated a sufficient cause for doing so, because she recused the judgment of that bishop whom she dreaded as her manifest enemy—which the theologians either knew or could easily imagine; also because she had been permitted to follow "our king" (i.e., Charles VII) by the Church after approving her faith; also because she constantly stated that she acted out of inspiration, which the Church reserved to the judgment of God alone, and she acted out of her conscience, which should not give way to the counsel of a prelate; he cites Innocent III's decretal *Inquisitioni*, which states that one should humbly submit to excommunication rather than go against the judgment of conscience.[63]

It seems to Bréhal's limited understanding, he says, that the decision of the University jurists was milder. They presupposed that Joan, fully in possession of her faculties (*compos sui*), pertinaciously affirmed and carried out what was said about her in the articles, and was charitably admonished by a competent judge. (He omits saying that the jurists declared such behavior explicitly heretical, which the theologians did not do.) Neither of the jurists' conditions were verified, he says. She never stubbornly asserted

[59] NT 2:577: "...citra tamen injuriam cujuscumque loquendo" (but short of speaking against anyone whomsoever).

[60] NT 2:577–78.

[61] NT 2:580.

[62] NT 2:580–86.

[63] NT 2:586, citing Innocent III, *Inquisitioni*, X 5.39.44 (CIC 2:908).

anything against the faith, and the incompetence of the judges and the nature of their exhortations have already been established.[64]

The jurists focused on two things: her separation from the Church and her failure to prove that she was sent from God. She refused only the judgment of the bishop of Beauvais, and rather appealed and submitted to the pope and the universal Church.[65] As for failing to prove her mission by miracle or Scripture, a political mission does not need to be proved; it can be judged by its goals, whether bad or good or indifferent. On the other hand, one could argue that there were miracles: a fragile girl delivered her country, foretold the future, and so on.[66] He says that the jurists refer to their deliberations as constituting "instruction" (*doctrina*). But if the instruction that results in the judgment of a person suppresses the truth out of fear or favor, there is no excuse for it. Let it not be thought that he is disparaging so famous a university. But he believes that, in keeping with canonical norms, punishment should take hold of those guilty of crime and not redound upon the innocent. He is sufficiently convinced that it was a very small number of persons overly favorable to the English who not so much extorted these deliberations by oblique means as enacted and issued them, so that, by this act of impiety, they hardly or only minimally represent the whole body of the University.[67] (This was a deft way of shaming the whole University: which, after all, fully endorsed the decisions of the two faculties; it could be read as a challenge to the University to admit wrongdoing and punish the wrongdoers. The trouble is, they would probably never see it, unless he somehow saw to it that they did.)

17.2.5 Weak Ending on the Sentences Against Joan

The last chapter deals with the sentencing, which was null for six reasons: Cauchon's lack of jurisdiction and Lemaistre's motivation of fear, Cauchon's corruption, Joan's recusal of them and appeals, the false charges, the obvious suspicion of malice, and content of manifest iniquity and intolerable error. After running through the three sentences and their defects, he also points out the "inexcusable error" in them, especially the last, namely: (1) she was pronounced to be excommunicated, just after the

[64] NT 2:586–87.
[65] NT 2:587–88.
[66] NT 2:589–91.
[67] NT 2:591–92.

judges had permitted her to receive the sacraments of penance and Communion; (2) she was then declared to be deprived of all the sacraments (citing fol. 116 of the record), which was against the law; (3) she was not absolved from excommunication; (4) she was declared a heretic, which was false, and even ex-heretics should not be called heretics in sentences; and (5) the sentence was passed after Joan had made many recusals.[68]

This is a rather anticlimactic ending to Bréhal's lengthy review. In fact, in the sentence passed after her abjuration, Joan was declared freed from the excommunication by which she was bound (even though she had never been said to be excommunicated before this time).[69] In the final sentence, it was related that by her relapse she reincurred the sentence of excommunication absolved at her abjuration.[70] In both the sentence interrupted by her abjuration and the final sentence after her relapse it was said that she always had access to the sacrament of penance.[71] When she was allowed to go to confession after the final sentence, her excommunication would have been automatically absolved, or considered no longer in effect.

Bréhal concludes that error in the sentence (presumably speaking of the last one) is not merely probable, but intolerable, and therefore null, or at least it should be annulled.[72] The distinction is that it was either void from the beginning or else, if it ever had any validity, it should be declared void from now on.[73]

He concludes his whole *Recollectio* by saying that both the proceedings against Joan and the sentence contain manifest injustice, which he undertook to declare, as ordained by the delegated judges and the consultors summoned by them.[74]

[68] NT 2:598–600.
[69] LR 393.
[70] LR 412.
[71] LR 412, 414.
[72] NT 2:600.
[73] This distinction (void from the beginning or void from now on) works in the case of a statute, but not in the case of marriage: an annulment declares a marriage void from the beginning, whereas a divorce (as now understood) makes void a previously valid marriage.
[74] NT 2:600.

17.3 The Verdict, July 7, 1456

After the review of evidence, including the above *Recollectio*, in Paris, as described above, the judges ordered another review and communications with consultants in Rouen.[75]

Then, on July 7, 1456, there appeared in the hall of the archbishop, before the archbishop of Rheims and the bishops of Paris and Coutances and one of the two heresy inquisitors of France, who were the delegated and commissioned judges, deputed by apostolic authority, of the nullity, iniquity, and injustice of certain judicial cases conducted by Bishop Cauchon and Sub-Inquisitor Lemaistre and their promotor, Estivet, against one Joan of Arc, and of the purging of charges falsely imputed to her, the following persons: Jean d'Arc, one of the principal plaintiffs, no longer represented by proctor; Guillaume Prévosteau, proctor of the plaintiffs Isabelle and Pierre d'Arc; and Master Simon Chapitault, promotor of the case, fortified by the counsel of Pierre Maugier, deputed advocate in the case. One of them produced the citation decreed against the current bishop of Beauvais, the sub-inquisitor in that diocese, and the promotor of criminal cases of the same diocese, and all others concerned in this case, and its execution, to hear the sentence on this day; and, since none appeared, he asked that they be declared in contempt; Archbishop Jouvenal complied, then pronounced the definitive sentence, which I summarize as follows:

> Having seen the proceedings performed in keeping with the pope's mandate in favor of the plaintiffs and against the duly cited above-said defendants, Bishop Hellande and others; having seen the petitions of the plaintiffs and their reasons and conclusions arguing for a declaration of the nullity, falsity, iniquity, and trickery of the pretensed trial in a matter of faith conducted against the deceased Joan by the one-time bishop of Beauvais, Cauchon, the pretensed sub-inquisitor of the said diocese, Lemaistre, and the Beauvais promotor, Estivet, all deceased, or at least to the voiding and nullifying of the abjurations and sentences and the expurgation of the deceased Joan; having long deliberated over the original records of the proceeding and the inquest of Cardinal Estouteville, and read the treatises of learned men showing the doubts to be elucidated, and also the articles put to witnesses and their depositions concerning Joan's life and also concerning her examination at Poitiers; our own promotor having fully joined himself to the

[75] NT 2:601.

plaintiffs and reproduced all material in the name of our office, we assigned this day to hear our sentence;

Reviewing all the above, and also the Twelve Articles beginning *Quedam femina*, which the judges pretended were extracted from the confessions of the said Joan, impugned by our promotor and plaintiffs as slanderously confected; having thoroughly deliberated upon all, and considered the opinions of experts in treatises and determinations, and the matter and form of the said proceeding, by which the experts deem (*quibus existimant*)[76] the deeds of the said Joan worthy of admiration (*admiratio*) rather than condemnation, while wondering (*admirantes*) at the adverse judgment against her, and also affirming the difficulty of determining whether her doings were "in spirit or in body," as with the private revelations of St Paul, which only God knows;

First of all, we judge the articles against her to be maliciously corrupted, declaring them void and ordering them destroyed;

And, having reviewed the sentences declaring her lapsed and relapsed, and the quality of the judges, together with the conditions under which the said Joan was held, weighing also her recusals, submissions, and appeals to the Holy Father, and the false abjuration extorted by the fear of death, and the opinion of prelates and solemn doctors that the crimes stated in the sentences were not dealt with in the proceedings;

Seated in tribunal, we give this definitive sentence:

We declare the said proceedings and sentences, containing manifest calumny, wickedness, and error of law and fact, to have been and to be null, invalid, without effect, and void;

But, nevertheless, to whatever extent necessary, we hereby annul and evacuate them of any and all legitimacy;

And we affirm that the said Joan, as well as the plaintiffs and her relatives, incurred no stain of infamy on account of these proceedings and sentences, and we declare expunged all stain to be expunged, and we now furthermore, to whatever extent necessary, do hereby expunge any such stain.

We order the solemn proclamation of this sentence in two places of this city, in the Square of St Ouen's, in the wake of a solemn procession; and, on the day following, in the Old Market, the place where the said Joan was horribly and cruelly burned to death; it is to be accompanied by a public sermon and the fixing of the cross to a perpetual memorial. There shall be further promulgation of this our sentence in cities and other noteworthy places of

[76] NT 2:608: referring to the conclusions of the experts; Duparc in his translation (4:227) takes it to refer to the conclusions of the delegated judges pronouncing the sentence (in that case, it would be *existimamus*).

this realm, as shall seem good to us, reserving any other further measures to our pleasure.[77]

The Twelve Articles were then taken in hand and pronounced to be false and mendacious, and order was given that they be torn to pieces (*lacerandi*), which was done then and there.[78]

We observe that in their sentence, as in the original supplication of the Arc family and the pope's following commission, the judges made no reference to the English foes who were ultimately responsible for her ordeal; they named none of the specific charges that Cauchon and his collaborators fabricated against her. For all its prolixity, the sentence could be justly summarized very shortly: Joan of Arc was falsely convicted. They said nothing in praise of Joan, except to report the experts' estimation of her admirable deeds. There is, then, no reason to suppose that the ceremonies that took place in Rouen after the trial made any reference to her outstanding Christian devotion and holiness of life.

Whether there was a large audience present at this conclusion to the trials is not stated. The sworn witnesses named were the two pro-tem judges, Bishop Lefèvre and Hector de Cocquerel; Nicolas Lambert, professor of theology; Nicolas Dubois, dean of the cathedral chapter of Rouen, along with two of its canons, Jean de Gouys and Guillaume Roussel (perhaps a nephew of the late archbishop); and eight advocates of the diocese, including Jean Roussel (another nephew?) and Jean Levieux, the one-time stand-in for Chapitault.[79] A different list of witnesses given at the end of the sentence includes four additional canons and Friar Martin Ladvenu. Jean d'Arc was also there, and Prévosteau and Chapitault, and they asked for copies of the sentence.[80]

It was indeed a victory for Joan, but a very modest one, and her honor was hardly restored.

[77] NT 2:605–10.
[78] NT 2:603.
[79] NT 2:603–04.
[80] NT 2:610–11.

CHAPTER 18

Historical Sequences

18.1 A Subdued Aftermath

18.1.1 Court of France

There is little historical reference to Joan's exoneration. No representative of the king was at the trial, during its course or at the end, and no royal proclamation of Joan's innocence was sent out to the realm. It was privately known, of course, that the participants were working for the king, and were paid for it in the following year from the king's coffers: £200 each to the three delegated judges, *L*£137 to Bouillé, £100 to Bréhal, and lesser amounts to Pierre Maugier and Chapitault and the notaries, and another £300 for compiling the six volumes of acts.[1]

A surviving copy of the trial record of Joan's exoneration, ornately decorated, was probably sent to King Charles, or to his half-brother Dunois, who fought with Joan.[2] One of the three active judges of Joan's case also received a copy of the trial proceedings, namely, Bishop Chartier, which was left among his effects at his death.[3] But whether he or the others returned to the case to insure further publications of the result, as they suggested in their sentence they might do, is not evident. Celebrations in

[1] Belon-Balme, *Jean Bréhal*, pp. 163–64 and n. 5.
[2] Duparc, *Procès en nullité*, 1:xii: Paris, Bibl. Nat. MS lat. 5970.
[3] Ibid., 1:xiii: Paris, Bibl. Nat. MS lat. 17013; Quicherat, *Procès*, 5:218.

H. A. Kelly, *The Trial and Retrial of Joan of Arc*, The New Middle Ages, https://doi.org/10.1007/978-3-032-07887-2_18

Orleans were recorded: fowl purchased on July 20, 1456, were sent as a gift to the mainly inactive judge, Bishop Olivier of Coutances, by the city of Orleans, as was a gift of wine, the latter being also for Inquisitor Bréhal. Six torchbearers were paid for the procession on July 21, ordered by the bishop and inquisitor, for the deeds of Joan the Maid.[4]

Why did Bréhal not make more of the outcome, and Dean Bouillé? And Cardinal Estouteville, who was, after all, archbishop of Rouen, where both trials took place, and who was instrumental in getting the nullity proceedings started? (He would continue to be archbishop there for another three decades.)

18.1.2 Papal Court

The judges-delegates sent a messenger (another Roussel—Robert, OP) to Paris to inform the papal delegate there of the outcome of the trial. An expedition was sent to the pope as well, led by the faithful Dean Bouillé and Inquisitor Bréhal and two other Dominicans, effected in the next months.[5]

What came of their meeting with the pope is not known. Belon and Balme reasonably assume that Calixtus would have been very pleased at the outcome; but as for his meditating some public rebuke of the perpetrators of this abuse of the power of the Church for base political purposes, as some historians believe, there is nothing in the historical record to confirm it.[6]

I myself was indulging in wishful thinking when I suggested recently that the review of the trial of Joan of Arc in 1456 should have made the papal curia suspicious of the government of Henry VI when the case of Reginald Pecock came to them in 1458.[7] Pecock, bishop of Chichester, had undergone a trial in November of 1457 in which he admitted errors but was restored to his original reputation, like Joan of Arc in the judgment of July 7, 1456. Pecock complained to Pope Calixtus that the

[4] Quicherat, *Procès*, 5:277–78.

[5] Ibid., p. 164 and n. 4. Payments of recompense for it were made for the year extending from September 1456 to September 1457.

[6] Ibid., pp. 164–65.

[7] Henry Ansgar Kelly, "Judicial Proceedings for and against Bishop Reginald Pecock: New Perspectives on the Mechanisms of His Downfall," *Viator* 52:1 (2021) 359–430, p. 389 and n. 124. I mistakenly say that Pope Calixtus himself proclaimed Joan's exoneration in a "resounding condemnation" of her trial.

sentence was not being carried out, and Calixtus replied in a bull dated June 13, 1458, commanding it to be done. It is doubtful that the bull ever reached Pecock or the Church authorities. Henry VI and his Queen, Margaret of Anjou, formally requested that the pope, by this time Pius II, replace Pecock as bishop of Chichester, asserting without proof that he had been a heretic at the time he was appointed. Pius approved this request in a bull of January 8, 1459, and acceded to a further request that he commission Pecock's trial of relapse in a bull of April 6, 1459. The second bull was sent from Siena, when the pope was on the way to a crusade conference in Mantua.[8] Since Pecock was the only bishop in the Middle Ages that had been convicted of heresy, Pius might have been expected to take a personal interest in his case, but it is very probable that he had not been informed, or fully informed, about it. Pius himself would very soon afterwards be assured of the unreliable and degenerate character of the Lancastrian government.[9]

It is also very likely that no one had informed Pius about the recent nullity trial of Joan of Arc, the *stupenda virgo* in whom he had definitely taken a personal interest long ago. His account of her, as we saw, was in his *Commentaries*, his great chronicle that was constantly undergoing revision. Leona Gabel characterizes this account as written "with a critical detachment mixed with admiration and wonder," and she finds it "curious that Pius does not write more accurately and thoroughly of a case that so interested him" after it had been completely examined under his predecessor.[10]

The curial officials of the papacy, however, must have remembered the nullity trial, because they assigned the same team of judges who effected it to assess another episcopal-inquisitorial "cause of faith" in 1461. Archbishop Jouvenal, Bishop Chartier, and Inquisitor Bréhal were commissioned to answer the appeal of a supplicant on a much lower level of notoriety than the family of Joan of Arc, namely, Guillaume Lefèbvre, one of the inhabitants of Arras who had been caught up in the prosecution of sorcery begun there by the local sub-inquisitor and the clergy in charge of

[8] See Constance Head, "Pope Pius II and the Wars of the Roses," *Archivum Historiae Pontificae* 8 (1970) 139–78, 144.

[9] Pius gives a speech to the earl of Warwick saying that Henry VI himself is a dolt, and that the realm is in the hands of his queen and those who defile the king's bedchamber (*Commentarii* 3.42, p. 231, Gragg 269). See Head, "Pope Pius II," p. 152.

[10] Gabel, Pius II, *Commentaries*, p. 436 n. 61.

the diocese. He had been excommunicated for fleeing the jurisdiction after being accused.

Lefèbvre's story is told in the *Memoirs* of Arras Chronicler Jacques Duclercq.[11] The judges, that is, Archbishop Jouvenal, Bishop Chartier, and Inquisitor Bréhal, sometime around June of 1461 sent two commissioners to Arras to hold an inquest or field inquisition, one of them being the Dominican sub-inquisitor of the diocese of Paris. The citation that they attached to the gates of the city (*aulx portes d'Arras*) was a call for witnesses who could testify about Lefèbvre. They heard several witnesses who had testified at Lefèbvre's purgation in Paris. Then the vicars-general in charge of the diocese were deposed, and they produced the record of the proceedings by which persons were executed and proclaimed as sorcerers (*vauldois*), which contained the accusation against Lefèbvre. The commissioners returned with copies of the court record, and the three judges, along with several doctors in theology, heard Lefèbvre's "propositions," and then declared him absolved and innocent of the said crime of sorcery.[12] Then, around September, Lefèbvre received authority to sue the Arras vicars-general for damages to his honor and for expenses.[13]

The judges were similarly minimal in their judgment, as in Joan's case, since they did not entertain criminal action against the judges and their collaborators, whether concerning Lefèbvre or their other victims. Contrary to Quicherat,[14] it was not their judgment that put an end to the

[11] Jacques Duclercq, *Memoires*, ed. Fredéric de Reiffenberg, 4 vols. (Brussels 1823), Book 4, chapter 28, 3:133–37.

[12] Ibid., pp. 135–37.

[13] Ibid., p. 137. This authorization may have been to pursue them at the Parlement of Paris. At the beginning of his chapter, Duclercq tells of such an action against the vicars-general by another target of their prosecution, Colard de Beaufort (pp. 133–35). At the end, he recounts that yet another accused person, Hotin Loys, the sergeant of Arras, also obtained a commission from the pope, who sent him to the dean and official of Cambray for adjudication, to receive punishment if he deserved it. He not only was not punished, but kept his position as sergeant (p. 137). Franck Mercier, *La Vauderie d'Arras: Une chasse aux sorcières à l'automne du Moyen Âge* (Rennes 2006), p. 321, records that Beaufort's family also brought his case for discussion before the cathedral chapter of Paris, where they consulted none other than Thomas de Courcelles, along with several other of its theologians.

[14] Jules Quicherat, *Aperçus nouveaux sur l'histoire de Jeanne d'Arc* (Paris 1850), pp. 154–55.

prosecution, which had already dissipated,[15] and their verdict affected only one victim.[16]

18.2 Thomas Basin's Summation of Joan in His History of Charles VII

One historian did give an account of Joan in light of the 1456 verdict, namely, Thomas Basin, in the history of Charles VII that he wrote after moving to Trèves in 1471, although the work remained anonymous or misattributed until Basin was established as the author by Jules Quicherat, who edited it.[17] We saw above that Basin was one of the jurists who contributed a consultation to the cause of overturning Joan's condemnation, which was included in the final dossier.

Basin added to Joan's devotion to Saints Catherine and Margaret a dedication to Christ and his Mother, and to St Agnes, and omitted mention of Saints Michael and Gabriel. Joan constantly maintained that she received divine revelations.[18] The French made great gains under her leadership, with God's aid.[19] After she was captured and brought to Rouen, it was decided that she should undergo an inquisition and trial of faith under Bishop Cauchon. Heresy inquisitors served as assessors, as did many theologians and jurists summoned from Paris for the purpose. All marveled at the answers that Joan gave to difficult questions. The assessors, who favored the English, wished her to be found guilty of heresy, but nothing valid could be found. Rather, everything revealed her to be a very devout person, who had vowed virginity (her virginity was proved by female examiners); she excused her male clothing as a defense of her chastity.[20]

But her captors, who called her a sorceress and wicked witch and feared her, wished her death. It is said that her judges promised her freedom if

[15] Mercier, *Vauderie d'Arras*, pp. 9–12.

[16] In Mercier's assessment (*Vauderie d'Arras*, pp. 319–21), the judgment was not as far-reaching as the action in favor of Joan of Arc in 1456, but it seems to have been identical in merely nullifying a previous judgment.

[17] Quicherat, *Procès*, 4:350; *Histoire des règnes de Charles VII et de Louis XI, par Thomas Basin, évêque de Lisieux, jusqu'ici attribuée à Amelgard*, ed. Jules Quicherat, 4 vols. (Paris 1845–49). See Mark Spencer, *Thomas Basin (1412–1490), The History of Charles VII and Louis XI* (Nieuwkoop 1997).

[18] Basin, *Histoire de Charles VII*, book 2 chapter 9 (ed. Quicherat, *Histoire*, 1:66–67).

[19] Ibid., 2.11 (1:71).

[20] Ibid., 2.15 (1:80–82); also in Quicherat, *Procès*, 4:351–53.

she rejected her revelations, and, beaten down by harsh treatment, she agreed. But when her imprisonment remained unchanged, word spread that her saints had reappeared.[21] When this was related to her judges, they convicted her as relapsed, and she was sent to the flames constantly invoking Christ and his Mother. All the remaining ashes were collected and thrown into the River Seine, lest they foster superstition.[22]

Basin then wonders if his readers expect him to give an opinion about Joan's life and deeds. Even though it would be rash to assume that her claimed revelations came from God, he answers, nevertheless, from the record of the proceedings against her, which he has read, he boldly affirms that she was not convicted of anything against the Catholic faith, so there was no basis for a judgment of heresy or relapse. Moreover, the process was defective on many points: she was tried by her capital enemies, whom she repeatedly recused; even though she was a simple girl, she was denied counsel, as he detailed in a treatise that he wrote at the request of King Charles, when he ordered the proceedings examined. Many others wrote similar treatises, and the proceedings, when reviewed by papal delegates, were quashed and the sentence against her revoked.[23]

As for the question of whether she was sent by God, given her capture and the afflictions imposed on her, no one can reasonably consider this an objection, in view of the suffering of Christ and the saints. Furthermore, in the Old Testament the Israelites were ordered by God to fight against enemies, but sometimes they were overcome. Who can know the mind of God? Basin does not say that Joan should be equated with saints and martyrs, but there is nothing incompatible with her having been sent from God against the English, who gravely oppressed the realm, to counter the pride of both the French and the English; or that God, because of the demerits of the French king or French people, ungrateful for the victories and benefits that He gave them through Joan (attributing them to themselves and their corrupt morals), allowed her to be captured. That God uses women in battles and conflicts, witness Deborah, Judith, and Esther. He concludes by saying that his readers are free to agree or disagree about what has been said of Joan and her mission, the revelations she recounted, and her capture and death.[24]

[21] Ibid., 2.15 (1:82–83); *Procès*, 4:353–54.

[22] Ibid., 2.16 (1:83–84), *Procès*, 4:354.

[23] Ibid., 2.16 (1:84–85), *Procès*, 4:354–55.

[24] Ibid., 2.16 (1:85–86), *Procès*, 4:355–57.

18.3 Jacques Meyer's Summary of Basin, 1561

Basin's account of Joan was not known to subsequent generations except by brief paraphrases made by Jacques Meyer in his *Annals of Flanders*, first published in 1561.[25] Meyer first cites "a writer contemporary with the Maid" on the siege of Orleans, rewording part of Basin's Chapter 11. But where Basin says that the victory was achieved by the divine will and mercy (*divino nuto atque miseratione*) under Joan's leadership, Meyer says, "It was the will of God to place the victory in the weak sex."[26] At the end of his paraphrase of the chapter, before going on with a brief summary of Chapter 12, Meyer adds, "Mirabilis Deus in sanctis suis!"[27]

Meyer starts summarizing Basin again (but, as before, using running quotation marks) in his Chapter 15, when Joan was captured at Compiègne, and continues without stopping through to the end of his Chapter 16, after the Trial of Nullity.[28] It was decided that Bishop Cauchon should hold an inquisition against her, whom they through envy accused of being a sorceress (*malefica*) and heretic. Questioning was conducted by many theologians and jurists summoned from Paris, but her answers revealed her piety and raised the admiration of all at her Catholic responses. Her English-favoring inquisitors used captious questions in order to entrap this holy virgin of Christ (*sanctam Christi virginem*) and accuse her of heresy, but they were not able. Still, the judges, who were her enemies, were determined that she should die. The occasion for her death was the report that after she renounced her revelations, Saints Agnes, Margaret, and Catherine appeared to her again, and she was convicted of relapse into abjured heresy. Her ashes were thrown into the Seine lest anything be saved as relics and venerated (*ne quid forte reliquarum servari aut coli possit*).

After Meyer quotes the writer as telling of the retrial and his own contribution of a *libellus*, and of the quashed sentence, he repeats nothing of Basin's discussion as to whether Joan was sent by God, but simply has him

[25] See Victor Fris, *Essai d'une analyse des Commentarii sive Annales Rerum Flandricarum (Annales Flandriae 1561) de Jacques de Meyere* (Ghent 1908), pp. 170–75, and Spencer, *Thomas Basin*, pp. 68–69, 274.

[26] Jacques Meyer, *Flandricorum annales*, ed. Antoine de Meyer, Liber 16, "Philippus Burgundio," in vol. 1 of *Annales, sive Historiae, rerum Belgicarum*, ed. Sigmund Feyerabend, 2 vols. (Frankfurt 1580), p. 312: "Dei voluntas erat victoriam ponere in sexu fragili."

[27] Ibid.

[28] Ibid., p. 317.

affirm it: "She was sent from God, lest anyone 'make flesh his arm,'" citing the prophet Jeremiah,[29] that is, "lest the pride of the English confide overmuch in their powers. They were glorying in their powers and not attributing their victories to God. God wished to show them that they acted foolishly and impiously in confiding in their powers alone, and produced a victory in the frail sex, as He did with Judith, Deborah, and Esther." Meyer concludes by saying, "Thus much and more did that anonymous author contemporary with the Maid say about the virgin."

It could be deduced from Meyer's report that the contemporary chronicler, in praising God in His saints and likening Joan to Old Testament heroines, calling her a holy virgin of Christ, and speaking of the English fear that her remains would be venerated as relics, was testifying to a cult of her saintliness in her own day.

18.4 Verdicts of Church History: *Annales ecclesiastici*

The famous chronicle of Church history begun by the Oratorian cardinal Cesare Baronio, *Annales ecclesiastici*, was completed by him only to the year 1198 at his death in 1607. Three historians produced continuations up to their own times, namely, Abraham Bzowski (Bzovius), OP (d. 1647),[30] Henri de Sponde (Spondanus), Bishop of Pamiers (d. 1643),[31] and Odorico Rainaldi (d. 1671), an Oratorian like Baronio. Giandomenico Mansi (d. 1769) chose Rainaldi's continuation for his edition of the *Annales*, followed in the edition of Augustin Theiner in the nineteenth century.[32]

Rainaldi first characterizes Joan as another Deborah, protecting the French not by lawless trickery but by singular military virtue, until finally, destitute of divine aid, she was captured at Compiègne and brought to Rouen and charged with the crime of magical art. He repeats the entire

[29] Jeremiah 17.5: "Maledictus homo qui confidit in homine, et *ponit carnem brachium suum*, et a Domino recedit cor ejus."

[30] Abraham Bzowski, *Annales ecclesiastici: post…Caesarem Baronium…*, 9 vols. (Cologne 1618–1640).

[31] Sponde, Henri de (Spondanus), *Annalium ecclesiasticorum continuatio*, 2 vols. (Ticino 1675–1682), vol. 2, year 1430.

[32] Cesare Baronio, Odorico Rainaldi, et al., *Annales ecclesiastici*, ed. Augustin Theiner, 37 vols. (Bar-le-Duc 1864–1883); see Mansi's Preface in vol. 20, pp. ii–iv.

paraphrase that Meyer printed of Basin's fifteenth and sixteenth chapters.[33] He then cites the similarly favorable report of another author, Jean-Papire Masson (d. 1611), who discovered the dossier of the 1456 trial in the Paris Church archives; it showed, on the basis of innumerable witnesses, that Joan was unlawfully condemned (*injuria damnatam*), which the judges, Archbishop John of Rheims and Bishop William of Paris, so declared.[34]

The celebrated work on canonization by Cardinal Prospero Lambertini, first published in 1734–1738, before becoming Pope Benedict XIV (1740–1758), first talks of the great fame that Joan achieved in aiding the French forces against the English, as noted by Pius II in his *Commentaries*. How she was transformed from a rustic maid to a leader of armies cannot be otherwise explained, he says, than that she was endowed with a prophetic spirit, about which the theologians and doctors of the University of Paris agreed; for they saw that she could ascertain the hidden thoughts of hearts, and a French defeat was revealed to her at the very day and hour it occurred, in spite of the distance from her. There was no doubt about her Catholic religion and the preservation of her virginity while in the army camps and her high morals, since the sentence of Peter, Bishop of Beauvais, which had convicted her of magic, heresy, and betrayed virginity, was revoked as unjust on the authority of the Supreme Pontiff Calixtus III, as is fully described in the continuations of Baronius by Spondanus and Bzovius, and also in Martin Del Rio's *Disquisitions on Magic*.[35]

Del Rio, a Dutch Jesuit whom Benedict cites, published his omnibus account of alleged incidents of magic and sorcery in 1599–1600; he says that Joan's prophecies were proved to be divine by the fact that they came true. After her exploits on behalf of the French, she was captured by the English, and, out of a mixture of envy, cruelty, calumny, and injustice, they burned her alive as a sorceress. But later, in 1456, Pope Calixtus committed her case to the archbishop of Rheims and bishop of Paris, who through innumerable witnesses established her innocence, modesty, chastity, and religion, and declared the sentence against her unjust, citing the acts of the

[33] Rainaldi, *Annales, anno 1430*, cap. 2 (28:80–81).

[34] Ibid., cap. 3 (28:81). See Jean-Papire Masson, *Annales quibus res gestae Francorum explicantur*, 4 vols. (Paris 1577), 4:505–08.

[35] Benedict XIV, *Opus de servorum Dei beatificatione et beatorum canonizatione*, 16 vols. (Naples 1773–1775), Lib. 3, cap. 45, section 9 (7:57).

trial that Papirius Masson had discovered in Paris.[36] Del Rio goes on to cite the fanciful account of the Augustinian friar Filippo da Bergamo in his *De claris mulieribus* of 1497 that two of Joan's judges who were still alive were tried and convicted and burned to death, while the bones of two others who had died in the meantime were dug up and similarly burned. Moreover, a church was ordered to be built in Rouen, paid for by the confiscated goods of the judges, to the honor of God and atonement to the virgin, and daily masses offered. Thus, the honor wrongly taken from her was restored barely more than twenty years later, by papal decree.[37]

After citing Del Rio, Benedict concludes by saying that, since there is never any mention of the Maid's sanctity or heroic virtue nor any judgment proving them, one can licitly infer that the gift of prophecy can exist apart from sanctity.[38] However, anyone who followed up on his reference to Del Rio would see that there was at least reverence to her memory, because of Filippo's bogus report. He must also have seen Rainaldi's account, which repeats Meyer's accolades of her as "a holy virgin of Christ" and so on.

It is hard to understand that Benedict could have misread the record so badly as to conclude that the University of Paris saw her as a genuine prophet, in light of its adverse judgment, which, among other things, found her wearing of male clothes to be abominably criminal, and concluded that her revelations were either lies or the inspiration of the

[36] Jean-Papire Masson (d. 1611), *Annales quibus res gestae Francorum explicantur* (Paris 1578), pp. 505–8. Masson notes that Pius II (Aeneas Sylvius) and the saintly Antoninus, Archbishop of Florence, have written in praise of her (p. 507).

[37] Martin Del Rio, SJ, *Disquisitiones magicae* (Mainz 1617) 4.1.3.6, regula 7, p. 526; ed. and trans. Peter Maxwell-Stuart and José Manuel Garcís Valverde, *Investigations into Magic: An Edition and Translation of Martin Del Rio's* Disquisitionum magicarum libri sex, 6 vols. (Leiden 2022–2023), 4:206–09. As for Filippo da Bergamo, see Jacobus Philippus Bergomensis, *De plurimis claris selectisque mulieribus* (Ferrara 1497), cap. 157 (fols. 144–145v): *De Janna, Gallica pulcella, optima juvencula.* Among other inventive changes, he puts King Charles personally in charge of the army at Orleans; after Joan conquers it, she fights against the English thirty times over the next eight years, finally capturing their leader, and Charles is crowned—in Orleans. At the end, Joan is burned by the English as a sorceress—in Rheims. Many years later, after Rheims is re-taken, Charles erects a bronze cross in her honor at her place of death. Then, after Charles dies, his son Louis XI petitions Pius II to send two jurists to judge the case, with results as recounted by Del Rio. Note: Quicherat, *Procès*, 4:521–28, uses a later version of Filippo's tale (from 1521), in which "Rheims" is corrected to Rouen.

[38] Benedict XIV, loc. cit.

diabolical spirits Belial, Satan, and Behemoth—a judgment that Cauchon specifically relied upon to justify his sentences against Joan.

18.5 The Historians Get a Grip on the Facts

Only in the eighteenth century, as Quicherat notes, were the acts of both the original trial and the exoneration trial drawn upon by French historians, and only in the nineteenth century did they come to discover "the secret of her grandeur," and none more than Jules Michelet.[39]

Michelet's lively and rhetorically embellished chapters on Joan of Arc came out in the volume of his *Histoire de France* that was published in 1841,[40] the same year that Quicherat published the first volume of his *Procès de condemnation et de réhabilitation de Jeanne d'Arc, dite La Pucelle*, containing Joan's trial of condemnation.

Michelet ends his description of Joan's execution with the lament of one of Henry VI's secretaries who had witnessed it: "We are lost, we have burned a saint!"[41] He goes on to say that this word, "saint," is no less important for its having been uttered by an enemy, for it will endure, the future will not contradict it: "Yes, indeed, in the view of Religion, in the view of the Fatherland, Joan of Arc was a saint."[42] In other words, he assumed that Joan was considered a saint at the time of her death and was still considered a saint.

There were undoubtedly persons in Joan's time who did think of her as a living saint, and saint in death and after death, but unfortunately their voices carried little weight and nothing came of it. I should note that the

[39] Quicherat, *Aperçus nouveaux*, pp. 163–65.

[40] Jules Michelet, *Histoire de France*, vol. 5 (Paris 1841), Book 10, chapter 3: "La Pucelle d'Orléans, 1429"; chapter 4: "Le cardinal de Winchester; procès et mort de la Pucelle, 1429-31." The chapters were included in full in subsequent editions: 1861, 1874 (the year of Michelet's death), 1876–1878, 1879–1884, 1886, 1894, and 1898. But in Michelet's reprinting of the Joan chapters as a separate book, *Jeanne d'Arc* (Paris 1853), he cut the second chapter short, as described in the next note. Both versions of the text are given in Jules Michelet, *Jeanne d'Arc*, ed. G. Rudler, 2 vols. (Paris 1925). For an English rendering of the book version, without Michelet's notes, see Jules Michelet, *Joan of Arc*, trans. Albert Guérard (Ann Arbor 1956).

[41] Michelet, *Jeanne d'Arc*, ed. Rudler, 1:120. In the 1853 book, Michelet's life of Joan ends here.

[42] "Cette parole, échappée à un ennemi, n'en est pas moins grave. Elle restera. L'avenir n'y contredira point. Oui, selon la Religion, selon la Patrie, Jeanne Darc fut une sainte" (Michelet, *Jeanne d'Arc*, ed. Rudler, 1:120).

secretary to whom Michelet refers above was not calling Joan a saint (*une sainte*), but only a holy person (*une sainte personne*).[43]

Quicherat was more clear-sighted. He said that Joan was the saint of the Middle Ages whom the Middle Ages rejected. She should instead be the saint of our modern times.[44] That is exactly what happened, thanks largely to Quicherat himself and his publication of her trial records.[45]

18.6 Trial on the Way to Canonization

Veneration of Joan as a saint quickly spread throughout France and the rest of the Catholic world. She was first set on the road to canonization in 1869, less than a generation since her full story had been made known, when Félix Dupanloup, Bishop of Orleans, wrote to Rome on her behalf. Three series of field inquisitions took place in Orleans between 1874 and 1888, comprising 101 sessions, and by the time that the case was admitted to the tribunal of the Sacred Congregation of Rites in 1892, commendatory letters from nearly 800 bishops had been received.[46]

At this time the term "martyr" had long been reserved for persons who were put to death specifically for defending the faith of Christ, even though there were examples in Church history of martyrs who had simply died an unjust death, like King Edward the Martyr as opposed to King Edward the Confessor. In the mid-twentieth century the term was again broadened: Maria Goretti was canonized in 1950 as a martyr for chastity and the Christian life, and Maximilian Kolbe was canonized in 1982 as a martyr for charity. The category of "confessor" was not open to female non-martyrs, for grammatical reasons, but "virgin" was available to Joan. To be declared a *virgo sancta* she had to be shown not only to have died a heroically virtuous death, as with a martyr, but also to have lived a life of heroic virtue.

By being admitted to the tribunal, Joan was given the title of "Servant of God." The first stage of her trial was to determine whether she had a

[43] The mason Pierre Cusquel in three depositions giving the words of the royal secretary Jean Tressart: NT 1:188: Joan was a faithful Christian and her soul was in the hands of God, whereas all who agreed with her condemnation were damned; NT 1:220–21: "We are all lost, because a good holy person was burned"; NT 1:453–54: "a holy person was burned."

[44] Quicherat, *Aperçus nouveaux*, p. 166: "La sainte du moyen âge, que le moyen âge a rejetée, doit devenir celle des temps modernes."

[45] For an account of Quicherat and his edition, see Philippe Contamine, "Jules Quicherat, historien de Jeanne d'Arc," *Jeanne d'Arc et son époque* (Paris 2020), pp. 337–55.

[46] Kelly, "Joan of Arc's Last Trial," pp. 206, 208.

sufficient reputation for sanctity (*fama sanctitatis*) to give her the title of "Venerable Servant of God." A prosecutor, officially called "Promotor of the Faith," but in common parlance referred to as "the Devil's Advocate," would attempt to establish that she did not. On this occasion, the role was filled by an advocate of the Congregation named Agostino Caprara. He acknowledged that she was one of the two most celebrated persons of the fifteenth century, the other being Christopher Columbus, and he admitted that she had many virtues, but they were not those of a saint; and even her admirable human virtues did not survive her last ordeal: "It seems, then, that two stages are to be discerned in the life of our Maid. The first was glorious and full of admiration, up to her captivity.... But when she was captured and subjected to judicial questions, that greatness of soul gave out, that splendor of divine revelations vanished, and grave faults are seen to have obscured the aforesaid virtues, whatever, finally, they were."[47] Even though Caprara was supposed to be reviewing her reputation for sanctity, he spent most of his fifty-page brief pointing out what he considered to be her actual shortcomings in character and devotion. For instance, even though he admitted that Cauchon was an unjust judge, he maintained that Joan should have had the humility to answer the questions put to her, as Christ did before Pilate; instead, she manifested contempt and arrogance, attitudes that were all too typical of her.[48] His position was that of Benedict XIV, whose opinion of her we saw above, which Caprara invokes more than once: her prophetic powers were not necessarily a sign of sanctity; dying for a private revelation was not martyrdom, and she did not accept death like a martyr, but with great anguish and fear.[49]

The appointed Defender of Joan's reputation, another advocate of the Congregation named Ilario Alibrandi, made a vigorous response against these allegations, coming to 170 pages in the record. He clearly prevailed, and the pope, Leo XIII, signed a decree on January 27, 1894, proclaiming Joan a Venerable Servant of God, and later in the year, the Congregation issued a highly laudatory account of her life.[50]

The second phase of her trial took place only in 1901; it dealt with Joan's practice of the theological virtues of faith, hope, and charity, and the cardinal virtues of prudence, justice, temperance, and fortitude. The

[47] Ibid., p. 207.
[48] Ibid., p. 211.
[49] Ibid., p. 210.
[50] Ibid., p. 215.

new Promotor of the Faith, Giovanni Battista Lugari, was tasked with raising doubts that she achieved the heroic level in each of them that was required of a canonizable saint. One point he makes is that most of the testimony in praise of her comes from the trial of nullity, which, he says was just as political as the trial of condemnation, except that it was in her favor.[51] He even made a case that she lacked military fortitude, and went on at length about her deficiencies in temperance, from her love of luxurious clothing to her carelessness of modesty—alluding to the duke of Alençon's testimony that he sometimes caught sight of her beautiful breasts after spending the night in the field with her.[52] Lugari's objections were rebutted by a new Defender, Giovanni Battista Minetti, and the matter was put to the Consultors of the Congregation.[53]

The Consultors came up with a large number of objections, presented by a third Promotor, Alessandro Verde, in a brief only twenty-four pages long. Defender Minetti made a massive response of 387 pages, submitted on February 12, 1903, followed by an unsigned *Defensio virtutum* of 198 pages.[54]

Another meeting was held in which the Consultors voiced their views again, which resulted in a third round of debate on Joan's virtues. This final assault was voiced once again by Promotor Verde. One noteworthy objection he makes is that, though the articles of condemnation were refuted at the Nullity Trial (or, as it is called here, using Quicherat's term, the "rehabilitation" trial), the sentence of this tribunal was never confirmed by the pope.[55]

This last discussion was held on November 15, 1903, under the new pope, Pius X. On the anniversary of Joan's birthday the following year, 1904, the pope announced that her practice of all the virtues in a heroic degree was established. It only remained to verify the requisite number of miracles worked through her intercession to declare her Blessed and Saint, which occurred respectively in 1909 and 1920.[56] Papal recognition of her rehabilitation could get no greater. Her feast day was May 30, the day on which she was burned to death after conviction as a relapsed heretic in a bishop's court.

[51] Ibid., pp. 216–17.
[52] Ibid., pp. 217–18. See NT 1:387 for Alençon's testimony.
[53] Ibid., p. 219.
[54] Ibid., pp. 220–25.
[55] Ibid., pp. 226–27.
[56] Ibid., pp. 227–28.

CHAPTER 19

Conclusion

The death of Joan of Arc, burned at the stake in Rouen in Normandy on May 30, 1431, was a judicial murder, with malice aforethought. Her main killer was the bishop of Beauvais, Pierre Cauchon, the judge who pronounced the sentence upon her as a relapsed heretic, without a trial, and delivered her over to her executioner. But he had many accessories, before and after the fact, especially those connected with the University of Paris, which, to its lasting disgrace, was decisive in conceiving the "trial of faith" against her, even without English instigation,[1] and affirming her condemnation. Thomas de Courcelles and the other five theologians from the University who joined Cauchon early on as assessors shared particularly in his malice. Other assessors were likely persuaded to participate because of intimidation by Cauchon or his English masters. But neither Cauchon nor any of his collaborators were ever brought to justice. Joan's supporters failed her both in life and death, until, almost a generation later, her "honor" was weakly restored and the judgment against her was voided.

In general, the above verdict against Cauchon has been accepted by modern historians, but occasionally revisionists offer excuses for him, which can be seen as further attacks on Joan's honor. For instance, it has been argued that his handling of the trial was a good-faith effort at fairness, and that his assurances of concern for Joan's spiritual welfare were

[1] See Denifle, *CUP* 4:510.

H. A. Kelly, *The Trial and Retrial of Joan of Arc*, The New Middle Ages, https://doi.org/10.1007/978-3-032-07887-2_19

sincere.[2] Just a few years after her canonization, George Bernard Shaw had also argued in the Preface to his play *Saint Joan* that Cauchon was being sincere, and that he genuinely found Joan to be a dangerous heretic, like Wyclif and Hus, showing the first vestiges of what would later mushroom into Protestantism.[3]

A similar judgment has been made more recently, that Joan was indeed guilty of heresy, primarily consisting of disobedience to the Church.[4] Disobedience, however, called at most for a sentence of contempt of court rather than an accusation of heresy. But what about the allegation that Joan refused to submit to the Church Militant? This supposed crime somehow made her both an apostate and a schismatic (starting her own church or joining an antipope), as well as a heretic. Of course, once she realized what her interrogators were talking about, she was more than willing to submit to the Church authorities who were superior in rank to the churchmen who were persecuting and tormenting her. But there was no obligation whatsoever to submit to the Church, and no crime in refusing to do so.

As for otheroffenses, admittedly, some of the theologians produced by the University of Paris were ready to admit that almost anything could be called an error in faith and even a heresy, as witness Pierre d'Ailly (created cardinal by the Pisan pope John XXIII), during the campaign against the so-called tyrannicide principles of Jean Petit in the Council of Constance. During this campaign, Cauchon had been outstanding in his insistence upon the rights of defendants to have all defenses of law against prejudiced judges and breaches of procedure, and to know the charges, whether the charges were justified or not.

Earlier, as bishop of Cambrai, in conjunction with the diocesan subinquisitor, d'Ailly had also shown himself unscrupulous in persecuting a woman, Marie Ducanech, in a heresy trial. But Marie had been able to

[2] Daniel Hobbins in the Introduction to his abridged translation, *The Trial of Joan of Arc*. For a response, see Henry Ansgar Kelly, "Questions of Due Process and Conviction in the Trial of Joan of Arc," in *Religion, Power, and Resistance from the Eleventh to the Sixteenth Centuries*, Karen Bollerman, Thomas M. Izbicki, and Cary J. Nederman, eds. (New York 2014), pp. 81–100, at pp. 81–87: "How Due Was the Process that Joan Received?"

[3] George Bernard Shaw, *Saint Joan: A Chronicle Play in Six Scenes and an Epilogue* (New York 1924), Preface. See, for instance, p. xlvi: "When the Church was not offering her favorite luxuries, but calling on her to accept its interpretation of God's will, and to sacrifice her own, she flatly refused, and made it clear that her notion of a Catholic Church was one in which the Pope was Pope Joan."

[4] Jacques Chiffoleau, "L'hérésie de Jeanne," p. 43. He also suggests that a series of smaller crimes could amount to the enormous crime of heresy (p. 31).

escape their clutches through appealing to d'Ailly's metropolitan superior, the Archbishop of Rheims. Unlike Cauchon, who had the backing of the English occupiers of Rouen, d'Ailly had been forced to comply with the workings of the ecclesiastical judicial system (he did attempt to resort to the secular authorities by appealing to the Parlement of Paris, but it declared against him).

Cauchon's metropolitan superior, Regnault de Chartres, Archbishop of Rheims, was Charles VII's chancellor. He had supervised or at least witnessed Joan's examination of orthodoxy at Poitiers. He could have intervened in her proceedings at Rouen, whether by advoking them to his court in Rheims or sending them to the pope. But he did not. In fact, any partisan of Joan could have appealed to the pope in favor of Joan, including Charles himself, but no one did, so far as we know. Auditor Lohier could have drawn attention to the travesty of a trial that was being enacted against her when he arrived in Rome, which he had protested against when he was in Rouen; but, if he did, it was to no avail.

Like all trials, Joan's trial was supposed to be an inquisition, as defined by Innocent III at the Fourth Lateran Council in 1215, in the decree *Qualiter et Quando*, and elaborated in subsequent canon law. A perfectly regular heresy trial against the lawyer Jean Ségueut, convoked under the chief ecclesiastical judge of the diocese and province of Rouen, Jean Basset, Official of Rouen, and the Inquisitor of France Jean Graverent, had just been concluded, in November of 1430. *Publica fama* that Ségueut held heretical views called for an investigation, which was undertaken; articled charges were presented to Ségueut; in his responses he was allowed defenses and counsel and appeals. Assessors were consulted at every step. He was properly convicted of clearly defined heresy and sentenced.

But in Joan's case, though *publica fama* of unnamed heresy was alleged, no proofs were presented that any such *fama* was justified. No charges were filed against her. Instead, she was interrogated for weeks, and offenses were formulated by twisting her responses (the Twelve Articles), not to charge against her, but rather to present to partisan or intimidated consultants for judgment against her. All defenses were denied to her, and all appeals rejected. At one point, charges were made, and Joan responded with denials (i.e., a trial was begun), but it was irrelevant to her conviction.

Both the theologians and canon lawyers of the English Burgundian faction who populated the University of Paris at that time professed to believe that there was enough in the Twelve Articles to send her to the stake if she did not abjure.

In the midst of being sentenced on crimes that were not proved, Joan agreed to accede to the judges. Acceding to the judges took the form of repeating an abjuration of actions somehow construed to be heresies or crimes against the faith which either were not crimes or were not against the faith or which she did not commit (like wearing male clothes, relying on visions of saints, not submitting to the Church). She was then sentenced to life imprisonment after allegedly confessing the crimes she abjured. Four days later, she was sentenced with no further trial to be delivered to the secular arm for another set of nonexistent crimes.

Then, after two decades of neglect and indifference, two investigations aimed at rectifying this miscarriage of justice were instituted but broken off, in 1450 and 1452, until finally, in 1455, a remarkably maladroit petition was sent to Pope Nicholas V, which landed instead in the curia of his successor Calixtus III. In it, Joan's mother and brothers brought a civil suit for damages to their honor, and to Joan's honor. According to this narrative, the chief villain in Joan's demise was alleged to be one "Guillaume" (not Jean) Estivet, promotor of causes for the diocese of Beauvais, who, "likely having been suborned by envious persons," brought false charges of heresy against Joan, which were upheld through the malicious connivance of the judges, Pierre Cauchon "of blessed memory," bishop of Beauvais, and Jean Lemaistre, pretensed sub-inquisitor of heretical depravity for the diocese of Beauvais.

Although the legal team that shepherded the case through the court on behalf of the plaintiffs was very competent, they had to work around the commission's absurd distortion of the facts of what had happened to Joan, and the awkward format of the trial, which required living defendants, meant that the present bishop of Beauvais and his current promotor were constantly cited to court and declared in contempt for non-appearance, and the nonexistent sub-inquisitor of heretical depravity was sought for in the Dominican house in Beauvais, all of which threatened to turn the case into a comedy of errors.

Of the three distinguished prelates the pope assigned to the case, Archbishop Jouvenel of Rheims and Bishop Chartier of Paris took the lead, and their sober verdict was indeed a victory for Joan, declaring the original judgment against her totally unjustified and void. But her honor was not restored to her in any meaningful way. At least, not for a long time.

When the trial records were freshly re-read after their new publication in the nineteenth century, and specifically by the canonization tribunal in the 1890s, to even raise the idea that there was any trace of heresy in her would doubtless have been considered ludicrous. The discussion then was not whether she offended against the faith in any way, but whether she sometimes did not live up to the high standard required for formal recognition as a saint. For instance, even though Cauchon was admittedly an unjust judge, some now complained about her deficiencies in temperance, love of luxurious clothing, or carelessness in the way of modesty. Such views, however, did not prevail among those whose votes mattered, and her canonization proceeded to the end.

Since that time, it has again become necessary to defend Joan against slurs of heretical leanings, and to explain the judicial procedures that were on and off the books in her time. One major difference is that the jurists of the fifteenth century were not as alert to the dangers of "defendant-tampering" as we are after the Miranda rights were imposed in the twentieth century. Before the Supreme Court ordered this imposition, we all had the right to remain silent before being charged. Now we know we have the right.

More, doubtless, remains to be said, now and in the future, and I hope others will join in, in the roles of *promotor*, *advocatus*, and *jurisperitus*, to work, as needed, for Joan of Arc's continuing and highly deserved honor.

Bibliography

Fiche Account

Kouamé, Thierry. University of Paris. http://studium-parisiense.univ-paris1.fr/individus/13716-thomasdecourcellis.

Manuscript

Rouen. Archives de Seine-Maritime: Seine-Inférieure, archives ecclésiastique, G 1154: Ségueut Case.

Printed Materials

Andreae, Johannes. 1475. *Questiones mercuriales super regulis juris.* Strasbourg.

Ayroles, Jean-Baptiste-Joseph. 1890–1902. *La vraie Jeanne d'Arc.* 5 Vols. Paris.

Bailey, Michael D. 2001. From Sorcery to Witchcraft: Clerical Conceptions of Magic in the Later Middle Ages. *Speculum* 67:960–990.

Bailey, Michael D., and Edward Peters. 2003. A Sabbat of Demonologists: Basel, 1431–1440. *The Historian* 63:375–396.

Baronio, Carlo, Odorico Rainaldi, et al. 1880. *Annales ecclesiastici*, ed. Augustin Theiner. 34 Vols. Bar-le-Duc.

Barrett, W.P. trans. *Trial of Jeanne d'Arc* (London 1931 [https://heinonline.org/HOL/Page?handle=hein.trials%2Ftrijedarc0001&collection=trials];

H. A. Kelly, *The Trial and Retrial of Joan of Arc*, The New Middle Ages, https://doi.org/10.1007/978-3-032-07887-2

New York. 1932 [https://sourcebooks.fordham.edu/basis/joanofarc-trial.asp], repr. New Orleans 2008.

Basin, Thomas. 1845–49. *Histoire des règnes de Charles VII et de Louis XI, par Thomas Basin, évêque de Lisieux, jusqu'ici attribuée à Amelgard*, ed. Jules Quicherat. Translated by Mark Spencer. 4 Vols. Paris. Thomas Basin (1412–1490). The History of Charles VII and Louis XI. Nieuwkoop 1997.

Beaune, Colette. 2004. *Jeanne d'Arc*. Paris.

Beaurepaire, Charles de Robillard de. 1869. *Recherches sur le procès de condamnation de Jeanne d'Arc*. Rouen: Google Books.

Beaurepaire, Charles de Robillard de. 1893–95. Éclaircissement sur Jean Lohier. *Bulletins de la Société de l'Histoire de Normandie* 7:284–290.

Bellaguet, M.L., ed. 1839–52. *Chronique du religieux de Saint-Denys*. 6 Vols. Paris.

Belon, Marie-Joseph, and François Balme. 1893. *Jean Bréhal, grand inquisiteur de France, et la réhabilitation de Jeanne d'Arc*. Paris.

Benedict XIV. 1773–75. *Opus de servorum Dei beatificatione et beatorum canonizatione*. 16 Vols. Naples.

1617. *Biblia sacra cum glossa ordinaria*. 6 Vols. Douai-Antwerp.

Bourgeois de Paris. See Tuetey.

Brissaud, Jean. 1912. *A History of French Private Law*. Translated by Rapelje Howell. Boston.

Bzowski, Abraham. 1618–4. *Annales ecclesiastici: post…Caesarem Baronium….* 9 Vols. Cologne.

Cazalas, Sébastien. 2020. *Jean Juvénal des Ursins (1388-1473): Étude des épîtres politiques*. Paris.

Chiffoleau, Jacques. 2014. L'hérésie de Jeanne: Note sur les qualifications dans le procès de Rouen. In *Jeanne d'Arc: Histoire et mythes*, ed. Jean-Patrice Boudet and Xavier Hélary, 13–55. Rennes.

Contamine, Philippe. 2009. Maître Jean de Rinel (vers 1380-1449), notaire et secretaire de Charles VI puis de Henry VI pour son royaume de France, l'une des 'plumes' de l'union des deux couronnes. In *De part et d'autre de la Normandie médiévale: Recueil d'études en hommage à François Neveux*, 115–134. Caen.

Contamine, Philippe. 2016. La réhabilitation de la Pucelle vue au prisme des *Tractatus super materia processus*: une propédeutique. In *De l'hérétique à la sainte: Les procès de Jeanne d'Arc revisités (Actes 2009 Cerisy conference)*, ed. François Neveux, 177–196. Caen.

Contamine, Philippe. 2020a. Le procès en revision de la condemnation de Jeanne d'Arc (1450-1456): raisons, obstacles, procédure, résultats. *Histoire de la Justice* 30 (1): 17–36.

Contamine, Philippe. 2020b. Jules Quicherat, historien de Jeanne d'Arc. In *Jeanne d'Arc et son époque*, 337–355. Paris.

Corpus Juris Canonici (CJC). 1582. Under the auspices of Gregory XIII. 3 Vols. Rome. See https://digital.library.ucla.edu/canonlaw/. Same contents as listed for Friedburg (q.v.), but with commentaries (glosses).

Coville, Alfred. 1932. *Jean Petit: La question du tyrannicide au commencement du xve siècle*. Paris.

Cuenca, Esther, M. Christina Bruno, and Anthony Perron, eds. 2025. *Law, Justice, and Society in the Medieval World: An Introduction Through Film*. New York.

Del Rio, Martin S.J. 1617. *Disquisitiones magicae*. Mainz.

Del Rio, Martin S.J., ed. and trans. Peter Maxwell-Stuart and José Manuel Garcís Valverde. 2022–23. *Investigations into Magic: An Edition and Translation of Martin Del Rio's* DISQUISITIONUM MAGICARUM LIBRI SEX. 6 Vols. Leiden.

Denifle, Henri (with Émile Chatelain), ed. 1889–97. *Chartularium Universitatis Parisiensis* (*CUP*). 4 Vols. Paris.

Denifle, Henri, ed. 1897a. *La désolation des églises, monastères, et hôpitaux en France pendant la guerre des cent ans*. Vol. 1. Paris.

Denifle, Henri (with Émile Chatelain), ed. 1897b. Auctarium Chartularii Universitatis Parisiensis. In *Liber procuratorum nationis Anglicanae (Alemanniae)*. Vol. 2. Paris.

Denzinger, Heinrich. 2012. *Compendium of Creeds, Definitions, and Declarations*, ed. and trans. Peter Hünermann. 43rd ed. San Francisco.

Doncoeur, Paul, and Yvonne Lanhers, eds. 1954. *Instrument publique des sentences portées les 24 et 30 mai 1431 par Pierre Cauchon et Jean Le Maître, OP, contre Jeanne la Pucelle*. Paris.

Doncoeur, Paul, and Yvonne Lanhers, eds. 1956. *La réhabilitation de Jeanne la Pucelle: la enquête ordonnée par Charles VII en 1450 et le Codicille de Guillaume Bouillé*. Paris.

Duclercq, Jacques. 1823. *Memoires*, ed. Fredéric de Reiffenberg. 4 Vols. Brussels.

Duparc, Pierre. 1841–49. *Procès de condemnation et réhabilitation de Jeanne d'Arc*. 5 Vols. Paris.

Eubel, Conrad, et al., eds. 1898–1978. *Hierarchia catholica medii aevi*. 8 Vols. Münster.

Eugene IV. 1990. *Acta Eugenii Papae IV*, ed. Giorgio Fedalto. Rome.

Eymeric, Nicolau. 1595. *Directorium inquisitorum* [1376], ed. Francisco Peña. Rome 1578, etc. I use the edition of Venice.

Favier, Jean. 2010. *Pierre Cauchon: Comment on deviant le juge de Jeanne d'Arc*. Paris.

Filippo da Bergamo (Jacobus Philippus Bergomensis). 1497. *De plurimis claris selectisque mulieribus*. Ferrara.

Finke, Heinrich. 1896–1928. *Acta Concilii Constanciensis*. 4 Vols. Münster.

Fraikin, Jean. 1973. La date de la redaction latine du procès de Jeanne d'Arc. *Quaerendo* 3:39–66.

Friedberg, Emil, ed. 1879–81. *Corpus iuris canonici* (CIC). 2 Vols. Leipzig. Containing *Liber Extra* (X), or *Decretals of Gregory IX* (AD 1234); *Liber Sextus* or *Sext* of Boniface VIII (1298); *Constitutiones Clementinae* or *Clementines* of Clement V (1317), and *Extravagants of John XXII* and *Common Extravagants.*

Fris, Victor. 1908. *Essai d'une analyse des Commentarii sive Annales Rerum Flandricarum (Annales Flandriae 1561) de Jacques de Meyere.* Ghent.

Gabriel, Astrik L., and Gray C. Boyce, eds. 1964. Auctarium Chartularii Universitatis Parisiensis. In *Liber receptorum nationis Anglicanae (Alemanniae) in Universitate Parisiensi*, vol. 6. Paris.

Garner, Brian, ed. 1999. *Black's Law Dictionary.* Vol. 7. St. Paul.

Gerson, Jean. 1960–73. *Oeuvres complètes*, ed. Palémon Glorieux. 10 Vols. Paris.

Gerson, Jean. 1706. *Opera omnia*, ed. Louis Ellies Dupin. 5 Vols, 2nd ed. Antwerp, The Hague 1728.

Gies, Frances. 1981. *Joan of Arc: The Legend and the Reality.* New York.

Gratian. *Decretum*, ed. Emil Friedberg, *CIC* 1.

Gregory XIII, Pope, ed. 1582. [*Corpus Juris Canonici* (CJC)]. 3 Vols. Rome. UCLA online edition: https://digital.library.ucla.edu/canonlaw/.

Griffiths, Ralph. 1981. *The Reign of King Henry VI: The Exercise of Royal Authority, 1422–1461.* Berkeley.

Guido da Baisio. *Rosarium* [1300]. Strasbourg ca. 1475.

Head, Constance. 1970. Pope Pius II and the Wars of the Roses. *Archivum Historiae Pontificae* 8:139–178.

Helmholz, R. H. 1990. Origins of the Privilege Against Self-Incrimination: The Role of the European *Ius commune. New York University Law Review* 65:962–990.

Hobbins, Daniel, trans. 2005. *The Trial of Joan of Arc.* Cambridge MA.

Institoris (Kramer), Henricus, and Jacobus Sprenger. 2006. *Malleus Maleficarum*, ed. and trans. Christopher S. Mackay. 2 Vols. Cambridge.

Jager, Eric. 2014. *Blood Royal: A True Tale of Crime and Detection in Medieval Paris.* New York.

Jouvenal des Ursins, Jean. 1978. In *Écrites politiques de Jean Juvénal des Ursins*, ed. Peter Shervey Lewis and Anne-Marie Hayez. 4 Vols. Paris.

Kelly, Henry Ansgar. 1976. *The Matrimonial Trials of Henry VIII.* Stanford.

Kelly, Henry Ansgar. 1989. Inquisition and the Prosecution of Heresy: Misconceptions and Abuses. *Church History* 58:439–451.

Kelly, Henry Ansgar. 1993. The Right to Remain Silent: Before and After Joan of Arc. *Speculum* 68:992–1026. Repr. In *Inquisitions*, article III.

Kelly, Henry Ansgar. 1996. Joan of Arc's Last Trial: The Attack of the Devil's Advocates. In *Fresh Verdicts on Joan of Arc*, ed. Bonnie Wheeler and Charles T. Wood, 205–238. New York. Repr. in *Inquisitions*, article IV.

Kelly, Henry Ansgar. 1999. Trial Procedures Against Wyclif and Wycliffites in England and at the Council of Constance. *Huntington Library Quarterly* 61:1–28. Repr. in *Inquisitions*, article V.

Kelly, Henry Ansgar. 2001. *Inquisitions and Other Trial Procedures in the Medieval West*. Variorum Collected Studies. Aldershot.

Kelly, Henry Ansgar. 2014. Questions of Due Process and Conviction in the Trial of Joan of Arc. In *Religion, Power, and Resistance from the Eleventh to the Sixteenth Centuries*, ed. Karen Bollerman, Thomas M. Izbicki, and Cary J. Nederman, 81–100. New York.

Kelly, Henry Ansgar. 2019a. The Fourth Lateran *Ordo* of Inquisition Adapted to the Prosecution of Heresy. In *Brill's Companion to Heresy Inquisitions*, 75–107. Leiden.

Kelly, Henry Ansgar. 2019b. Luther at Augsburg, 1518: New Light on Papal Strategies. *Journal of Ecclesiastical History* 70:804–822.

Kelly, Henry Ansgar. 2021. Judicial Proceedings for and Against Bishop Reginald Pecock: New Perspectives on the Mechanisms of His Downfall. *Viator* 52 (1): 359–430.

Kelly, Henry Ansgar. 2023. *Criminal-Inquisitorial Trials in English Church Courts: From the Middle Ages to the Reformation*. Washington.

Kelly, Henry Ansgar. Joan of Arc. Inquisitorial Trial of Faith in *The Passion of Joan of Arc*. In *Law, Justice, and Society in the Medieval World*, ed. Cuenca et al., 60–72.

Kors, Alan Charles, and Edward Peters, eds. 2001. *Witchcraft in Europe, 400–1700: A Documentary History*. 2nd ed. Philadelphia.

Lanéry d'Arc, Pierre. 1889. *Mémoires et consultations en faveur de Jeanne d'Arc par les juges du procès de réhabilitation*. Paris.

Lea, Henry Charles. 1887. *A History of the Inquisition of the Middle Ages*. 3 Vols. Philadelphia.

Levy, Leonard W. 1968. *Origins of the Fifth Amendment: The Right against Self-Incrimination*. New York. Repr. with new preface, 1986.

Lyndwood, William. 1679. *Provinciale, seu Constitutiones Angliae* [1434]. Oxford. Repr. Farnborough 1968.

Mansi, Giandomenico. 1759–98. *Sacrorum conciliorum nova et amplissima collectio*. 54 Vols. Venice.

Marchand, Jean, intro. 1955. *Le procès de condamnation de Jeanne d'Arc: Reproduction en facsimile du manuscript authentique, sur velin no. 1119, de la Bibliothèque de l'Assemblée Nationale*. 2 Vols. Paris.

Masson, Jean-Papire. 1577. *Annales quibus res gestae Francorum explicantur*. 4 Vols. Paris.

Mercier, Franck. 2006. *La Vauderie d'Arras: Un chasse aux sorcières à l'automne du Moyen Âge*. Rennes.

Meyer, Jacques. 1580. *Flandricorum annales*, ed. Antoine de Meyer, Liber 16, "Philippus Burgundio," in vol. 1 of *Annales, sive Historiae, rerum Belgicarum*, ed. Sigmund Feyerabend, 2 Vols. Frankfurt.

Michelet, Jules. 1841. *Histoire de France*. Vol. 5. Paris.

Michelet, Jules. 1853. *Jeanne d'Arc*. Paris.

Michelet, Jules. 1925. *Jeanne d'Arc*, ed. G. Rudler. 2 Vols. Paris.

Monstrelet, Enguerran de. 1857–62. *Chronique*, ed. Louis Douët-d'Arcq. 2 Vols. Paris.

Moranvillé, Henri, ed. 1891–97. *Chronographia regum Francorum*. 3 Vols. Paris.

Müller, Heribert. 2003. 'Et sembloit qu'on oyst parler un angèle de Dieu': Thomas de Courcelles et le Councile de Bâle; ou, Le secret d'une belle réussitée? *Comptes rendus des séances de l'Académie des Insciptions et Belles-Lettres* 147:461–484.

Neveux, François. 1987. *L'évêque Pierre Cauchon*. Paris.

Newhall, Richard A. 1934. Payment to Pierre Cauchon for Presiding at the Trial of Jeanne d'Arc. *Speculum* 9:88–91.

Ostorero, Martine. 2002. Itinéraire d'un inquisiteur gâté: Ponce Feugeyron, les Juifs, et le sabbat des sorciers. *Médiévales* 43 (Fall): 103–117.

Oxford Dictionary of National Biography Online. https://www.oxforddnb.com/.

Peters, Edward. 1988. *Inquisition*. New York.

Pius II. 1937–57. *The Commentaries of Pius II*. Translated by Florence Alden Gragg. Intro. and notes Leona C. Gabel. Northampton MA.

Pius II. 1984. *Commentarii rerum memorabilium que temporibus suis contigerunt*, ed. Adrianus van Heck. 2 Vols. Vatican City.

Provvidente, Sebastián. 2019. *Stylus theologicus et iuridicus*: La *causa* Jean Petit à Constance (1414-1418) et les débats sur le tyrannicide. *Médiévales* 77:129–151.

Quicherat, Jules. 1841–49. *Procès de condemnation et réhabilitation de Jeanne d'Arc*. 5 Vols. Paris.

Quicherat, Jules. 1850. *Aperçus nouveaux sur l'histoire de Jeanne d'Arc*. Paris.

Russell, Joycelyne Gledhill Dickinson. 1955a. The Congress of Arras. *History* 40 (1): 31–41.

Russell, Joycelyne Gledhill Dickinson. 1955b. *The Congress of Arras, 1435*. Oxford.

Sacrae Rituum Congregatione, Aureliensis: Beatificationis et Canonizationis Ioannae de Arc: Positio super introductione causae. Rome 1883. Part 3: *Summarium additionale: Excerptum ex processu Aureliae condito anno 1885 super dubio "An sit signanda."* (Rome 1885).

Schafer, Ernst. (1904–05). Die älteste Instruktionen-Sammlung der spanischen inquisitionen. *Archiv für Reformationsgeschichte* 2:1–55, 109–177.

Shaw, George Bernard. 1924. *Saint Joan: A Chronicle Play in Six Scenes and an Epilogue*. New York.

Sponde (Spondanus), Henri de. 1675–82. *Annalium ecclesiasticorum continuatio*. 2 Vols. Ticino.

Stevenson, Janet H., ed. 2022. *The Register of Richard Praty, Bishop of Chichester, 1438–1445.* Woodbridge.

Sullivan, Thomas. 2011. *Parisian Licentiates in Theology, AD 1373-1500: A Biographical Register.* In *The Secular Clergy*, vol. 2. Leiden.

Tanner, Norman P., ed. and trans. *Decrees of the Ecumenical Church.* 2 Vols. London 1990.

Tarrant, Jacqueline, ed. 1983. *Extravagantes Iohannis XXII.* Vatican City.

Taylor, Larissa Juliet. 2009. *The Virgin Warrior: The Life and Death of Joan of Arc.* New Haven.

Thorndike, Lynn. 1944. *University Records and Life in the Middle Ages.* New York.

Tisset, Pierre, ed. 1960a–71. *Procès de condamnation de Jeanne d'Arc.* 3 Vols. Paris.

Tisset, Pierre (with Yvonne Lanhers), ed. 1960b–71. *Procès de condamnation de Jeanne d'Arc.* 3 Vols. Paris.

Tuetey, Alexandre, ed. *Journal d'un Bourgeois de Paris, 1405-1449.* Paris 1881. Translated by Janet Shirley. *A Parisian Journal, 1405–1449.* Oxford 1968.

Valois, Noël. 1896–1902. *La France et la grand schisme d'Occident.* 4 Vols. Paris.

Varin, Pierre, ed. 1848. *Archives administratives de la ville de Reims: Collection de pièces inédites, etc.* Vol. 3. Paris.

Vidal, J. M. 1913. *Bullaire de l'inquisition française au xive siècle et jusqu'à la fin du grand schisme.* Paris.

Warner, Marina. 1981. *Joan of Arc: The Image of Female Heroism.* New York.

White, Arthur. 2014. *Plague and Pleasure: The Renaissance World of Pius II.* Washington.

Wolfe, Bertram. 1981. *Henry VI.* New Haven.

Index[1]

[1] Note: Page numbers followed by 'n' refer to notes.

H. A. Kelly, *The Trial and Retrial of Joan of Arc*, The New Middle Ages, https://doi.org/10.1007/978-3-032-07887-2

M

The manufacturer's authorised representative in the EU is Springer Nature Customer Service Centre GmbH, Europaplatz 3, 69115 Heidelberg, Germany. If you have any concerns regarding our products, please contact ProductSafety@springernature.com

Printed and bound by CPI Group (UK) Ltd, Croydon, CR0 4YY
17/09/2026
02218454-0013